269
286
290
303
307
321
338
350
358
371
313 — ANTI-MECH. STATEMENT
384
396 — imp. theme

[❀]

Ego and Instinct

EGO
AND INSTINCT

*The Psychoanalytic View
of Human Nature—Revised*

BY

DANIEL YANKELOVICH

&

WILLIAM BARRETT

Vintage Books
A Division of Random House
New York

VINTAGE BOOKS EDITION, September 1971

Copyright © 1970 by Daniel Yankelovich and William Barrett

All rights reserved under International and Pan-American
Copyright Conventions. Published in the United States
by Random House, Inc., New York, and simultaneously in
Canada by Random House of Canada Limited, Toronto.
Originally published by Random House, Inc., in 1970.

ISBN: 0-394-71181-5

Library of Congress Catalog Card Number: 70-85601

Manufactured in the United States of America

To Hassie and Nicole

Preface

"Never explain, never apologize," runs the old maxim. And therefore never write a preface. But since the authors of this book are a social scientist and a philosopher, and neither is a psychoanalyst, the reader may wonder how they came to collaborate in the first place and why, further, they chose a subject that would seem to lie far beyond their own special interests.

The collaboration was not originally intended. It grew—at the time it seemed more by happenstance, in retrospect it looks more inevitable—out of a number of informal conversations. These talks were mainly philosophical, and they ranged far and wide. Gradually, however, our questions came to turn around a central one—that of finding a sensible and comprehensive philosophy within which to view the nature of man in relation to certain social and scientific problems. The lack of such a philosophy seemed to both authors a disquieting gap in contemporary culture.

Both met, so to speak, coming from opposite directions. The place of their meeting was the region undeservedly left empty between their separate disciplines.

The social scientist had originally been trained as a philosopher, but had quit that field because of the irrelevance, as he saw it, of its academic practice. In his professional work in the social sciences he had ploughed through mountains of documents on man under varying social conditions. Here just the opposite kind of irrelevance was to be found: an array of findings and techniques that were brilliant but bewildering, penetrating but fragmentary—the poverty of chaotic riches. If there was a figure at all in the carpet, one could hardly trace it. What was needed was some unifying scheme of ideas; and thus he found himself drawn back into philosophy.

The philosopher, for his part, had also experienced the narrowness of a good deal of academic philosophizing. Philosophy, which had originally begotten all of the sciences, seemed to have lost touch with those that dealt with human matters and to have resigned itself, like Hamlet, to discussing "words, words, words." For example, though some contemporary philosophers take David Hume as an admired model, they consider only a handful of formal and epistemological problems from his writings, forgetting that his main work is entitled *A Treatise on Human Nature* and really does deal with that subject. In the other camp, the Existentialists do speak a great deal about man and the human condition; but their emphasis on personal choice and decision is, typically, so one-sided that the gritty reality of human nature recedes into the background and virtually disappears.

But why psychoanalysis? A more formal accounting for this choice of subject will be found in the body of the text; but here we may speak a little more personally about why psychoanalysis became the point of convergence of our thinking.

We came of age at a time when Freud's influence was at its peak. Today people blame Dr. Spock for the excesses of youth. When we were young, this honor was often reserved for Dr. Freud. Because of him, our parents lost their bland self-assurance, and enlightened young mothers talked furtively of sibling rivalry, penis envy and the woman down the block who slept in the same bed with her twelve-year-old son. As students in college, we learned about Freud by day and urged our own interpretation of his message on nubile girls by night. One of us became an editor of *Partisan Review* at a time when Freud's influence dominated the literary scene; the other was trained as a clinical psychologist in a setting where to be or not be a Freudian was the decisive issue. Every cocktail party featured a hip guest who laughed at the wrong places, evangelized on the purgative value of psychoanalysis and applied his new Freudian vocabulary to the other guests. We worked and thought in a world which had swung from the Marxian-tinged social de-

terminism of the thirties to the Freudian-tinged psychological
determinism of the forties and fifties.

Now the pendulum has swung back toward social determinism, and in some quarters Freud is distinctly out of favor.
Youthful activists carry placards with such puzzling mottoes
as "Freud Is a Fink!" and "Freudian Fascism Must Go!"

But what these young activists do not know, indeed cannot
know, is that the historic issues raised by Freud have only now
reached their full expression. At the heart of many of the great
social issues of our day—war and peace, the uses of technology,
race and poverty, the revolt of youth and the aims of society
—lies the question of whether social engineering can remake
society and the individual to specification, or whether an inherent human nature imposes its own forms and limits. We
must know the answer to that question, or we may perish.
When so many feel estranged from themselves, what precisely
is it that are they estranged from? Hidden beneath the barbaric
jargon of psychoanalysis there is the germ of an answer to
these questions. But the answers are surprisingly unfamiliar to
a generation that thinks it knows what psychoanalysis really
says.

The psychoanalytic theory we once thought we knew so well
has changed today, almost beyond recognition. The new "ego
psychology" of Erikson and Hartmann has accommodated itself to many of the discoveries made by Freud's old enemies,
the men who rejected Freud's emphasis on a human nature
dominated by instinct. Today, psychoanalysis itself is being torn
in many conflicting directions. In both its aspirations and un-
certainties, psychoanalysis can be seen as the most drastic human expression of the quandaries that beset the sciences of man.

In the past, whenever psychoanalysis strayed from its own
narrow preserve of studying the private neurosis of the middle-
class individual it proved a bust. Whether the subject was
Woodrow Wilson and World War I, as interpreted by Freud
and Bullitt, or the labor strikes of the thirties, as interpreted by
Ernest Jones, or the Hiss-Chambers case of the forties, or the
student revolt of the sixties, those who applied psychoanalysis
as an explanation inevitably did so in a crassly reductionist
fashion, scanting reality and overplaying the unconscious motives of the individual. Such misapplication is due not to

an inherent and incorrigible defect in psychoanalysis itself but to certain problems in its philosophical foundations.

In today's climate of social reform it seems to the authors that there is an excellent reason for fastening upon psychoanalysis and trying to rescue some of its profounder, if less flattering, insights into human nature by presenting them in a new philosophical framework. It will be disastrous if in the current wave of revolt the minds of the gifted young become clouded (as in previous revolutions) by utopian illusions.

In Samuel Beckett's play *Endgame*, at one point the son reviles the father for having begotten him. "I didn't know . . . ," the old man stammers in reply. "You didn't know what!" roars the son. "I didn't know it would be you." When we first began our conversations, we did not know it would end in psychoanalytic theory and in this book. In any case, the matter is now out of our hands, and has to be left in the reader's.

We wish to acknowledge here the great debt we owe to some of the members of the Boston Psychoanalytic Association, in particular to Dr. Leon Shapiro, Dr. Paul Myerson, Dr. Robert Gardner, Dr. Avery Weisman, Dr. Helen Tartakoff, Dr. Joseph Nemetz and Dr. Sanford Gifford. Both as individuals and as a formal study group, their sympathetic scrutiny of the manuscript helped to assure some degree of faithfulness to the great body of unwritten psychoanalytic experience.

The psychoanalytic community has the reputation of being inhospitable to outsiders, especially outsiders who criticize. Our psychoanalysts proved to be the opposite. They struggled to find a common meeting ground with us, and they were genuinely interested in testing the new philosophical theories we proposed.

Finally, we wish to thank Dr. Robert Coles, also of Boston, who read the manuscript and offered many valuable suggestions. To Jane Thompson, Marie Valenta and Joyce Nicholson who typed immeasurable revisions of the manuscript with such forbearance we express our warmest gratitude.

D. Y.
W. B.
New York, 1969

Contents

PART III

A Fresh Start Philosophically

PART IV

Toward Reconstruction

PART V

Beyond Psychoanalysis

PART ONE

FREUD AND THE HUMAN EGO

ONE

Two Worlds ... Two Truths

A few years ago a well-known public figure in the communications world, whom we shall call Mr. N., ended a long period of depression and emotional turmoil by taking his own life. For several years he had been under the care of a noted psychoanalyst, almost as prominent as himself. In the months preceding N.'s suicide, the psychoanalyst had dropped virtually all of his other responsibilities to place himself at the disposal of his patient and friend. When N. died the psychoanalyst felt a sense of poignant personal loss, much like the grief of the immediate family. Some time later a colleague of the psychoanalyst, who had also known N., wondered aloud whether his suicide might have been prevented if the psychoanalyst had been a slightly different sort of person. "Don't get me wrong," he said. "In many ways my colleague is a most gifted and unusual psychoanalyst. Certainly, he's a lot smarter than I am. But I wonder whether I might have been able to save N. if *I* had taken care of him."

He went on to explain: "My colleague is a brilliant man and a thorough intellectual. So, of course, was N. They locked themselves indoors for hours on end, analyzing, analyzing, analyzing. Maybe, just maybe, if I had taken N. outside of that damned library and walked with him—long walks through the countryside . . ." His voice trailed off. After a long pause he added: "I'm a more physical type, more down to earth. Maybe if it had all been a little simpler and more basic—less intellectual —N. might have shaken himself out of it."

To turn abruptly from death to birth, we recall a famous anecdote Freud liked to tell about himself. It concerns an interview with an old Jewish midwife that he had conducted with a number of other young physicians when they were finishing their medical training in Vienna. All were members of Brücke's Institute for Physiology and very proud of their strict allegiance to scientific method. "Why does a baby cry at birth?" asked one of the young scientists. Without hesitation, the old midwife answered, "Because it is afraid." The group—except for Freud—broke out into laughter at the innocence of this unscientific response. Freud later recalled that he exchanged a glance of silent understanding with the midwife and felt that they were the only two in the room who understood the literal truth of her response.

These two incidents show us one side of psychoanalysis—intuitive, unscientific (or at least nonscientific), coping with imponderables, and concerned with the most elemental aspects of human existence. But there is another side. Freud worked unceasingly to make a science out of psychoanalysis, and to do so, he spent much of his time elaborating a set of concepts which he called his "metapsychology." Some parts of the metapsychology were borrowed from the current physical sciences and philosophy, and other parts were drawn directly from his clinical experience. The purpose was to set out in some systematic scientific form the vivid clinical descriptions of his patients and their problems that he had written up in his case histories. (Revealingly, Freud referred to his case histories as his "short stories," not giving them much scientific status in their own right.) In his formal scientific papers and in those of his disciples we find references to no fewer than six metapsychological points of view—topographical, genetic, economic, dynamic, adaptive* and structural; the last is the famous subdivision of personality into id, ego and superego. We also find terms such as "the psychic apparatus," primary and secondary process, libidinal energies, cathexes and counter-cathexes, and so on. By means of such concepts, Freud attempted to bring together his insights into the human condition with what he

---

* The adaptive point of view was added to the metapsychology by Hartmann and others.

considered to be the requirements of scientific explanation. These efforts to translate insight into science continue unabated among his successors up to the present time.

The other human sciences draw a similar, if less sharply defined, line between their descriptive presentations of topics and scientific explanation. The raw materials of sociology and social psychology, for example, include race riots, the conditions of poverty, student protest, drug addiction, delinquency, changing work and leisure habits, social values, the shifting character of the American family—and other events that reflect our society. Academic psychology concerns itself with such basic processes as perception, learning, motivation, thinking, and behavior. Yet, the scientific concepts of these disciplines—social structure, reference groups, cognitive dissonance, anticipatory socialization, operant conditioning, autonomous central processes, and others—like the concepts in Freud's metapsychology, have a quite indirect relationship to their subject matter; often, they seem curiously unrelated to the events they explain. To the observer, the things that are studied and their scientific explanations seem to refer to two quite different worlds and to two quite separate truths. On the one hand, there is the familiar, concrete world of human experience, where rich and famous men who have "everything to live for" nonetheless take their own lives, where babies cry on entering this world because they are afraid, and where black citizens riot because they are angry, poor, and out of patience. When reduced to scientific formulas, however, these human events seem to disappear in abstract and remote causes that are rarely within our experience.

This discrepancy between the two worlds, of everyday experience and of science, does not bother us in a science like physics, probably because we are long accustomed to it. We see before us the flashing orange and blue color and leaping shape of the fire in the grate and we may feel a pleasant and sleepy warmth diffused through the room. Physics tells us that the warmth we feel is "really" only the accelerated agitation of molecules—which we do not experience, at least not as such. The gulf here between our personal experience of the fire and its causal explanation—a gulf that Whitehead called "the bifurcation of nature"—does not trouble most of us (though philosophers have been agonizing over it for the last three hundred years); custom and habit have dulled the shock. But in the case of the newer sciences that deal with man, this splitting of experience into two realms of discourse causes an acute intellectual discomfort and raises many troubling problems, just because the material is so personal in nature.

One might think that the scientists of man, reflecting on the nature of their study, should have been alert to the dangers of adapting a physical, i.e., mechanical, mode of explanation to human experience. Since they study man and society, presumably they must seek to understand man as he lives and works, loves and hates, succeeds and fails, within his specifically human world. On the other hand, psychology and the other human disciplines would seek to be *sciences*. The legacy of scientific thought that they inherited was that the world of physics (the world of molecules, atoms and electrons moving in empty space), was utterly different from the world of our human experience. Human experience, indeed, according to the inherited doctrine, was the arena where objective reality was modified by the personal, subjective element, the one coming in as physical stimuli and the other passing out as subjective projections onto an external environment. How could the points of view of both worlds be maintained? What weight should be given to one or the other? Indeed, how can one even begin to weigh or measure such incommensurables against each other?

The men who founded modern psychology, sociology, and psychoanalysis as empirical sciences at the end of the nineteenth century were not held back by such metaphysical niceties. The physical mode of thought, in its Newtonian form, stood at the height of its power and influence; and these thinkers were tempted to work within that model. To be sure, they did not propose immediately to explain human behavior from the motions of atoms and molecules. (That was a possibility to be left in the back of one's mind.) But they aimed to imitate the physicists' methods. They searched for invariant and deterministic laws to explain human behavior. And if they could not plausibly make use of physical atoms and molecules, they would at least have their psychological equivalents—atoms of elementary experience, conditioned responses, sensations or units of psychic energy that could be linked together in some causal pattern as determined and regular as their physical counterparts. Moreover, they would marshal and apply to the study of man the full institutional and technical arsenal of the physical sciences: laboratory experiments, statistical controls, mathematical modes of measurement, publication of results, replication of experiments, stress on specialization, and above all, the systematic testing of hypotheses.

We have now had almost a century of this vigorous scientific attack, and much of it has come in the past few decades. As of the present time, the results are mixed and confusing. There is much that is positive. One can point to a massive accumulation of specific scientific findings, fact piled upon fact, experiment upon experiment. One can also point to isolated insights of great brilliance, fragments of illumination. At the same time, however, one has the sense of want in the midst of plenty. In spite of great amounts of information, there is at the center no unified perspective within which one can understand the individual and his society. In principle, the reflective person ought to be able to turn to these human sciences for an understanding of his human situation. He should find in psychology a unified conception of human nature and the human condition; in sociology, guidelines about how to best organize society for man's needs (or at least adapt man to society); in psychoanalysis, insight into his own personal anxiety and conflict. But he is not likely to find these things he is looking for. Indeed, his journey through these disciplines may leave him more fatigued, discouraged, and bewildered than when he began. As the philosopher Heidegger perceptively remarked:

> No other epoch has accumulated so great and so varied a store of knowledge concerning man as the present one. No other epoch has succeeded in presenting its knowledge of man so forcibly and so captivatingly as ours, and no other has succeeded in making this knowledge so quickly and easily accessible. But also, no epoch is less sure of its knowledge of what man is than the present one. *In no other epoch has man appeared so mysterious as in ours.* (Heidegger, 1962, p. 206.) (Our italics.)

The problem is not a matter of inadequate means. That is to say, more of the same will not solve it: more experiments, more finely differentiated concepts, more precise measurements, more government grants, more scientific journal articles, more scientific organizations, valuable as all these may be, would only heighten the contrast between data and truth, information and understanding. The problem is ultimately philosophical and lies in our basic ideas and grasp of the material. Science, where it touches upon the human world, is not at all points congruent with the latter, and at some points may be violently out of touch. The scientific study of man does not yet draw close to ordinary human experience.

This book will focus mainly upon psychoanalysis because it exemplifies in a crucial and striking way the distortions in philosophic perspective that afflict the other behavioral sciences as well. Psychoanalysis is one of the most original, and consequently characteristic, products of our period, and, as such, seems to share in all the ambiguities of our ambiguous century. In its theoretical position it stands in an ambiguous relation to science and art; in practice it occupies a position between medicine and psychology. By attempting to make a science out of the existential events of our human experience, it seems to raise the whole question of "the two worlds" in the most radical form.

Unlike most other branches of behavioral science, psychoanalysis is involved with the human person concretely—and too much cannot be made of this point. In discussing psychoanalytic practice, we will sometimes use the expressions "clinical material" and "clinical data" with a certain irony; the analyst, in his practice, cannot forget that his "clinical materials" are in fact flesh-and-blood people, and that his "clinical data" are usually the troubled problems of those people who come to him concerned or even anguished over their lives. In certain branches of scientific psychology, the experimenter may concern himself with monkeys, rats, dogs, fishes, earthworms or computers. Behaviorist psychologists may deal with human subjects, but often are concerned only with a fragment of the person—as a perceiving mechanism or as a performer of learning tasks. The human personality as a whole is excluded by the very selectivity of the experimenter's goal in research, the tools that he uses, his philosophical frame of reference—and even his idiosyncratic interests. For odd as it may sound, there are psychologists who do not profess to be interested in people and who on occasion will even say so. The psychoanalyst, however mechanistic his official language, cannot escape some kind of encounter with the human person who is his patient and who, in fact, is presenting a human plea to another human whom he has chosen as *his* doctor.

Initially, we propose to concentrate on that segment of psychoanalysis known today as *psychoanalytic ego psychology,* a topic that has assumed great prominence since Freud's death. This emphasis may seem odd in light of the fact that the revolution accomplished by Freud is usually spoken of as the dethronement of the ego before the forces of the unconscious. And, with the proper qualifications, this description is still correct; Freud himself compared his place in history to that of Copernicus and Darwin, who also had dethroned human *hybris* and given mankind a sobering lesson in humility. Copernicus had shown that the earth was not the center of the solar system, and that consequently man did not occupy the central place in the cosmos. Darwin had made clear that the human species was not the product of a special creation that placed man apart from and above the other animals but was in fact the outcome of a long chain of evolution from the lowest and humblest forms of organic life. Now, with Freud, came the most humbling news of all: the lordly ego, center of meaning and value, could no longer be taken as the master within its own house, the human psyche; instead, it bends in servitude to unconscious forces.

Freud was not the first to take note of the unconscious; many philosophers before him had recognized its importance and reality. But their treatments of it rather resemble the voyages of St. Brendan and Leif Ericson to America, transient and unnoticed deeds that resulted in no permanent settlements. Columbus is America's discoverer because he brought the new world for the first time before the awareness of the old. Since Freud took clinical possession of the new continent, he will rightfully go down in history as the discoverer of the unconscious. And whatever one's cavils, one has to recognize that his is the prime psychological discovery of the century, and that it marks a genuine revolution in man's thinking about himself.

But revolutionaries must learn to govern. This practical need has always made it necessary for revolutions, no matter how extreme or pure, to compromise with the conditions and knowledge that preceded them. Every revolution has to learn to be more than one-sided, or it will perish, and the psychoanalytic revolution is no exception. Post-Freudian analysts, taking their cue from revisions Freud himself made in the theory in the 1920's and 1930's, have had, bit by bit, to accommodate themselves to an older wisdom and accord the ego a more prominent role. The source of this trend toward modification was the physician's commitment to cure his patient; clinical experience found that the ego, once regarded as altogether weak and ineffectual, did indeed play a powerful role in the therapy itself.

Learning to give the human ego its just role in the economy of the human psyche was perhaps the most difficult problem Freud wrestled with throughout his long professional career. At the very beginning of his investigations, Freud accepted the conventional nineteenth century philosophy that mental life begins and ends with consciousness. As the importance of unconscious instinctual forces unfolded in his investigations, he began to downgrade consciousness, freedom, and choice, and came to believe that these were mere epiphenomena, effects rather than causes, similar to the spray that is churned up by the ocean but powerless to move the depths beneath it. Reality lay elsewhere, in the workings of unconscious biological forces blindly obedient to the laws of nature.

In the last third of his life, however, Freud began to reassess the role of ego function. He saw a need for a better understanding of the balance between ego strength and instinctual drive, and attempts to achieve this caused him considerable trouble in his later years; he wavered back and forth more than on any other single major psychoanalytic concept. In the end he remained faithful to the main thrust of his work, emphasizing the primacy of the biologically fixed instinctual drives as the prime movers of human life. But his followers picked up where he left off in his reformulations of ego, and as a consequence the history of psychoanalysis from Freud's death to the present time is, to a significant extent, that of ego psychology.

The importance of ego function in the therapeutic process had been brought to the foreground by the attempt to remove a specific obstacle to therapy. In 1936, when Freud was still alive and struggling with this problem, his daughter, Anna Freud, in a psychoanalytic classic, *The Ego and the Mechanisms of Defense*, pointed out what Freud and other psychoanalysts had long experienced in practice: that the ego defenses play a major, if negative, role in the therapeutic process: most of the hours people spend in psychoanalysis are devoted to working through the resistances thrown up by these defenses.

Step by step, psychoanalysts have added to the significance and complexity of the ego's functions within the whole psychic life. Current emphasis on ego strength and conflict-free ego function (Hartmann), identity (Erikson), ego autonomy (Rapaport), the self (Jacobson), hope (French), responsibility (Weisman), and so-called early object relations (Spitz, Wolf, Mahler, and others)—all deal in one way or another with the psychology of the ego. It is gradually becoming clear, however, that these contributions outstrip both the philosophical and psychological underpinnings of the basic theory. The superstructure has become top-heavy. To make a comparison with the history of another science: Ptolemaic astronomy during the Middle Ages could always accommodate its already complicated system of cycles and epicycles to a new astronomical discovery by adding another epicycle to explain an irregular movement. The theory could thus be maintained logically forever, but at a certain point it simply became implausible and cumbersome, and the simpler course was to scrap it. Some of the newer theories within psychoanalysis seem to be adding epicycles in the same way.

Some psychoanalysts have begun to worry about this clash between the new emphasis on ego and the older psychoanalytic emphasis on the instinctual drives, but most are not overly concerned with this or similar problems of the metapsychology. One prominent analyst conjectured privately that few psychoanalysts grasp the total structure of psychoanalytic theory. This failure arises not from a lack of intelligence but the lack of any sound practical *motive* for grappling with the intricacies of the metapsychology. Most practitioners simply do not see how the metapsychology can help them to cope with the concrete problems of their patients. (The best theoreticians, it should be noted, are not necessarily the most gifted therapists.) Under the pressure of a special case or a special interest, an analyst may have occasion to dig more deeply into some one or another aspect of the theory. But many are not concerned with or interested in the metapsychological, that is, the more general and abstract side of the theory.

To claim that many psychoanalysts do not understand certain aspects of their own theory may sound like a paradox in an age when most educated people are sure that *they* understand psychoanalysis. But the fact that so many people think they grasp the essential principles of psychoanalysis serves as an obstacle to true understanding, preventing the full complexity of psychoanalysis from being recognized. Psychoanalytic theory still remains one of the most complex, inaccessible, and misunderstood theories in contemporary culture.

The conflict between ego and unconscious, between ego and instincts, that emerges within psychoanalytic ego psychology serves, in effect, as a remarkable philosophical case history; if it did not exist, one would almost have had to invent it. For it is the contemporary expression of the central philosophical issue of modern Western thought. In its eighteenth century version, this issue took the form of materialism versus religion; in the nineteenth century materialism versus idealism; and today, in the final third of the twentieth century, it has taken the form of *scientific* materialism versus existentialism.

Certain long-standing problems in psychoanalysis have increasingly become polarized around this philosophical tension between scientific materialism and existentialism. The most abstract level of psychoanalytic theory, its metapsychology, represents in almost pure form the late nineteenth century version of scientific materialism (i.e., the human person is conceptualized in analogy with a material object as a "psychic apparatus" powered by energies whose accumulation and discharge are as lawfully regulated as any machine). Psychoanalytic practice, on the other hand, is, in psychoanalyst Avery Weisman's apt phrase, "existential at its core" (i.e., it is dominated by the human encounter between two subjects and the transformations that take place in both of them). Thus, psychoanalysis has one foot firmly planted in scientific materialism and the other equally firmly in existentialism, which is at violent odds with the former and indeed was largely conceived in opposition to it. A rigorous adherence to both philosophies would tear psychoanalysis apart.

Oddly enough, the practical consequences of adhering to two mutually exclusive philosophies have been less traumatic for psychoanalysis than might have been expected. Psychoanalysts have found a way of living more or less comfortably with two incompatible philosophies. Most of them avoid the full brunt of the conflict by failing to take their own metapsychology at face value; instead of using it as an active scientific theory, they pay obeisance to it as an inert, if sacred, object. They bow to it in their writings, they translate their clinical findings into its ritual language (sometimes with considerable loss of meaning and clarity), and each of the many times it is damaged by a new clinical discovery, they lovingly restore it (Hartmann and Rapaport are the main architects of restoration since Freud's death). But it is a measure of the futility of such tinkering that it serves only to ensnare psychoanalysis more deeply than ever in a web of concepts so complex and so involuted that many psychoanalysts can barely manage to follow its theoretical twists and turns, let alone reconcile its inconsistencies. For example, psychoanalysts cannot, without playing semantic tricks on themselves, explain the phenomena of identity and the therapeutic alliance in the terms of their own metapsychology. Instead, they have grown accustomed to living with the inconsistency of the "two truths."

One principal reason, therefore, for choosing psychoanalysis as our paradigm case is that its two main facets (its clinical practice and its metapsychology) illustrate perfectly the conflicts that are created in a human science when a basic inconsistency of perspectives is left unreconciled. The various efforts by psychoanalysts, including Freud himself, Hartmann, Erikson, and others, to reconcile the irreconcilable, efforts on which great intelligence, ingenuity, and energy have been spent, strongly suggest that the problem cannot be resolved until one is willing to go beyond its symptomatic expression in psychoanalysis (in the impasse of its ego theory) to its philosophical origins.

Why should the psychology of the ego be so central to this effort? First of all, the ego, in one of its chief aspects at least, is the nuclear center of our consciousness. There is no consciousness, as Kant long ago pointed out, unless it is accompanied by the "I think." As such a nuclear center, it is the locus of all meaning, and consequently of the possible meaningfulness of the individual's life itself. The problem of the continuing "I" is the problem of self-identity, which has now become so acute for psychoanalysis as well as for our civilization as a whole. Then there is the difficulty of describing the fundamental structure of the human ego, which is not a simple physical object and for which the analogies borrowed from the physical sciences are obviously both inadequate and distorting. From Socrates to the present time, philosophers have known that man's conception of himself is an inherent part of that self: we become different beings in the light of a changed idea of our own being. This is the ontological issue, which raises questions about the very nature of the human person as a subject for inquiry. Further, a root epistemological question arises if the inquiry is to be carried on scientifically: how the methods of science are to be adapted to fit the subject. Then, too, the ego as the actively evaluating center of the human personality brings forward the whole question of what values are and what their status is. Finally, unlike some of the more archaic strata of the unconscious psyche whose functioning is not usually related to the urgent issues of the day, the ego does live out its life within historical time, and its essential fate is coupled with that of its culture and its epoch. Here radical questions arise about the cultural and historical dimensions of man's being. Do human history and culture transform human nature? Or is the whole time-order of human history merely a peripheral episode within the immensely longer and immensely slower time-order of natural evolution?

The new psychoanalytic ego psychology opens up a Pandora's box of basic problems. If these were confined to psychoanalysis, it would concern no one but the members of that remarkable profession. But psychoanalysis has become so enmeshed in the academic disciplines and in the general culture that its intellectual conflicts have a wider relevance. More importantly, the problems involved touch upon the most fundamental philosophical questions about man's nature and culture. Far from being a matter of provincial scientific interest, a shift in basic psychoanalytic premises would imply a corresponding shift in our general outlook.

The history of science is full of instances of large philosophical issues provoked by a persistent probing into seemingly narrow technical matters. Einstein's revolution and the changing world view that came with it grew out of a series of experimental failures to find the ether drag called for by Newtonian theory. The freedom of modern mathematics from empirical premises grew, in part, out of Lobachevski's technical failure to prove that it was impossible for parallel lines to meet in space. The Copernicus-Kepler-Galileo revolution that only now after three centuries is drawing to a close, grew initially out of a concern with fairly narrow measurement errors ensuing from Ptolemaic theory. (Even Galileo believed, on religious grounds, that the orbits described by the planets formed perfect circles, circular motion having certain mystical qualities of perfection.) And Freud started his second and more famous career (he was a research physiologist in his early professional years) with the technical problem of searching for the physiological etiology of female hysteria.

In each of these famous instances, as a narrow and stubborn problem within a specialized field of inquiry received closer scrutiny, it became evident that previous efforts to solve it had failed because of a flaw in basic theory. In the process of correcting the theory, new views of nature were created and new shifts in perspective emerged that permanently changed the features of our human world.

Such is the case with psychoanalytic ego psychology. It is but a fragment of a single discipline. Yet, it leads us to reexamine the fundamental ideas on which psychoanalysis is built. Conversely, a solution to the central dilemma within psychoanalysis can contribute to solving the larger philosophical problem of the two worlds and the two truths. Roughly speaking, we can therefore say that the problem may be approached either from the side of philosophy, where it is posed in a general way, or from one of its more special embodiments, such as psychoanalysis, where it emerges when one attempts to develop specialized theories about certain forms of human motivation and behavior. The philosophers on whom we shall draw, such as Whitehead, Heidegger, and Wittgenstein, have all, in their separate ways, worked at finding a way around the impasse created by the doctrine of the two worlds—the world of physical science and the world of man. The collection of insights, hints, and dicta thrown out by these thinkers moves toward a resolution of the paradoxes. If they have, starting from one end, dug a tunnel two-thirds of the way through the philosophical mountain, our procedure will be to start from the other end, from psychoanalysis, in the hope that the two paths will meet.

TWO

Freud I (Pre-1895)
The Case of Miss Lucy

Freud's character suggests depths and complexities that psycho-analysts delight in rediscovering when they read his clinical cases and the personal notes that accompany them. The question of his personality falls outside our scope here, but the qualities of Freud's mind do concern us, since they are seen in operation in the parts of his theory we shall be analyzing. And what strikes one is a complexity of mind not usually visible in popular summaries of his thought. It has often been noted with what asperity Freud dealt with deviationists within the movement in his zeal to preserve the core of psychoanalysis. Yet rigidity is one of the last things one could charge against him in view of the varied formulations of his own doctrine. Everywhere he exhibits the tentative and hesitant character of his theoretical concepts and interpretations—and most of all in his case studies, where he was directly in contact with his material. These case studies, in fact, are a central achievement of his genius.

It is a difficult task to trace the patterns of theory as they wind through the labyrinth of these cases. The division of Freud's thought into three stages—Freud I, Freud II, Freud III—which we borrow with modifications from David Rapaport, is not an ironclad compartmentalization. It does, however, present the most salient points that need to be examined for any reconstruction of theory.

Freud did not set out to become a revolutionary; on the contrary, his mind was of a decidedly conservative cast. He remarks in one place that the revolutionary as such is an undesirable character. It is sometimes thought that he was referring here merely to the social or political revolutionary, but in fact the remark expresses his own general intellectual temperament. In matters of philosophy, particularly, he was quite willing to accept an inherited framework without critical questioning; and this curiously conservative aspect of his theorizing will emerge as a major point in the following analysis. The people he treated, and their histories, were his laboratory, and his genius lay in patient, stubborn observation, following step by step where these unlikely cases—which had previously been deemed unrewarding and unappetizing material for psychology—led him. They led him, of course, to the point where he was forced to become a revolutionary himself.

In one general respect the opposing tendencies of Freud's mind fit his historical situation. Freud very much belongs to his time and place; and to say this is of course no denigration. What was the significance of the particular historical juncture in which Freud arrived? On this point Erik Erikson offers a most suggestive phrase. Freud was, Erikson remarks, "at the end of the era of absolute reason." What Erikson seems to have in mind here is that the nineteenth century was the continuation of the rationalism of the Enlightenment, while our century by contrast—with its wars and totalitarian terrors as well as its scientific discoveries about human nature—can no longer continue in the supreme confidence that rational consciousness is the absolute center of the human personality. In laying bare this darker side of man Freud is, of course, a leading if not the leading pioneer. Yet it is paradoxical that in doing so he employs the theoretical framework of a reductive rationalism that belongs to nineteenth-century positivism. The paradox is further heightened by the fact that there was much of the poet in Freud; some of his key concepts—the Oedipus complex, the forces of Eros and Thanatos—have a sweeping poetic power. Indeed, some academic psychologists are still unwilling even to entertain these ideas because they are "mere poetry" and therefore not scientific. Positivist and poet—that is one way of stating the opposing aspects of Freud's mind.

They are aspects of the tension that make his thought richer; but within his whole theory they rest in very unstable equilibrium.

The case of Miss Lucy is not one of Freud's more complicated and labyrinthine studies. In its very simplicity, however, it reveals in the most clear-cut manner his earlier views of the role and function of the ego in human personality. The year was 1892, and Freud had not yet created psychoanalysis. His treatment of Miss Lucy, and the fundamental concepts by which he understood her illness, are rather startling if one looks back at them from the point of view of later psychoanalytic theory.

Miss Lucy was an English governess working for a well-to-do family in Vienna. She was referred to Freud by her physician after she had complained of being pursued almost continuously by the smell of burned pudding—a sensation she found quite distressing. She also suffered from low spirits, constant fatigue, loss of appetite, diminished efficiency and "heaviness in the head." After several sessions, Freud discovered that the sensation of the smell of burned pudding had first occurred after Lucy's employer had scolded her rather severely for permitting his children to be kissed on the mouth by a casual friend. The father had a horror of this kind of contact for children. He held their governess responsible for seeing to it that they were not exposed to this unseemly breach of the Victorian health code.

In another session, Freud's probing had already brought to light an incident that preceded the scolding: Lucy had had a rather tender discussion with her employer, who was a widower. The talk had raised hopes in her about being able eventually to replace his dead wife. When, however, her employer took her to task in so cold and impersonal a manner, these hopes were destroyed. It was this experience that eventually brought on the symptoms, though they did not appear right after it. Several other related events took place at later times and served to reinforce the disagreeable and anxiety-evoking character of the original scolding.

CONVERSION REACTION

Conditions of Hysteria

When Lucy came to him late in 1892, Freud had already treated a number of women for hysteria and had developed a clear-cut theory of how its history unfolds. He had discovered several types, and Miss Lucy's case was the most prevalent kind, involving marked methods of defense on the part of the patient. The patient attempts to defend herself against having to face the consequences of a disagreeable experience by deliberately pushing the memory of it out of consciousness. The defensive maneuver does not quite succeed and the excitation associated with the disagreeable idea is not eliminated or discharged, but instead emerges in the guise of the hysterical symptoms.

Freud traced the development of hysteria in the following steps:

1. The patient must have undergone a "traumatic experience," that is, an experience that (a) stirs up a considerable amount of emotions and excitation and (b) gives the person a feeling of intense "unpleasure" at the time. (Freud had not yet defined "unpleasure" as anxiety, and it was only later that he turned to defining anxiety.)

2. The trauma must represent to the patient some idea or ideas incompatible with "the dominant mass of ideas constituting the ego."

3. The incompatible idea is "*intentionally* repressed from consciousness." (Our italics.)

4. The excitation accompanying the incompatible idea is converted into somatic tension (which manifests itself in such symptoms as fatigue, depression, loss of appetite, paralysis, and the rest).

5. All that remains in consciousness is a mnemic (remembered) symbol that is connected with the event by the process of association, which may well be a disguised association. (For Lucy the mnemic symbol was the smell of pudding that had burned when she and the children had forgotten about

it. Freud, however, discovered that the smell was a surrogate for the heavy odor of cigar smoke that had been in the air at the time her employer had severely reprimanded her.

6. If the memory of the traumatic experience can be brought into consciousness, and the patient can be made to see the connection between the experience and its affects, then the paralyzing quality of the latter is discharged and the symptoms disappear.

It is worth looking a little more closely at this conception of hysteria. The symptoms, according to Freud, are brought on by the incompatibility between an idea as it is symbolized in a traumatic experience, and "the dominant mass of ideas constituting the ego." Though he does not tell us directly what these phrases mean, Freud's answers are nonetheless implicit in the case material.

The "dominant mass of ideas constituting the ego" for Lucy was her conception of herself as future mistress of the house, with the possible life and status she might have as wife and surrogate mother in the household, and the conception centered on her perception of her employer's attitude toward her. Her second perception of his attitude—the discovery that her employer regarded her merely as a governess—was obviously not compatible with the first. Note that we are not talking about logical incompatibility alone; a person may certainly hold two incompatible ideas at the same time without the profound psychological repercussions of this episode. The magnitude of those repercussions was the result of a clash between two emotionally charged perceptions. cognitive dissonance

It is important to notice that these perceptions are not, in Lucy's case, isolated experiences; their import has to be taken in connection with Lucy's understanding of herself and her possible place in the world, of the possible life and status she might have as wife and surrogate mother in the household.

At this early stage of his thinking Freud is not concerned with the *content* of his patient's ideas, beyond noting the frequent association with sexuality. (It is not until after *Studies on Hysteria* was published that Freud came out flatly with the statement that if one traces the symptoms to their origins one must inevitably arrive at a root sex experience.) (Freud, 1896,

p. 434.) At this early period Freud was primarily concerned
with tracking down whatever of his patients' ideas seemed to
carry conflicting emotions with them (whether or not those
ideas or emotions had specifically sexual content), and finding
out what happens when the emotion is strangulated. What
emerges in the case we have summarized as the "dominant mass
of ideas" does not include, or only very indirectly, any specifically sexual material; rather, the ideas at issue are Lucy's own
conceptions of herself, her views of her place in the world, her
values, hopes, ideals, and her specific notions about what is correct and proper and what is shameful and embarrassing. The
constellation of these ideas, as Freud presents the case, is what
constitutes the personal identity of Miss Lucy.

In discussing this case Freud also makes a number of comments of the kind one does not usually associate with the
famous determinist and scientist. He speaks plainly and clearly
of Lucy's act of volition in suppressing the memory of her
employer's scolding. His view at this time was that when a
repudiated idea is suppressed from consciousness, it forms the
basis of a whole new group of ideas; it becomes in effect a
nucleus around which all ideas and experiences that would
"imply an acceptance of the incompatible idea" subsequently
collect. This entire complex of ideas will have to be suppressed
if the ego's conception of itself is to be defended. Hence, the
intricacy of detective-work in ferreting out the nuclear idea in
the complex. The whole effort of defense is, initially at least, a
conscious one; and Freud explicitly states that "the splitting of
consciousness in these cases of acquired hysteria is accordingly
a deliberate and intentional one." And he has qualified it
morally: "The mechanism which produces hysteria represents
on the one hand *an act of moral cowardice* and on the other a
defensive measure which is at the disposal of the ego." (Our
italics.) Pushing the unpleasant idea out of consciousness may
be an expedient thing to do at the time, but, as Freud adds, "a
greater amount of moral courage would have been of advantage
to the person concerned." (Freud, 1895, pp. 121–24.)

At this stage, then, we see that Freud attributed a considerable autonomy to the ego—more indeed than he was ever to
concede to ego processes again. The idea of voluntary suppression of ideas from consciousness, as well as the further judg-

ment that Lucy's volition lacked moral strength, are not compatible with Freud's later determinism. This style of comment was soon to disappear from his writings (if not from his informal discussions), and he was to squelch it vigorously wherever it appeared in the writings of others.

We can sum up Freud's thinking at this stage by listing three aspects of the ego that appear in these early writings:

1. *The Ego as Consciousness.* Freud had studied with the philosopher Brentano, who stressed the intentionality of consciousness. That is, consciousness always intends or means something; it is always consciousness *of*. The ego, in this aspect, is that which grasps meanings and performs intentional acts. As such, it is coextensive with consciousness itself. There are no floating thoughts without an "I" who thinks them.

2. *The Ego as Agent and Object of Defense.* Here the ego engages in defensive maneuvers to guard itself against unwanted and threatening ideas.

These two aspects of the ego, consciousness and defense, are further combined into a single dynamic principle: "An idea becomes pathogenic when its content is in opposition to the predominant trend of the patient's mental life, so that it provokes him into defense." (Freud, 1900, p. 109.)

By "dominant trend of the patient's life" Freud clearly means the pattern of ideas, the structure of intentions, that give the patient's life its particular form of meaningfulness. He was thus very close to Brentano's notion of consciousness as intentionality, which was then current.

3. *The Ego as Subject.* Here the term, less formal and systematic than in the previous two aspects, is frequently used as a loose synonym for the whole person.

Yet here too, Freud's usage is connected with a formal philosophical tradition. It was the general philosophical tendency at that time to equate consciousness with the whole person as *subject*, which was then contrasted with the "external world" as *object*. Only many years later, most formally in 1923, did Freud sharply distinguish between the whole person and the ego—the latter being coextensive with only a part of the person's mental processes.

In all three aspects of the ego—consciousness, defense, and subject—we are struck by the importance Freud attributed at that time to the individual's power of will, intention, and volition. And we are all the more struck when we realize that this emphasis diverges from the views of two prominent contemporaries—his collaborator Breuer and the eminent French psychiatrist, Janet. Many years after *Studies on Hysteria*, reviewing the course of his own development, Freud wrote: "Janet attributed to hysterical patients a constitutional inability to hold the contents of their minds together." Janet held this inability to be a structural and hereditary difficulty, and therefore did not touch upon the ego's function as consciousness and defense; and for this very reason Freud rejected Janet's view. On the other hand, Freud states that Breuer "supposed that the pathogenic ideas arose during hypnoid states" (Freud, 1922, p. 109); that is, that Breuer attributed the destructive character of the trauma not to incompatibility with the patient's other ideas but to the fact that the trauma took place when the patient found himself in this altered state of being. Thus both Breuer's and Janet's explanations of hysteria would bypass the factors of volition, conflict of ideas, and the intentional function of the ego. And precisely for this reason, Freud rejected both explanations. In this opposition to two distinguished contemporaries we have the strongest indication of how central a role the ego played in Freud's early thinking.

Keeping these three aspects of the ego's function—consciousness, defense and subject—firmly in mind, let us proceed now to Freud's second phase, during which psychoanalysis in a strict sense really emerges.

POSTSCRIPT

For the sake of both convenience and precision, we shall follow the historical scheme advanced by David Rapaport, one of the outstanding scholars of psychoanalysis, which divides the history of psychoanalytic ego psychology into four phases. Phase I—approximately 1883 to 1902—covers the period of Freud's collaboration with Breuer, the publication of Studies on Hysteria, *Freud's abortive attempts to develop a* Project for a Scientific Psychology *(discovered only a few years ago), and the publication of the monumental* Interpretation of Dreams *in the last year of the century. In this phase, the ego is mainly identified with consciousness and with defense. A concept of ego as person holds a central position in the theory.*

Rapaport's second phase, from 1902 to 1923, covers the development of psychoanalysis proper. It was in this first quarter of the century that Freud made his most brilliant discoveries, correcting, amplifying, and enormously enriching psychoanalytic theory as it was first set down in the work on dreams. In its treatment of the ego this phase differs from the first in two key respects: ego considerations fade into the background while the instinctual side of man's life—especially the sex instincts—receives concentrated attention; and the concept of ego as instinct is superimposed on the earlier definitions.

The third phase cited by Rapaport, 1923 to Freud's death, is the most complex. The notion of ego as a group of instincts is dropped in favor of the concept of ego as structure. We have now entered the familiar Freudian landscape of the three-part division of personality into ego, id, and superego. In some respects, the ego is restored to the foreground of attention; in other respects, its importance is diminished. Throughout this period, Freud constantly re-examined his theory of ego function, seeking to place the ego in its proper relation to man's instinctual life. He was dissatisfied with his solutions, and he kept coming back to the question of where and how the ego fits and what importance is to be given to it.

The fourth phase deals mainly with the development of ego psychology after Freud's death. It begins with Anna Freud's important work, The Ego and the Mechanisms of Defense (written in 1936, several years before Freud died), and is carried up to the present time through the work of Hartmann, Kris, Erikson, Arlow, Brenner, and others. Hartmann's notion of conflict-free spheres of ego-function together with Erikson's enrichment of the concept of identity, plus all the increased emphasis by analysts on the "therapeutic alliance," give ego psychology a far more central position in psychoanalytic thinking than it has ever enjoyed before.

In tracing the story of psychoanalytic ego psychology, we have departed slightly from Rapaport's dates by placing the beginning of the second phase in 1895 rather than in 1902. The 1895 date seems more appropriate since it marks the beginning of Freud's independent work, and it brings with it the two discoveries that Freud, himself, cites as the true start of psychoanalysis—the technique of free association and Freud's discovery of the sexual etiology of the neuroses.

There is, we realize, a false exactness in setting precise dates on a movement of ideas: psychoanalysis is too rich and too complex to be boxed into neat time units. Care has been taken with certain dates, however, when these have a direct bearing on important turning points in the theory.

THREE

Freud II (1895–1923)
The Discovery of Instinct

In the second phase of Freud's development six new aspects of the ego and its functioning were added to the three delineated in his earliest discoveries. In addition to conceiving it under the aspects of consciousness, defense, and subject, the ego was now seen to be:

4. Intrinsically bound up with the instinct for self-preservation;

5. Intrinsically connected with the instincts of aggression and hate;

6. Intrinsically bound up with libidinal pleasure;

7. A structure that emerges from the well-known "secondary process." The "primary process" is the name for all those laws that cover the workings of the unconscious or the id; and by contrast the secondary processes cover the workings of the preconscious (which is on the threshold of consciousness) and the ego. In effect, this comes to defining the ego as what is not id.

8. Controlling access to motility (motion, or action). The ego elaborates plans and decides for or against action. It can thus release or inhibit motion on the part of the human being; and

9. The receptor of sensory data.

Since the original three aspects of the ego were not rejected, the conception of the ego is now greatly enriched, and in this new phase each aspect of its function covers a vast domain of mental life.

As psychoanalysis evolved, these various meanings would appear, be defined, transformed, disappear and then again reappear later in slightly changed form. Some meanings, such as the "ego as source and goal of instinct" and the "ego as a weapon of hate and aggression" were eventually qualified out of existence. But at one time or another they all played their part in the development of psychoanalytic theory.

What is one to make of these nine organizing concepts? At first glance it would seem that they overlap and are confusing, that there is no need for so many subdivisions. The very concept of ego could be meaningless if it were used as a catch-all term to refer to whatever forces are found in the many conflicts Freud investigated and also, on the other hand, to refer to the concrete person in whom these conflicts are taking place.

Why should there have been this confusing proliferation of meanings at this stage? True, the subject matter of psychoanalysis is extraordinarily complex; and some writers give this as a reason for the multiplication of meanings attached to the ego at this period. But Freud was too gifted in coping with complex subjects to allow mere complexity to lead him into confusion. Yet he was not always as precise as he might have been. Sometimes when asked why he used a certain word he would answer in self-deprecation that it was pure Viennese *"Schlamperei."* Yet, neither Viennese "carelessness" nor the complexity of the subject explains why the theory of the ego is so steeped in ambiguity at this stage.

The reason may well be that at this stage in the development of psychoanalysis, Freud and his followers were simply not concerned with the conscious and voluntary aspects of the ego. As Anna Freud and others have stated, analysts in this formative period steered away from the study of the ego because of their belief that "the value of their scientific and therapeutic work was in direct proportion to the psychic strata upon which attention was focused." (Freud, A. 1936.) These psychic strata were assumed to lie beyond and beneath the ego. In fact, many analysts felt that the very term "psychoanalysis" should be reserved for the new discoveries of unconscious psychic life, and that the conscious values of the individual, the adjustment of children and adults to their world, and other "rational" concerns were not the proper object of this new discipline. In other words, psychoanalysts in this period tended to concentrate on one side of psychic conflict—the instinctual and the repressed. They tended, therefore, to think of the other side as being the ego—whatever this other side happened to be. Since they were not interested in this side of the psyche, they were not concerned with differentiating or describing it accurately.

If there is any consideration of ego forces at this earlier period, it is because of the observed presence of conflict in Freud's patients. Conflict is probably the key notion throughout all Freud's thinking. (Erikson states that psychoanalysis is the view of man as conflict.) In all of Freud's most far-reaching theories, one basic human experience is pitted against another: love is set against hate; civilization opposes the individual; the instincts of self-preservation conflict with the sexual drives; the pleasure principle, although often supposed to be served by the managing reality principle, fundamentally clashes with the latter; and in Freud's ultimate metaphysical statement, the two basic instincts of life and death are always to be found in a state of tension one with the other. Indeed, in this last and most metaphysical of his antinomies—between the will to life and the will to death—Freud was only making explicit a view he had long harbored that the organism always seeks to ward off stimuli and to return to a state of quiescence (the death wish). To this Nirvana principle he opposes the organism's thrust to action which will satisfy those drives that move it toward relations with objects within the world.

During Freud's most productive adult years—from the age of thirty-nine to sixty-seven, 1895 to 1923—he was preoccupied with that side of human conflict that comes in the first few years of the life of the individual, and in the life of the race (the archaic traces of man's long prehistory), in other words the side that is unconscious and hidden from view within the present. Freud saw these unconscious impulses in a state of active turmoil—pressing for release, distorted by rage, fear, and frustration, held down at the cost of tremendous expenditures of energy, yet still managing to break through, and threatening to ruin his patients' lives. His insights into these various forms of conflict were to color his total view of man.

Clearly, any man's most fundamental philosophical outlook will be revealed by how he judges the balance of the forces of life and death, being and nothingness, vitality and decay. Does he see the individual destroyed by civilization or enhanced by it? Does he perceive all nature, all being, all life, pulled inexorably back to inertness and death? Or is the thrust of life, as he sees it, always creating new things under the sun? No man can escape the fact of conflict—it is a dominant theme of life. If you know how a man feels about the way the most basic conflicts get themselves resolved, you have grasped a key aspect of his philosophy of life.

Many writers have suggested that there is a profound streak of pessimism in Freud. Since his thought kept pulling him toward the negative side of each of his antinomies, he could not, apparently, escape the feeling that non-being was stronger than being and that man was drawn inexorably toward the void of nothingness. Though this was to some extent his temperamental tendency, it would be wrong to overemphasize this aspect of Freud's emotional make-up. He also saw himself as a conquistador, an explorer who strove to reach new shores of understanding, and his life was dedicated to the creative endeavors of understanding. However his own thoughts may have turned toward the void, he remained a thoroughly active, involved and committed person until the age of eighty-three!

His pessimism is not necessarily explained through his temperament. Nor was it a strict consequence of his empirical discoveries of the destructive modes of neurotic conflict. The source of this so-called "pessimism" lay rather in a prior commitment to a metaphysical framework that forced him, by its inexorable logic, to impose a negative view on his data. This last contention may strike the reader at this point as being too great an interpretive leap, and indeed we have to postpone its substantiation to a later part of this chapter when we shall be able to show how his dependence upon the Helmholtz school of physiology set Freud's thinking in a mold that inevitably led him to view man in a negative and reductive fashion. To prepare for that conclusion, we have first to set forth in more detail the theory of the ego in this second phase—a theory which in fact turns out to be neither clear nor straightforward, but rather tangled in its development.

Ego as Instinct

The first fundamental shift in Freud's thinking about the ego is his change from the ego conceived as a dominant mass of ideas to the ego conceived as a kind of nuclear center of various instincts—particularly those instincts that center on the individual's struggle for survival.

His instinct theory as a whole grew out of a series of hypotheses Freud gradually evolved out of his clinical observations. From 1895 to 1900, the beginning of Phase II, his theory of neurosis crystallized around four key points: (a) that repressed sexuality was to be found in *all* neurotic conflicts; (b) that neurosis was rooted in early, not adult, sexual experience; (c) that the traumatic early sexual experience took the form of an actual seduction of the patient by a parent or some other adult* and (d) that the cause of the neurosis was not repressed sexuality alone but a conflict between sexuality and the ego.

Freud's hypothesis of the sexual source of all neuroses emerged from a prolonged search for the traumas that lie behind hysterical symptoms. Referring to cases like that of Miss Lucy, he kept asking why a commonplace occurrence (the relatively mild event of Lucy's scolding by her employer) should become a trauma intense enough to produce severe hysterical and somatic symptoms. He concluded that the experience could possess such shattering force only because of its link with some earlier sexual trauma. "Eventually it became inevitable to bow before the evidence and to recognize that *at the root of the formation of every neurotic symptom is to be found traumatic experiences from early sexual life*." (Our italics.) (Freud, 1896.)

Note that Freud did not attribute all pathogenic symptoms

---

* Freud had suspected this at an earlier time, when he collaborated with Breuer, but was not able to reach agreement with the latter on its importance.

to early sexual trauma. Neurotic symptoms are distinguished from the symptoms of "common nervousness and anxiety"; adult sexual disturbances, he held, were the cause of the latter, and they were relieved when the abuses were relieved. Further, the symptoms of neurosis were distinguished from the psychoses, the psychosomatic disorders, and many other human disorders of psychological origin; contrary to what many simplifiers insist, Freud traced only one category of psychological disturbance back to early sexual disturbance. *Neurosis*

He insisted, too—and this is most germane—that the neuroses are not traceable to sexuality alone, but to the conflict between sexuality and ego. Over a period of years, and scattered through many papers (1896, 1911, 1914, and 1923), the following picture emerges: The sexual impulses are repressed and prevented from direct satisfaction because they are not "ego-syntonic," that is, they are incompatible with the individual's ethical standards, with his conception of himself, and with his calculations of prudent versus dangerous satisfactions. One becomes aware of the strength of the ego's repressive functions when one tries to bring these sexual impulses into consciousness.

The repressive effort, however, does not always succeed in blocking expression of the sexual instincts even when dangerous to the ego and even when their pressure can cause the individual to regress to ever earlier stages of his development. When a vulnerable point is reached, the repressed impulse breaks into consciousness, in a disguised form that is appropriate to the particular stage. It obtains, in so doing, some sort of discharge and satisfaction. The result is a symptom that is a compromise between the wish for something and what is permitted—in short, a "substitute sexual gratification." And these are the symptoms of the two transference neuroses: hysteria and the obsessive-compulsive state.

In these transference neuroses, the reservoir of sexual energy is available to be transferred onto external objects which provide the "substitute sexual gratifications." In psychoses, just to the contrary, sexual energy, instead of being transferred to substitute objects, is withdrawn from external objects altogether and pulled back onto the self; these psychoses emerge fundamentally as kinds of narcissistic disorders.

A Major Setback

Significantly, not all of Freud's firm hypotheses were to work out as he expected. He continued to find confirmations of his view that the origins of the neuroses are sexual in character and relate to early sexual development, but one key hypothesis failed to hold up under closer examination. It was a failure that caused him much distress. As he began to realize how important early sexual experiences were, he came to believe that actual seduction by parents and other adults was the key to the neuroses. To his consternation he discovered that in most cases the seductions were imaginary. "When I realized that these sexual approaches had never actually occurred, that they were just fantasies made up by my patients or perhaps even suggested by myself, I was at my wit's end." (*Origins of Psychoanalysis*; Freud.)

This realization that fantasies and childhood misinterpretations, not actual seductions, lay at the source of many neurotic disturbances, was to have far-reaching and permanent consequences for the development of psychoanalysis. If it was not a real but an imaginary seduction that brought about the neurosis, then it would seem that external facts in the life of the person counted less for psychoanalytic understanding than the internal play of forces within the psychic system itself.

Thereafter Freud tended to play down the role of actual life experiences and play up the importance of sheerly instinctual pressure and the indirect ways through which this pressure discharges itself. Though in later years he did come upon cases (e.g., the Wolf Man) where fantasy *and* actual seduction were present, he never again considered that the external world and the patient's actual experience had a central role in the individual's development.

This bit of background may help to explain why Freudian man always seems so worldless and ahistorical. One rarely sees Freud's patients as part of a world larger than the family, and the family as it existed in the patient's childhood but not in his own adult present. The individual's relation to society, to other adults, and beyond to the involvement in a unique personal and historical situation—all these fade into the background. Detached from that background, Freudian man stands forth as a bundle of intrapsychic conflicts—a solitary individual engaged in constant struggle with his own instinctual pressures against a vague backdrop of a society that provides him with a small measure of gratification and relief from tension, but only at a tremendous psychic cost.

The Genetic Point of View

In 1905 Freud brought together the results of his pioneering research into early sexual development in *Three Essays on the Theory of Sexuality,* and presented the view that the sexual instincts are expressed through a variety of bodily functions. At one stage or another the mouth or the anus or the genitals become a focus for sexual feeling. At first, acting independently of the individual's other needs, the sexual instincts develop in successive stages until at last they evolve, in accordance with an ontogenetically fixed pattern, into a "more or less complete synthesis." The time of each stage may be influenced by environmental interactions, but the sequence and nature of the program for development appears to be fixed.

The three major steps in development are the oral, anal, and genital stages. These three stages are so well known that they need not detain us here beyond noting Freud's observation that "development through these three stages is ordinarily passed through quietly and unobtrusively," though when anything occurs to throw this development off its fragile balance, the grounds are laid for future troubles. The difficulties may not be manifest at the time, but troublesome transitions from one sexual stage to the next give rise to predispositions that can later turn into neuroses and perversions.

The grand design of the three essays on sexuality may be summarized briefly as follows: The sexual instincts—quanta of excitation—are remarkably flexible as to aim (mode of discharge) and object (desired object) and both aim and object change as the individual progresses through each of the major stages of sexual development. The adult sexual perversions show the full range of object choice and organ mode (orifices, etc.) characteristic of each of the various stages. Normal sexuality, on the contrary, integrates all of the "perversions" (perverse tendencies) as components of a fully developed genital sexuality.

The approach of *Three Essays* has thus come to be known in metapsychology as the genetic point of view—a view that applies evolutionary and historical concepts to man's psychological development, emphasizing in particular the close relationship between ontogeny (the development of the individual) and phylogeny (the development of the human species). This emphasis upon the genetic aspect is only one of four or five ways in which Freud was struggling at this time to pull together his clinical observations in some sort of systematic conceptual framework; and in our judgment it is one of his most valuable innovations in psychology. In a later section we shall contrast it with the other "points of view" of Freud's metapsychology—the topographic, the economic, the dynamic, and the structural.

From Idea to Instinct

We are now in a position to see more clearly the major shift that Freud's thinking was undergoing at this point. He had come to regard neurosis as a conflict of instincts rather than as a conflict of disagreeable and incompatible ideas concerning the self, something deeper than the clash of a repressed idea with the conscious image of the self (as with Miss Lucy); rather, the source of neurotic conflict extends backward into the fundamental disturbances within early sexual development. In most cases these disturbances were not due to actual seductions or other gross interferences with sexual development from *external* agents or causes; the trouble, rather, arose from the difficulty *intrinsic* to the developmental process itself—from that touch-and-go task of progressing normally from one sexual stage to the next. What was called for, consequently, was a thorough exploration of how the sexual instinct develops; and, accordingly, the concept of instinct became central to Freud's thought.

In his important paper, *Instincts and their Vicissitudes* (1915), Freud went into considerable detail in explaining what he means by instinct. We draw upon his account to contrast the concepts of instincts and ideas.

1. An instinct is a quantum of energy; a force; a need; a stimulus; an impulsion; an excitation. All of these terms are used at various times to capture the essence of instinct as an active agent driving the organism toward seeking some form of satisfaction and relief. An idea, on the other hand, is a mental representation or image without force or energy.

2. Instincts arise within the organism, frequently manifesting themselves by physical sensations (as, for example, a gnawing sensation in the stomach). The source of an idea, on the other hand, may be some external experience. Thus, in Freud's early conception, the disagreeable idea posited as the cause of hysteria was thought to be the memory trace of some actual event that took place outside of the organism.

3. An instinct acts as a constant force that is always maintaining pressure, unlike an idea, which may come and go and cannot be thought of as exerting a constant pressure. You can escape from an external stimulus by flight or by withdrawal or by some other relatively simple physical movement. The process of mastering the constant pressure of an internal stimulus is much more complicated.

4. Within the organism, the instinct is linked with a specific organ or body zone. Freud referred to the instinct as a borderline concept between the mental and the physical. In most of his references, however, instinctual impulses are conceived after the model of mechanical or chemical processes.

5. Instincts are inborn and have a specific biological purpose to fulfill. Here Freud ties psychoanalytic thought specifically and directly to Darwinian evolutionary theory. An idea is

not inborn, nor need it fulfill any inherent biological purpose.

6. Instincts aim at satisfaction that can be achieved only by abolishing the conditions of stimulation. To be sure, the instincts may be inhibited in this aim, but their pressure toward such satisfaction never ceases. Ideas, on the other hand, at least as ideas, do not automatically press toward satisfaction.

7. Finally, the instincts are flexible; they can achieve gratification through a wide variety of objects. In the pregenital expressions of sexuality, object choice always has a narcissistic quality, such as the choice of one's own body. In the final adult form of genital sexuality the object of the sexual instinct may be another person of the opposite sex, but any number of substitute objects can be found even at the end of a complex developmental process. At this point Freud was so impressed by the malleability of the sexual instinct that he was led into the bolder hypothesis that the instincts are not really qualitatively different. The ultimate differences among various instinctual impulses lie, he stated, in the differing quantities of excitation that accompany them and in their origins in one or another somatic source.

Though it is clear that the subject of the instincts was in the forefront of Freud's thinking at this time, the instincts did not hold the spotlight alone. Wherever any description of instinct is made, there is nearly always the accompanying reference to something quite different and antithetical in nature—variously called "the mental," "the mental apparatus," or "ideas." What we know of the status Freud gave this "mental apparatus" comes mostly from what he says of its relation and interplay with the instincts, rather than from specific description of the apparatus itself. Freud states that "the instincts are the true motive forces." (1915, p. 63.) The instincts represent "quantities of excitation" that trigger the mental apparatus, while the mental apparatus, in turn, is governed by the need to free itself of this excitation: it discharges energy, and regulates the direction of the energy. Together, in interaction, they provide an abstract model of the organism in its psychic aspect. Once

again, Freud's basic thinking runs along the line that the interplay of opposites—which may be either cooperative or in dire
conflict—provides the key to the working of the human psyche.

In spite of the many descriptive phrases Freud applied to
the instincts, he had not succeeded in fixing them in any hard
and fast form; and he himself was aware of this as he went on
to shift (both in this particular period and later, in his third
phase) his interpretations of the specific ways in which instinct
functioned. But the same general picture persisted: it is the
instincts that provide the energy, while the mental apparatus
provides the basic direction of human life. The instincts are
conceived of as "demands for work" made on the mental apparatus. The logical consequence of this general picture is,
oddly enough, that the specifically and qualitatively different
forms in which instinct manifests itself become a less crucial
problem. Thus, in a classic paper on instinct theory, Bibring
observes: "How the disturbing stimuli [the instincts] are
classified is a secondary matter compared to the adoption of
the view that the mental apparatus has a fundamental way of
working in relation to all stimuli, whether they emanate from
within or without." (Bibring, 1936, p. 126.)

In other words, if the instincts are the sources of energy
that trigger the mental apparatus into action, it does not matter
very much how the specific form of these instincts is defined
since the regulative mechanisms shape the behavior that ensues
until the stimulation is removed and the mental apparatus can
return to its normal state of quiescence. Indeed, the whole point
is already implicit in Freud's view of instincts as quanta of
energy rather than qualitatively distinct manifestations. If we
think of instinct as a kind of reservoir or pool of homogeneous
energy, then the specific ways in which this energy is siphoned
off is relatively secondary. What fundamentally differentiates
one instinctual impulse from another is its relative amount of
force.

Hence, in dealing with the specific forms instincts take,
Freud was left singularly free to tinker with his own theory.
In his first and clearest formulation (the one we have been
principally dealing with here), he postulated two groups of
instincts (i.e., two specific forms instinct could take)—the
sexual instincts, which serve the biological purpose of preserv-

ing the species; and the ego instincts, which serve the biological purpose of preserving the individual. These two sets of instincts might cooperate, as when man may incidentally receive ego gratification from the act of procreating; but Freud was more ready to see conflict springing up between them and he goes so far as to remark that in the service of preserving the species man is "only an appendage to his germ plasm."

In his second formulation of the instinct theory, Freud blunted the hitherto sharp distinction between the sex and the ego instincts by sexualizing the ego. That is, the ego itself could become an object of emotional attachment; and of course any such attachment means a discharge of sexual energy in the direction of the object. Accordingly, the ego instincts were now subdivided into two parts—a libidinized component (via the concept of narcissism) and a nonlibidinal component (referred to at this stage simply as "ego interests"). This development came in 1914, in his paper *On Narcissism*; but a year later (in *Instincts and their Vicissitudes*), he further qualified the ego instinct by stating that its nonlibidinal component also contained an aggressive element. The sexual instincts remained relatively homogeneous, but the ego instincts now are seen as containing three components: a libidinal aspect, an aggressive aspect, and a neutral aspect of "interest." (Though this last is left rather unspecified, it would seem to correspond with the usual conscious and practical concerns of the ego as it moves about its business in the world.)

Some years later, in 1923 (when he had moved into his third phase), Freud introduced an even more basic change, dropping the ego instincts altogether and replacing them with a group of aggressive instincts. Thus, he retained his basic concept of dual instincts, independent but capable of an infinite variety of fusions, interactions and conflicts. The ego, having lost the status of an independent "primordial instinct," was now presented as a structure of the mental apparatus that evolved out of the "vital stratum" of the self (its instinctual heritage). (Freud, 1923.) Though this position belongs to the third and final phase, its anticipation can be noted as early as 1914, when Freud remarks: "It is impossible to suppose that a unity comparable to the ego can exist in the individual from the very start; the ego has to develop." (Freud, 1914, p. 35.)

To add to the confusion of the total picture, in his last period Freud further "simplified" his instinct theory by postulating two primal instincts, for life and for death. Though these correspond roughly to the previously postulated instincts of sex and aggression, they do so only in a remote and highly generalized way, and they raise very new points of view of their own.

Clearly, it is difficult to follow the twists and turns of these changes in the instinct theory. (For a fuller account, see Freud 1905, 1914, 1915, 1917, 1920, and 1923, and Bibring 1936.) But it is just as clear that each change in the theory represented a determined effort on Freud's part to grapple with specific problems encountered in his practice. The attribution of a libidinal component to the ego instincts came about as an attempt to take into theoretical account the fact of narcissism as it appeared both in schizophrenia and in normal human development. The addition of an aggressive component was to take into account the confusing presence of sadistic and masochistic tendencies in his patients. And so on. One may disagree with the theoretical suggestions he offers, but one has to concede that his intent and his procedure are resolutely empirical throughout: namely, to follow the facts where they take him, no matter how much the theory has to be patched and mended in the process.

Of course, Freud himself was aware of the hesitant and awkward nature of a good deal of his *ad hoc* tampering with theory; and at about this time he makes a most revealing comment on theory in its relation to its empirical material:

One dislikes the thought of abandoning observation for barren theoretical discussions, but all the same we must not shirk an attempt at explanation. Conceptions such as that of an ego-libido, an energy pertaining to the ego instincts and so on, are certainly neither very easy to grasp nor is their content sufficiently rich; a speculative theory of these relations of which we are speaking would in the first place require as its basis a sharply defined concept. But I am of the opinion that that is just the difference between a speculative theory and a science founded upon constructions arrived at empirically. The latter will not begrudge to speculation its privilege of a smooth, logically unassailable structure, but will itself be gladly content with nebulous, scarcely imaginable conceptions, which it hopes to apprehend more clearly in the course of its development, or which it is even prepared to replace by others. For these ideas are not the basis of the science upon which everything rests: that, on the contrary, is observation alone. They are not the foundationstone, but the coping of the whole structure, and they can be replaced and discarded without damaging it. [1914, p. 34.]

This remarkable passage could bear a much more extended comment than we have space for here. What is perhaps most salient is Freud's insistence that theory is no rigid or sacrosanct structure to be preserved at all costs, but has instead to be constantly reviewed and revised in the light of new empirical findings. The reader may be slightly winded by having had to follow these various shifts and turns, shadings and countershadings in the development of Freud's views on instinct; but a much more meaningful picture of his thinking, as well as of his qualities as an empirical observer, is brought before us by witnessing this organic development instead of a petrified summary that would present, in Freud's own words, "a smooth, logically unassailable structure."

Instinct defined as energy and force, no matter how Freud varied his descriptions of it, remains the constant factor opposed to the "mental apparatus," with its regulating principle of homeostasis—the return to a steady state. The two remain the fixed core of his theory through all his other gropings and hesitations. But when we examine the treatment given these two, we find that Freud follows an entirely different procedure for each. He introduces the empirical theory of instincts with sound scientific prudence, stating that it is a provisional and working hypothesis, and he modifies it as he encounters different cases in practice. The "mental apparatus," on the other hand, remains unmodified throughout; much less is said of it, and it persists like an unchanging shadow in the background. Moreover, and this is a capital point, when Freud introduces the concept of the mental apparatus, he does not bring it forward as a mere working hypothesis, as he did the concept of instincts. Rather, he states that it is a "necessary postulate." We begin to suspect that he is operating here not as the empirical researcher, but as a metaphysician taking over a piece of philosophical baggage without critical scrutiny.

And this indeed turns out to be the case to a remarkable degree. Rarely in the history of science have we had so striking an instance of the bold and gifted empirical researcher, who persistently modifies his conclusions in the light of his case materials, combined with the unconscious metaphysician, who rests dogmatically within an unexamined framework. It is not that Freud was by nature dogmatic; but he was philosophically ultraconservative. He wished that psychoanalysis might become a strictly empirical discipline, and above all, he did not want to fish in the troubled waters of philosophical reflection. To plunge into those waters, he feared, might make the discoveries of psychoanalysis look like matters of mere speculation. The result was that he simply accommodated himself to the reigning "scientific" philosophy of his milieu—the physiological school of Helmholtz.

On the face of it, indeed, there would seem to have been every empirical reason for Freud to question the concept of a "mental apparatus," or nervous system, that is dominated by a need to abolish its sources of stimulation. Consider the language with which he introduces this concept: "We must make use of certain *necessary postulates* [our italics]. The nervous system is an apparatus having the function of abolishing stimuli which reach it, or of reducing excitation to the lowest possible level, an apparatus which would even, if this were possible, maintain itself in an altogether unstimulated condition." (Freud, 1915, p. 63.) The aim of the nervous system, in short, is to seek Nirvana—a stimulus-free condition. The "mental apparatus" acts like the governing mechanism of a steam engine, discharging pressure at certain times in order to maintain a steady state in the whole. But is this search for quiescence the only role that mind plays in human affairs?

The word "mind" may seem a little out of key here. Freud, indeed, uses the term "mental" in the expression "mental apparatus" with a constantly uncomfortable ambiguity, as if he would prefer all the time to be speaking of the nervous system itself. Very well, we can jettison the terms "mind" and "mental," but raise exactly the same kind of question with regard to the nervous system itself. Does it seem at all plausible that the extraordinary process of organic evolution that developed the more complex and higher nervous systems took place merely to find a more elaborate means of escaping stimuli? If Freud had pursued the evolutionary point of view that he had borrowed from Darwin, Haeckel, and others, and explored in connection with the instincts, he would certainly have questioned this Nirvana-like view of the nervous system. Does it not seem that the more complex and higher nervous system of man may even be involved in a restless search for stimuli? It is by means of this complex nervous system that man, unlike the other animals, breaks out of his biological habitat, creates new environments for himself, and now soars restlessly into space. It would seem that Pascal spoke more acutely of human nervousness, when he described man's condition as one of perpetual "inconstancy and restlessness." Human mobility and restlessness are blazoned on the pages of history, and it is hard to see how they could be the product of a nervous system whose essential function is to diminish stimuli, and if possible to eliminate them altogether.

Freud's conception of the mental apparatus comes out of the older physiological laboratories with their experiments, quite exciting when he was a young worker in the subject. When a drop of acid was poured on the leg of a decapitated frog and the creature twitched and twitched, the experimenters concluded that this was an attempt to scrape off the irritating stimulus—and the further judgment was that what was revealed there was the essential and whole truth about the nervous system. The philosophy that dominated the physiological laboratories of Freud's day was that of the Helmholtz-Brücke school of physiology, whose influence upon the formation of Freudian theory we have now to make clear.

Freud's Philosophic Commitment: The Helmholtz School

It used to be the common impression that Freud kept himself so aloof from philosophizing that there were no philosophic influences or colorations at work upon his thinking. More recently, as we have come to know more about his life and his earlier background, quite the opposite has turned out to be the case; and, in particular, the story of the influence of the Helmholtz School has been told many times in recent years (especially since the discovery of Freud's correspondence with Fliess). Bernfeld reported it first in 1944, and more recently Jones, Kris, Erikson, Rapaport, Shakow, and others, have all recorded their versions. It is a story of great intellectual interest in itself, but we shall present it here only in as much detail as will make clear the fundamental theoretical questions that are at issue.

The Helmholtz School emerged as one of the most important intellectual movements in Germany toward the middle of the nineteenth century, and by the 1860's had become for many intellectuals the most modern symbol of what science really was. To understand its importance and its attraction for young people, it must be compared to the position of prestige certain forms of positivism held in this country several decades ago. In the Germany of the eighteen-forties and fifties, it was not merely a specialized branch of science, but offered a conception of science itself that could absorb technical philosophy and deal effectively with human values.

The forward march of the German Enlightenment, symbolized by reason as embodied in science, had been momentarily interrupted by certain forms of post-Kantian Idealism, Romanticism, and by the "Naturphilosophie" associated in the early part of the century with the names of Schelling, Goethe, and Herder. Somewhere around the middle of the century there occurred the momentous event commonly called "the collapse of German Idealism." In the wake of this collapse many rival claimants arose. In social philosophy, for example, Marxism emerged as a rising international movement. In natural science and the philosophy of nature, the movement that came to be known as the Helmholtz School of Physicalistic Physiology, named after its outstanding representative, ended for many the romantic episode of "Naturphilosophie" and re-established the hegemony of a strictly scientific *Weltanschauung*.

The movement bears a resemblance to the Vienna Circle of the nineteen-twenties and thirties—a group of logicians and physicists who gathered around a few key figures possessed of a program of philosophical reform. There is the same mixture of emotional opposition to religion, to metaphysics and idealistic philosophy; the same intense exaltation of Science and Scientific Method almost as a code of values rather than a mere neutral method of inquiry; the same fervent denunciation and exclusion of opposing points of view; and the same crystallization of the movement around a program of reform personified in a few outstanding leaders.

If this picture of a passionate ideological movement fails to square with the conventional image of the scientist as a cool, objective, dispassionate and rational person, it is because this latter image is, and always has been, less than the whole truth. The typical scientist is often dispassionate about his specific findings, but never about his metaphysics. We sometimes fail to realize that science has a long history as an ideological movement set implacably against tradition and authority (especially where tradition and authority have been represented by the church and its philosophical apologists). Thus, to see science in its full context we have to see it not only as the impersonal advance-guard of technological progress, but also as a historical movement with a sense of mission. Science was born in controversy and martyrdom; and the issues of basic values and metaphysical commitments for which it stands remain as alive and vital today as they have been throughout the past three centuries. Nor are these issues yet resolved (as anyone who works in the social sciences, psychology, or philosophy departments of a large university will testify); every so often they break out again in the form of a militant ideological movement.

The Helmholtz School was just such a movement in the

middle of the last century. Its chief representatives, besides Helmholtz himself, were Dubois-Reymond, Brücke and Ludwig. In 1842 Dubois-Reymond set forth this credo for the movement:

> Brücke and I *pledged a solemn oath* to put in power this truth: No other forces than the common physical chemical ones are active within the organism. In those cases which cannot at the time be explained by these forces one has either to find the specific way or form of their action by means of the physical mathematical method, or to assume new forces equal in dignity to the chemical physical forces inherent in matter, reducible to the force of attraction and repulsion. [Bernfeld, 1944, p. 348.] [Our italics.]

Notice the emotional solemnity of the language here: they have "pledged a solemn oath," and an oath not merely to abide by a truth but to put that truth in power—an expression of crusading militancy.

In 1845, they solemnly transformed this program into a school by creating a group called the Berlin Society for Physical Physiology. In 1847, at a meeting of this society, Helmholtz launched his own career by reading a paper aimed at giving physiology a firm foundation in the basic principles of Newtonian physics. The paper dealt with the application to the human organism of the principle of conservation of energy— the very principle that was to become the foundation for Freud's thinking about the "mental apparatus." Both Helmholtz and Brücke had been trained as physicists, and their explicit intention was to reduce all aspects of the human organism to physical-chemical processes. Their goal was not merely to add to scientific understanding, but also to destroy once and for all the vitalist philosophy of their respected teacher, Johannes Muller. And it was precisely this philosophical aim that gave the movement its emotional intensity.

The philosophy of the Helmholtz School was conveyed to Freud by one of its chief founders and representatives, Ernst Brücke, whom Freud spoke of as "the greatest authority who affected me more than any other in my whole life." (Jones, 1953, p. 29.) Brücke's Physiological Institute was well known to Freud quite early, and his actual relationship with the man

began in his very first year in the university, when he took
Brücke's course in physical physiology. Later he became
Brücke's laboratory assistant. He credits Brücke with giving
him the fateful advice to abandon his career in research physiology (on which he could hardly support himself) and to set up
in private medical practice. It was Brücke's influence that enabled him to receive the coveted prestige of Privatdozent, thus
assuring him of the academic prestige needed in the Vienna of
his time to get enough patients to make a living. And it was
the reserved and distant Brücke whose emotional defense of
Freud's candidacy enabled him to receive the traveling fellow-
ship that sent him to Paris, where he attended the famous
lectures of Charcot on the nature of hysteria.

There were also other personal relationships, besides that with
Brücke, that led in the direction of the Helmholtz school of
thought. Once he entered private practice, Freud's closest professional relationships were formed first with Joseph Breuer and
then with Wilhelm Fliess. Although Breuer is usually referred
to simply as "a practicing physician in Vienna," he was, in fact,
a distinguished scientist who made a number of lasting contributions to medicine. He happened also, significantly enough,
to be a staunch member of Brücke's Physiological Institute,
where he lectured. As for Fliess, he too was a fervent follower
of the Helmholtz School; and it was from him that Freud
received the coveted two-volume work of Helmholtz's lectures
as a Christmas present in 1899.

Thus, for more than a quarter of a century, from 1873 to
1902—and in his most intellectually formative years to boot—
Freud was closely associated with, and directly influenced by,
Brücke, Breuer, and Fliess, all of whom maintained steadfast
allegiance to the thought of Helmholtz. It would have been
extraordinary if Freud had not assimilated the mode of thought
that prevailed in this milieu. Nor was it merely a matter of
personal relationships. The climate of thought, which the Helmholtz School represented, seemed at the time unassailable. The
later discoveries within physics itself that were to change the
thinking of physicists in our own century had not yet arrived;
in the middle of the nineteenth century the Newtonian mode
of thought had achieved such triumphs that it seemed the universally binding model for all science, that of man as well as

nature. If there were to be scientific explanations of any subject matter, then these explanations must be in accord with that model. And what is that prescribed mode of explanation? It requires first that any complex phenomenon be reduced to elementary components, particles or atoms as the case may be; and then, in order that the movements of these elementary particles be calculable, they must be governed by the law of inertia. Thus movement, or change of movement, arises only from a definite quantum of force, such that if this quantum is known the resulting quantum of change may be calculated. Furthermore, in order that the whole system may be constant for the purposes of calculation there is invoked the principle of conservation of energy: energy is never gained or lost but only transformed.

It is now possible to see out of what intellectual background Freud's concept of the "mental apparatus" emerges. It is nothing less than a psychological surrogate for the Newtonian postulates of inertia and conservation of energy. Its function is only regulatory (though just how it regulates is left unspecified), and regulatory only to secure a steady and constant state. The "mental apparatus" is, in fact, an inertial system; and like all inertial systems it initiates nothing, but only holds to the status quo. There is no compelling empirical reason why Freud should have introduced this concept. The compulsion, in fact, was entirely *a priori,* although very plausible in the metaphysical climate in which Freud grew up. It was a compulsion resting on a metaphysical dogma that rested in turn on the highly abstract and selective mode of explanation that had worked successfully within Newtonian physics. Freud had enough on his hands without also accomplishing a fundamental philosophical critique of this Newtonian brand of scientific materialism. It was more convenient for him to fit in with the prevailing mode of thought. And to say this is not in the least to denigrate his greatness. It is well to remember those somber and penetrating words of Hegel: "As to the individual, everyone is the son of his time, and therefore philosophy is its time comprehended in thought. It is as silly to imagine that any philosophy could transcend its own time as that an individual could jump out of his time."

How deeply Freud was committed to the thinking of the

Helmholtz School is shown by his *Project for a Scientific Psychology* (1895), which he communicated to Fliess. The purpose of the *Project*, he states, is to "represent psychical processes as quantitatively determined states of specifiable material particles." The basic unit, the specifiable material particle, is the "neurone," conceived as the building block of the nervous system. The neurone could be either empty or charged with a certain quantity. Neurones tend to rid themselves of these quantities; and, consequently, the entire nervous system endeavors to keep the sum of excitation constant, in accordance with the Newtonian laws of inertia and the conservation of energy.

Freud dropped the *Project* so far as it aimed at reducing psychic processes to material particles; but he never ceased to follow through its fundamental line of thought. Thus in 1900, in the famous Chapter VII of his *Interpretation of Dreams*, he simply translated the thinking of the *Project* into psychological language. In place of the nervous system made up of neurones he substituted the notion of "psychic systems" and the "mental apparatus." In place of the "quantity of charge" (upon the neurone) he substituted the notion of "cathexis" or psychic energy. In the place of the "principle of inertia" he substituted the pleasure principle (which was to be the regulative mechanism governing the mental apparatus). And in place of the principle of conservation of energy he substituted the economic viewpoint, in accordance with which the mental apparatus distributes the various pleasurable gratifications of instinct. The names have changed; but the whole psychic constellation still functions in strict analogy with a Newtonian system.

And as late as 1929, in his article on psychoanalysis in the *Encyclopaedia Britannica*, Freud still harks back explicitly to Brücke's basic position as the theoretical foundation-stone of psychoanalysis. Following Brücke, he states that human organisms are to be conceived of as systems of small particles moved by forces according to the principle of the conservation of energy. The organism is regulated by a principle which keeps the sum of forces constant. And as we get to know more about these forces, we see that they are not so varied as they first appear to be, but can be reduced to the two fundamental forces in physical nature: attraction and repulsion. We see here, in an explicit fashion, the source of Freud's concept of Eros and Thanatos—the life instinct and the death instinct. Neither in the *Project* nor in his later writings was Freud ever to free himself of his commitment to the metaphysics of his respected teacher and mentor.

Many psychoanalysts claim to regard the *Project* as simply an interesting historical document, an abortive attempt by Freud to reduce psychology to physics. In fact, however, Freud never really abandoned the thinking of the *Project*. (Indeed, as his theory evolved after 1900, the incorporation of Brücke's thought increased rather than diminished, as we shall see in the next chapter.) The translation of his terminology from the physical into the psychological, far from abandoning Newtonian materialism, merely continues the same mode of thought in metaphorical garb. For what is fundamental to this mode of thought is that it insists that explanation must always proceed by reduction to elementary entities—no matter if they now be called quanta of libido or psychic energy instead of neurones. This insistence requires that the phenomenal world we experience be set aside almost immediately for the "real" world of elementary forces that alone are causally efficacious. To put it another way: explanation of the macroscopic, as it were, must always be by way of the microscopic. In this connection, it is odd, by the way, that Freud never questioned the possible conflict of his Newtonian and Darwinian inheritances. It would seem hard to understand, as we have already suggested, how the evolutionary place and relatedness of the human nervous system could possibly be understood simply by analyzing its subcutaneous particles in movement according to a Newtonian inertial model, and without regard to the far-ranging relations and effects that the system leads to within the organism's environment.

One of Freud's outstanding characteristics as a thinker was his respect for the single, empirical fact. He was a faithful observer, a lucid, honest reporter, and a bold discoverer. His empirical insights and his agonizing efforts to get them right stand as a permanent contribution to man's original thinking about man. As long as Freud remained close to his case materials he gave us one conception of human reality; he held his metaphysics in abeyance, and reported what he found. But his metaphysics are borrowed second- and third-hand from other fields. Immediately behind Freud stand the awesome figures of Darwin and Newton, and his theory is unthinkable without them. Indeed, almost all of its major flaws stem from his misapplication of the metaphysical foundations of seventeenth century physics and nineteenth century biology to man's mental and emotional life.

This, then, is the paradox of Freud's greatness as a thinker: his stunning and original insights into the human condition were, when he reverted to his formal metapsychological theorizing, worked over relentlessly so that they would fit into an inherited philosophical mold. The task that philosophy must now share with psychoanalysis is to elucidate a new framework that will do greater justice to Freud's empirical discoveries.

FOUR

Freud III (The 1920's and After) The "Psychic Apparatus"

In Freud's final phase, he continued to build theories in a tentative and questioning manner. He had never been quick to readjust his formal theory to accommodate new clinical discoveries, and frequently a new concept lay fallow for decades before it was integrated and systematized within the theoretical structure. The 1911 publication, *Two Principles of Mental Functioning*, and the 1914 paper, *On Narcissism*, hung in limbo for years before being integrated into the formulations of the 1920's.

But by the twenties there were quite a number of important clinical observations on the influence of unconscious guilt and on the negative therapeutic reaction that could not be accounted for in the formal theory as it stood. So in the years from 1923 to 1926, for the third and final time, Freud reformulated his analysis of the nature of psychic conflict.

His first version (in the case of Miss Lucy) had presented conflict as the collision between an unconscious wish and the preconscious moral and realistic standards of the individual. The wish, being incompatible with the individual's *mores*, was prevented from entering consciousness. Conflict was thus conceived of as taking place between two strata of the psychic apparatus—the preconscious and the unconscious. (In the jargon of psychoanalysis, this approach came to be known as the topographical point of view.)

In the second version (Phase II), Freud saw the source of the neuroses in conflicts among instincts—the sexual instincts of the dynamic unconscious against the self-preservation instincts of the ego. In his more speculative writings, the opposition was presented in broader terms as the instinct of life (Eros) versus the instinct of destruction and death (Thanatos).

Now in 1923, with *The Ego and the Id,* Freud began his final reformulation of basic psychic conflict. He pointed out that since both sides of a conflict can be unconscious, it was no longer useful to define conflict essentially as a struggle between conscious or preconscious forces and unconscious forces. The topographical approach had been concerned primarily in locating the place (*topos* in Greek)—whether in the conscious or unconscious—where the conflict erupted. Since it is not so important to know where as to know what the conflict is, and how it affects the individual, this topographical approach had to be supplemented and partially replaced by the *structural* point of view. In this scheme, conflict is defined as a clash between the two major psychic structures: the ego (or superego) and the id. So far as consciousness enters the picture, it is to be considered simply as a possible aspect of certain ego functions.

On this same occasion, Freud also revised his previous notion of conflict as a struggle between the sexual instincts and the self-preservation instincts. Instead, the aggressive impulses—hitherto associated with the self-preservation instincts—were reassigned to the id; and these combined instincts (sex and aggression) were now seen as pitted against the ego.

The reformulation started in *The Ego and the Id* was further advanced three years later in *The Problem of Anxiety* (1926). Here, the whole psychoanalytic concept of anxiety is to be recast. Freud remarks that he had been mistaken in his earlier conception of anxiety as undischarged libidinal energy. Instead, it now seemed to him more accurate to conceive anxiety as an ego function. Any new situation that resembled an earlier event linked with trauma (such as the threat of separation) causes anxious stirrings in the individual that act as a signal of danger. The ego then mobilizes the defensive capacities to prevent the individual from being flooded with the anxieties that are linked to the earlier trauma.

All told, then, the major changes in the 1920's may be summed up in a preliminary and schematic form:

1. Conflict is no longer an opposition merely between instincts or psychic strata, but more predominantly an opposition between psychic systems (the structural point of view).
2. The impulses toward destructiveness and aggression are removed from the ego and regrouped under the id.
3. The conception of anxiety is changed—from converted libido to an adaptive control process of the ego.
4. The superego emerges as a group of semi-autonomous ego functions—the result of introjected parental moral standards and prohibitions.
5. The effort is now made to give as much attention to the *repressing* forces in psychic conflict as to the *repressed*—an aspect of psychic life that had been partially neglected in the formative years of psychoanalysis.

Unlike Freud's earlier, momentous discoveries, such as infantile sexuality and the importance of unconscious motivation, these changes in theory had very little impact on the general culture. They were of interest primarily to the psychoanalytic profession. Yet despite this narrower appeal, these new formulations are of enduring significance, and indeed mark a decisive turning point of psychoanalytic theory. Kris, for example, refers to these new formulations of the 1920's as a "decisive reorientation of psychoanalytic theory." Other prominent theorists agree; Arlow and Brenner state that "the full significance of these theoretical developments . . . is not yet fully realized."

On close inspection we find this "decisive reorientation" somewhat elusive. Some aspects of a new orientation are clear enough: the shift in emphasis from id function to ego function is a far-reaching change; the regrouping of psychic functions under the categories of ego and id is a simplification many psychoanalysts have found quite helpful; and the light thrown on the dynamics of unconscious guilt and resistance represents an important clinical advance. Nevertheless, there still hovers in the air the question of whether these changes really mark the decisive reorientation to which Kris referred. Are these changes, singly or in combination, as Arlow and Brenner suggested, developments whose full significance are not yet apparent? As one observes contemporary analysts struggling with the new ego psychology, one cannot escape the feeling that something more far-reaching and profound is at issue than the specific changes in theory enumerated above. And if what is at issue here were to be squarely met, then indeed we would have, in Kris's term, a decisive reorientation. There seems to be little doubt that Kris—a sensitive and gifted thinker—was responding to a change below the surface of Freud's explicit formulations, a change far more radical than Freud was able to bring to expression because of his restrictive philosophical framework.

Freud, after all, was sixty-seven when *The Ego and the Id* appeared, and seventy when he wrote *The Problem of Anxiety*. These are remarkable contributions from his later years; but at that age, he could not be expected to change his philosophical base—in fact, he did not. When viewed closely, the formulations of *The Ego and the Id* bear a striking resemblance to his first metapsychological paper—the *Project* of 1895. This latter work, it will be recalled, was an abortive effort, quickly abandoned, to reduce psychology to physiology. Twenty-eight years —Freud's mature career as a psychoanalyst—separates the two works, and in that interval, he accomplished the main body of his clinical work. While the impetus to write the *Project* was plainly theoretical, the stimulus for writing *The Ego and the Id* was clinical. The puzzles of the character neuroses, the presence of unconscious resistance in therapy, and the paradoxes of unconscious guilt—all these impressed upon Freud the need for a more adequate formulation than the one the old topographical scheme provided. But while *The Ego and the Id*, like the other writings of the 1920's, sought to do greater justice to the facts turned up in practice, the new clinical concepts were in fact merely grafted onto the old philosophical framework, which was left almost intact.

The result is that certain aspects of the new look of the 1920's, once we dig beneath the surface, turn out to be a very old look indeed. (It is this fact that obscures what is decisive about the new orientation.) The vital center of the meta-psychology has now become "the psychic apparatus" divided into its major parts: ego, id, and superego. The reader must not confuse this concept with that of "the mental apparatus" discussed in the previous chapter. The mental apparatus is a mere part—and in Freud's handling of it, often a negligible part—of the total psyche. The psychic apparatus, on the contrary, is the system of the whole psyche, that is, ego plus id.

An apparatus is always a mechanism of some kind, and that indeed is what the psychic apparatus turns out to be. To be sure, it is not made up of cogs, wheels, pins, and bolts like the ordinary machine; the parts that make it up are said to be formed by the instinctual energies organized into "systems of functions." Nevertheless, these instinctual energies in their ebb and flow, discharges and inhibitions, are regulated in a strictly determined fashion by natural law. The psychic apparatus, in short, is a thoroughly Newtonian engine, and the supposed laws by which it is governed are markedly similar to Newton's laws of motion.

Now, this elevation of the psychic apparatus (garbed in the new language) to the center of the theory turns out to be a curious regression. In 1905 Freud had advanced the genetic point of view for understanding how psychosexual development evolves. The clinical fruitfulness of this approach had caused the idea of the psychic apparatus to languish throughout the middle years of psychoanalytic development. (Actually, psychoanalysts do rely most heavily on the genetic point of view in their clinical work.) The supposedly new formulations of the 1920's, the so-called "decisive reorientation," take the old 1895 framework out of the closet, dust it off, and give it a new prominence.

In giving the psychic apparatus this central role, Freud created glaring difficulties for the whole psychology of the ego, difficulties that plague his followers up to the present day. The heart of those difficulties can be found in the conflict between a developmental point of view and that of a Newtonian mechanism. How can an organic ego, gradually developing and maturing, come out of a mechanical framework? A Newtonian engine stays put. It may wear out and be scrapped, but it never grows up. It can only transform the energy put into it according to fixed patterns; it does not develop new patterns. The psychic apparatus is conceived as such a homeostatic and strictly conservative engine. How then can the ego develop out of this apparatus?

These considerations lead us to assert that this last stage of Freud's theory, while it may mark an advance clinically (by permitting clearer descriptions of *intrapsychic* conflict) is nevertheless retrogressive philosophically, obscuring rather than elucidating the basis for a "decisive reorientation."

We shall return, when we discuss the post-Freudians, to the search for the true meaning of the "decisive reorientation." In preparation, we must scrutinize more closely the three principal concepts that make up the new theory: namely, the psychic apparatus as a whole, the id with its instincts, and the ego, taken in that order. (The superego, although all-important clinically, is logically derivative from these other concepts and will not, therefore, concern us at the moment.) The detailed examination that follows will, in turn, make possible a deeper comprehension of the philosophical assumptions that are intrinsically woven into the theory. The introduction of philosophy into the matter is not gratuitous; it cannot be avoided; and it is, moreover, in line with the ultimate intentions of Freud himself. For Freud's final statement of psychoanalytic theory—the unfinished *Outline of Psychoanalysis* published after his death—begins with a chapter entitled "The Psychic Apparatus" and with these words:

> Psychoanalysis makes a basic assumption (the nature of the psychic apparatus), the discussion of which is reserved to philosophical thought . . . (1940, p. 144.)

It is high time we took these last words to heart. Perhaps that "philosophical thought" has been "reserved" too long—to the immense detriment of psychoanalytic progress.

The Psychic Apparatus

We begin with a picture (Exhibit I). This diagram, we believe, is well worth reflective contemplation, though all such pictures

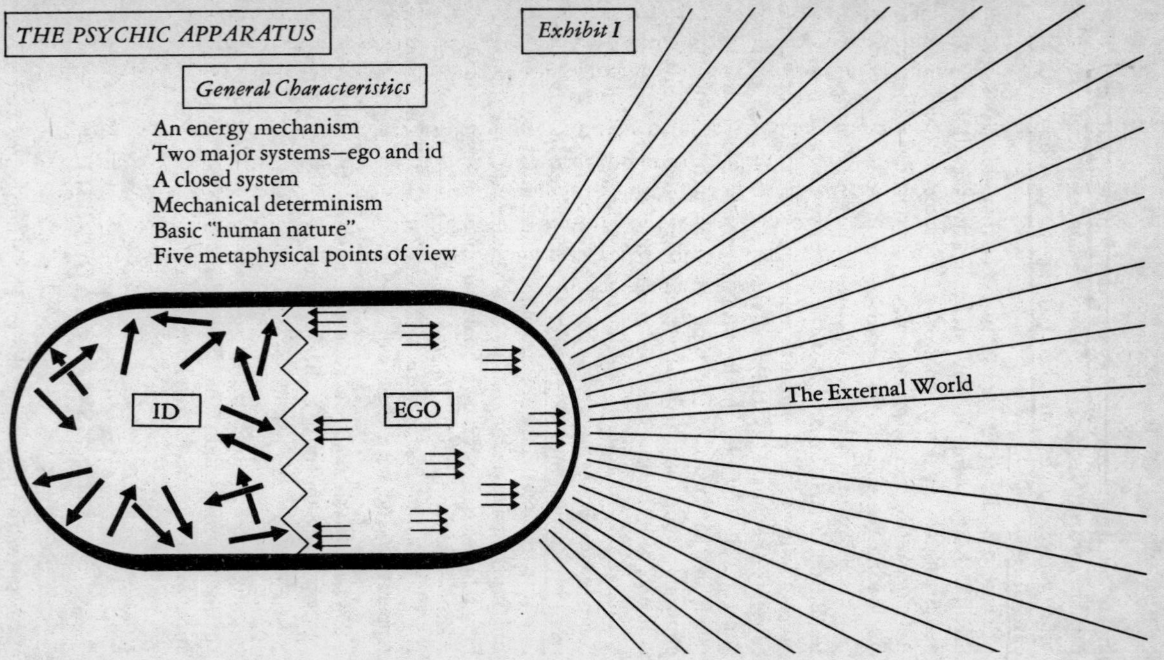

THE PSYCHIC APPARATUS

Exhibit I

General Characteristics

An energy mechanism
Two major systems—ego and id
A closed system
Mechanical determinism
Basic "human nature"
Five metaphysical points of view

The External World

EGO

ID

THE ID

The center of hereditary dispositions
The exclusive source of energy
The exclusive source of motivation
Sex and aggression
Primary processes
a) *Regulating principles*
b) *Feeling states*
c) *Energy characteristics*
d) *Perpetual modes*
e) *Learning principles*

THE EGO

Grows out of undifferentiated matrix
Development of reality principles
Identifications substitute for object cathexes
Superego develops
Uses borrowed energies
Anxiety at the "danger signal"

_____

KEY

● The *egg-shaped parabola* encloses the psychic apparatus of the individual in its totality.

● The *heavy black line* around the parabola symbolizes the region of the unconscious.

● The *lighter line* at the head of the shape continuous with the heavy black line represents consciousness.

● The *jagged dividing line* down the middle of the egg is the basic line of conflict between the two major systems of the psychic apparatus—the id (on the left) and the ego (on the right).

● The *large field* on the right, outside the parabola, into which the psychic apparatus penetrates only slightly, represents external reality.

● The *heavy black arrows* going every which way in the id stand for the unorganized masses of energy (cathexes) available to the instinctual drives. The *neat, well-contained packages of arrows* in the ego region on the right represent energies borrowed from the id, organized and bound into structures in the ego.

have to be taken with certain reservations. It has been observed that when we enter the realm of the human psyche, the prospect of visual representation vanishes. Nevertheless, Freud himself used convenient diagrams, and there is also more than a grain of truth in the ancient Chinese saying that one picture is worth ten thousand words. Such a diagram has to be considered a kind of metaphor, of varying degrees of closeness. At the same time, the psychic apparatus itself is a colossal Newtonian metaphor imposed upon the psychoanalytic data. Perhaps it takes one metaphor to catch another, or at least to bring out the extraordinarily metaphorical character of the latter. There is the further consideration, too, that a Newtonian machine is one that is, by the very quantitative and spatial concepts that define it, essentially representable; and a Newtonian machine, as we have said, is what the psychic apparatus is conceived to be.

Looking carefully at the diagram, and keeping in mind the continuity of Freud's development from his earliest phase, we are bound to notice that the picture is not at all a good resemblance to Miss Lucy. Miss Lucy may not have been an impressive person but in Freud's spare and masterly report of her case, a certain tang of that English Victorian spinster does come through. Nothing of this is to be seen in our picture. The reader may think that these remarks are made in levity; on the contrary, we are taking the theory in dead seriousness and rendering in the starkest simplicity what it really says. For the theory does in fact hold that this picture is what Miss Lucy really and ultimately reduces to. The psychic apparatus is supposed to give us the reality (the "real reality" in Plato's phrase) of Miss Lucy's psyche; all the other observed phenomena of her personality would then be merely peripheral effects. Our diagram thus helps make clear at the outset that we are confronted here, not with a clinical report, but with an exercise in traditional metaphysics.

General Characteristics
of the Psychic Apparatus

The most general characteristic of the psychic apparatus is that it is an energy mechanism (see Exhibit I). The biological instincts, rooted in the physico-chemical processes of the body, provide its vital psychic energies—the instinctual cathexes. (*Cathexis*, from the Greek, is a taking hold of; hence, a charge of energy attached to some object. Within consciousness, the cathexis appears in the form of an emotional affect or feeling toward some object.) How these energies are mobilized, patterned, and distributed between the two major systems of ego and id, determines the fate of the psychic apparatus.

Energy is transmitted within the apparatus from id to ego and then is discharged onto the external world (or back onto the organism itself in the form of controls, repression, secondary narcissism, etc.). A considerable amount of the energy, however, is not discharged but "bound" by the ego. Despite this extraordinarily important function, Freud nevertheless held that the ego has no independent energies of its own but simply utilizes those that flow from the id. Some of these energies when organized within the ego system are used, in turn, to control and channel other id energies.*

Of the two parts of the apparatus, the id is the older phylogenetically and the more important. Like the ego, it too is subdivided into parts, though it has a more fluid structure. One part is the repository of inherited dispositions and is present at birth; the other part stores up experiences and emotions repressed in the early years of the child's development.

Freud considered the id to be prior to the ego both onto-

---

* The process whereby id energies are "neutralized" by the ego and then used for ego purposes is a murky spot in the theory and has, in recent years, become a subject of controversy. (See Chapters Six and Seven.)

genetically and phylogenetically. That is, the ego developed
from the id in the early history of the race, and this process
is recapitulated in the development of every infant. Though
he expressed this view in many ways on different occasions,
Freud's final description is perhaps the most clear-cut and
sweeping:

> Under the influence of the real external world around us,
> one portion of the id has undergone a special development.
> From what was originally a cortical layer, equipped with
> organs for receiving stimuli and arrangements for acting
> as a protective shield against stimuli, a special organization
> has arisen which henceforth acts as an intermediary be-
> tween the id and the external world. To this region of our
> mind we have given the name of ego. (1940, p. 145.)

Later thinkers have somewhat revised this account of how each
human individual develops from infancy. We shall see how in
subsequent chapters.

Each of the two systems, the ego and the id, has its own
regulating principles. Though the purpose of the ego is to "safeguard" the id, the two systems are in constant opposition and
tension in relation with each other. The regulating principles
of the id dictate that its energies press blindly and remorselessly
toward release; the regulating principles of the ego seek to prevent such a simple and direct consummation. The psychic
economy of the individual consists largely of countless tiny
confrontations, and a few heroic ones, between these two opposing laws built into the structure of the individual's being.
It should be apparent from what has been said so far that
Freud conceived the psychic apparatus primarily as a *closed
system.* (In Exhibit I this is symbolized by the unbroken line
—both heavy and light—which contains it completely.) Of
course, streams of influence reach it from the external world.
But once these have activated it, the apparatus proceeds to
operate within its own intrapsychic territory according to its
own autonomous laws. Its connection with the world is not one
of essential involvement, but only of causal interplay.
We have here a very obvious descendant of the classic notion
of the mind as a Cartesian subject. According to Descartes, the
conscious subject is cut off from the world of external objects.

It has causal intersections with the world of objects, but it is not in any sense essentially enmeshed with the world. Just how subject and object, mind and matter, meet in causal interaction is not explained by Descartes. The mystery persists in Freud; somehow physical and chemical forces are transformed into instinctual energies, but this "somehow" remains unspecifiable. Nevertheless, apart from an inexplicable causal relation, for both Freud and Descartes the psyche is a self-enclosed system, really distinct from the world, and in fact in rather precarious relation to it.

A second cardinal characteristic of Freud's apparatus—and again an indication of how thoroughly his thinking falls within the Cartesian-Newtonian framework—is that this closed system operates in completely deterministic patterns. Ernest Jones writes,

> Freud never wavered in this attitude [belief in determinism] . . . He would have endorsed the view of the great anthropologist, Tylor, that "the history of mankind is part and parcel of the history of nature; our thoughts, wills and actions accord with laws as definite as those which govern the motion of the waves." Freud believed in the thoroughgoing meaningfulness and determinism of even the apparently most obscure and arbitrary mental phenomena. (Jones, 1953, p. 366.)

Notice that "meaningfulness" and "determinism" are used by Jones as virtually equivalent terms. A mental phenomenon is meaningful only if it occurs as a result of conditions, is clearly predictable, and would always result from those conditions and objects. Why should this be so? Why should it be "meaningless" for such an event to occur outside such a chain? To assert that determinism is the only "meaningful" way to grasp human history is pure metaphysics, and not at all a generalization drawn from empirical observation.

This habit of thought was, for Freud and others of his generation, the result of a pervasive climate of opinion. Physicists a century ago would have found it "meaningless" to speak of physical events other than within a strict scheme of Newtonian determinism. Today, such nondeterministic events are the physicist's daily bread. The impossibility of such a conception was merely a mental barrier through which the physicists had to break; once beyond it, they found that what had seemed an *a priori* necessity was a very expendable habit of thought. How many psychologists today, one wonders, still live in the older climate of opinion?

The psychic apparatus thus turns out to be a deeply philosophical conception, and as such represents Freud's view of the general nature of man rather than a special empirical theory of psychopathology. His theory of psychopathology describes the mishaps to which the psychic apparatus is prone in the course of its development and functioning. The apparatus is thus a more fundamental concept than either the neuroses or normality. Neurosis can be described as a dysfunction of the apparatus; normalcy as the apparatus' developing and operating with relatively few hitches. Once again, the psychic apparatus shows itself to be the bedrock concept that grounds the metapsychology.

Some analysts have tended to minimize the importance of Freud's psychic apparatus by referring instead to his elaboration of the five metapsychological points of view: the topographical, structural, genetic, economic, and dynamic. Of these five, we have already touched upon the first three; it remains to indicate briefly the nature of the economic and dynamic points of view.

The question of economy, as it arises in connection with the psyche, has to do with what might be called the problem of management of energies. The quantities of energy (cathexes) set off by the instinctual drives have to be weighed against the quantities of energy bound by the ego and mobilized to expedite or to oppose the discharge of the energies. At a certain point it may become too costly to maintain ego defenses against the instinctual drives; the ego may then give in or be swamped altogether. If, on the other hand, the ego should still continue to use all its available energies to ward off the instinctual drives, a crippling neurosis may result. The economic point of view refers, in brief, to the relative quantities of energy at issue in intrapsychic conflict. The dynamic point of view, on the other hand, looks at the opposition of energies in the psychic apparatus not in terms of quantities but in terms of the content, process, and specific interplay within psychic conflict.

No doubt, these five approaches, ways of regarding the data of the psyche, provide very fruitful and suggestive leads. However, they are not the core of the metapsychology, since the same basic assumption of the psychic apparatus underlies them all. They are, as it were, five different ways of mapping a terrain.

Let us clarify this point by another analogy. Suppose we are trying to understand the situation in Vietnam. We could discuss the matter from many points of view—the military point of view with respect to the balance of armed forces, or the point of view of internal social and economic problems, or the ethical point of view of what harm (or good) is being done morally on both sides, or the point of view of *Realpolitik* —the jostling for world power by the United States, China, and the Soviet Union. And so on. All of these perspectives are valuable; and each may very well bring to light some facet of the problem obscured by others. They are all, as it were, helpful maps. But underlying them all is the assumption that a country called Vietnam exists (quite apart from all our various "maps") in a particular geographical location with a particular population, set of physical characteristics, social and economic circumstances, and the rest; this is the reality that all the talk is about.

The psychic apparatus is the reality that is talked about through all the various metapsychological points of view. It is futile to argue, as some psychoanalysts have, whether or not the structural should replace the topographical approach. The issue of which point of view to use on any particular occasion is a purely pragmatic one. An analyst may, on one occasion, find it helpful to organize his data into unconscious, preconscious and conscious categories; while on another, to split up conflicts into ego-id groupings. The results may be confusing to the outsider, but that does not mean that within psychoanalysis there need be any serious confusion on this issue.

Thus, whichever way we turn we come back always to the basic fact that the psychic apparatus is the core of Freud's formal theory in this last period. It is this concept that exhibits the fundamental mode of thought, the basic philosophical presuppositions, in which the theory as a whole is cast.

Yet, the concept of the psychic apparatus may very well be

in conflict with Freud's empirical findings, particularly with reference to the therapeutic aims of psychoanalysis. We shall return to this issue in later chapters but it is worth calling attention to here, at the point at which it arises. Suppose, for example, that a patient (perhaps through his own reading) comes to understand and believe the theory of the psychic apparatus. The system is one that essentially seeks a homeostatic equilibrium within its own fixed boundaries, a prospect that is not promising for development or growth beyond the impasse in which the patient now finds himself. Locked within its own walls, the psychic apparatus does not open essentially toward possibility and the future; there is no room in it for choice or freedom. What then is the point of the therapeutic session at all—unless it be a mere analytic autopsy of the system into which the patient is locked? Actually, a literal belief in the psychic apparatus, supposedly erected as a generalization of the facts discovered in therapeutic sessions, would make any meaningful change impossible.

We have here an extraordinary tension created between the therapeutic goal of the theory and the eventual end at which the theory arrives, if taken literally. This situation puts the practicing psychoanalyst into the difficult position of holding to one set of operating assumptions about human nature to permit his day-to-day progress, while adhering nominally to a metapsychology which contains quite different assumptions. (Many, if not most psychoanalysts, cope with this embarrassment by ignoring large parts of the metapsychology.)

The Id and the Instincts

The operations of the id are basic to the whole psychic apparatus, and have consequently to be described in some detail if we are to comprehend how the apparatus as a whole is supposed to work. This description will have to involve some repetition; but that is unavoidable if we are to grasp concretely and adequately what the whole Freudian view of the human psyche comes to. It is an arduous task sifting through the Freudian corpus of writings to separate the amazing clinical insights from the metaphysical husks in which they are enclosed—one gains a new sympathy for Psyche, sifting her millet from the grain. Yet the job has to be done; and perhaps it will try the reader's patience less if we put the material down in a rather summary and abrupt outline form:

Thus, the id may be schematized as having the following five major characteristics (see Exhibit I):

1. *It is the center of hereditary dispositions:*
   The id is the seat of the biologically derived instinctual drives. It is the vital core of the individual, his continuity with nature.

2. *It is the exclusive source of energy:*
   The id is the source of *all* energy. This is its most important characteristic. Energy moves from the physico-chemical processes of the body (where it is generated) to the psychic apparatus. Entering the psychic apparatus by way of the id, energy moves through the ego, and is then discharged onto objects in the outside world or is used by the ego to hold back other id energies.

3. *It is the exclusive source of motivation:*
   The id sector of the psychic apparatus is the source of all human motivation. This is a point of cardinal importance, imposing the demand on theorists that all evidence of motivation, however remote from the instinctual drives, must be ultimately related to them. Concepts such as displacement, projection, sublimation, and relative autonomy are introduced into the system for the purpose of tracing all human motives ultimately to id processes.

4. *It is the source of the sex and aggression instincts:*
   The instinctual energies of the id are subdivided into the libidinal and the aggressive drives. Due to the fluidity of instinctual drive energies, differentiation between libidinal and aggressive energies cannot be sharply maintained. Overwhelming clinical evidence supports the observation that all degrees of separateness and fusion occur between these two types of impulse.

5. *Its basic laws of functioning are the primary processes:*
   So broad is Freud's notion of primary process that at one

time or another he subsumed under this one term more than
eighteen logically distinct meanings—including the various
regulating principles of the id, the feeling-states that accompany the release of energies, the characteristics of these
energies, the modes of perception that accompany them.
The analysis that follows presents a schematic inventory of
the primary processes, abstracted from Freud's metapsychological papers (1900, 1911, 1915, 1917, 1920, 1923,
1926, 1933 and 1940).

We are departing from Freud's characteristically loose use
of terminology and assigning a fairly definite single meaning
to each primary process so that we will be in a better position,
when discussing the ego, to see the contrasts between the primary and secondary processes. The philosophical issues raised
by this aspect of the theory have been obscured, in part, by the
purely linguistic confusion.

Exhibit II lists the primary processes; the definitions follow.

Exhibit II

THE PRIMARY PROCESSES

Regulating Principles
Pleasure principle
Constancy principle
Nirvana principle

Feeling States
Pleasure or relief (at relative discharge of energy)
Trauma (actual or threatened "flooding" of the system)
Rest or repose (equilibrium)

Energy Characteristics
Mobility
Displacement
Condensation
Unconsciousness

Perceptual Modes
Distorted time sequence
Distorted spatial relationships
Lack of distinction between reality and hallucination
Drive satisfaction

Lack of connectedness between cathexes and words, images and memory—these are preconscious processes. (The averbal nature of primary process meanings.)
Suspension of logical association

Learning Principles
Repetition of pleasurable perceptions and experiences
Avoidance of trauma

REGULATING PRINCIPLES

Pleasure principle:
  Instinctual cathexes, unless they are prevented from doing so, will press toward full and immediate discharge.
Constancy principle:
  The organism tends to maintain a state of equilibrium (homeostasis) among its vital energies.
Nirvana principle:
  The organism tends to eliminate all pressures and energies, and to maintain its homeostatic equilibrium at a zero state of tension.

FEELING STATES

Pleasure or relief (at relative discharge of energy):
  When instinctual energies are discharged, the organism experiences a feeling of either positive sensations of pleasure, or more simply relief from tensions unburdened.
Trauma (actual or threatened "flooding" of the system):
  As we have noted, Freud recast his formulations of anxiety in 1926. According to the newer formulation, traumatic anxiety occurs when the young organism is flooded with more energies and tensions than it can handle. Later experiences that threaten a recurrence of the trauma give rise to the anticipation of the trauma and produce a sample of it (anxiety).
Rest or repose (equilibrium):
  Freud does not give so much attention to this feeling state as to relief or anxiety, but it is logically implied by the con-

cept of the Nirvana principle. It occurs when the organism succeeds in achieving a comparatively tensionless state.

ENERGY CHARACTERISTICS

Mobility:
Characteristically, id energies are to be found in disorganized, mobile, and unstable states.

Displacement:
Because they are highly mobile, id cathexes are readily displaced in aim and object. These displacements are ordinarily revealed in dreams and neurotic symptoms. In a dream, for example, a sexual attachment (libidinal cathexis) to one person may readily be displaced onto another person or onto an animal, object, idea, or fragment thereof.

Condensation:
An image or symbol in a dream may be supercharged with instinctual cathexes condensed from many sources. The part may stand for the whole or the whole for the part.

Unconsciousness:
The mobility, instability, displaceability, and condensation of energy processes all take place unconsciously. This characteristic is inferred from fragmentary manifestations of unconscious processes such as in dreams, symptoms and what Freud called the psychopathology of everyday life (jokes, slips-of-the-tongue, etc.)

PERCEPTUAL MODES

Distorted Time and Space:
Included under the primary processes are various nonrational modes of perception. The Kantian categories of time and space are distorted in perception that is governed by the primary processes. Time loses its orderly sequential character and space collapses as a stable form of three-dimensional orderliness in which objects are perceived in stable, spatial equilibrium in relation to each other and to the perceiver.

Lack of distinction between hallucination and reality:

Perception governed solely by the primary processes permits no distinction between hallucination and reality. We see this most clearly in dreams. In waking life the primary processes are overlaid by other modes of perception (appropriately termed "secondary processes" by Freud). But in sleep, a state in which energies are distributed differently and the secondary processes are partially suspended, the primary processes give rise to hallucinary perceptions.

Drive satisfaction:

If the primary processes were the only modes of perceiving, then what we see, sense, feel and hear would be determined solely by considerations of drive satisfaction. We would fail to perceive neutral objects; objects, that is, that do not contribute to immediate drive satisfaction; objects would be classified solely as satisfying or not satisfying.

The averbal nature of primary process meanings:

Freud has suggested that cathexes in their unconscious state are not connected with words or images. The phenomenon of human memory develops when connections are formed at a preconscious level between the unconscious cathexes of the primary processes and words, categories, and images belonging to the domain of the preconscious and secondary process.

Suspension of logical association:

Nonlogical associations are created, by condensation and displacement, etc.

LEARNING PRINCIPLES

Repetition of pleasurable perceptions and experiences:

Psychoanalysis contains a learning theory, but it is scattered throughout the whole corpus of psychoanalytic writings and is rarely presented in explicit or systematic fashion. Our present discussion of primary process would not be complete without reference to several types of learned behavior that result from the encounter between the primary processes and the world. The tendency to repeat pleasurable perceptions and experiences is one such learning principle.

Avoidance of trauma:

As we have seen, Freud believed that anxiety has its roots in trauma—the flooding of the organism with more psychic energy than can be assimilated or discharged at any one time. Traumas are most likely to take place in the early years of development before the child has learned to handle large amounts of instinctual cathexes and yet is exposed to fears (e.g., separation from the mother) that are likely to release large amounts of tension. A counterpart of the tendency to repeat pleasurable perceptions and experiences is the tendency to avoid trauma by flight from an external source of danger or by repression when the danger emanates from an internal source. (In Freud's writings, this tendency is implied by the pleasure principle but is logically and empirically independent.)

In summary, according to the theory of primary processes, a disequilibrium in the balance of the individual's instinctual energies produces a pressure for discharge and a return to a steady state; time loses its sequential character and events occur simultaneously; images of events in space are superimposed on one another; logic is suspended—incompatible and paradoxical ideas exist side by side; meanings form clusters of associations held together by shared emotion rather than by the laws of logical relatedness; the unconscious processes condense varied and complex events into simple, concrete symbols borrowed from the inventory of memories in the preconscious.

Condensation, timelessness, the paradoxical pairing of opposites, the suspension of the categories of sequence and space—these, and other of the phenomena described as primary processes, are firmly rooted in clinical experience. Logically, they are easily separated from a mechanistic framework such as the psychic apparatus, but historically Freud joined the two in his own version of human evolution.

Freud believed that the primary processes represent the oldest and most archaic parts of the psychic apparatus. Their origins can be traced back to the dim prehistory of man's development. They have not, however, been left behind in the long history of evolution: they are still an essential part of our everyday functioning, but are not so obvious or so open to inspection as conscious and preconscious processes because of the evolutionary overlay of secondary processes. Freud allowed that the phylogenetic "primacy" of the primary processes might be factually incorrect. He agreed that prehistoric man could probably not have survived for a single day if his responses and perceptions were governed solely by primary processes. But with respect to *ontogenesis*—the development of the individual from embryo to adult—Freud believed that the primary processes do literally precede in time the development of the secondary processes. It was his view that the infant comes into the world as a mass of primary processes, and that the secondary processes related to ego functioning develop out of a series of frustrating experiences inevitable in a world where even an infant's every need cannot be satisfied instantaneously.

The Ego

As we try to sift out what Freud has to say about the ego, we are struck by the difference of quality and tone from his descriptions of the id. The ego and its functions are less concretely defined and less oriented toward clinical experience. They have an almost deductive flavor—as if the reasoning were, "Well, if the id behaves one way, then logically the ego must behave the opposite way." Thus, if the primary processes describe how id energies press toward discharge, then the secondary processes (associated with the ego) describe how they are channeled and controlled. If, more precisely, the pleasure principle is defined as "mindless" pressure toward release—the tendency of instinctual energies to discharge themselves at any time, any place, with no relation to the consequences—then one must posit an opposite principle for the ego, and define it precisely in terms of its ability to prevent that immediate discharge. If the instinctual energies of the id are defined as mobile, unstable, and disorganized, the ego's functions will be defined in terms of structure, stability, and high organization.

Yet, in conceiving the ego as what the id is *not*, Freud is nevertheless led to make it subject to the same kinds of Newtonian principles as he postulated to account for id processes.

Ego phenomena, however, are far less susceptible to descriptions in terms of transformations of energy and motion.

It is with the elaboration of the ego concept that psycho-analysis is gradually being led into a crisis of fundamentals. This crisis occurs because the implications of psychoanalytic ego psychology make the metapsychology increasingly irrele-vant and/or contradictory. Let us examine how Freud's de-velopment of the ego leads to this impasse, and then look at various attempts since Freud's death to break out of it.

Although he modified his views slightly toward the end of his life, Freud held fast to the conviction that the ego grew out of the id and began to develop only after the first few months of life. As we have seen, he stated as early as 1914 that:

> It is impossible to suppose that a unity comparable to the ego can exist in the individual from the very start; the ego has to develop. But the autoerotic instincts are pri-mordial.

Freud made this point more explicit in 1923. The ego, he said, is the surface of the id, "that part of the id which has been modified by the direct influence of the external world . . ." (P. 15.)

In 1926, Freud once again restated this belief, even more ex-plicitly. In *The Problem of Anxiety,* he complains about both critics and followers taking analytical abstractions too literally:

> . . . we take abstractions too rigidly and from out of a complicated state of affairs we pick now one aspect and now another exclusively. Separation of the ego from the id . . . is forced upon us by certain findings. Yet, on the other hand, the ego is identical with the id, is only a specially differentiated portion of it. (P. 24.)

We have already quoted, from the *Outline of Psychoanalysis* (1940), Freud's final, systematic statement on this cardinal point of theory. It is worth repeating: "Under the influence of the real external world which surrounds us, one portion of the id has undergone a special development . . . an organization . . . which acts as an intermediary between the id and the external worlds. This region of our mental life has been given the name of ego." (1940, p. 15.)

We have taken pains to show that this belief of Freud's endured over a long span of years because it is so basic to Freud's fundamental outlook. Note that the id is never referred to as part of the ego, but only that the ego grows out of the id. This id is primordial—man's basic nature. The ego is a late-developing bloom (phylogenetically and ontogenetically), it lacks energies and motivations of its own, operates on borrowed energies, and is subject to a mode of functioning that develops only after the infant is born.

The ego develops slowly and falteringly, accelerating in the third month of life. By age two, the discrimination between self and others is fully developed and the processes of individuation have been firmly established. Between three months and two years, the essential characteristics of ego structure have fully emerged.

The process unfolds somewhat as follows: the infant starts out life as a bundle of uncontrolled instinctual urges. There is no differentiation of self from non-self, of subject from object, of hallucination from reality. Edith Jacobson refers to the infant at this stage as an "undifferentiated matrix" of libidinal and aggressive forces. The infant, says Jacobson, is "characterized by a low level tension in a general diffused dispersion of . . . undifferentiated energy . . . within the primal structurally undifferentiated self." (1964, p. 14.)

Slowly the process of differentiation begins, and the unstable division of psychic drives into their libidinal and aggressive components takes place.

During the first three months, the tendency to repeat pleasurable sensations (noted under the primary processes) manifests itself—a tendency associated with the experience of being fed and fondled by the mother. It is believed that the ability to hallucinate the source of gratifications first develops at this stage. The decisive point comes when the baby can "hallucinate" the mother even when the mother is not actually present. This act keeps the infant from crying for a fleeting moment, momentarily quieting its uneasiness. The theory holds that in this one tiny crucial moment, we have a model for all subsequent ego development: an instinctual drive pressing for immediate and peremptory satisfaction has been quieted and briefly held back. Slowly and gradually, the experience repeats itself in varying forms and on countless occasions, laying the groundwork for the elaborate control systems of the ego.

It soon happens, however, that the mere hallucination of the mother fails to produce the expected satisfaction. And this event, too, is fraught with far-ranging developmental consequences. In his brief but important paper in 1911, *Two Principles of Mental Functioning*, Freud first described how the reality principle develops out of the experience of frustration.

Stage 1: The infant's state of psychic rest is disturbed by peremptory instinctual demands.

Stage 2: The object desired (the mother, the breast, the bottle) is presented to the infant as an hallucination.

Stage 3: The expected satisfaction does not materialize, and this leads to abandonment of the effort to satisfy the need by means of hallucination alone.

At this point Freud makes a momentous leap:

> The psychic apparatus had to decide to form a conception of the real circumstances in the external world . . . the new principle of mental functioning (the reality principle) was thus introduced; what was presented in the mind was no longer what was agreeable but what was real even if it happened to be disagreeable. (1911, p. 291.)

Thus, the sequence is: arousal of internal need; hallucinated fulfillment; increase in the quantity and intensity of the need; absence of real satisfaction; motor discharge in the form of crying, screaming and thrashing about of arms and legs; satisfaction and fulfillment provided by the mother; reality testing (mother is real).

We see, then, that it is frustration that breeds learning and leads to the development of intelligence and controls. The archetypal experience of the failure of hallucination to satisfy the press of instinct gives rise to reality testing. Here, it is held, is the origin of the ability to perceive reality.

According to Freud, the failure of hallucinations to satisfy the instinctual drives causes a number of alterations to take place in the psychic apparatus. These alterations in that part of the id in contact with the external world slowly give rise to an *ego* structure; they are very far-reaching:

1. Consciousness becomes heightened.
   Before the decisive failure of hallucinated gratification the sole task of consciousness was to attend to events that provided tension release (pleasure). Now consciousness takes on the added task of learning to discriminate and to comprehend sensory qualities.
2. Focused attention develops.
   Instead of passively waiting for sense impressions to occur, the organism develops a more active mode of attending to them. A special function of attention is introduced into consciousness, giving the infant the beginnings of control over perception in case an urgent internal need should arise.
3. Memory develops.
   These experiences also lay the basis for memory, a method of retaining the results of active consciousness.
4. Perception of reality develops.
   Prior to the development of these capabilities, anything unrelated to the pleasure-unpleasure series was "excluded from cathexis" (or repressed). Now a new category of judgment is introduced. The rudimentary judgment "true-false" begins to be made by comparison with memory traces.
5. Effectiveness begins.
   Heretofore the means of unburdening the psychic apparatus of stimuli was to use motor discharge for expressive movements and expressions of affect. Now motor discharge is used in a new way—to "alter reality."
6. Control develops.
   Slowly a capacity develops in the psychic apparatus to tolerate increased tension and to postpone discharge.
7. Thought begins.
   The process of thought intervenes between tension accumulation and motor discharge. Freud conceived of thought as a form of trial action. Small quantities of cathexis are used to pretest the action without involving actual motor discharge.
8. Cathexes become less mobile.

The process of thought requires that the fluid and mobile cathexes of the id be organized more tightly, or "bound." Freud believed that this process was originally unconscious till it became connected with verbal residues.

It is in this manner that Freud conceived the origins of the so-called secondary processes—the development of thought, consciousness, attention, memory, reality testing (discriminating reality from hallucination), and effective action. Frustration triggers these processes, but other principles of development quickly come into play. The next major stages of ego development have to do with the infant's perceptions of, and his relations to, persons and objects external to himself.

Throughout the first few months of life there is some discrimination between self and object, but it is weak and unstable. The child has a limited capacity to make this distinction and the boundaries between self and object are blurred. The symbiotic relationship of infant with mother is, of course, difficult for an adult to grasp from the point of view of the infant's perceptions. Apparently, however, the primitive mechanisms of *introjection* and *projection* characterize this early period of life. The infant wavers between a gradually developing separation and a primitive need to fuse with the mother and to become one with her—making the mother part of the self by incorporating and devouring the breast in the phases of oral gratification.

It is in this period of fluid and weak boundaries between self and object that the first early object cathexes occur. Freud's concept of object cathexis is that of charging self, external objects, images, etc., with forms of psychic energy and emotional meaning. A point of crucial importance in the Freudian conception is that at some stage in the development of the child, by some process or another, an object cathexis is replaced by an identification. This is the next momentous stage in the development of the ego. What does this concept mean and how does it occur?

We start with the so-called mother-child symbiosis: from the vantage point of the child, the mother-child relationship in its earliest stages is considered to be virtually that of a single entity both emotionally and perceptually. The repeated frustrations, satisfactions, and separations of the first few months generate infantile fantasies of total incorporation of the mother and an intense wish, as separation between mother and child becomes more and more marked, to re-establish the lost unity.

Freud stressed the role of separation in creating the first major traumas that lead to anxiety and to the creation of the danger signal. In recent years, Bowlby and others have studied and called attention to the significance of the separation anxiety that occurs in the sixth or seventh month of life. These very early fantasies of being one with the mother are considered to be the *anlage* (or groundwork) for future object relations and identifications.

When writing *The Ego and the Id* in 1923, Freud remarked that several years earlier (in his 1917 paper, *Mourning and Melancholia*), he had described the process whereby "an object which was lost was set up again inside the ego—that is, an object cathexis has been replaced by an identification." (P. 18.) He goes on to say that at that time he hadn't realized how typical the process is—the fact that it is one of the essential processes of building up the character of the ego. In other words, when one has lost a love object or is forced to give it up, one compensates by identifying with it (by setting it up inside one's ego). To make this very abstract idea concrete, visualize a mother putting her child to sleep. The mother kisses the child and pulls up his blanket. Later when the mother is absent the child secures the same effect by imagining her doing it and thus sets her image up within his consciousness and the identification process is launched. This is what Freud means by the "reinstatement of the object within the ego."

Gradually, as the child matures, his need to become merged with the mother slowly recedes and is replaced by selective identifications. In the child's behavior we now begin to see his struggle between the desire to retain the symbiotic relationship to mother and at the same time to achieve some degree of independence. Once past this stage, the ego continues its further development and alterations through later stages—through the crisis of the Oedipal conflict, and the development of superego formation, the next critical stages of ego growth.

We need not at this point go beyond our summary of the first two momentous stages of ego development—the beginnings of impulse control and identification. These do not, of course, occur at any single moment in time; they are spread out with innumerable retrogressions, hesitations and stumbling throughout the first few years of life.

The specific processes and mechanisms that characterize these first few decisive stages are not made clear by Freud. He is concerned primarily with pointing out that the stages occur, and that an ego structure does emerge. However, even when fully developed, Freud does not attribute as much potency to the ego as to the primal stuff of the id—the great force of nature represented by the sexual and aggressive drives. More accurately, perhaps, we see Freud wavering time and again on the key issue of how much emphasis to ascribe to each of two main sides of man's life: the blind sexual and aggressive drives that urge him forward, and the mechanisms of control and calculation that serve him increasingly as he develops from infant to child to man.

Freud believed that a shift takes place at some stage in the child's development from a preoccupation with immediate satisfaction (the pleasure principle) to postponed satisfactions (the reality principle). The way in which the transition occurs is obscure. Furthermore, the two motivations are related. This is how Freud describes the relationship:

> Actually the substitution of the reality principle for the pleasure principle implies no deposing of the pleasure principle, but only a safeguarding of it . . . a momentary pleasure, is given up but only in order to gain . . . an assured pleasure at a later time. (1911, p. 223.)

Freud saw the renunciation of the pleasure principle and the substitution of postponed gratification as the source of the most far-reaching aspects of man's life. He traces art, education, and religion to the struggle involved in the renunciation of the pleasure principle for more distant gratifications.

In summary, then, the Freudian ego safeguards and serves the instinctual motivations, both libidinal and aggressive; it does so through its access to both the sensory and the motor mechanisms; and in the process it calls upon many mechanisms, mainly upon the postponement and delay of gratification. The ego also serves the id by finding objects for instinctual gratification, by testing their suitability through memory, thought, and experimentation, and by developing selective identifications out of an extraordinarily complex process. The process involves the following sequence: frustration; hallucination; lack of satisfaction with hallucination; reality discrimination; control of impulse discharge; object cathexis; identification.

Perhaps we could see Freud's meaning most clearly if we supposed that there were no ego. Presumably, man would then be a dimly sentient creature, barely able to discriminate his pleasant or painful sensations from the external world—a bundle of nonconscious forces labeled sex, hunger and aggression. He would appear as a mindless, thoughtless, brutelike creature who would eat, procreate, fight, sleep—and quickly die out. Death would come swiftly indeed. Lacking intelligence, the ego-less man would soon perish from starvation; if by chance he escaped hunger, he would die from exposure to the elements or as prey to physically stronger creatures. If, miraculously, he did survive these dangers, he would be destroyed while fighting over a sex object or be killed by others in a moment of uncontained rage.

Even more inimical to survival and civilization would be the unrestricted workings out of the death instinct. Most psychoanalysts are embarrassed about Freud's attachment to the death instinct. To them, it is a matter of pure speculation. What they see in their clinical practice is merely aggression; they are uncomfortable about leaping beyond aggression to postulate a transcendent death instinct. But Freud himself was implacable in drawing out the implications of his metapsychology. And the death instinct is a valid, indeed an inevitable, implication of psychoanalytic metapsychology. For Freud, the aggressive impulses are merely a diversion toward the external world of the workings of the death instinct. Without ego controls, the direct, untrammeled expression of the death instinct would soon result either in the death of the individual by virtue of his own self-destructive urges, or in an inevitable collision with others by virtue of the unhindered release of his rage to return to an inorganic state of being. Indeed, the death instinct is already presupposed in the concept of the Nirvana principle—the notion that the organism seeks to discharge its energies in order to return to a state of quiescence.

There is no doubt that the creature described above is the one Freud perceived under the controls of the ego and beneath the patina of civilization. To insure the survival of this creature, man's ego develops. Its main function is biological and evolutionary: to safeguard this inner man; to permit his instincts to gain satisfaction with relative impunity; to take into account the intractability of an external world, and to exchange impulse for prudence and calculation.

The main point to remember is that the Freudian ego has no purpose of its own. It is "the servant of the id." Given the nature of the psychic apparatus as an energy system dominated by the pleasure principle, the ego must perform its safeguarding functions in terms of energy control. The forms of control may be varied: the energy can be stopped in its tracks and prevented from discharge, the object of discharge can be changed, the impulse can be transformed and mutilated, it can be isolated, it can be caught and bound by the ego and used for repression, it can be incorporated with other less dangerous forms of energy discharge, etc., etc. But the ego can never, within the frame of the psychic apparatus, be conceived in terms other than energy control or pain avoidance.

Freud elaborated this implication of his theory, explicitly assigning to the mature ego a number of specific functions. Let us quickly review what these are.

The Characteristics
of the Mature Ego

Except in one brief period, Freud always regarded the instincts as the exclusive source of psychic energy (White, 1963). When he consolidated his views in 1923, he resolved any early doubts he may have had and placed the locus of psychic energies squarely in the id. But if the id, as the seat of the instincts, is the sole source of psychic energy, how can intrapsychic conflict, which Freud conceptualized in terms of energy, take place between ego and id? This question has hovered in the air ever since, and has never been fully resolved. In *The Ego and the Id* it caused Freud to describe the ego as being virtually power-less (since it has no energies of its own). It was in this work that he introduced his now familiar metaphor of the ego being like the rider of a powerful horse impotent to control it in any way and "obliged to guide it where it wants to go." (1923, p. 30.) In 1926, Freud solved the problem to his own satisfaction: the initially powerless ego, he postulated, gains its strength by mobilizing the dynamism of the pleasure principle; i.e., by "borrowing" energies from the id.

This issue of where the ego gets its energies, though it seems highly abstract and even a little unreal, masks a point of great practical and theoretical significance. Its meaning will become abundantly clear if the reader substitutes the word "motives" for "energies." If the id is the exclusive source of psychic ener-gies, then the drives of sex and aggression define the root mo-tives of human life. The ego is then merely a calculating and control mechanism to help ensure their fulfillment. Such is the view implied by the notion that the ego has no energies of its own and derives whatever force it has from the "all but omnip-otent pleasure principle." But what about the so-called reality principle? In most of Freud's formulations it is the reality prin-ciple that is supposed to regulate the ego.

In distinguishing between pleasure principle and reality prin-ciple Freud got somewhat caught up in semantic difficulties. Usually he did not have to pay a heavy price for his careless-ness with words, beyond causing his followers a certain amount of confusion. Often the context explains the particular mean-ing Freud attributed to a word on any occasion of its use. In several instances, however, carelessness in terminology did bring with it a more serious penalty. Such is the case with the con-fused and overlapping meanings of the two parallel pairs of terms (1) primary process versus secondary process and (2) pleasure principle versus reality principle. Both the concepts of secondary process and reality principle seem to be logically rather than empirically derived—they are given meanings that are logically opposite to primary process and pleasure principle. To add to the confusion, Freud has given each term several major meanings which are not necessarily related to one an-other either logically or empirically. More specifically, the meanings of secondary process include both the control over instinctual cathexes *and* also conscious mental processes such as thinking logically, discriminating reality from illusion, perceiving objects in an ordered time sequence, etc.

The reality principle, though less general, also has a number of overlapping meanings: in general, it means the ability to calculate and weigh opportunities for "pleasure," i.e., the calculations that enable the individual to give up direct and immediate gratifications that may be dangerous for indirect and future gratifications. Some of the meanings of secondary process and reality principle are similar, but secondary processes is the more generic term.

Now then, if the id is dominated by primary process and the pleasure principle, and the ego by secondary process and the reality principle, does this mean that the ego does have a motive of its own in the form of the reality principle? Is the reality principle a method for sneaking in independent motives and instincts through the back door after they had been banished from the ego? Indeed, why should frustrating experience lead, as Freud supposed, to more control over reality instead of to disaster, unless there were already built into the organism some prior regulating principle? Logically, there is no reason why frustration should not simply lead to more frustration, which it does under some circumstances.

These are some of the issues, and there are many others, that caused Freud and those who followed great difficulty. The reality principle, in particular, has dangled in mid-air unrooted in the basic theory. Although Freud continued to refer to the reality principle throughout his lifetime, it is significant that in *The Problem of Anxiety* the controlling mechanism of the ego is *not* the reality principle, but the pleasure principle. It is worth inspecting the anxiety theory of 1926 a little more closely to see how this can be.

Consider first a situation not involving trauma. Let us suppose that a moderate accumulation of instinctual energy is experienced by the individual in that form of tension which Freud called "unpleasure." In theory, the psychic apparatus mobilizes itself to discharge the tension and proceeds to do so adequately.

Consider now an instance of traumatic anxiety. In infancy

and early childhood the psychic apparatus is not well enough developed to manage large amounts of energy and tension efficiently. Freud describes some typically dangerous situations that arise during the early years of childhood—the absence of the mother, the threat of loss of love, etc. These situations trigger an unusual amount of instinctual energy that cannot effectively be discharged or bound. The result is trauma, the flooding of the organism with feelings of intense unpleasure and stress.

After describing such traumas Freud states that the violation of the organism by vast waves of anxiety arouses the pleasure principle; i.e., forever after, the organism through an almost reflex action, avoids a recurrence of these traumas. It does so by a mechanism Freud calls the "danger signal." On future occasions whenever there is anticipation of events similar to those that caused traumas in the past, the release of a small amount of anxiety is enough to mobilize the defensive powers of the psychic apparatus. As Freud stated it:

> We like to conceive of the ego as powerless against the id. When the ego struggles against an instinctual force in the id it merely needs to give a signal of distress to attain its purpose with the aid of the *all but omnipotent pleasure principle*. (1926, p. 18.) (Our italics.)

Flight, avoidance or repression follow—or any of the other myriad methods the organism possesses to protect the integrity of its energies.

Through this formulation of anxiety in 1926, Freud avoided a trap he almost fell into in 1923, but he may have set an equally dangerous one in its place. In 1923 he seemed to set up ego and id as rigidly opposed systems inherently in conflict with one another. He corrected this impression in 1926. His analysis of anxiety presents a single psychic apparatus dominated by a single set of principles: the ego is simply the organized part of the id in contact with external reality, regulating by means of energies borrowed from the id, and calling upon the aid of the pleasure principle.

With the psychic apparatus divided into ego and id, all of the energies and motivations of the individual are grouped on one side in the id and all of the perceptual-control mechanisms are grouped on the other side in the ego. This seems to be a neat arrangement, but it encounters difficulties almost immediately.

The signaling function attributed to the ego is in keeping with its role as the perceptual side of the psychic mechanism. But the idea that the id can be used against itself by mobilizing its own regulating principle, the pleasure principle, to keep it in check requires close scrutiny. In this particular instance at least, Freud seems to be playing semantic tricks on himself. We have seen that he used the concept of the pleasure principle for three major meanings: the first and the most fundamental is the tendency for instinctual impulses to press for full and immediate discharge. But Freud also used the pleasure principle to refer to the feeling state of relief or pleasure that accompanies such discharge of energies. This meaning tends to confuse matters from time to time, but otherwise it is harmless. It is the third meaning of the pleasure principle that involves Freud in a flagrant contradiction: namely, the use of the pleasure principle to refer to the tendency of the organism to avoid disagreeable experience as well as to seek pleasure. Now the avoidance of disagreeable experiences will frequently involve preventing one's impulses from achieving full and immediate satisfaction. If I covet my neighbor's wife and act out my covetous impulse in the presence of her husband, the consequences may be extremely disagreeable. So I hold back my covetous impulses. But not even Freud can use the same term to refer both to the tendency to release energy and the tendency to hold it back. If meaningful discourse is one's objective, one cannot use the same word to convey opposite meanings. Also, if the pleasure principle is to be used to refer to the control over impulses whenever anxiety threatens, what meaning will be left over for the reality principle?

It is not easy to see how this confusion can be resolved, except by keeping faith with the clinical data. There is overwhelming clinical evidence for the narrow and specific meaning of the pleasure principle: the fact that libidinal and aggressive impulses when aroused press toward release. Our main hope for unraveling some of the logical puzzles Freud has built around the psychic apparatus is to confine the use of the pleasure principle to this one meaning.

There is, in addition, overwhelming clinical evidence that the core of the ego's control mechanisms consists in the ability to impose delay upon the gratification of impulse. Using such a broad term as reality principle for this narrow and constricted meaning can be misleading. However, it is probably advisable to do so to preserve continuity with Freud's terminology. We propose, therefore, that the more general meaning Freud gave to the reality principle—the tendency of the organism to maximize its pleasure over time by the constant exercise of prudence—be ignored at least so far as the metapsychology is concerned. It is likely here that Freud mistook a cultural value peculiar to the European middle classes for a universal characteristic of the human species. The reality principle will, therefore, be considered to mean only the development of control over impulse.

FIVE

Postscript to Freud

The sharpness of some of our criticisms should not be misunderstood: we regard Freud's achievement as a major breakthrough in twentieth century thought. And yet this breakthrough is expressed in a theory that, simply as theory, leaks at every seam. This apparently contradictory state of affairs is not at all unprecedented in the intellectual history of mankind. Contradictions of this sort do not mark the end of the road for any discipline; on the contrary, they can be immensely productive, calling as they do for a basic shift in thinking.

On the essence of his discovery Freud was altogether clear. In a conversation with Ludwig Binswanger in 1927 he remarked: "Man has always known he was a spiritual [*geistige*] being; it remained for me to show him that he was also instinctual." (Binswanger, pp. 182–3.) These words give us as brief and incisive a characterization of the whole thrust of Freud's thought as could be desired. To bring man face to face in uncompromising confrontation with his instinctual nature was the Freudian breakthrough. And to trace the rootedness of psychic life in the instinctual must remain an essential, if not the essential, continuing task of psychoanalysis, however it may develop in the future.

It is imperative that the emphasis upon the instinctual be retained; but what is also required is that we develop a more accurate conception of what the human instincts are and how they operate. Many humanistic psychologists who have criticized Freud for his reductionism seem to end up by bypassing the fact of instinct altogether. In doing so, they paint a more "optimistic" picture of man in place of the "pessimistic" one Freud offers, colored as this latter is by the darker sides of the instincts. We are not pleading here for any such "optimism." Neither optimism nor pessimism has relevance to the effort to understand, which seeks only to see things as they are. The main question when we confront the instinctual forces of human life is not whether we paint a light or a dark picture of human nature but whether or not we understand this side of man adequately.

It is our contention that Freud in his formal theory gives an inadequate account of the nature of human instinct. The mechanistic model of the psychic apparatus must necessarily distort our understanding of the operations of instinct; and further, many of Freud's characterizations of instinctual life derive from descriptions of cases of deranged instinct—instinct that is damaged, mutilated and prevented from full expression. Perhaps the instinctual side of man, when it is not maimed, has a far different character. Perhaps, the more deranged we are from aspects of our nature which we share with other species the more we project upon them dark and forbidding attributes; it may be asked whether some of the worst forms of human blindness do not arise from a disastrous estrangement from instinct.

Instinct, as such, does not push toward immediate gratification. In many of its manifestations among the animal species, instinct in fact plays an inhibiting and regulatory role. Among the more social animals we discover inhibitions against forms of aggression that would, if unchecked, end by exterminating the species. Moreover, the sexual act in many animal forms has to be carefully timed in relation to the reproductive cycle; and in these cases the amount of sexual activity would have to be judged by the standards of some humans as severely inhibited. In general, it would seem that the instincts of the animal are part and parcel of the organic form that characterizes and also limits that animal as a member of a definite species, and in some adaptive way relates the animal to his world and to other creatures, both of his own species and of other species.

Why did Freud characterize instinct as a force pushing toward immediate gratification? One reason, we have seen, lies in the artificial Newtonian model within which he thought. A force, in the Newtonian scheme, must push forward in a straight line; if it is not actually pushing, it does not exist as a force. But there are also clinical reasons why Freud was led to characterize instinct as a greedy child rushing toward immediate gratification. These lay in the neurotic material with which he had to deal. Deranged instinct becomes obsessive for the patient. He cannot escape it. He keeps coming back to it, in one form or another, time and time again. Under duress he may neurotically regress toward an infantile stage where like the child he must have immediate satisfaction. Freud, speaking in a candid moment to a friend, referred with exasperation to his patients as *"Die Narren!"* (the fools). He was delivering himself, in a passing mood of exhausted patience, of a human and not a clinical judgment of the tiresome childishness of some neurotics. Yet this neurotic distortion was what he encountered overwhelmingly in his consulting room, and on the basis of this empirical material he made his essential characterization of instinct.

Instinct in the human appears to be much less rigid than in the animal. In taking our clue for the understanding of instinct from the observations of naturalists, we do not in the least intend to "reduce" man to the animal. The relative freedom from instinct in the sense of rigid automatisms is what makes man, in the words of Nietzsche, "the most problematic of the animals," and also creates specifically human problems in our handling of instinct. Yet if we are to understand man as a natural being, we have to see him against the background of millions of years of evolution that have shaped him. As most students of animal behavior remind us, there is much more of the human in the animal, and more of the animal in the human, than most people commonly think. In a highly social animal like man, in particular, a good deal of our communal habits, good and bad, may repose very heavily on a foundation of instinct. Perhaps even our moral feelings are instinctually rooted and their violation can take place only when there has been an estrangement from instinct.

⟨In short, if the Freudian breakthrough lies in confronting man with the instinctual side of his nature, then we have to recognize that the instinctual, however we characterize it, cannot be compartmentalized in one psychic system (the id) nor properly conceptualized as forces blind to the survival of the species. The eminent existential psychiatrist Ludwig Binswanger, who was for many years a close and devoted friend of Freud, was willing to concede that the Freudian description of *homo natura*—the natural man—was valid, but that it had to be supplemented by an understanding of man as an existential and historical being. On this point we are in radical disagreement with Binswanger. It is true that the Freudian apparatus cannot yield any adequate account of man as he is concretely situated in history and enmeshed in his urgent and personal tasks within his world. But to concede the Freudian concept of the natural man as correct, and then to try to graft an existentialist overlay upon that, is precisely to create a picture of man as a centaur—a radically divided being whose two parts are too dissimilar to be united. ⟨The point is that Freud's description of man as a natural being is not only inadequate but a positive distortion of our instinctual nature.⟩

The so-called ego could not develop on the basis of the instincts if the latter were merely blind subcutaneous itchings that it was supposed to render quiescent. From the evolutionary point of view, the human ego could develop in all its complexity only within a limiting framework of instinct. Perhaps it is that limiting framework that modern life threatens to tear asunder.

The truth is that though he loved to flourish it as a banner, Freud never carried through the evolutionary or genetic point of view in analyzing human nature within the formal theory. In the end, as we have observed, the Newtonian wins over the Darwinian legacy. If the genetic point of view has led us to question Freud's fundamental characterization of instinct, from that same point of view his description of the ego becomes even more questionable. For here, in the case of the ego, we come upon a kind of development that is unique and complex, and for which his concept of the psychic apparatus provides no accommodation. The development of the ego is a develop-

ment in identity of the self and of the sense of identity. What
sense of its own identity can an ego harbor whose purpose is
supposed to be merely to keep the boiler pressure steady?

And indeed it is no surprise that the first major gaps in the
theory should have emerged in the various developments within
ego psychology from Anna Freud and Heinz Hartmann to
Erikson. We turn now to observe those developments in some
detail.

PART TWO

FREUD'S HEIRS:
THE EGO RESTORED

[✳]

SIX

Heinz Hartmann,
the Conserver

The two key transitional figures linking Freud to present-day psychoanalysis are Anna Freud and Heinz Hartmann. Both have made major contributions to psychoanalytic theory; both have responded to a deeply conserving impulse to continue Freud's work; both have attempted to build a bridge from psychopathology to normal psychology; and both offered their major ideas to the psychoanalytic movement while Freud was still alive.

The reader will recall that Freud's "decisive reorientation" in the 1920's replaced a one-sided emphasis on instinct with a more balanced emphasis on instinct in relation to the control mechanisms. Freud introduced the shift but did not live long enough to confront all of its consequences. By calling attention to the controlling functions of the ego, he brought to light a gap in psychoanalytic theory which he could not himself fill. How, specifically, does the individual adapt to the often conflicting demands of reality, instinct, and superego? How is the transition from the dominance of the pleasure principle to the reality principle effected? Into what channels do the sex and aggressive impulses ultimately flow to provide a "normal" life? How does the ego adapt to change so as to maintain a reasonably ordered life for the individual in the midst of an accelerating pattern of social change?

If we divide the ego into its *defensive* and *adaptive* functions, we can most readily see how Anna Freud and Heinz Hartmann tackled some of these questions. Anna Freud concentrated on those relating to defenses; Heinz Hartmann addressed himself to the ego's adaptive processes.

The simplicity of Anna Freud's prose in *The Ego and the Mechanisms of Defense* (1936) at first obscured the importance of her contribution. She integrated and synthesized all that had been written up to that time on the ego's mechanisms of defense, and in so doing, showed the ego and its workings in a new light. Where previously the ego's defenses had been regarded as obstacles to successful therapy (the defenses were technically regarded as "resistances") she showed that these resistances were, in fact, highly adaptive, at least in their origins. She further demonstrated that the task of working through the resistances was an important part of the patient's cure, not a hindrance to it. Consequently, she was also able to show how each individual's defenses (intellectualization, reaction formation, ego restriction, etc.) were characteristic of his total adaptation to life, forming a distinctive part of his personality.

In time, *The Ego and the Mechanisms of Defense* became a classic in psychoanalytic circles. It persuaded most psychoanalysts that a major gain in understanding could be won by paying close attention to the defensive maneuvers of the ego. Unlike Heinz Hartmann, whose classic paper *Ego Psychology and the Problem of Adaptation* followed a few years later (1939), Anna Freud conceived her early work within the narrowest definition of psychoanalysis. She considered the mechanisms of defense to be part of the purview of psychoanalysis only because Freud had shown the roots of these defenses, along with the instinctual drives, to be unconscious. For many conservative psychoanalysts, even today, the proper domain of psychoanalysis is the unconscious—the more conscious aspects of mental life, including the processes of normal growth and functioning, are the concern of other branches of psychology.

It was Heinz Hartmann, whom many believe to be the main architect of the post-Freudian period, who launched the program for enlarging the scope of psychoanalysis beyond the unconscious and the neurotic. Many, perhaps most, psychoanalysts would agree with psychologist George Klein that "the framework of contemporary psychoanalytic ego psychology is as much Hartmann's achievement as Freud's." Hartmann's name is not as familiar outside of psychoanalytic circles as Jung's or Adler's or even that of Erich Fromm, Karen Horney, Wilhelm Reich, Otto Rank or Abram Kardiner. Most works on the post-Freudians stress these individuals, who came later, and who tended to emphasize how their work differed from Freud's. But in actual practice, Hartmann's work has been more important and influential. Though he emphasizes his continuity with Freud rather than his differences, his own innovations in the theory have a far-reaching significance because they are accepted, by and large, and followed in practice, by a great many psychoanalysts.

Just as *conflict* is the central notion in Freud's work, *adaptation* is central in Hartmann's. While Freud's stresses the ego's conflict-ridden limitations, Hartmann's work stresses the ego's conflict-free achievements. Throughout Western intellectual history, philosophies emphasizing the harmony of life have always followed close upon philosophies emphasizing strife, and vice versa. Freud's concepts of *Eros* and *Thanatos* portray the eternal tension between the thrust of life to create new and harmonious modes of being while fighting against the tendency of all living things to return to inertia and to death. Freud's was the great tragic-romantic vision of death-in-life, of "being" interpenetrated with "nonbeing." It should be kept in mind that Freud's enormous influence in the modern world does not reside primarily in medicine (Freudian psychiatry is still suspect for many orthodox physicians). Nor does it reside in the social sciences: for most social scientists, psychoanalysis is a very small part of a large smorgasbord, the other dishes being labeled Marx, Durkheim, Weber, Sullivan, Parsons, Mead, etc. Freud's most explosive impact has been on the literary and humanist tradition of our culture. And with good reason, for those nurtured on the great literature of the West have had the best possible preparation for Freud's tragic vision of life.

Compared to Freud, Heinz Hartmann is another breed altogether: not a revolutionary, but a practical, earthbound traditionalist. His vision is not tragic, but liberal and constructive. He is a conserver, not a breaker-of-new-ground; a person who would rather heal a wound than open it up, the kind of thinker who must follow in the footsteps of a revolutionary if a tradition is to be established, maintained, and institutionalized.

What Hartmann tried to do can be seen most clearly by referring back to one of Freud's last papers, *Analysis: Terminable and Interminable*, written in 1937 when he was over eighty years old. Hartmann has said that it may "prove to be the most farsighted of Freud's last papers." It is undoubtedly one of the master's major contributions, in which Freud struggled once again with the problem that had preoccupied him for half a century: the cause and cure of the psychoneuroses. The neuroses, he states in this penultimate summing up, are caused by a combination of two sets of factors, constitutional and accidental. No two individuals enjoy the same constitutional endowment. In some people the instincts are weak and readily controllable, while in others they are excessively strong and resist taming, creating a predisposition to neurosis. The accidental factor refers to chance psychic traumas undergone in the early years of life. Freud notes that this accidental type of neurosis offers a far more favorable opportunity for cure than the constitutional type.

Early repressions endure, Freud adds, because of the relative strength of the forces involved. A child's ego is at its most immature stage of development. The undeveloped and immature ego is unable to control the flood of instinctual pressure aroused by infantile trauma in any way except through indiscriminate repression. But the security won by the repression comes at a high cost. The warded-off impulse continues to press toward satisfaction; it lives "an independent life of its own."

These same "quantitative" considerations heighten the likelihood of a neurosis breaking out at vulnerable stages in the maturational processes—for instance, at puberty and at menopause. At these transitional stages of life, instinctual forces are strengthened from physiological sources, upsetting the internal balance.

There are several points of interest in this analysis. The first is Freud's very strong reaffirmation of the primacy of a balance-of-forces theory and of the so-called quantitative factor. He repeatedly emphasizes the "irresistible power of the quantitative factor in the causation of illness." (1937, p. 226.) The crucial assessments in determining neurosis are, he states, all quantitative: how intense was the trauma? How strong are the instincts? How much does the ego have to be strengthened to bring it into better balance with the demands of the instincts and of reality?

In placing this much stress on quantities of forces in relation to each other, Freud is once again asserting the importance of the metapsychology as *the* mode of explanation: "We have had occasion to recognize the paramount importance of the quantitative factor and to stress the claim of the metapsychological line of approach . . . in any attempt at explanation." (1937, p. 234.)

Freud's proposals for curing neuroses follow directly from his analysis of their cause: if psychoneurosis is caused by an imbalance of forces the cure lies in righting the balance. Specifically, psychoanalysis must strengthen the patient's ego by replacing insecure and harmful repressions with reliable ego-syntonic controls, "allying ourselves with the ego . . . to subdue portions of the id which are uncontrolled." (1937, p. 234.)

When it comes to strengthening the ego, however, Freud feels that he is on shakier ground than when he is analyzing the causes of the neuroses. He concludes pessimistically: "What we have to say about strengthening the ego will prove to be very inadequate." (1937, p. 234.) It is in this section of Freud's classic paper that the fatigue of his eighty-plus years may be showing itself. As always, the logic of his presentation is impeccable, the prose strong and lucid. But his commitment to habitual ways of thinking is too ingrained to overcome. Throughout the preceding half century, Freud had played down the strength of the ego in relation to the power of the instinctual drives—which were perhaps his greatest discovery.

Too many aspects of his theory point to an inherently weak ego for him to be sanguine about the chances for greatly strengthening the ego:

(1) The Freudian ego clearly starts off its career as a weaker force than the instincts from which its energies must be borrowed. The ego, growing out of the id, is a secondary growth, while the id, the seat of the instinctual drives, is primary. The id stands for the millions of years of primate evolution, preceded by the billions of years of evolution of

nonhuman life on the planet. The ego, being derivative, must borrow its energy from the id.* And, since the metapsychology is, in part, an energy theory, this borrowed energy became the busiest *deus ex machina* in psychoanalytic theory; it is held responsible for just about every act not clearly sexual and aggressive in origin. Yet, despite much scientific-sounding talk of borrowed and neutralized energies, the actual processes whereby psychic energy is transferred from id to ego, from ego to object, and from objects back to ego, remains shrouded in mystery. This is usually the place where most theorists find themselves bogged down in the metapsychology, and the more they struggle, the deeper they sink.

(2) Freud tended to think of the ego as devoid of goals, needs and purposes of its own. In Freud's work, the ego is regarded as a means only; it is the "servant" of id and super-ego. In his final statement in the *Outline of Psychoanalysis* (1940), Freud repeats essentially what he said in 1923 about the ego as servant: "An action by the ego is as it should be if it satisfies simultaneously the demands of the id, of the super-ego and of reality—that is to say, if it is able to reconcile their demands with one another." (1940, p. 146.) In this same final work, Freud also repeats a conclusion that remained, with one exception, unchanged in his thinking for over fifty years: namely, that the pleasure principle, the regulating principle of the id, is the fundamental law of psychic life. This conclusion reinforces the primacy of the id, for Freud adds that the ego too serves the id by striving after pleasure and seeking to avoid unpleasure.

(3) The ego stands for learned experience while the id stands for heredity: "It will be observed that, for all their funda-mental difference, the id and the superego have one thing in common: they both represent the influences of the past—the id the influence of heredity, the superego the influence, essen-tially, of what is taken over from other people—whereas the ego is principally determined by the individual's own experi-

---

* Psychologist Robert White has elaborated on a suggestion made by Freud that the ego might have independent energies of its own. As White makes clear, however, this possibility was not developed sys-tematically either by Freud or by Hartmann. (White, 1963.)

ence, that is by accidental and contemporary events." (Freud, 1940, p. 146.) The thrust of Freud's writings for nearly half a century leaves little doubt about his belief that the past carries more weight than the present, and that our biological heritage, represented by the id, is far stronger than the effects of individual learning and experience, represented by the ego.

It is interesting to note that the line of attack taken by those who have abandoned the psychoanalytical fold has chiefly opposed Freud's biological orientation. Erich Fromm, Abram Kardiner, Karen Horney, and others of the so-called culturalist school have all tended to reverse Freud's emphasis, placing greater weight on the individual's life experience than on his biological heritage. Fromm, in particular, takes a Marxist position which commits him to a belief in the almost infinite malleability of the individual in response to social and economic forces. He thereby drives a wedge between himself and Freud, since the Freudian and the Marxist point of view on this matter are opposed to each other. In fact, much of the controversy about the nature of man and society tends to revolve around precisely this issue of whether man is shaped mainly by his culture or whether biological "human nature" transcends cultural differences.

Not too many of those who work within the classic psychoanalytic tradition today accept unquestioningly Freud's premise that what is innate is stronger than what is learned through life experience; and psychoanalysts have also begun to challenge Freud's other assumption that the split between id and ego parallels the distinction between the instinctual and the learned —all of the instincts belonging with the id and all of learning and experience belonging with the ego. This latter question is more important and fundamental than the controversy over whether the environment is a stronger influence than the instincts, or vice versa.

(4) There is one final element of Freud's theory that contributes to the concept of a weak ego. In *Analysis: Terminable and Interminable,* Freud refers once again to a force within man that "defends itself by every possible means against recovery and . . . is absolutely resolved to hold on to illness and suffering." (1937, p. 242.) And Freud adds the clinical evidence of masochism, of the negative therapeutic reaction, and

of the sense of guilt. To Freud, these manifold tendencies of man argue for the presence of the instinct of aggressiveness or destruction which he traces back to "the original death instinct of living matter."

In summary, then, the Freudian ego is weak (1) because it is conceived as a secondary development: it evolves out of the id and borrows its energies from the instinctual drives; (2) because it has no goals of its own but as servant to other stronger psychic functions borrows its goals from them; (3) because it represents the individual's puny life experience pitted against the greater force of millions of years of evolution represented by the instinctual drives of the id; and (4) because it has to fight against the negative force of the death instinct.

Hartmann's Contribution

How can the neuroses ever be cured if one holds simultaneously to the views that cure requires a greatly strengthened ego and that the ego is inherently weak and cannot be strengthened significantly? "Victory," Freud said, "is always on the side of the big battalions." (1937, p. 240.) But the "big battalions" are rarely with the ego; they are aligned with the instinctual drives, the pleasure principle, the superego, the demands of the real world, and the pull of death. Such a conclusion is most discouraging to physicians committed to curing the neuroses. And indeed, in the 1937 paper, Freud is not sanguine about the chances for lasting cure. His own clinical experience had shown him that some neuroses can be cured, and yet, the theory makes lasting cure unlikely. "The business of analysis is to secure the best possible psychological conditions for the functions of the ego," Freud states. (1937, p. 250.) But his description of these "best possible psychological conditions" merely underscores the enormity of the task confronting the ego.

There is nothing that Freud says about the ego to suggest that the balance of forces can shift in any fundamental way in its favor. According to Freud, the ego is strong mainly under negative conditions: when a signal of anxiety is given, the ego can mobilize the "all but omnipotent power" of the pleasure principle to bring about avoidance of pain. Otherwise the ego is weak. And yet, Freud had repeatedly implied that maturity and mental health come about from replacing the pleasure principle with the reality principle. "Where id is, there ego shall be" is one of his most famous mottoes. According to the strict implications of the metapsychology, however, all that this means is improving the efficiency of the ego as a calculator of pleasure and as a reconciler of pleasure with security. Such a conception of man's ego—a calculating function for conducting cost/effectiveness studies to maximize pleasure and minimize pain—does not fit well with the tragic vision of man's life conveyed in Freud's *Civilization and its Discontents*, or with his sweeping concept of the interplay of the instincts of life and death, of creativity and destructiveness in human life.

Thus, Freud left his followers with a terrible dilemma at the very heart of the psychoanalytic enterprise: an official theory that suggests the neuroses cannot be cured, and a profession whose reason for being is to cure them. Hartmann's contribution was to lead psychoanalytic theory out of this dead end. And he did so tactfully, painlessly, authoritatively and unobtrusively. Small wonder he enjoys such great influence in psychoanalytic circles, for he accomplished a major piece of theoretical surgery without shedding a drop of blood.

Hartmann modified the concept of ego as servant by developing the notion of ego as autonomous. Though its autonomy is relative and subject to regression, the postulating of an autonomous rather than a dependent ego leads to quite different emphases and conclusions. In the language of Freud's military metaphor, Hartmann placed many more battalions at the disposal of the ego—which, he insisted, must be more than "a developmental by-product of the influence of reality on the instinctual drives." (Hartmann, 1950, p. 119.)

Since the notion of a weak ego is intimately woven into Freud's theory, it is intriguing to watch Hartmann achieve his feat of logic while preserving intact the psychic apparatus, as well as the varying "points of view" of the classical metapsychology.

We have seen that the heart of the metapsychology consists of the psychic apparatus bifurcated into ego and id. (In giving such scanty attention to the superego, we do not underestimate its clinical importance; but it is not directly relevant to the theoretical issues.) The bifurcation contains several critically important premises. It assumes, as we have already noted, that the id, man's archaic heritage, is phylogenetically prior to the ego, and at the same time, curiously enough, that instinct in man does not behave the same way as instinct in animals— man's instinct does not serve adaptive or survival purposes.

It is the assumption of enmity between ego and instinct that Hartmann bears down on, though "bearing down" may be too strong an expression, since he approaches the topic rather gingerly. Nevertheless, approach it he does; and the approach is a great step forward. If the instinctual drives of the id are estranged from reality, and if they do not serve the purposes of survival and adaptation, then, reasons Hartmann, the ego, which has adaptation and survival as its major functions, must have biological roots of its own. Freud had also briefly entertained the possibility that the ego, like the id, may have its own genetic roots. But he offered this suggestion tentatively and later backed away from it. His exact language is most revealing. It does not, he says, "imply any *mystical overvaluation* of heredity if we think it creditable that even before the ego has come into existence, the lines of development, trends and reactions are already laid down for it." (1937, p. 240.) (Our italics.)

Freud cautiously concluded that ascribing a preformed path of development to the ego does not violate a scientific explanation of human growth processes. Hitherto, such suggestions had seemed to him to border on mysticism and vitalism—points of view that had been roundly condemned by Brücke and Helmholtz in Freud's formative years.

It is precisely this conclusion that Hartmann picks up and elaborates. The ego, he states, does not develop solely as a result of learning and experience; it follows its own timetable of inborn processes analogous to the development of physiological processes. The timing of the appearance of grasping, walking, the motor aspect of speech, and other ego functions follows a biological schedule. Furthermore, and this is the crucial point, certain of these inborn ego functions develop independently of the instinctual drives. Therefore, Hartmann concludes, all ego functions are not, as Freud suggested, the outcome of conflict between instinctual drives and reality. (Hartmann, 1939, p. 8.)

The reader will recall the model of how the reality principle develops, discussed in Chapter Four. According to Freud, perception of reality, reality testing, and other ego functions develop only when the instinctual drives fail to gain immediate satisfaction. (Freud, 1911.) Hartmann is now saying something quite different, and with it changing a major plank in the theory. He has singled out the ego functions of perception, memory, motility, and the stimulus-barrier thresholds as existing prior to and independent of conflicts involving the instinctual drives. These ego functions, he states, are "inborn and conflict-free."

Such a revision does not, Hartmann reasons, contradict Freud, since he agrees with Freud that many aspects of the ego do grow out of conflict. In his own view, Hartmann has not so much changed the theory as extended it by showing that conflict is not the only possible route of ego development: "Not every adaptation to the environment, or every learning and maturation process, is a conflict. I refer to the development outside of conflict of perception, intention, object comprehension, thinking, language, recall-phenomena, productivity, to the well-known phases of motor development, grasping, crawling, walking and to the maturation and learning processes implicit in all these and many others." (Hartmann, 1939, p. 8.)

Hartmann states explicitly that it does not make sense to define the ego negatively as the nonbiological part of the personality. If the ego does not develop solely out of instinctual conflict, then it need not grow out of the id, but can be present from the very beginning. What Hartmann is leading up to is to introduce the notion that both id and ego develop out of an "undifferentiated phase" characteristic of the first few months of the infant's life. Out of this undifferentiated phase there grows an autonomous ego, says Hartmann, in exactly the same way "as we consider the instinctual drives autonomous agents of development." (Hartmann, 1950, p. 119.)

The functions of perception, memory, and motility are what Hartmann calls functions of primary autonomy. Their roots are part of the biologically given, and they thus give the ego a certain independence of the instincts. Consequently, the ego has now gained more strength vis-à-vis the instincts. Hartmann has thus revised the Freudian division of effort between learning (ego) and biological inheritance (id).

These are not the only "battalions" Hartmann adds to the ego. Another force is recruited under the rubric of "functions of secondary autonomy." Turning to the ego functions that arise as defenses against the instinctual drives, he introduces the notion of change of function, as for example, the defense mechanism of "reaction formation," one of the most paradoxical of the ego's mechanisms of defense. A case in kind would be that of a person fighting against powerful impulses of cruelty who would have to swing to the other extreme and develop a consistent kindness in order to manage and control his more brutal desires. Eventually, the kindness may come to have an autonomy of its own.

David Rapaport cites the experience of Anna Freud with children at the Hempstead Nurseries in England. She found that many children who were blatantly anal-sadistic at one phase of their development later became nice youngsters with an aversion to cruelty. The personality characteristics of kindness and gentleness may have originated as the defense mechanism of reaction formation, but these qualities evolve as the child develops, and they become relatively autonomous and independent of their origins.

Hartmann's point is that forms of behavior that started out as defenses against instinctual drives can "turn from a means into a goal in their own rights"; they become, in Hartmann's words, "ego apparati of secondary autonomy." (Hartmann, 1939, p. 23.)*

It should be clear that these changes in theory vastly enlarge the scope of ego function and give it many "battalions of its own." If there are functions of the ego that arise independently of the instinctual drives, if the ego has biological roots of its own, and if, further, some ego functions that developed in relation to conflict come to have autonomy, then the Freudian

---

* The late Harvard psychologist, Gordon Allport, introduced almost the same concept with virtually the same words in 1937. He referred to the "functional autonomy" of motives, pointing out that motives originally serving one purpose may become an end in themselves.

concept of a weak ego has been changed to the Hartmann concept of a potentially strong and autonomous ego.

One important qualification must be made. Hartmann and his associates are careful to qualify the ego's capacities by referring to their *relative* autonomy. Much clinical experience has accumulated to show that the ego's autonomy can, if pressures are strong enough, collapse into serious regressions. Rapaport, for example, has summarized some of the conditions under which the ego's autonomy can be undermined. (Rapaport, 1958.) He refers to the writings of Bruno Bettelheim about concentration camp experiences which showed that ego autonomy can be surrendered under conditions of systematic degradation. As another example, he cites the sensory deprivation experiments of Hebb and others, in which various devices such as totally soundproof rooms, blindfolds, padding on arms, legs, torso, etc., keep the subject from receiving sensory stimulation for prolonged periods of time. Under such conditions, strange things happen to one's cognitive processes. The subject loses the ability to pursue orderly thought; trivial experiences take on an incredible intensity and a delusional quality; and confusion and disorientation take place, undermining ego autonomy. Rapaport also mentions, as posing yet another potential threat to ego autonomy, the physiological changes in puberty and menopause. Finally, he cites the Gill and Brenman work, *Hypnosis and Related States* (1959), which shows how the autonomoy of certain ego functions can collapse or be suspended under conditions of altered consciousness.

Thus, we are presented in Hartmann's work with the concept of an ego far stronger than the Freudian ego, but one whose autonomy is vulnerable to threats not only from within but from changed environmental conditions.

Hartmann has always insisted that the changes he introduced are logical extensions and refinements of Freud's thought, not deviations from it. He points out that initially psychoanalytic theory had to be preoccupied with conflict, since resolution of conflict is indispensable to the therapy of the neuroses. Ego functions relatively free of conflict did not, he notes, become the subject of psychoanalytic attention until the goals of psychoanalysis itself were enlarged. Hartmann believes that conflict-free ego functions have less clinical significance than those involved in conflict. His interest in the conflict-free aspects of ego relates, he emphasizes time and again, to his desire that psychoanalysis become a general psychology and not merely a special theory of psychopathology.

Hartmann integrates his theories of a strong ego with Freud's metapsychology by adhering faithfully to the major concepts of the metapsychology: the psychic apparatus, the intrapsychic systems of ego, id, and superego, and the unit of psychic energy. He accepts without qualification the unit of psychic energy as the basic concept of the metapsychology. He then proceeds to define his innovations in terms of units of energy by building on Freud's suggestion that energy originally libidinal in origin can be neutralized in order to serve the purposes of the ego. In Hartmann's view, as the ego develops out of the undifferentiated phase, it borrows energies from the instinctual drives which become neutralized in the process. Hartmann refers to the "ego's capacity for neutralization" as one of the chief criteria of ego strength. He points out that this process of transforming instinctual energy into neutralized energy continues through the lifetime of the individual; he further notes that such energy does not always shed all traces of its origins in the instinctual drives: there are degrees of delibidinized and deaggressivized energy. The degree of neutralization achieved depends on the type of activity at issue and on the success of the transformation: incomplete neutralization can spell trouble for the individual.

Hartmann is not dogmatic about the sources of such neutralized energies. While he refers to Freud's statement that "nearly all the energy of the psychic apparatus comes from the drives," he raises the question of whether there might be other sources of ego energy, and he frankly states: "The question whether all energy at the disposal of the ego originates in the instinctual drives, I am not prepared to answer." (Hartmann, 1950, p. 131.) For all practical purposes, however, this qualification is ignored and references to psychic energies made by Hartmann refer exclusively to the powerhouse of the sex-aggressive instincts as their exclusive source.

While this outline of Hartmann's major innovations does not do justice to the full subtlety of his thought, it does indicate the main thrust of his changes in the theory. Hartmann's master concept is adaptation, and he leaves no doubt about the importance he ascribes to it. He believes it to be the conceptual bridge between pathology and normal psychology, and between psychoanalysis and the social sciences. A base in psychopathology is, he states, too narrow to support a general psychology. The concept of adaptation broadens the base and leads directly, in his judgment, to the fulfillment of the ambitions of psychoanalysis to become a general psychology.

SEVEN

Adding Epicycles

Freud postulates a relatively weak ego, Hartmann a relatively strong ego. In terms of its practical consequence, the choice could hardly be more important. Freud's interpretation implies that when caught in a neurotic trap there may not be much one can do to change oneself—not even by psychoanalysis (a method Freud certainly did not underestimate).

Many people share a similar view of self-change. As they grow older, they see how intractable human nature can be. "People don't change"—one hears the familiar phrase many times. But the main business of psychoanalysis as a profession is to produce change. For people struggling with problems whose successful resolution requires a decisive change in themselves, the idea that human change is improbable or even impossible is, of course, a counsel of despair. Hartmann's innovations, holding out greater hope for human change, fall on more receptive ears—especially to Americans—than Freud's. There is, however, a problem. In the interest of maintaining continuity with Freud, Hartmann retained all of the conceptual awkwardness of the old metapsychology—even though his new concepts are incompatible with it. Seen in retrospect, Hartmann had the choice of grounding the new concepts on empirical evidence or forcing them to fit the metapsychology by a logical adjustment, i.e., by using units of "neutralized energies" to account for the transition from a weak to a strong ego. Unfortunately, he chose the latter course, thereby helping to create some of the problems that plague psychoanalysis today.

Consider Hartmann's major proposal—the autonomy of the ego. Clinical experience suggests that there are enormous individual differences in ego strength: some patients are able to endure frustrations, to delay gratifications, and to relive painful experiences without falling apart, while others are not. Hartmann's collaborator, Kris, speaks of "regression in the service of the ego." By this Kris means that a person may have to abandon his customary controls and regress temporarily to earlier stages of development in order to rebuild a new solution to an old problem. For example, in the treatment of the so-called character neuroses, the psychoanalytic procedure calls for undermining the patient's defenses—his life-long ways of dealing with problems. Most psychoanalysts believe that it takes a strong ego to undergo the painful experience of psychoanalysis itself—having old and familiar modes of defenses destroyed before new methods of coping can be learned. (Paradoxically, therefore, the classic form of psychoanalytic therapy is of little use to those who need it most—those whose egos are weakest.)

There are many patients who cannot endure the frustration of psychoanalysis. Regression may precipitate a psychotic episode or an acting out that is destructive to the patient himself or to his family and friends. For example, at a recent psychoanalytic meeting on the subject of regression, one analyst described a patient, the mother of several children and the head of a well-organized household, who took to her bed and did not leave it for several days even to go to the bathroom. She let herself go in every way. Normally well-groomed, she became dirty and unkempt, regressing to the worst infantile condition. The analyst described this grown woman, who had regressed to the point of wetting the bed, as "a new-born babe discovering the cruel world."

In their daily practice, psychoanalysts encounter an extraordinary range of human reactions of both endurance and frailty. What is it that makes one person capable of coping with frustrations and able to maintain normal human relationships while undergoing a great emotional crisis, while someone else will crack up under seemingly trivial stress? What makes one person rigid and another flexible? Why is one man able to control his impulses while relaxed and living normally, while another can control his impulses only by imposing the most restrictive rigidities on himself, and a third can exert no self-control whatever?

These are the concrete realities that lie behind the abstract concept of ego autonomy. The clinical experiences of psychoanalysts suggest that the development of a strong versus a weak ego is primarily a matter of early experience. Today, most clinicians place great emphasis on what they call the individual's early object relations. By object relations they mean, oddly enough, not involvement with objects but the mother-child relationship and other close human relationships in the child's early years. They stress the importance of the mother's attitude in creating ego autonomy: her encouragement of the child to be free, to be autonomous and to make his own decisions.

The mother-child relationship is, of course, highly complex. In his early years the child can have, depending on the qualities of his mother and father, thousands of confirming experiences of his own trust, hope, and autonomy, or thousands of experiences that are frustrating and destructive.

If we look at this emphasis on early "object relations" carefully—and it is one of the most important insights psychoanalysis has to contribute—we will note its curious relationship to Hartmann's proposals. The analysis of early mother-child relationships contributes clinical evidence within psychoanalysis to support Hartmann's concept of an autonomous ego. The evidence is not formal from a scientific point of view, but it is persuasive by virtue of the common experience of thousands of analysts with tens of thousands of patients. But how does this evidence relate to Hartmann's proposals? Ego strength, if we are to believe psychoanalytic clinical experience, does not appear to depend on the "apparatuses of primary autonomy"—perception, memory, and motility. These serve a strong or weak ego indifferently. Nor does it depend on "the apparatuses of secondary autonomy" (defense mechanisms such as reaction formation which lose their original defensive purpose and come to serve an adaptive function in the individual's life). Rather, the ego's strength appears to depend primarily on the quality of the child's early human relationships. It appears that Hartmann was correct about ego autonomy, but for reasons having little to do with his metapsychological concepts of primary and secondary apparatuses. Indeed, how can one ever hope to describe accurately the mother-child relationship and how it helps to create a strong ego in terms of the Freudian psychic apparatus and quanta of energy? Is such a frame of reference truly relevant? These are the kinds of questions raised when one connects the metapsychology with clinical data.

At the time Hartmann first advanced his changes in the late 1930's and at that particular stage in psychoanalytic development, his proposals served an important institutional purpose. They unquestionably contributed to holding the psychoanalytic movement together in the years following Freud's death. Both as a profession and as a science, psychoanalysis might have been struck a mortal blow if, in the years following Freud's exile to England, there had not been within the movement itself an attempt to maintain its integrity both as theory and as institution.

Any movement has its rigid conservatives, whose concept of preservation is to change nothing. Hartmann has proven himself to be the very opposite—an enlightened conservative who introduced change where change was needed in order to maintain and to preserve. But today a different situation prevails: the psychoanalytic movement is in greater danger of developing hardening of its institutional arteries than it is of being torn asunder by schisms. On the theoretical side, enough time and experience have passed to justify reopening the question as to whether the limited changes suggested by Hartmann are radical enough. In his hands, psychoanalytic metapsychology has been patched up and stretched as far as it can go. These repairs were badly needed. But their final effect may be the opposite of what Hartmann had in mind; they help to demonstrate that the psychic apparatus is not serviceable even under the best of conditions, and that it makes no sense to waste the effort to salvage it.

One purpose of any viable theory is to abet and precede discovery. But if the theory is inappropriate, its relationship to discovery can be reversed: instead of the theory leading to new discoveries, new discoveries are made by other means and tremendous energy is then expended in "adding epicycles" to save the theory. Further, when this happens, the tempo of discovery slackens; no fruitful theory arises to lead to new discoveries; and the outmoded official theory keeps getting in the way, deflecting the energies of workers in the field. We suggest that this double-negative effect is operating today in psychoanalysis. Thinkers of great skill and ingenuity like Heinz Hartmann put their best energies into adding epicycles to help an inherently inadequate metapsychology keep up with discovery.

We shall, in future chapters, return often to one or another of Hartmann's proposals: his thought is central to contemporary psychoanalytic theory and practice. But to conclude the present discussion, let us examine more closely the logical problem that has caused Hartmann's contributions to have, at least in part, the opposite effect to the one he intended.

Hartmann has stressed on more than one occasion that psychoanalytic concepts (including his own) may lack a rationale and still have great heuristic value. A nonlogical formulation that accurately reflects clinical experience is to be preferred, he argues, to a logically neat concept that fails to do justice to clinical reality. Who can argue with such a principle? But paradoxically, it is Hartmann himself, the master metapsychologist, who most consistently violates this principle. His justification of the concept of neutralized energies on heuristic grounds masks a deep metaphysical commitment, not an effort to be faithful to clinical data even at the cost of logical neatness.

A heuristic theory, i.e., a theory that is supposed to do a lot of practical good even though its justification is not clear, usually takes the form of an analogy or model, characteristically borrowed from some other science. This is certainly the case with the psychic apparatus, where the underlying model compares human to mechanical functioning. Built into the very structure of the metapsychology is the assumption that man can be studied as if he were an inanimate object. The model presupposes, as do many "scientific" psychologies, that man as an object falling through space and man as a subject living out his life can both be treated by the same kinds of laws—like the law of gravity.

In the nineteenth century, the machine model of human functioning conjured up the picture of a hydraulic system or a steam boiler. In the twentieth century, the model of frequent choice is that of the servo-mechanism—the computer or other type of information system utilizing the feedback principle. But whether the machine model is a steam engine or a computer matters less than whether, in order to be scientific, one has to be mechanistic, and whether a machine model, however marvelous the machine may be, is the best scheme of abstractions for capturing the essence of human life.

The application of mechanism to human life has been popular in academic and scientific circles since the seventeenth century. Though whole libraries have been written denouncing it, the practice nevertheless persists—today more actively than ever. Because psychoanalysis covers the most vital aspects of human life, application of the machine model seems least appropriate here. Other psychologies that use the machine model as their dominant scheme of abstraction, notably behaviorism, tend to focus on the more peripheral aspects of human life where the model may be faintly applicable. (However, in recent years we have seen the growth of "conditioning therapies" applying behaviorism directly to man's intimate emotional experiences.)

This is not an issue about which one can be dogmatic. There is no one correct way to conceptualize a subject matter as complex as the psychic life of the individual person. But we must constantly expose schemes of abstraction about human life to criticism by keeping in mind the similarity of theories to models and to maps. A model is merely an analogy and it should be scrapped as soon as it becomes evident that the integrity of the subject is being ravaged by the effort to assimilate it to a false model. Furthermore, a map is merely a high-level abstraction; it excludes far more than it symbolizes and what it excludes may be of the essence.

One can easily mistake the map for the reality to which it refers (the fallacy of misplaced concreteness), and one often fails to recognize the superimposed model for the limited analogy that it is (the fallacy of false categorization). Too simple maps of human life falsify our experience; and when the emotional and valuative life of the individual is at issue, models based on nonhuman categories break down almost as soon as they are tried.

Our thesis is that for the science of psychoanalysis, the Freudian psychic apparatus is a false model and the orthodox metapsychology based on this apparatus is the wrong kind of map. It is like asking a tourist to find his way around France with a contour map of Paris. The map symbolizes only one small part of the whole. Even for this small part, it tells the tourist how many feet he is above sea level when what he really wants to know are the names of the streets and the location of the landmarks.

Hartmann and his followers are residents of the area to be mapped. With their insiders' viewpoint, they can overlook the grosser inadequacies of even a poor map and use it quite well among themselves. One needs only the crudest kind of guidepost when exchanging information with others who share your experience. If it proves misleading to outsiders, so much the worse for the outsiders.

Many analysts have little sympathy for the plight of the non-psychoanalyst trying to decipher the metapsychology. But not Hartmann: he has vigorously advocated the integration of psychoanalysis with the social sciences, and he is the chief representative of psychoanalysis's claim to be the general psychology of our time. Hartmann is a thinker of stature, and the issues he raises are central. But the psychic apparatus is an inadequate scheme of abstractions for capturing human life, and patching it up does not make it adequate. There is a real need to get behind the map to the underlying reality itself in order to re-emerge with a new, more appropriate scheme of abstractions. Hartmann's defense for logically shaky psychoanalytic concepts is that they work clinically. But while Hartmann's changes in the metapsychology do not directly contradict the clinical data, neither do they explain or add understanding to the data. Furthermore, the plausibility of his line of reasoning—that the existing metapsychology does more justice to clinical experience than any alternative—is seriously weakened by the fact that most of the metapsychology did *not* originate in Freud's clinical experience but stemmed directly from his indoctrination in the pure Newtonian metaphysics of the Helmholtz School. The Freud who wrote the great case histories (like the Wolf Man) is the greater Freud, the man of original genius. The Freud who wrote about the psychic apparatus, the pleasure principle and the reality principle is the lesser Freud, the man who borrowed a second-hand metaphysics from his teachers.

It should be clear by now that what is at stake is not a narrow, technical problem within psychoanalytic theory. What we have to deal with are the fundamental questions about the nature of man, the requirements for a science of man, and the philosophical framework in which that science can be developed. By carrying the logic of the metapsychology as far as it can go, Heinz Hartmann has helped to pose these issues in the sharpest possible terms.

[❋]

EIGHT

Erik Erikson— The Meaning of Identity

In discussing current psychoanalytic ego psychology, Rapaport singles out Hartmann and Erikson as the two outstanding post-Freudian figures. Summarizing their relationship to each other and to Freud, Rapaport states:

> Erikson's contribution constitutes an organic extension of Freud's theory. They and Hartmann's contributions are consistent with and complementary to each other. Yet Erikson related his theory in an explicit fashion mainly to the concepts of Freud's id psychology, less to the concepts of Freud's ego psychology, and only slightly to Hartmann's theory. Nor did Hartmann attempt to formulate the relation between his and Erikson's theory. *Here a task of integration faces ego psychology.* (Rapaport, 1959, p. 16.) (Our italics.)

This statement of Rapaport's is as interesting for what it does *not* say as for what it does. It is true that in certain respects Erikson and Hartmann do complement one another. Hartmann proposed the concept of ego autonomy; Erikson particularized it with exquisite clinical insight. Hartmann announced a program of building a bridge to normal psychology; Erikson provided the specific material of nonpathological human strength with which to build the bridge. Hartmann emphasized the importance of nonfamily institutions; Erikson detailed how individual identity is molded by and in turn molds nonfamily institutions.

Thus, on one level, Rapaport is correct in stating that Hartmann's and Erikson's views do complement each other. Indeed, in the last few years, these two outstanding figures have grown closer to one another; one finds repeated reference in Erikson's most recent works to Hartmann's theories and views—and Hartmann has returned the compliment. But at a more fundamental level, Hartmann and Erikson represent opposite poles of thought and styles; philosophically their contributions are at serious odds with one another. Only the fact that no systematic effort has been made to integrate their theories hides this most intriguing paradox from view.

Freud's death left the psychoanalytic community with a perplexing dilemma. There is a wealth of practical therapeutic experience which suggests that many neuroses can be cured, but Freud's theory of the ego, carried to its logical conclusion, implies that finding a lasting cure for the neuroses is unlikely if not impossible. Hartmann and Erikson, each in his own way, have struggled mightily with the problem. Each has offered his own solution, and in the process has posed a new dilemma. Each has postponed, for various reasons, the inevitable crisis of fundamentals that must sooner or later break out between the currently popular theories of ego autonomy and the almost universally accepted Freudian division of labor between ego and id within the psychic apparatus.

Hartmann stresses the autonomy of the ego—man's strength and freedom, but he defines man's freedom in terms of Newtonian forces and energies—a contradiction in terms. In his effort to remain faithful both to Freud and to psychoanalytic experience, Hartmann tried to reconcile the irreconcilable.

The behaviorists in psychology and some positivists in philosophy, having built their systems on scientific materialism, take a more logically consistent position. They state unequivocally that man's will is an illusion, an epiphenomenon, and that freedom does not exist. Hartmann denies these dicta. He insists that man's autonomy does exist, and further that it exerts an influence on human affairs beyond that ascribed to it by Freud. It is, in fact, Hartmann's development of this theme that has won him such prestige among his psychoanalytic colleagues. He has, therefore, come to represent the apex of influence for re-appraising the autonomy of the ego, while, at the same time, he has brought the theory to a logical dead end by his effort to preserve precisely those elements of the metapsychology that make it impossible for the ego to be autonomous.

Hartmann has papered over this logical difficulty at the heart of the theory. Although he is a distinguished clinician, his scientific papers are almost wholly devoid of clinical examples and case histories. Furthermore, he writes at so high a level of abstraction, and his efforts to reconcile theory and data are so convoluted, that his writings pose extraordinary problems. Maybe psychoanalysts are so fatigued by the time they follow the maze of abstract reasoning to its end that they fail to ask critically what relationship Hartmann's revisions in the metapsychology may have to clinical experience.

When we turn to Erik Erikson we confront an entirely different kind of mind. But doing justice to the subtlety of his thought will prove to be a difficult task. Like Freud, Erikson is an accomplished prose stylist; but unlike Freud, he started his career as an artist. His work exhibits the unity of a painting, not that of a formal logical structure. Erikson is a thoroughgoing clinician, whose best insights are often embedded in his case histories, and he sets forth his psychoanalytic themes in a context enriched by the texture and detail of many vivid examples. By extracting his concepts from the matrix of detail, one risks losing a great deal.

The risk is well worth taking, however. Not only is Erikson one of the most gifted minds in the psychoanalytic pantheon, he probably stands among the very gifted men of the age. Yet his most important contributions remain obscure for many reasons, one being that he himself has blurred the extent of his divergence from the psychoanalytic movement; it seems he must feel that his debt to Freud is too great to warrant magnifying the differences between them. His own "identity" is that of a clinician in good standing within the psychoanalytic fold; he is accepted as one of the very few nonmedical psychoanalysts and for his clinical ability he has earned the respect of his medical colleagues who ordinarily do not take kindly to outsiders plying their trade. Being less of an abstract theorist than Hartmann, possibly he himself has not pursued his ideas to their inexorable conclusion. He has moved intuitively, in a different direction from his psychoanalytic colleagues; but logically, he has not fully thought himself out of the conventional philosophical tradition. And however modest and oblique he may be, however reluctant to disturb the institutional setting of psychoanalysis, however skillful in blurring the divergence between him and the official theory, the fact remains that, unlike Hartmann, the logic of Erikson's thought creates a yawning gap between him and the prevailing orthodoxy.

One suspects that as a clinician Erikson is bored with the formal philosophical underpinnings of psychoanalysis. As he casually remarked a few years ago in a paper presented before his colleagues of the American Psychoanalytic Association, "here as elsewhere I have left metapsychological questions to experts in this kind of thinking." (Erikson, 1959, p. 2.) The lessons of history show all too clearly that one ignores these seemingly remote issues at one's own peril.

It is possible that the price Erikson has paid for leaving these matters to "experts in this kind of thinking" is higher than he might wish: other analysts, even though they enormously respect his insights, have found it difficult to apply them in their own clinical practice. Like William James, he is admired for his gifts of intellect, presence, and insight, but his concepts are honored outside of clinical psychoanalysis more than within. Furthermore, Erikson is systematically misunderstood—and not only by his students at Harvard. At a recent dinner meeting in Boston of psychoanalysts and social scientists, Erikson presented a brilliant paper on ritualization as a form of human relatedness. A long discussion followed; by late in the evening Erikson was exhausted, and when pressed by an insensitive question, he reacted in one of his rare moments of impatience. "Some people," he said irritably, "insist on misunderstanding what I am getting at. They accuse me of being a Pollyanna, of seeing only the nice side of people. Don't they understand that when I talk about hope and about basic trust I am not referring to good manners or to the niceties of personality, but to the minimum conditions for human survival itself!"

Identity

Of all the ideas associated with Erikson, none is more popular, and more confusing, than his concept of identity.

Freud first described the process of identification* in his paper *Mourning and Melancholia* (1917). Then, in his book *Group Psychology and the Analysis of the Ego* (1921), he took the next step in specificity, analyzing how the process of identification precedes the establishment of object relationships. Several years later, in *The Ego and the Id* (1923), he further generalized the concept, taking it far beyond crisis situations like mourning. Identification, Freud observed here, is the earliest form of emotional infantile experience. He presented this series of steps in his description of ego development: identifications; object relationships; the building of ego structure.

As the process which precedes and helps to establish early object relationships, identification can readily be perceived as fundamental to psychoanalytic theory; the vicissitudes of early object relationships are as important to the clinical practice of psychoanalysis as the psychic apparatus is to its metapsychology.

There are, however, difficulties in understanding Freud's precise meaning of identification. Psychologist Robert W. White has recently analyzed its many ambiguities and has shown that Freud employed the term in at least five different ways, including identification as imitation, as introjection, and as the creation of an emotional tie. He concludes: "Some of the meanings depend upon the love object being lost or renounced, but others do not. Some point to a lasting change in the character of the ego, but others deal with superficial and temporary change. The concept has obviously come to mean too much, too easily." (White, 1963, p. 102.)

Erikson, although his use differs from Freud's, also gives

---

* Freud uses the term identification, Erickson uses identity. Throughout this discussion we are using the two words synonymously.

identification a central position in ego development. And he continues Freud's habit of using the term in a multiplicity of meanings (though these are not the same as Freud's). We can readily distinguish three major meanings of identity in Erikson's work: (1) identity as imitation; (2) identity as the feeling of continuity about one's existence; and (3) so-called ego identity. The third meaning is the most elusive and the most important. It presupposes the other two, but goes far beyond them. This third meaning will gradually unfold as the first two are set forth.

Since something like Erikson's concept of identity is a popular theme of contemporary existentialists (Erikson's ego identity is similar in many respects to Sartre's "existential commitment"), it will be helpful to compare and contrast the Eriksonian and existential treatments of the same themes.

MEANING 1—IDENTITY AS IMITATION

The first, the narrowest, and the most precise meaning of identification is that of a psychological mechanism involving imitation (i.e., a young boy imitating the way his father walks). Erikson himself does not give undue prominence to this meaning of identification. Indeed, he gives examples of imitations which do not by themselves create ego identity and he also gives examples of ego identity being destroyed without destroying the person's previous imitations. Imitation is not synonymous with ego identity, but it is one part of a complex process by which ego identity is achieved. The imitation may be of persons, acts, values, roles, attributes, styles, etc. It may be a partial imitation, as when a little girl scolds her dolls in the way she herself is scolded, but without adopting her mother's mannerisms. Nor does imitation require a bond of love: the imitation of their Nazi guards by some inmates of concentration camps, as described by Bruno Bettelheim, is an example of imitation in a negative emotional context.

In discussing this meaning of identification, White points to a common thread in the full range of a person's imitations, whether the object of the imitation is loved and admired or feared and rejected. Its purpose, and the hoped-for result, says

White, is the achievement of effectiveness and competence. Imitation of someone who is feared but respected offers the imitator a powerful method for coping with anxiety and for achieving an admired form of competence. In fact, it is White's proposal that identification be confined to this single meaning of imitation, and that all other meanings be dropped (i.e., those that connote a libidinal or aggressive tie, or the primitive processes of projection and interjection, or primitive forms of object relations). (White, 1963, p. 112.)

White certainly has a point in urging that some degree of conceptual clarity be introduced if the term identity is to refer to five Freudian plus three Eriksonian meanings, plus the additional meanings others like Melanie Klein bring to bear—all of which have different purposes and achieve different results. But restricting the meaning of identity to imitative processes would not do justice to the phenomena Erikson seeks to describe. In fact, Erikson stresses how limited a role imitation plays in personality formation. He points out that an individual's imitations may be partial and may even contain contradictory elements. The boy who "identifies" in bewildering succession with the fireman at one age, the baseball player later on, then the doctor or engineer as well as father, friends, and teachers, needs to bring together all of these loose ends into some self-consistent structure. This job, states Erikson, belongs to the synthesizing ego. The ego seeks to integrate the various contradictory elements, previously achieved by partial imitations, into a single coherent whole. It is the process of transmuting mere imitations into a unique sense of self that creates one aspect of true ego identity.

We begin here to distinguish between imitation and ego identity. They are closely related: one is a partial process and the other is an end result created by it. But ego identity calls upon many other processes as well; a synthesizing ego plus a particular stage of maturation plus an upheaval in personality are all presupposed before true ego identity can be achieved. The synthesizing ego, acting on the sum of all of these partial processes, consolidates them, forges them into a unity, and transforms them to create the unique sense of self known as ego identity.

What do the existentialists have to say about the meaning of identity as imitation? Except negatively, this psychological process holds little interest for most of them. The French existentialist, Gabriel Marcel, has in particular flagellated our culture for its tendency to create pseudo identities—personalities that are little more than their imitations. In our epoch, says Marcel, the individual has become too identified with his functions: he becomes the sum of his imitations; there is a hollowness at the core.

Erikson would agree: imitation is not enough; something else must happen before mere imitations can be transformed into true ego identity. Erikson also shows that imitation can easily go wrong. He cites Jung's concept of the *persona* (i.e., a social personality that is mainly role-playing) as an example of a weak ego yielding to a strong cultural prototype. In other words, imitation can undermine true ego identity unless other processes are also present. Mere imitation leads to cultural stereotypes like the conformist junior executive in the gray flannel suit that novelists have parodied.

On this single point, if on no other, psychoanalysts and existentialists are agreed: something else besides imitation is required to produce an authentic ego identity. When this something else is scanted the results may be grotesque. For Erikson the added element is a synthesizing process that reaches a critical mass at the end of adolescence, a process of fusion and transmutation brought about by the workings of the synthesizing ego. Without this explosive synthesis, the sum total of imitations would be a miscellaneous heap, something like a badly deteriorated Walter Mitty.

For existentialist Gabriel Marcel, the missing element is the sense of *being*. It is not, says Marcel, the sexual drive that is repressed in our time, but the sense of being. He is referring to the lack in modern man of a sense of belonging to a larger whole. However infinitesimal he may be, man remains an inherent part of a cosmic order, though his sense of relatedness to it has been submerged.

MEANING 2—IDENTITY AS THE SENSE
OF CONTINUITY

Erikson includes in his definition of identity the sense of a persistent sameness within oneself, "a subjective sense of continuous existence and a coherent memory which may be lost in a state of amnesia." (Erikson, 1965a.) Whenever Erikson discusses identity he makes at least passing reference to this meaning—a person's sense of sameness and continuity. But he sometimes dismisses this meaning by referring to it as "mere" identity.

In contrast, it is unlikely that any existentialist writer would apply the qualification "mere" since concern with continuity of being is a major preoccupation of existential thought. For the past twenty-five years, a school of existentialist psychiatry has flourished on the Continent, particularly in Germany, France, and Switzerland. Many existential psychiatrists have a debt to Freud, although typically (with the notable exception of Binswanger) they are critical to the point of dismissing him. Where psychoanalysts in this country have concentrated on the study of the psychoneuroses, European existential psychiatrists have concentrated on the psychoses. The difference in emphasis is a key to why American psychoanalysts attach less importance to this second meaning of identity. Most American psychoanalysts in private practice accept for treatment only those individuals whose egos are strong enough to endure the rigors of psychoanalytic therapy.* It is unlikely, therefore, that most American psychoanalysts are as sensitized to the ravages of weak and threatened egos as the European existential psychiatrists. For these men there is nothing "mere" about identity in the sense of a person's conviction of his sameness and continuity over time. They see identity in this sense as a tremendous achievement—made horribly clear in those who lack it.

---

* In recent years there have been many exceptions, notably in the work with psychotic patients of Fromm-Reichmann and Rosen. Nevertheless, it remains true that the predominant bulk of psychoanalytic practice remains concentrated on private practice with neurotic individuals of means.

We are dealing here with a meaning of identity that is fundamental to the understanding of man's nature. "A rose is a rose is a rose," said Gertrude Stein. But can one say the same thing about a man? Consider the case of the great German poet, Hölderlin. A profound student of ancient Greek culture, Hölderlin pursued a scholarly life writing his poetry until he developed a psychosis in his late thirties. Hölderlin lived on for many years; he did odd jobs for people and puttered around as a gardener for most of the time, but was never again to read a book or to write his lyric verse. One day he ran into a man carrying a book of Homer's poetry. They chatted briefly. Taking the book and inspecting it, a bewildered expression fell across Hölderlin's face. For a moment, it seemed, a confusion set in—as if some ancient painful memory had stirred in him. But the moment passed; Hölderlin returned the book and quietly walked back to his gardening chores.

What can we say about the identity of Hölderlin the poet in relation to Hölderlin the befuddled gardener? The careful phenomenological studies of the psychoses by Medard Boss, Minkowsky, Von Gebsattel, Binswanger, and other European existential psychiatrists suggest that one facet of psychosis consists in the disturbance of this sense of identity. No other meaning of identity is even possible without presupposing this fundamental definition of the self as a stable structure that endures in time.

This concept opens a window onto the fundamental difference between the being of objects and the being of man (and other living creatures): identity in this sense is not a material object with the property of simple location.

Neither is it the process of successful imitation. Nor is it to be resolved into the instincts of sex, aggression, hunger, and flight. Nor is it fully explicable in terms of the reality principle, for this meaning of identity is presupposed by the reality principle itself. We are coming closer here to the notion of the sheer *is*-ness of the person and to the reason why self-identity cannot be understood in analogy with the world of physical objects. Even in the psychoses, where the sense of self is threatened, it is never totally destroyed.

Inquiry into the nature of the psychoses suggests that if this sense of identity is threatened, a man will sacrifice everything else in his life to preserve it. The catatonic schizophrenic sits in a state of stupor, unattentive and unheeding to all that is going on about him; but his external rigidity hides from view the epic struggle going on within him to preserve his sense of inner coherence.

The British psychiatrist Laing (1962) has described what happens when this sense of identity is threatened. He calls it a state of ontological insecurity and vividly describes its manifestations: generalized feelings of unreality; a blurred sense of selfhood precariously differentiated from the rest of the world; a lack of a sense of temporal continuity; a threat to awareness of personal cohesiveness; and a feeling of insubstantiality or the sensation of experiencing oneself as partly divorced from one's body. For such a person, relationships with others are not a source of gratification but a dire threat. The ontologically insecure individual is more preoccupied with preserving than with gratifying himself; the most ordinary circumstances of his life constitute a continuing and deadly threat. The unremitting focus of all his attention is to prevent himself from losing himself, with the result that his world of experience becomes increasingly impersonal. It is not that external events cease to affect him, but that they affect him too much so that he must turn his back on them. The threshold of his resistance to threats to his identity is so low that almost anything can cross it.

Laing goes on to describe the various forms of intolerable anxiety to which such a person is subjected. There is, for example, the anxiety of engulfment, when he fears that even the most casual forms of relatedness will swallow up his precarious sense of being. For such a man, to be hated is sometimes less threatening than to be engulfed by love. It is difficult to treat someone thus threatened with conventional psychotherapy, since he will have a negative reaction to a correct interpretation: to be understood is to be swallowed up, stifled, drowned. Only in isolation can he achieve a nominal measure of security. He cannot even ask from life the minimal demands of love and acceptance. His first requirement from the world is that it simply let him be.

Another threat to self-identity assumes the form of emptiness: the person feels like a vacuum but dreads that the vacuum may be filled by the more powerful personalities of others. To fill the emptiness is to threaten even this negative sense of being. Feeling empty and like a vacuum is itself a form of identity—it is, at least, his own emptiness.

In this connection, there is an enlightening story about the brilliant logician and philosopher, Morris Cohen. When Cohen taught philosophy at New York City College in the twenties and thirties, the philosophy and psychology departments were still held together by the loose bond of sharing the same group of offices. Sometimes students seeking psychological counseling would mistake members of the philosophy faculty for their psychological colleagues. One day such a student wandered into Morris Cohen's office, mistaking him for the guidance counselor. "Doctor," the student said plaintively, "I feel empty and without meaning. I feel that I don't exist." Cohen, who was notorious for his abrupt manner with students, looked at the boy quizzically and asked, "Who is it, then, that's making the complaint?" Whereupon Cohen put on his hat and departed, leaving the boy in a state of bewildered Socratic enlightenment.

The preoccupation of a bright adolescent college student with his own existence may be a legitimate object for such wry commentary, but for the psychotically afflicted person who lives in a state of dread and anxiety, needing unceasing reconfirmation of his own existence, we see in tragic form the frailty of identity. We see also the enormity of the achievement for those so fortunate that they take their own identity for granted without even recognizing it as a category of existence. The preservation of a core of meanings that defines the continuity of the self as it endures from day to day cannot be taken for granted by psychologists; it is evidence of a considerable amount of successful integration of biological development with affective experience.

A restless middle-class housewife, bored with suburban life and social pressures, may set out to find a more meaningful spiritual significance to her life. But certainly she is seeking a new identity in a different way from the person whose very sense of his own existence is threatened. This latter meaning of identity is implicit in Erikson's concern with basic trust and hope. But it must be admitted that he hardly develops this fundamental meaning; he tends to take it for granted. He concentrates his attention on aspects of identity that could not exist without presupposing this more primal meaning.

MEANING 3—EGO IDENTITY

Jean-Paul Sartre said, "first a person exists and then he defines himself." Though the slogan makes too rigid a distinction between existence and self-definition, it is a striking way to characterize this last meaning of identity as self-definition. However, Sartre overemphasizes the sheer givenness of existence together with the abrupt change of identity rather than the step-by-step development of the personality, the process of becoming. It is self-definition that preoccupies Erikson under the name of ego identity.

In focusing on Erikson's concept of ego identity, we find a whole family of meanings and processes. Since it would be unfair to the texture of Erikson's thought to impose too rigid a straitjacket of logic and precision on this key concept, we shall briefly present some members of the family of meanings that group around his term ego identity.

One popular meaning that Erikson has explicitly disowned is the definition of ego identity endemic among students; i.e., as some kind of encapsulated answer to the questions, "Who am I?" and "What am I?" (Erikson, 1965a). But he provides no simple, easy-to-grasp alternative. In *Childhood and Society*, the work that clearly established Erikson as a major figure, he writes about the combat neuroses he encountered in war veterans: "What impressed me most was the loss in these men of a sense of identity. They knew who they were; they had a personal identity. But it was as if subjectively their lives no longer hung together—and never would again. There was a central disturbance of what I then started to call ego identity." (Erikson, 1950, p. 38.) Clearly, Erikson here is using ego identity in a different sense than awareness of continuity or the results of imitation, neither of which had been lost by these war victims.

In the years that followed, Erikson pursued his investigations of ego identity at the Austen Riggs Clinic in Stockbridge, Massachusetts, where he worked extensively with disturbed adolescents. Drawing on this experience, he has since described in rich detail how ego identity comes into being. It is formed, he states, toward the close of adolescence as the crystallization of certain comprehensive gains which the individual must have derived from his preadult experiences. Although the maintenance of ego identity is a life-long process, it takes on its lasting shape and character in this period of transition between childhood and adulthood. Colleges and apprenticeships of various kinds reflect society's recognition of youth's need for a "psycho-social moratorium" during which an individual can complete the process of achieving a lasting pattern of inner identity. (Erikson, 1959.)

Erikson's superb descriptions of what the adolescent goes through to achieve self-definition have won him well-deserved fame. In presenting the complex interplay of all of the strange new personal experiences the adolescent undergoes during this period, Erikson also stresses the society's role in providing institutionalized settings for these vital experiences. He emphasizes, in addition, the importance of other people, particularly the adults who evoke the adolescent's intense ambivalence. Those who surround a growing boy or girl must be prepared to give more than mere recognition to youth's objective achievements. The young person's "gradual growth and transformation must make sense to the people who make sense to him." (Erikson, 1959.) The adolescent needs this support to help him to maintain powerful ego defenses against a growing intensity of impulse; to align his most important conflict-free achievements with work opportunities; and to resynthesize childhood development in a way that accords with roles offered by the society.

Thus, Erikson sees the psychosocial task of achieving a lasting ego identity as an enormously complex process. It culminates in the transformation of a huge miscellany of imitations accumulated throughout youth's earlier years into the unified sense of selfhood that fits the individual for social and adult life. He portrays the ego's attempts to incorporate the most powerful positive and negative identities of the youth's past, good and bad, masculine and feminine, beautiful and ugly, in order to "make one battle and one strategy out of a bewildering number of skirmishes." Hopefully, all fragments and loose ends of infantile and youthful identifications are collapsed, consolidated, and condensed into a single set of meanings approximating some kind of unity.

When, in later years, the person's experiences are compatible with this structure of meanings, he feels a sense of fitness, a feeling of oneness with himself, with his environment, and with his life. Erikson quotes approvingly a letter by William James to a friend in which he describes the feelings that accompany this kind of experience. "This is when," James said, "a person feels himself to be most deeply and intensively active and alive. At such moments there is a voice inside which speaks and says, 'this is the real me.'" Erikson adds, "Thus may a mature person come to the astonished or exuberant awareness of his identity." (Erikson, 1965a.)

It is interesting to note how Erikson's concept of ego identity approximates Sartre's notion of existential self-definition, but without the ring of defiant and dizzy self-choice and with much more concreteness and insight. Consider Sartre's concept of the existential decision. "A person," Sartre says, "is a coward in a different sense from being 6 feet tall." The individual's final self-definition is the sum of all his existential decisions. There is a sense in which a coward "chooses" to be a coward. Sartre's "existential decision" is too cerebral to capture Erikson's meaning precisely, but it comes close enough to make us realize that both are fixing their sights on the same sort of phenomena.

Sartre developed his point of view primarily from the early Heidegger. The later Heidegger would reject the notion of an existential decision as being too activist, as stressing the act of will too much, as overemphasizing doing over being. The later Heidegger stressed being open and responsive to existence rather than filling a role or function or acting out a part. A key aspect of identity for Heidegger is simply how a person comprehends his own being. Erikson's concept of ego identity takes Heidegger's emphasis into account, but as a psychologist, Erikson is more concerned with the genetic question of how such feelings of identity develop, while the existentialist philosophers preoccupy themselves with the nature and meaning of the end result. Yet the two efforts of thought move in the same direction.

FURTHER MEANINGS OF EGO IDENTITY

In a wonderfully vivid discussion of George Bernard Shaw, Erikson adumbrates yet another facet of ego identity, quoting Shaw's statement: "My identification was with the mighty dead." He refers here to Shaw's ego identity as presenting a form of transcendence, a way of reaching beyond one's own self and even beyond the limits of one's own times and culture. (1959, pp. 102–110.) Lionel Trilling once observed that many a man has been saved by the idea of another country. The ability to reach beyond the parochialism of one's immediate experience constitutes a powerful resource for those who can achieve it.

Still another member of Erikson's family of meanings refers to ego identity as a variant of a cultural prototype. Erikson uses the concept of group identity to refer to the methods of organizing and transmitting the group's experience in child training. He cites Freud's use of the term "inner identity" to refer to those aspects of values and personality that Freud felt he shared with the tradition of Jewry. (Erikson, 1965a.) In another example, Erikson contrasts the group identity of the Sioux Indians to that of our own culture. The group identity of the Sioux combines a passive resistance to the present with dreams of restoration to the powerful past. Our federal educators responsible for Indian affairs preach a way of life to the Sioux that runs counter to their own group identity in every respect: a way of life oriented to the future rather than to the past, and one that values money, ambition, and schooling, rather than dreaming about former grandeur. These educators stress inner reform, while the Sioux look to outer restoration for the return of their once glorious identity. (Erikson, 1959, pp. 21–22.)

These examples are sufficient to show how charged with ambiguity the concept of ego identity is. At various times, it is presented as a structure of meanings, a form of transcendence, a form of social relatedness, a form of self-definition and a particular quality of experience. But if the definition seems too rich and all-embracing, the phenomena themselves are partly to blame. Ego identity is the outcome of a complex interplay among biological heritage, the unfolding of individual potentialities, the responses of family and other significant persons, and the accumulated values of the culture. None can be ignored if we are to capture the essential way in which a human being manages to become a whole and single person.

The confirming testimony of the philosophers on this subject is not accidental. The modern existentialists are being responsive, as is Erikson, to one of the main themes of our day: the disharmony between ourselves and the quality of modern life. We are victims of identity confusion, and that is why we are so preoccupied with the problem. There are, say the philosophers, pressures in contemporary life that make it impossible for the individual to say truthfully, "this is the real me." The elements essential to create a comfortable, and unobtrusive, ego identity are not synchronized. Erikson describes the process of ego identity as a result of the mutual influence of society's impact on the individual's potentialities, and the creative role the individual plays in transforming society. Thus, for sound ego identity to come into being there has to be a good balance between the individual's potentialities and the culture's ability to actualize them. We come close here to one of the great modern themes to which Erikson is responsive in a far more subtle, indirect and possibly ambivalent fashion than the angry existentialists.

The Epigenetic Crisis

Complex meanings and phenomena such as those we have been discussing can hardly be described in the language of Freudian metapsychology. Erikson recognizes that the metapsychology cannot grasp them. He observes that the concept of psychic energy utilized by Freud and the theory that instinctual energy is expressed, transferred, displaced, and transformed "in analogy to the preservation of energy in physics no longer suffices to help us manage our data. . . ." (Erikson, 1959, p. 23.) Erikson explicitly rejects instinctual energy as a mode of explanation for identity, but what does he substitute for the psychic apparatus and the quantitative point of view? This question brings us to Erikson's master concept, which he defines as the epigenetic point of view.

Erikson's definition of epigenetic development through various life stages is undoubtedly his most familiar concept. Seen in the light of the epigenetic principle, each individual develops through eight fairly well-defined stages. Each stage exhibits a unique combination of needs, susceptibilities, and vulnerabilities, concentrated on one or another aspect of growth; and each stage culminates in an encounter or crisis, the outcome of which leads to the development of a vital human quality.

The *first* life stage is man's infancy; its epigenetic crisis develops around the growth of basic trust and hope. Developmental failure at this stage creates defects so serious that they may ultimately lead to severe addiction or psychosis.

The *second* stage takes place in early childhood. Its epigenetic crisis centers on the child's development of a sense of separateness, autonomy, and will.

In the *third* stage, the play-age develops a sense of initiative and the *anlage* [the potential ground] for adult purposefulness.

The *fourth* stage—the school age—leads to a crisis over the child's developing a sense of industry, confidence, and effectiveness.

The *fifth* stage—that of adolescence—covers the crisis of identity; failure in this stage breeds identity confusion.

The *sixth* stage, occurring in young adulthood, involves the struggle between intimacy and isolation, the successful outcome of which is a capacity for enduring love.

The *seventh* stage is that of maturity. Its crisis occurs over the struggle between generativity and stagnation; its successful resolution creates the structures of care, concern, and responsibility for others.

In the *eighth* and final stage, that of old age, a struggle ensues between integrity and despair. Bitterness and disgust mark its failure, while wisdom is the reward for a successful outcome. Erikson defines wisdom as the "detached and yet active concern with life as with death." (Erikson, 1965b.)

Because of Erikson's stress on society's role in shaping the individual's identity he has sometimes been grouped with the cultural relativists, like Sullivan and Fromm, who emphasize the importance of environmental influences over the biological and instinctual. Actually, however, Erikson's concept of epigenesis is profoundly biological. The epigenetic principle, he states, is derived from the growth of organisms in the womb. As part of our phylogenetic inheritance, we are born with a maturational blueprint, a biological ground plan, in accordance with which the various aspects of personality (hopefully) develop in sequence. Each part has its own time of ascendancy during which it should fully develop and be integrated into a more or less smoothly functioning whole.

Erikson defines the fifth epigenetic stage, adolescence, as the stage of identity crisis and of a concern with fidelity. We have already alluded to this time of life when the individual seeks to synthesize a unified ego identity out of the accumulated partial identifications of his childhood. This fifth stage is also a period of physiological maturation; the adolescent has to cope with powerful impulsive drives as well as with the personal and social task of preparing for a future role in the society. During this period, inner demands mesh with external tasks to create a particular quality of experience. The adolescent mind becomes ideological, striving after some intellectual synthesis, some overriding system of ideas that will explain the nature of things in a way that will satisfy the youth's mixed cravings. Youth demands something to believe in, and also someone to believe in —a lover, a friend, a mentor, a hero. Erikson intends the term "fidelity" to mean this overwhelming need to believe in and be true to something and to someone. The concept of fidelity encompasses the individual's ideas, emotions, and state of being during his search for a lasting ego identity.

With these thoughts in mind, consider now his discussion of the Dora case, one of the most famous of all Freud's clinical case histories, presented in a paper entitled "Psychological Reality and Historical Actuality" which Erikson read to his psychoanalytic colleagues during their 1961 midwinter meeting. (Erikson, 1964c.)

At psychoanalytic congresses, participants typically meet in splintered groups for several days. The final meeting takes place on a Sunday morning. It is the custom of the American Psychoanalytic Association to honor some distinguished member of their group by asking him to address the Sunday morning plenary session. It was on such an occasion that Erikson brought up once again the case of Dora, a girl who had developed hysterical symptoms after being sexually approached by a Mr. K., who was a friend of her father's and a well-known Viennese socialist.

Erikson began by summarizing Freud's interpretation. Freud, he pointed out, presented the case as an instance of quantities of instinctual excitation that had become transmuted into hysterical symptoms, the result of repressed instinctual strivings. Dora's symptoms were the outcome of her conflict between sexual desire (the repressed instinctual drives) and moral repugnance.

In an aside, Freud suggested that Dora may have wanted him to show more of a warm personal interest in her. But he states that he didn't see how "acting a part" could have helped her. So he retained his own somewhat impersonal objectivity. His theory at that time (1905) was that Dora would gain relief from her symptoms primarily by her own insight into the true nature of her unconscious responses. Objective insight, not a personal relationship with her physician, would help her the most. His therapy, therefore, took the form of interpreting the nature of her unconscious motivations, helping the girl to see the "truth"—the objective, literal, unvarnished truth.

Freud described Dora's return visit a year after she had interrupted her brief three months' treatment. Dora told Freud at that time that she had confronted her family with her knowledge of their various infidelities, and had pressed everyone to acknowledge what was going on—her father's adultery with the wife of Mr. K., Mr. K.'s sexual advances to Dora herself, the father's seeming acquiescence in Mr. K.'s advances to his own daughter in order to keep his own relationship with Mr. K.'s wife unchallenged, etc. Freud was distressed by this particular use of "the truth," and he concludes his discussion with the enigmatic comment: "I do not know what kind of help she wanted from me."

Erikson goes on to observe *how different the meaning of truth was for the young girl and for the middle-aged physician.*

Erikson's interpretation is that truth for the girl meant fidelity, i.e., keeping faith with someone, not a factually accurate account of infidelity.

Truth in the sense of fidelity, Erikson adds, is always pointed toward the future. It is not merely a matter of having a "personal stake in the accuracy, veracity and authenticity, in the fairness, genuineness and reliability of a person's methods and ideas." (Erikson, 1964c, p. 170.) It is also a matter of expanding the possibilities of freedom, i.e., keeping faith with someone who will point the way toward hope and fulfillment in the future. While Freud's kind of truth carries with it "the danger of hopeless determination"—the opposite of freedom—the truth of fidelity would have given the girl a firm foundation on which she could fulfill her own future potentialities.

Commenting on Freud's interpretation of Dora, Erikson remarks, "What we would consider an interpretation, to youth easily becomes a statement of doom." With this one soft-spoken comment, Erikson has opened up a nest of vipers. Consider its most elementary meaning: that a factually accurate interpretation made by an analyst to a patient, which illuminates repressed instinctual strivings and which enlarges the consciousness and awareness of these, can "easily become a statement of doom." This apparently simple, but fundamental, point will emerge again in our later discussions of what is required for a newer and more basic theory.

A built-in drama is enacted at each of the eight successive stages, each stage sooner or later leading to a crisis caused by a shift in instinctual energy and vulnerability. The individual does not grow smoothly, accumulating maturity and strength in an unbroken linear progression; rather, development proceeds from struggle to struggle, and each struggle focuses on different life problems. Among the lowest forms of life, at the bottom of the phylogenetic scale, the fate of the organism is decided by a few rigid automatic mechanisms (go to the light; go away from the light). In man, the fate of the organism is decided by biologically rooted potentialities fulfilling themselves amid the infinite complexity of the individual's world. Potential characteristics become concrete and actual by virtue of a number of decisive encounters within the social world and also within the impersonal world of objects and time. The age-old philosophical argument of whether essence precedes existence or existence precedes essence is bypassed. The concept of epigenesis suggests that essence and existence occur together; one has no meaning without the other; separated, they must be regarded as a high form of abstraction from concrete reality. Both the essence and the existence of human life emerge when the organism-in-its-environment is seen as a single indivisible whole and not as two separate and precariously united Cartesian abstractions.

Erikson suggests that the person is constituted anew many times. Each stage of development becomes "a new configuration of past and future, a new combination of drive and defense, a new set of capacities fit for a new setting of tasks and opportunities, a new and wider radius of significant encounters." (Erikson, 1964a.)

If something goes wrong in any of the epigenetic crises, such as in Dora's case, mistrust, shame, doubt, guilt, a sense of inferiority, identity confusion, isolation, stagnation, or despair can ensue, depending on at what stage failure occurs. On the other hand, the successful resolution of an epigenetic crisis is said to lead to the step-by-step development of hope and basic trust, a sense of autonomy and will power, initiative, purpose, competence, fidelity, love, care, integrity and wisdom.

In recent years, Erikson has come to refer to these latter qualities as basic virtues. He introduces the term "virtue" into the psychoanalytic lexicon cautiously and self-consciously ("I would like to share with you briefly the kind of thinking which may motivate a psychoanalyst to use such a word"). In his explanation of so curiously unscientific a word as virtue, Erikson refers to former meanings of virtue in Roman and Christian times, pointing out that virtue has always meant basic strength: "I therefore put the word to our use to underscore the fact that only basic strength can guarantee potency to any value; that ego strength develops from an interplay of personal and social structure; and that it emerges as do all human capacities in stages of development—that is to say, in stages of changing actuality." (Erikson, 1964c, p. 175.)

In another place, Erikson refers to the etymology of virtue as meaning *inherent quality,* as in "the undiminished potency of well-preserved medicines and liquors." Virtue and spirit, he notes, once had interchangeable meanings. He asks the question, "by virtue of what strength does man acquire that animated or spirited quality without which his moralities become mere moralisms and his ethics mere goodness?" He concludes: "I will call virtue, then, certain qualities and strengths and I will relate them to that process by which ego strength may be developed from stage to stage and imparted from generation to generation." (Erikson, 1964a, p. 113.)

Erikson's master-question is concerned with human strength. How, Erikson asks, do people manage to function, cope with life, endure, develop ties with others and a relationship with society; how do they manage to live, work, build, care for others, and face death while being continually involved in life? His answer, in brief, is in his concepts of ego identity, epigenetic development, and human virtue. Freud's master-question was: What is the cause of, and cure for, the neuroses? His final answer was that the neuroses are caused by an imbalance of forces whereby the "battalions" at the disposal of the instinctual drives outmatch those at the disposal of the ego. The contrast defines the two poles of contemporary psychoanalytic thought.

Erikson has rediscovered prescientific truths, and he has accordingly used a prescientific word to define them. What is new is their redefinition in a psychoanalytic context, and the detailed analysis of how they develop. Erikson shows that the virtues do not grow automatically; they are not the result of acts of moral resolution or religious dedication; nor are they defined in opposition to lust, depravity, and weaknesses of the body; nor does he suggest that human nature is inherently good or inherently evil. His is a thoroughgoing naturalistic picture of the emergence of the human spirit in the psychoanalytic context of developing ego strength.

His vision shares with Freud's its dramatic quality, since the virtues are the outcome of struggle and conflict, but he differs from Freud in enlarging the arena of conflict from an internal, intrapsychic battle to one inextricably embedded in the context of others, of society, and of the individual's total world. For Erikson, the unit is not the quantum of energy; not the instinct as quantitative excitation; not one psychic structure pitted against another; not even the individual as a whole. The unit is the indivisible person-in-his-world.

To designate the same phenomenon Heidegger used the composite phrase "being-in-the-world." Erikson speaks of the actuality of the individual to define the noncerebral aspects of the latter's world, distinguishing actuality from Freud's notion of reality. He does so in order to avoid the connotations of the term reality as customarily used in psychoanalytic theory. "Reality," Erikson points out, "usually designates the cerebral intellectualized world of veridical perception; perception free of distortion . . . the world of phenomenal experience perceived with a minimum of distortion and a maximum of customary validation agreed upon in a given state of technology and culture." (Erikson, 1964c, p. 165.) Actuality, in contrast, is the world of participation—the concrete experience of the individual that is largely preconscious and unconscious. (This concept resembles Husserl's concept of the *Lebenswelt*—the world of lived experience.)

The human virtues, then, develop or fail to develop in a sequence that is dictated, in part, by phylogenetic patterns built into our genes, but the unfolding of the maturational process needs for its completion specific life experiences, or in Erikson's terminology "stages of changing actualities." Without such experiences, the phylogenetic patterns remain mere possibilities, infinite in number. The virtues develop by means of decisive encounters that characterize each stage of actuality; and they develop in time—the structured sequential time of biological development, not abstract quantitative Newtonian time.

NINE

The Gambit Declined

Erikson's concepts take him far beyond traditional psychoanalytic theory and cause him to diverge from Freud on three basic issues: he presents man's ethical reality (superego) as rooted in biological development, not opposed to it; he shows that the normal personality cannot be deduced from the neurotic and that a neurosis is qualitatively as well as quantitatively different from normal behavior, i.e., one can understand the neurotic in the light of the normal, but not the other way around; and he believes, though he does not make an issue of it, that psychoanalytic metapsychology, Hartmann to the contrary, is inadequate to the data it purports to describe. These are giant steps that Erikson takes beyond most of his colleagues.

Not surprisingly his formulations have brought him into conflict with other prominent psychoanalysts. Edith Jacobson, a noted psychoanalyst and worker in the field of ego psychology, criticizes the eight stages and the concept of epigenetic crises as "not too informative, and somewhat misleading" (Jacobson, 1964, p. 25), and she goes on to suggest that ego identity as Erikson uses it is both ambiguous and far too broad. She states that Erikson fails to distinguish between an individual's identity as it can be described objectively and the subjective experience of striving for identity. She holds that he places too much emphasis on adolescent and post-adolescent stages and not enough on earlier stages of identity formation. She also disagrees with the idea that "man is forever threatened with loss or breakdown of his identity." This, she says, is not borne out by clinical observation. "Serious identity problems appear to be limited to neurotics with specific narcissistic conflicts and to borderline and psychotic patients." (Jacobson, 1964, p. 29.)

In essence, Jacobson is suggesting that a gap exists between Erikson's concepts and clinical practice. Jacobson and other psychoanalysts, including some who greatly admire Erikson, doubt the relevance of his concepts to clinical practice. Paradoxically, many other psychoanalysts respect Erikson's concepts precisely because they are so relevant to clinical practice. One of Boston's leading psychoanalysts, who believes that Erikson's major contribution is his notion of the epigenetic crisis, adds: "Erikson is a true clinician. He is tuned in to the problems people really struggle with." Indeed, this psychoanalyst and many others praise Erikson for being so responsive to people's real problems and concerns. (Personal conversation with Paul Myerson.)

Which point of view is correct? Why do some psychoanalysts find that their patients are troubled by quite different problems from those Erikson describes while others find him to be cogently relevant?

The disparity has a ready explanation. Most patients in analysis are people whose adult lives have been made wretched by some unresolved childhood drama (a still crippling envy of an older, better-loved sibling; a wound caused by the ambivalent love of a frustrated mother; the scars made by an unreasonable and demanding father nursing his own disappointed life, etc.). But not all human problems are rooted in neurosis. Some psychoanalysts seem, like bats, able to see into the infantile darkness clearly enough, but are blinded by the light of the adult world when they come out of the cave of the patient's childhood. Erikson's peculiar gift is to distinguish the profound difference between neurotic anxiety and the anguish of life itself, apart from any pathology. The two may occur together, and indeed are often intertwined, but they are different states of being. Erikson has balanced the traditional psychoanalytic preoccupation with the roots of neurosis in childhood with an attempt to understand the full depth and complexity of the adolescent's and adult's life in the world.

The customary psychoanalytic approach to defining what is "normal" behavior rests on the shaky assumption that abnormal behavior differs from the normal only in degree, not in kind, and that therefore one can readily extrapolate from the abnormal to the normal. One of Erikson's most positive achievements is that he takes the opposite stand. Psychopathology, he believes, cannot be understood except as a variant of normal behavior. Deducing the norm from forms of deviancy has foisted an appalling distortion on our understanding of man. In combating reductionism by developing a conception of normal human development, Erikson has plunged into the deepest waters of psychoanalytic theory—into the question of man's being, of what it means, concretely, to be human at all.

Psychoanalysts have always assumed a continuity between neurosis and the normal human condition. Their metapsychology has forced them to see the distinction between normal functioning and psychopathology as a purely quantitative one: a matter of how energy accumulations are balanced on the side of ego or id, a matter of "battalions." In relying upon psychoanalytic concepts to attempt to understand the general human condition, and yet in going far beyond them, Erikson has indeed opened a gap between normal psychology and psychopathology that may not be easily bridged.

But it is not the gap that Jacobson suggests. Even if Jacobson were correct on the specifics of her criticism, her angle of vision on Erikson is far too narrow. The crucial question is not whether his concepts have relevance to neurotic states, but whether he has been successful in freeing the psychoanalytic view of the human condition from pathological connotations and also from connotations that adhere to it from its own cramped philosophy. There is no question more central to the theme of this work.

Erikson is fascinating to watch as he approaches his data in an effort to avoid reductionism and yet stay within a general psychoanalytic framework. Consider his analysis of one of Freud's own dreams. The well-known "Dream of the Three Fates" is about Freud's desire to be fed by the hostess of an inn at which he dreamt he was staying. The dream occurred after Freud had been traveling and had been obliged to go to bed without his dinner. The search for food automatically brings to his psychoanalyst's mind suggestions of regression to the oral stage. But, Erikson adds:

> . . . if in the analysis of a dream we come to the conclusion that it reaches back into problems of the oral stage, do we also find evidence for the assumption that the dream, besides references to food, to mouth, to skin and to modes of incorporation, also concerns itself with the psychosocial problem of *basic trust, with the first vital virtue of hope and with the cosmic order?* (Erikson, 1964c, pp. 178–179.) (Our italics.)

Other analysts might also have found in the dream a concern with trust, hope, and the cosmic order alongside of oral cravings. But within the framework of the metapsychology, it is hard to resist the temptation to reduce the former to the latter. In his analysis of the dream, Erikson is struggling against the psychoanalytic tendency to explain away structures of meaning such as trust, hope, and a belief in a cosmic order as epiphenomena reflecting the instinctual drives.

His struggle, and its consequences, can be seen clearly in a more elaborate example where such "higher" structures of meaning are involved—the case of Martin Luther as developed in Erikson's remarkable book, *Young Man Luther*.

Erikson begins the book by indicating, with a genial and sophisticated irony, how other interpreters of Luther have been trapped within their own *a priori* interpretive schemes. He cites a psychiatrist (a non-psychoanalytic one) who projects a body-mind pathology upon Luther that violently distorts facts, a believing Protestant historian who sees all sorts of divine portents and effects in Luther's life that may or may not be there, and a sociologist who sees Luther's motives as primarily social and economic. Erikson then offers us his own interpretation, alluding to an identity diffusion and an identity crisis in Luther on the occasion of his entry at the age of twenty-two into the Augustinian order.

Erikson's interpretive scheme, in its most general form, holds that every human life is fundamentally a search for meaningfulness and for an ego identity within that meaningfulness. But he applies this framework by tracing Luther's identity crisis mainly to his family situation, that is, to his response to an overstern father and a loving mother whose love for him as an infant had built up his sense of basic trust, a predecessor to his later Christian faith. Yet man's search for meaning must also take place within the world beyond the family, a human world that is always his world, and therefore radically temporal and historical.

This last point gains greater force when we are dealing with a world-historical figure like Luther. What is the meaning of Luther's life? At one level at least the answer to this question is plain enough, and we must not overcloud it initially with undue subtleties. We have first to let the phenomenon be what it is, and grasp its large-scale and evident structures as those within which the qualifying details are to be eventually fitted. Well, then, the simplest meaning that constitutes the core of Luther's life is that he led a religious revolution. As a result, the history of Christianity was to change, and social and political upheavals followed, but these were not mainly the points around which Luther's own meaningful preoccupations centered. His mind was on theology, and specifically on a certain point in theology—the absolute priority of faith for the believing Christian. The achievement of his life demanded of him a strong intellect, able to hold fast to a single point, and a stubbornness of will to stick with the point once he got hold of it. These, then, are what we know *prima facie* about the psychology of the man Luther that was demanded for the accomplishment of his life's work.

For this task he needed formidable intellectual equipment, a mastery of the political, philosophical, and theological doctrines of his time. We must not forget this intellectual equipment even though in other contexts Luther spoke out against "the whore, Reason"; for when he did so speak, he was also speaking as an intellectual. How would he get this necessary intellectual preparation better than in the monastery of the Augustinians, where he would have opportunities for contemplation and study? Why should there be a diffusion of identity in his choosing to go into the monastery? To be sure, Luther at that age does not have the identity of the man who later had fathered a theological revolution. In the same way, we might say that Einstein as a youth in the *Gymnasium* does not have the identity of the later Einstein who had created the theory of relativity; but at the *Gymnasium* he was surely the same person, a younger Einstein. Indeed, looking at Luther's life backward from its accomplished goal (thus from its meaning-ful culmination), we can say that he could not have made a more appropriate choice than to enter the monastery (the Augustinian order was on a very high intellectual level) that would uniquely equip him for what he eventually was to do with his life.

On the other hand, Luther's father wanted him to go into law. But is the opposition here different in kind than between, say, a contemporary father who might want his son to go into business and the son who decides to go into public service? No convincing argument can be made out from this difference between Luther and his father here as to the nature of their relationship in its most intimate terms. Erikson implies (and here his method is one of graceful insinuation) that Luther's entry into the monastery was a failure to meet the challenge of an overstern father and a temporary relapse back to the shel-tering mother (whose surrogate here would be Mother Mon-astery). But this is plainly contrary to Erikson's main emphasis that in interpreting human psychology we are to be guided fundamentally by the patterns of meaningfulness within a life. The monastery, as we have seen, would be a place where Luther could acquire the preparation—intellectual and contemplative —necessary for the world that would be the meaning of his life. Moreover, we do not have enough facts to establish the nature of Luther's emotional relationship to his father. People then did not hover over their children as we do now and record every passing symptom. Luther in later life spoke of having been caned often, but we have to remember that he often spoke out of a morose mood and frequently singled out and exag-gerated the unpleasant aspects of his experience. Nor would the fact of being whipped as a child in the fifteenth century have the same emotional significance as being whipped in the twentieth century. A whipping by one's father would not have automatically established the male parent as a monster in the eyes of a child of Luther's time.

So far we have seemed to move mainly on the terrain of historical details, but the relevance of these for psychoanalytic interpretation will shortly be clear. Meanwhile, one other large matter of historical fact raises questions about Erikson's constructions of Luther's character and its psychosexual origins. We are beginning to understand a little more fully nowadays the sources of Luther's thought in late Medieval Nominalism. There is a common tendency to think that the critical and nominalistic modes of thought brought in by Occamism are such that they already establish Occam and his followers as modern secular figures—a Bertrand Russell, say, in a friar's frock. On the contrary, the more particularistic and critical the nominalists became in their thinking, the more theologically positivistic they became in their insistence that the true data of the Christian religion were faith in revelation and the written word of the scriptures. The sweeping rationalism of a St. Anselm in the twelfth century, who speaks of faith seeking understanding, as if the former could pass over into the latter, and the more moderate rationalism of St. Thomas in the thirteenth century, where reason brought one majestically to the very portals of faith, were now gone, and attention turned more and more to the scrupulous and meticulous scrutiny of the factual letter of revelation. Luther is a culmination of this movement. Inevitably, then, his attention would be turned more and more to the scrutiny of the Bible, and he would discover in some parts of it very somber accounts of the wrath and judgment of God. And if, in turn, he did become obsessed with this aspect of God, its true source lay in the intellectual movement which led him to take account of the wrathful Yahweh found in the scriptures rather than in any putative projection of his own possibly stern (but just as possibly affectionate) father. So too, reading St. Paul more and more closely, as the new positivism of the text demanded (from the fourteenth century onward the Occamists had referred to theologians like St. Thomas as the old-fashioned ones—"*antiqui*"—and themselves as the "*moderni*"), Luther would have been struck with the sheer historical situation of Paul's confrontation with the Greeks and the Jews, and the nature of Christian faith that emerges from that encounter. The Greeks demanded wisdom—that is, rational philosophy; and the Jews saw in the incarnation of God in a man nothing but absurdity. Against these formidable opponents, St. Paul can only walk the thin razor's edge of a precarious faith—and a faith, at that, which bears the marks of absurdity. Hence, Luther's insistence on the priority of faith is a perfectly understandable development of a whole movement within theology, and is not compelling evidence that as a child he had developed trust at this mother's breast and was projecting this infantile experience onto a religious doctrine. (Though there is nothing incompatible in the fact that he may have gained his own personal, basic sense of trust at his mother's breast.)

Now, the upshot of all this is to suggest how Erikson's controlling presuppositions have shaped his psychological interpretations throughout. There is nothing wrong in harboring an *a priori* framework of interpretation. Indeed, it is absolutely necessary in approaching any subject-matter at all. Many psychoanalysts, apparently, have been unaware that they never go naked to meet their phenomena but approach them with a preconceived structure within which the phenomena are to be placed and related, and further that this structure is just as likely a source of error as are mistakes about the matters of fact which it embraces.

The interpretive ontological structure of Erikson, roughly described as a Freudian infancy with an Eriksonian adolescence, would seem to be a great advance over the traditional metapsychology. To the basic Freudian insistence on the development of the infant out of frustration of pre-emptory instinctual demands within the family setting, there are added the later struggles of the individual (on the soil of that early shaping) for self-validity and meaning in a larger setting. Such an interpretive framework is in many ways a remarkable achievement. Yet the two parts of the synthesis still stand in unstable equilibrium with each other, as the study of Luther reveals most vividly perhaps of all Erikson's books. For, if we trace Luther's life as a structure of meaning, certain "explanations" having to do with unknown infantile experiences become merely gratuitous and unexplanatory relapses into another form of reductionism that would seek to derive the whole person from the psycho-social phenomena of infancy and adolescence.

The truth is that Erikson has thought beyond Freud to a degree that, in his reticence and loyalty to the psychoanalytic movement, he does not stress; and yet, at the same time, because he does not have an explicit philosophy of science to substitute for Freudian metapsychology, he too must inevitably lapse into reductionism. Moreover, if the reductionism is subtle and elegant in his hands, it becomes less so in the hands of those who seek to apply his concepts without having his personal sense of balance and perspective.

One final word on Luther as a historical figure. The more we examine Luther, as with every great man, the more we find him immersed in his time, the more he appears to borrow and to bring to fruition themes and motifs that had already been launched into the current of his culture. Whether a great man merely expresses his time or creates it is an unreal question. The more decisively he shapes his time the more deeply he borrows from it, bringing to a head thoughts and insights that were already in the air but halting and half-formed. A great man is in this respect only a reminder of how deeply embedded in history man's being is, and this would seem to be a fact which psychoanalysis must also take into account in the case of more ordinary people. The concepts and methods of the natural sciences cannot explain the human person *in toto* because, among other reasons, one essential characteristic of man is his historicity, his immersion in history up to his neck. How, on the basis of mechanistic theory, psychoanalysis can hope to do justice to this pervasive feature of human existence, remains an open question. And Erikson himself—just because of his wide historical erudition and his sensitivity to the conditions of society and culture within which each human destiny is played out—leads us to raise this question.

Anyone familiar with the work of the German phenomenologists Husserl and Heidegger cannot fail to be struck by similarities in Erikson's outlook and theirs. There are also similarities to Whitehead's concept of organism as an emergent structure. This is not to say that Erikson has borrowed from these thinkers, or even that he is familiar with their work (he may or may not be; it is beside the point). Rather, it is tempting to speculate that the similarity may be due to the fact that Erikson has responded to the spirit rather than to the letter of Freud's discoveries, and to the fact that Erikson's extraordinarily sensitive clinical sense has helped him to remain phenomenologically close to what he found in working with human lives; while Heinz Hartmann, who remained more faithful to the literal meaning of the metapsychology, may have been led up the garden path of trying to salvage an inherently inappropriate scheme of abstractions. Erikson has wrestled with the more immediate and concrete lived experience of his patients. Inevitably, the confrontation of Erikson's thought with the phenomena has brought him to the brink of a radical change in the philosophical underpinnings of psychoanalysis.

In the seventeenth century, the famous philosopher and mathematician, Pascal, deplored the evolving mechanistic philosophy of his day. During the romantic period, a century later, poets such as Wordsworth and Coleridge deplored the same tendencies. Toward the end of the nineteenth century idealistic philosophers deplored in England and Germany; Bergson deplored in France; and William James, the pragmatist, deplored in this country. In our own period, and within the profession of psychology, such noted psychologists as Henry Murray, Gordon Allport, Nevitt Sanford, A. A. Maslow and Isidor Chein have all deplored. After three hundred years of imprisonment in a one-sided philosophy of science, it is clear that deploring is not enough.

Erikson does more than deplore. He suggests, he hints, he insinuates. Unfailingly polite and tactful, his most telling criticisms are gently whispered. In several places, Erikson speaks of wisdom as the reward for the final epigenetic crisis of old age. Although most psychoanalysts are hesitant to describe one of their living brethren as a possessor of wisdom, some of Erikson's colleagues, psychoanalysts of considerable stature, use this supreme accolade in describing him. Erikson does indeed possess the quality of wisdom. Strange to say, however, just as deploring is not enough, so personal wisdom is not enough either. Erikson has gone to the very edge; his thought has carried him far beyond Hartmann's theory to the point where radical incompatibilities in psychoanalytic theory flutter into view. He has defined the problem, has raised the right issues, has pointed to the direction of its solution—but he has personally declined the gambit. Unfortunately, nothing less than an explicit philosophy of man, not personal wisdom nor mere rejection of the old philosophy, can accommodate the complexity of human life.

Man does not first exist in a world of Freudian forces, energies and cathexes, and then later search for meaning. This is the paradox one is struck with if one tries to swallow both Freud and Erikson as completely compatible. The inexorable logic of accepting a Freudian metapsychological base with an Eriksonian superstructure can readily lead to the positivist conclusion that the very search for meaning is meaningless. The anxiety of meaninglessness—the defining anxiety of our day —is a symptom of our entrapment in scientific materialism. Erikson personally understands that this is the case, but he plays it down in his formal work in order to avoid making the divergences with the Freudian tradition too sharp. He defines his basic concepts in terms of meanings and intentions, in terms of becoming, of transcendence and of virtues rather than in terms of forces and energies. But he does not carry through this philosophical framework when it would bring him into open conflict with the official psychoanalytic framework.

The psychoanalytic theory of the psychic economy does not leave room for experience that results in a transformation of the whole person. And yet, this is what Erikson means by the epigenetic principle when he says that "the person is constituted anew at each stage of development." His writings appeal both to youth and adults because he smuggles the concept of the human spirit through the back door of psychoanalytic theory. He is responding to the human need for meaning and for self-understanding, to the need for a sense of relatedness to a cosmic order, and above all, to the universal search for a bedrock basis for ethical reality in a secular age.

Erikson describes identity as a structure of meanings, and epigenesis as a series of crises and transformations. In the creation of a valid ego identity, a person does not change because he imitates a model, but because the encounter with some living fellow creature serves as a catalyst that enables the person to transform himself and shape his own self. The difference is critical: the former process might be explained in metapsychological terms, but the latter cannot possibly be.

In his search for a more viable philosophy for psychoanalysis than the metapsychology, Erikson affords us the curious picture of a prominent psychoanalytic theorist who ignores four-fifths of Freud's metapsychology and uses the remainder idiosyncratically. Erikson almost never discusses his materials in terms of the topographical or the dynamic or the economic or the structural point of view (although he accepts the basic distinction between ego and id). And he has evolved his own version of the genetic point of view.

Yet there cannot be any doubt on how Erikson feels about the traditional metapsychology:

> The "points of view" introduced into psychiatry and psychology by Freud are subject to a strange fate . . . since on their medical home-ground they were based on physical facts such as organs that function, in the study of the mind they sooner or later served as improper reifications, as though libido or the death instinct or the ego really existed. Freud was sovereignly aware of this danger, but he was always willing to learn by giving a mode of thought free rein to see to what useful model it might lead. He also had the courage, the authority and the inner consistency to reverse such a direction when it became useless or absurd. Generations of clinical practitioners cannot be expected to be equally detached or authoritative. Thus, it cannot be denied that in much clinical literature, the clinical evidence secured with the help of inferences based on Freud's theories has been increasingly used and slanted to verify the original theories. This, in turn, could only lead to a gradual estrangement between theory and clinical observation. (Erikson, 1964b, p. 77.)

Erikson here is talking about his own estrangement from the metapsychology. He implicitly depends upon a philosophy at odds with the scientific materialism that underlies the classical metapsychology, but he has not developed such a philosophy explicitly to the point where he can lean on it for support.

In departing from the metapsychology, Erikson, on the surface, appears to be less faithful than Hartmann to the Freudian heritage because he abandons most of Freud's theoretical machinery. But a strong case could be made that, in ignoring the metapsychology, Erikson has kept faith with the deepest element in Freud—the biological thrust of his thought. Far more than Hartmann, Erikson returns again and again to early sexual origins as the grounds of human development, although he treats these early facts of biological-cultural development in other than a mechanical and reductionist fashion.

Thus, on the critical issue of what philosophy shall support psychoanalysis, Erikson stands for the exactly opposite solution to Hartmann's. Both have attempted to preserve and at the same time to advance psychoanalytic insight, but each has interpreted this task in a radically different way. Hartmann's mode of preservation is to maintain and repair the metapsychology; Erikson's is to discard the metapsychology but retain the insight within a new implicit philosophical setting.

Earlier we quoted Rapaport's statement that Hartmann and Erikson complement each other by particularizing each other's generalities. It should now be clear that this complementarity is more apparent than real. When we move from Hartmann to Erikson we move from the world of forces and energies to the world of meanings, possibilities, genuine development, and ethical realities. In making this move we have truly made a decisive leap; for we have not only changed our unit of analysis, we have begun to change our philosophy.

TEN

Four Strategies—
And Stalemate

Much of what is elusive and involuted about the formal theory of psychoanalysis flows from the various strategies invented by Freud and his followers to reconcile clinical data with the metapsychology.

Freud's own strategy was to avoid a direct conflict between his scientific philosophy and his clinical theory by juggling two modes of explanation simultaneously. Working with an explicit metapsychology that defined the ego as analogous to an object, he nevertheless made use of an implicit clinical theory that gave the ego a very different status. This clinical theory was, in fact, based on a great many assumptions that had been formally banished from his metapsychology. By switching back and forth between the two modes of explanation—depending on whether he was describing a case history or writing a meta-psychological paper—Freud was able to deal with a broad spectrum of human activity on which the metapsychology, had it been followed literally and exclusively, would have closed the door.

In the excitement of the new discoveries about unconscious motivations, Freud put aside the problems of theorizing on conscious mental life. In part this was deliberate; he felt that the problems of consciousness were already familiar and, in fact, were emphasized at the expense of the unconscious. By the early 1920's, however, he had discovered that "the ego, too, could be unconscious," and so he decided to abandon his earlier equation of consciousness with ego. It was at this point that he introduced a change in direction that led ultimately to the conceptual impasse between human experience and its scientific explanation with which we are concerned in this work.

While making his revisions in the 1920's, if Freud had challenged his philosophical premises as well as his findings, we might have a very different picture of psychoanalytic theory today. The second-hand philosophy was not at all necessary to, and in fact did not jibe with, his great discoveries. But Freud spent the last decades of his life consolidating his past discoveries, and there were no further radical changes in philosophical premises. He chose to remain with the concept of a psychic apparatus, but now split it up between learned functions (ego) and unlearned instinctual drives (id) instead of among degrees of consciousness. In this way, he was led to replace the topographical mode of categorization which had proven too restrictive with the so-called structural point of view, which contains even more serious difficulties.

Freud's new method of dividing up the psychic apparatus (including the subdivision of ego into superego and ego proper) quickly became "official" doctrine, hailed as a decisive reorientation by leading psychoanalysts. But were they not, perhaps, too quickly won over by its heuristic advantages? The new ego-id-superego framework is so all-embracing, so usefully descriptive of the kinds of conflicts analysts encounter, and yet so wonderfully simple that it seems to encompass all fundamental truths about the psyche. Furthermore, at the time Freud proposed the new formula it did offer the inestimable benefit of taking the ego out of the shadows and permitting direct attention to be focused on it.

And so, many of Freud's successors, psychoanalysts of great discernment, may have failed to see that while the earlier conception (ego equals consciousness) was merely too limited to account for the full range of ego phenomena, the later distinction (ego equals the results of learning and experience) can be extremely misleading.* Recent theorists such as Arlow and

---

* Not all psychoanalysts have moved in this direction; but the great majority appear to have done so.

Brenner (1964) have even suggested that the earlier topographical point of view has now been rendered obsolete and might well be abandoned. Adopting their proposal might, however, prove to be retrogressive: the rendering of psychic life in terms of varying degrees of consciousness is descriptive of experience; the ego-id distinction, for all its utility, artificially categorizes the facts of human development. Most ethologists tell us that learning, the modification of behavior by experience, cannot be sharply contrasted with instinct; learned behavior and instinctual behavior are not found in nature as separately organized functional structures. Furthermore, the early psychoanalytic definition of instinct on which the ego-id dichotomy is based needs radical reformulation (see Chapters Twenty and Twenty-one). Freud's introduction of the ego-id concept set the stage for the difficulties that inevitably ensued.

After *The Ego and the Id* and Freud's related works in the 1920's and 1930's, psychoanalytic ego psychology was radically advanced by Anna Freud and Heinz Hartmann, as we have described; Erik Erikson was the author of the third psychoanalytic strategy we considered. Erikson does an injustice both to himself and to psychoanalysis by blurring the fact that his philosophical framework and the classic metapsychology are irreconcilable. His refusal to make his argument clear is political and personal: he does not wish to become more of a center of controversy within psychoanalysis than he already is. But the result, of course, is that his proposals must stop short of bridging the impasse between clinical experience and formal theory that now blocks the development of psychoanalysis.

Other contemporary workers in psychoanalysis have also avoided coping with all the implications of the metapsychology. Jacobson, Spitz, Bowlby, Mahler, Greenacre, Wolff, and many others have added to specific psychoanalytic findings on early ego development with an ever-increasing refinement of observation and insight within their own areas of specialization. But they too have left the basic framework unchallenged.

Perhaps the most philosophically sophisticated strategy in the post-Freudian period is the one proposed by Avery Weisman in *The Existential Core of Psychoanalysis* (1965). Weisman has thought profoundly about the nature of the therapeutic encounter between psychoanalyst and patient, and he has successfully defined the full scope of the philosophical dilemma in psychoanalysis. His colleagues should, he proposes, acknowledge the existential core of psychoanalytic practice and find a way of reaping the benefits of both the existential and what he calls the "categorical" point of view without reducing either one to the other. (Categorical, in Weisman's terminology, has virtually the same meaning as scientific materialism.) His book accomplishes two purposes: (1) it shows that the philosophical issue in psychoanalysis is an urgent concern for practicing clinicians and not a remote theoretical matter that can be left, as Erikson suggests, "to experts in this kind of thinking"; and (2) it offers a thoroughgoing critique (and partial reformulation) of the metapsychology by a theorist who is identified with the orthodox psychoanalytic "establishment" (Weisman is a training analyst associated with the Boston Psychoanalytic Institute, one of the most prestigious and authoritative centers of psychoanalytic activity).

It is not easy to summarize Weisman's work and the task is made more difficult by his invention of a new vocabulary to describe aspects of experience for which conventional language is not well equipped. For our limited purposes we need not document his full contribution; we can confine our attention to Weisman's proposed strategy for reconciling the existential with the categorical aspect of psychoanalysis.

"Man is the knowing subject, the world is the object known." This statement, which occurs early in his work, clues us in to Weisman's basic approach. His strategy is essentially epistemological, and the major thrust of his work is, in effect, a theory of knowledge written from a psychoanalytic perspective —a highly original approach. When philosophers write about epistemology they generally look for the *logical* and *analytical* grounds of the belief that we have knowledge; Weisman on the other hand, traces the *psychological* and *affective* roots of our knowledge. One of his major concerns is with tracing how we form our convictions about the nature of truth and reality —not in any esoteric sense, but in the ordinary sense of the convictions of certainty we develop about our own existence, the existence of others, the realities of job and family, and the solid tangibility of our physical possessions. A psychological explanation of how we know what we know is particularly interesting when logical proofs are lacking—as they are to a surprising degree when this rudimentary sense of the reality of our everyday experience is at issue.

Weisman's major concept is that of *reality sense*. "Many familiar psychoanalytic concepts and theories," he states, "are irrelevant and inadequate explanations for the events we find in psychoanalysis. That is why the significance of reality sense for the existential experience of psychoanalysis is our principal theme." (P. 83). By reality sense Weisman means quite literally how we develop our sense of reality. ("The unfractionated experience of whatever commands the conviction 'this is real.' ") Weisman links inextricably our sense of what is real with our sense of what is true: "From the existential point-of-view the value judgment—real—is identical with the value judgment—true—because whatever is judged true or false is secondary to an initial judgment that our affirmations are real . . ." Our sense of what is real is the common beginning point for both the emotional and the cognitive life of man.

He describes how this sense of reality develops into the complex network of personal and objective meanings of the adult. Earlier we noted how central the concept of meaning is to both psychoanalytic theory and practice. Weisman also emphasizes this conclusion: "The proper study of man," he states, "begins with how his meanings are created." But his use of meaning as a master concept depends utterly on the distinction between *objective* and *personal* meaning. Objective meanings are arbitrary linkages established by convention between symbols and objects, while personal meanings develop out of the individual's unique life experience on its affective side. In the discussion of the Dora case, for example, we saw that the personal meaning of the truth was not the same for all parties concerned. Weisman comments on an implication of the distinction: "One reason why intellectual insight is ineffective in psychoanalysis is that the patient is unprepared to relate the meaning of what the analyst says (i.e., objective meaning) to his own body of personal meanings." So long as the dialogue remains in the domain of logical and conventional objective meanings, rather than being thoroughly immersed in the patient's personal meanings, effective therapeutic change is unlikely to take place.

It is our personal meanings that give us our sense of reality, and at their core we find those absolute convictions which Weisman calls *acceptances*. Acceptances, he states, are our primitive axioms of certainty so strong that no alternatives are even conceivable. They are the implicit grounds on which other ideas are rendered true and false; they take the form of deep-rooted attitudes toward experience rather than consciously formulated propositions or even distinct ideas; and they shape the questions we ask of nature. Their unspoken certainty permits no compromise. Thus, our acceptances which direct our sense of what is real and what is unreal become a precondition for any other form of judgment. They are both "logically and psychologically prior to the formation of meanings in both senses of the word and derivative value judgments." When we analyze a person's values and convictions what we perceive are not these actual sources of belief—the acceptances—but conscious derivatives of them. It is from this base of acceptances that one's personal meanings gradually build up.

Weisman points out how different the method of thought is for forming personal meanings from the method by which we form objective meanings. He emphasizes the importance of antitheses and paradoxes (the anger in sorrow, the love in hate); he describes how personal meanings tend to vary with the mood of the viewer (when a patient is depressed, every event seems to forebode disaster), and he shows how personal meanings, in contrast to objective meanings, often modify the very nature of the object apprehended. Furthermore, one's base of personal meanings is greatly expanded by what Weisman calls the process of affective equivalence, i.e., seemingly disparate events come to have the same personal meaning by participating in the same affect. Weisman gives the example of a patient who ostensibly reacted quite differently toward his employer and his wife—with truculent compliance to the one and altruistic dedication to the other. But, in fact, the patient brought to both relationships an affectively equivalent mood compounded of a wish to be taken care of, a disguised envy, and a profound bitterness.

The individual's core of acceptances, extended by affective equivalence and other forms of personal meaning, gradually leads into the more familiar world of objective meanings. In

Weisman's terminology we then move from acceptances to *conditionals*. While acceptances are absolutes, attitudes derived from them eventually come to lose some of their original absolutist conviction of certainty. Man emerged into the dawn of the thinking process, says Weisman, when his derived attitudes offered him a choice among alternatives. With choice, reality testing begins and ushers in the more familiar rules of objective thought, i.e., trial and error learning, provisional generalization, and ultimately, the forming of hypotheses about the nature of truth. We have moved now onto the logical terrain of concepts and propositions, the world of science and philosophy.

The developmental processes associated with our sense of reality appear to evolve through three stages. The first is the formation of acceptances; the second is an "unsettled aspect of existence" when opportunities for choice among competing acceptances lead to the first forms of reality testing; and the third stage is the formation of conceptual thought and formal propositions, the world of objective meaning. "To subject a cherished belief to open examination," says Weisman, "is to change its sense of reality from certainty to doubt. When this noble event happens . . . acceptances become conditionals."

We have an obvious and striking parallel here to Freud's description of how primary-process thinking develops into the rational, orderly "secondary" thought processes. But the difference between the two concepts is more relevant than their similarities. In discussing the primary processes, Freud stressed the distortions in time and space and the characteristics of condensation, displacement, and symbolization (see Chapter Four), while Weisman stresses the imperfect transition from the conviction of certainty to doubt, the affective equivalence of personal meanings, the role of paradox and antitheses, and the unity and concreteness of the act of knowing with all of its affective accompaniments. Also, Weisman does not suggest a biological rootedness for his acceptances (save only for the feeling of conviction they generate). But most important of all, Weisman gives his "primary processes"—the individual's core of personal meanings—an important role to play in determining truth and reality (though subject to verification by objective procedures), whereas in the Freudian schema, the id, the source of primary process, has no part to play in determining truth; truth and reality are tied wholly to the secondary processes associated with the ego.

The contrast between personal meanings and objective meanings leads directly to Weisman's analysis of the interplay between the existential and the categorical. Weisman emphasizes that this distinction is not simply another dichotomy; there is no need to choose between them. The question, he states, is not whether one is more valid than the other, but which is the more reliable way in any given situation to discover what is real and what is illusory. The difference between the existential "I" and the categorical "ego," he points out, is parallel to the difference between the sensation of warmth and light from the sun as a personal unshared experience, in contrast to "an analysis of this same event according to the perception of regulated body temperature." Each in its own way is both real and true.

At issue, then, is the difference between an event and various abstract descriptions of the event. As the precondition for any abstraction, we must always start with the existential event of my personal existence—which precedes knowledge and indeed, in its dense immediacy, eludes being wholly captured by abstractions. The unique lived experience of the patient and physician in their therapeutic encounter constitutes the "existential core" of psychoanalysis. Abstraction begins with phenomenological descriptions of this experience, i.e., case histories of patients and of therapeutic encounters, particularly when these are relatively uncontaminated by theory. At the next level of abstraction comes the categorical mode of analysis, i.e., the description of psychodynamics as the interplay of forces within the personality, and at the very highest level of generality, we enter the domain of truly scientific discourse, that of psychophysical analysis.

While the various levels of abstraction have their proper role to play in theory making, they can never serve as a wholly adequate substitute for the existential. Weisman's philosophical position on this key point is quite clear and he states it explicitly: "Existence," he says, "is prior to knowledge." Our descriptions and analyses of existence at one or another level of abstraction can never be "literal expressions of the world." They play an important and valuable role in describing, highlighting, and confirming aspects of experience, but their rigid limitations as modes of knowing must always be kept in mind. The correct strategy for encompassing the existential and categorical aspects of psychoanalysis follows logically: it is to have us embrace both, and learn to move more easily between them. They are to be regarded as complementary rather than as mutually exclusive modes of knowing.

While this sketchy account merely hints at Weisman's thought, we have perhaps indicated enough of its direction to show that for all its originality, it nonetheless remains fixed within the tradition of Cartesianism—which will be described at length in the next section. Weisman's acceptances are unseen realities operating from behind the scenes as the "cause" of our most cherished beliefs. Their logical status is analogous to Freud's concept of the instincts: we never see them directly, we only perceive their effects and their aims. Furthermore, they are regarded as wholly internal states of mind: "The sense of reality arises from the centrifugal reality of the 'I' *who cannot escape his subjective orientation* . . ." (our italics). And once again, "None of us ever enters directly into the sanctum of another person's subjective experience and literally sees the world through his eyes." We remain enclosed in Cartesian subjectivity, looking from an inner world out onto an external reality; and, from this standpoint, the mind of another person remains private and inaccessible, as with Descartes.

Weisman's description of man as knower is, in effect, an analysis of Cartesian man from a psychoanalytic point of view. This is a new and fascinating perspective; but it remains bogged down in dualism. Possibly, it is Weisman's own acceptances that have led him to the conviction that reality must always begin and end with the totally subjective experience of the single individual. We are not arguing that this conviction is wrong at a certain level of generality; we are simply pointing out that Weisman shares the distinguished company of those legions of philosophers and scientists who in the past three hundred years have felt compelled to describe the nature of human experience within one or another form of the Cartesian framework.

In making his proposal to regard the existential and the categorical as complementary modes of knowing, Weisman reflects a familiar psychoanalytic appreciation of the value of bringing multiple and shifting perspectives to the examination of the same clinical material. There can be no doubt that looking at a confusing subject from a number of different points of view can be quite useful. In the present instance, however, we believe that to apply what is, in effect, a principle of complementarity, is to leave unresolved the central philosophical issue. Weisman has stopped one step too soon in his analysis. After going as far as he does to define the philosophical nature of the problem, nonetheless he proposes a solution that accepts the crucial premises of the old philosophy. Weisman agrees that nature in all of its existential concreteness is not bifurcated into Cartesian subjects and objects, and that experience presents itself as a seamless unity. But given the limitations of our minds, we must, he believes, approach these concrete, unified events of experience now from one mode of knowing (with the detachment of science) and now from another (with the immediacy of existential involvement). Such a tactic has obvious advantages to practicing clinicians, and it is an ingenious strategy for bypassing the philosophical stumbling block. But we are concerned here not with bypassing it but with confronting and, if possible, removing it because of its larger implications for the culture in which we live.

The recounting of these four strategies—Freud's, Hartmann's, Erikson's, and Weisman's—brings us to the present and completes the first part of our story. So far, it emerges as a story that runs into an impasse from which there seems to be no exit. Why should these very gifted minds have such difficulty in breaking out of what is, after all, an impasse of the mind's own making? Perhaps we can guess at an answer by venturing to borrow psychoanalysis' own vivid terminology and speak—with all due respect—of a philosophical neurosis, which has congealed at the very center of this discipline.

Like all neuroses, this one too has its genesis in "childhood." In its earliest years psychoanalysis was exposed to the hostility, misunderstanding, and sometimes open derision of an alien world. It responded by walling itself up from the environment that rejected it, and by clutching tightly the set of ideas that had seemed, originally, to provide its identity. The resulting philosophical neurosis now comprises a firmly entrenched system of intellectual defenses that was once adaptive, and is still stubbornly clung to long after its adaptiveness has ceased—and when, in fact, these defenses impede adaptation. Like any defense mechanism, this scheme of ideas continues to be tenaciously held and it exacts a great drain of energy to maintain: the analyst can spend an inordinate amount of time and effort in trying to squeeze his clinical findings into the framework of the formal metapsychology. Then, too, like all neurotic structures, this scheme of ideas creates intrapsychic conflict—in this case, between the psychoanalyst as physician and the psychoanalyst as theorist. And, as often happens, the conflict when fully activated exerts a paralyzing effect, since it prevents the analyst from going beyond his theory to pursue fresh developments in his own material as well as in the outside world.

The comparison of the assumptions in psychoanalysis to neurotic defenses may be exaggerated here for the sake of emphasis. But it is not made in a spirit of denigration or in an effort to win empty verbal points at the expense of psychoanalysis. On the contrary: we are utterly sympathetic to the goals, as we also admire the discoveries of both psychoanalysis and the other human sciences. The aspirations to create a science of man can be, we believe, a great positive force in modern life. A science of man need not be a jailhouse of the human spirit nor turn man into an impersonal object—provided we have a more concrete and adequate grasp of what scientific understanding in these fields comes to; that is, provided we can cure ourselves of the "philosophic neurosis." But unless the conflict in basic ideas presently frustrating the human sciences can be resolved, their promise and their dream may never be fully realized.

The nature of the assumptions that comprise this philosophical neurosis have to do mainly with three topics: how psychoanalysis answers the ancient Platonic question of what is most real in human life; how it answers the question of what place, if any, human freedom has in a science of man; and how it defines the nature of the human self. Considered together, ideas on these subjects have dominated Western thought in one or another version from its Graeco-Hebraic origins. In the early years of modern science they were given a particular interpretation, one that helped the physical sciences to prosper but loaded the dice against the sciences of man.

In the history of the West there are not more than a half-dozen occasions when the dominant philosophy of an epoch gave way to a fundamentally new outlook. Today there are signs that new philosophical modes of understanding are beginning to arise, perhaps for the first time in several hundred years. Psychoanalysis is not a mere accessory to such stirrings; it is the most appropriate vehicle through which such a new philosophy could emerge. At one time physics played the role of midwife to new philosophies. Today psychoanalysis is a more likely candidate for the honor: this time the new philosophy must develop out of a science concerned with human experience rather than with inanimate nature.

PART THREE

A FRESH START
PHILOSOPHICALLY

ELEVEN

Why a Metapsychology?

There remains a fifth strategy, more simple and drastic than any of the previous four: a straightforward act of surgery that would eliminate the metapsychology altogether.

In view of the many difficulties associated with the imposition of the metapsychology, this strategy has great appeal to many psychoanalysts. The metapsychology is almost always the focus of criticism both within and outside psychoanalysis. The term itself has a somewhat ambiguous status—the "meta" indicating an unresolved relation to the actual content of psychoanalysis. Suppose one were to scrap this metapsychology as a dated and now unprofitable piece of metaphysics. Does anything of psychoanalysis remain? Indeed, very much does remain, for psychoanalysis has accumulated a vast body of experience year in and year out, in session after session with patient after patient. Why not, then, take this clinical and empirical observation as the essential activity of psychoanalysis, and its results as the really valid knowledge that the analyst has to impart, without feeling called upon to erect a basic metapsychological theory at all?

This proposal has been put forward in a persuasive form by psychologist George Klein (1966); and since to dispense with the metapsychology altogether would greatly simplify our task, we have now to consider the merits of this proposal carefully.

To begin with, we have first to take a careful look at this empirical core of psychoanalysis as a whole—the parts of psychoanalysis that lie beneath the metapsychology. The first and the most secure part of psychoanalysis is its data-base. The raw data, the psychoanalytic observables, are obtained by a combination of methods whose scientific excellence has generally been underestimated. The psychoanalytic interview is, in point of fact, an excellent combination of phenomenological and experimental techniques. The phenomenological aspect emerges principally in relation to the prime rule of such an interview —namely, the technique of free association. The subject is encouraged to reveal his total psychological mass by adhering strictly to the rule that he verbalize all thoughts, images, and feelings as they occur to him without attempting to censor or without regard to the normal social amenities. He lets be whatever comes to the surface, however embarrassing, childish, irrelevant, or socially unacceptable the thought or feeling that he has thereby to express. All this is obviously in line with the essential point of the phenomenological approach: that the basic data must be allowed to show themselves in all their fullness and concreteness. (Phenomenon is from the Greek verb *phainesthai*, to show or reveal itself.)

The orthodox psychoanalytic situation has the respondent lying on a couch, not facing the interviewer, in order to minimize face-to-face encounter. This technical rule is intended to encourage the development of the transference relationship, which could scarcely be built up as well in the context of the normal two-person social situation. The interviewer, the physician, is trained to listen to the responses of his patient in an attitude of "free-floating attention" without prejudging and without imposing Procrustean interpretations. Again, these procedures are in line with the general principle of phenomenology that we must have recourse "to the things themselves" without, initially at least, distorting them by preconceived notions.

In a typical training situation, the young analyst will rush in with premature interpretations and explanations for the patient's problems. Learning restraint in interpretation is one of the most valuable lessons analysts derive from their training. One cardinal rule of psychoanalysis runs: "When in doubt—wait and listen."

In practice, the therapeutic commitment of the physician may play havoc with the phenomenological aspects of the psychoanalytic interview. The doctor has not only to observe but to cure; and, accordingly, the scientific research elements in the analytic situation will often be sacrificed to therapeutic goals. Nevertheless, it is important to note, as Freud himself did, that even within the therapeutic restrictions, the psychoanalyst has at his disposal a superb research instrument. An immense fund of data is obtainable from even a single individual, especially one who is highly motivated as well as disciplined to express the stream of his psychological processes of thought and feeling. A full-scale psychoanalysis will extend over a period of several years and average hundreds of hours. The incredibly detailed output about the single individual gained in this way constitutes an invaluable source of data which is scarcely matched in the research repertory of psychology as a whole.

Moreover, beyond these phenomenological possibilities, the analytic interview provides a unique, if subtle, opportunity for experimentation. True, the psychoanalytic situation does not reproduce the classic controlled experiment. The analyst is not a detached god who can play with the life of the patient. However, one must remember that rigidly controlled experiments have as their prime purpose the testing of hypotheses and not the gathering of observable data. The usual gathering of data, so far as it employs experimental methods, proceeds by means of interventions in a situation under fairly well-defined conditions, followed by careful observation of the results of such interventions. Though he must be judicious and circumspect, the analyst constantly intervenes in his patient's life-situation by offering certain interpretations, and he constantly observes the latter's reactions to those interpretations. Events in the patient's day-to-day life outside the interview-hour also intervene and the analyst is in a privileged position to catch the patient's reactions to these. In both cases, intervention by the analyst and by external events, the precise observations of the patient's reactions become an invaluable part of the total body of observables.

The analyst's interpretive interventions are not random and unselective, but designed to achieve that psychological state in the patient known as the *transference neurosis*. The analyst begins by treating the ego defenses of the patient in order to get at the repressed material they safeguard. One major finding of psychoanalysis is that such a procedure (if a therapeutic alliance has already been established) causes the patient to project onto the analyst attitudes, emotions, and responses appropriate to some emotionally significant person in the patient's past life, typically parents and siblings. To expedite the development of the transference, the analyst keeps his real personality vague and in the background.

For many years the therapeutic efficacy of psychoanalysis was believed to reside exclusively in the working through of the transference relationship. Recently, however, more emphasis has been placed on the real relationship between the therapist and the patient—the therapeutic alliance. The complicated interplay between these two relationships—the *real* one of the therapeutic alliance, which is between the two actual human beings, doctor and patient; and the *projective* relationship of the transference neurosis, which is really between the patient and the people of his childhood via the psychoanalyst—is a current focus of interest within the psychoanalytic community. What we wish to emphasize, however, is the fact that this interplay as a whole, this gradual establishment of the transference relationship within the context of the therapeutic alliance, provides a remarkable human experiment, ideally designed to elicit a body of data that is not available to any other technique within the whole body of psychology.

Of course, many scientists tend to dismiss this data as "merely" subjective or private interpretation. They recognize its richness while deploring the privacy, lack of controls, difficulty of distinguishing between data and interpretation, and the element of subjectivity that is always associated with clinical data. These objections do have some weight. From a purely scientific point of view, the therapeutic commitment of the analyst and his frequent lack of research interest or training can play havoc with the data and make them scientifically unusable. The method of compilation itself—typically, summary notes made by a physician who is more concerned with helping his patient than with advancing knowledge—tends to make the data unusable by anyone but the analyst himself. It is true that in recent years steps have been taken to introduce more objective methods of data-gathering by the use of tape recorders, cameras, and other instruments. But it must also be confessed that these steps are still in their infancy, and the analytic interview still remains, by and large, an intimate, but scientifically rough-and-ready affair.

In the end, however, these objections against the empirical credentials of psychoanalysis are not conclusive, but have to do with questions of technique rather than of principle. The same or similar objections would have to be made against many other fields of research. Where the data are subtle and complex, subtle and complex modes of perception may be required; and, consequently, there is the greater danger of subjective coloring or distortion in interpretation. Yet for this danger there is also a recourse—the only recourse against subjective bias that is open to all the sciences—namely, the free communication with fellow scientists in the light of which a one-sided or personally colored view can come to be tested by the findings of others and by more formal research procedures. Admittedly, this process might be a little more difficult, a little slower, and more groping in psychoanalysis than in other disciplines, because the ordinary analyst, usually overworked in his practice, does not have enough time to bring the full materials of his cases before his fellow scientists. But to argue because of this difficulty against the empirical basis of psychoanalysis is equivalent to arguing that there can really be no ore in a gold mine because conditions of terrain and location make the labor of extraction painstaking and time-consuming. The argument is made all the weaker when we already know that there is no other mine within the whole of psychology that provides so rich an ore for understanding the individual person in his intimate depth and complexity.

In addition to its data-base, the large body of specifically clinical findings of psychoanalysis also help to validate its empirical credentials. These findings are stated as propositions, of varying levels of generality. Some of these propositions are peculiar to psychoanalysis, some belong to our general everyday discourse about the development of human beings. Rapaport and Gill (1959) distinguish three levels of generality of psychoanalytic concepts apart from the most general level of the metapsychology itself: "empirical propositions," "specific psychoanalytic propositions," and "general psychoanalytic propositions." For our purposes we need not break these down so fine; and, in fact, we believe it confusing to do so. Let us refer to all such propositions collectively as findings (or hypotheses), thus distinguishing them on the one hand from the observables (the raw data) and on the other hand from the metapsychology (statements about the psychic apparatus). Examples of "findings" are:

—Around the fourth year of life boys begin to regard their fathers as rivals.

—The sexual development of the child is interrupted at about the sixth year by a latency period that lasts until puberty.

—The anxieties of early childhood, especially those relating to separation from the mother, frequently play a major etiological role in the psychoneuroses.

—Major repressions take place in early childhood.

—Adult obsessive-compulsive neurotics display certain character traits and attitudes toward money, cleanliness, and order that have their origins in early toilet training.

It is unlikely that anyone has ever attempted to count these varied hypotheses, but hundreds of them have been advanced within psychoanalytic doctrine. To call them "findings" does not imply that they have been subject to formal proof. Informally, however, they are tested over and over again in everyday clinical experience, and they stand up as generally valid guideposts for psychoanalytic practice.

These data bear no relation to the present metapsychology; they would remain just as they are without the orthodox metapsychological theory. Their validity (or lack of it) rests on clinical evidence, not on the *a priori* constructions of metapsychology. On this point, which we have stressed throughout, we are in agreement with Professor Klein. We would also agree with him that the range of empirical materials provided through clinical observation is enough to keep psychoanalysts busy full-time. Yet, having granted these points, we must disagree with his thesis that analysts keep their noses at the clinical grindstone and forgo any attempt to build a more basic theory.

First of all, it is always a dangerous procedure for the scientist, wearied and disillusioned by an unacceptable theory, to plunge into the waters of a pure, rough-and-ready, no-holds-barred empiricism. The impulse to theorize, turned out at the front door, returns by the back. The history of science abounds in cases where a total rejection of philosophical questions, along with the hard-headed resolve to deal with the facts and only the facts, has produced its own dogmatic and usually unconscious forms of metaphysics. As the economist Keynes remarked in another connection, the person who insists that he is without any philosophy whatever, usually has an unconscious philosophy inherited from some defunct metaphysician. Research can run around in circles if it is not guided by some fundamental conceptions of the field it studies and the nature of the objects that lie within that field. In the case of psychoanalysis, we have to ask what, after all, the human person is. In what fundamental terms are we to conceive of human personality with any tolerable degree of adequacy? The terms that we choose will focus and even shape our clinical experience through and through. The notion of psychoanalysis as a body of empirical findings, held together in a rather loose-jointed amalgam, leaves the theory floating in the air with no solid mooring. In the analogous case of medicine, the clinical observations of physicians over the centuries accumulated an indispensable body of experience; but to insist that medicine restrict itself to being no more than a vast compilation of rule-of-thumb observations would deprive this science of its roots in anatomy, physiology, and chemistry.

We agree with Freud's insistence that "the nature of the psychic apparatus must be reserved for philosophic reflection" —which implies that the philosophical underpinnings are indispensable but at the same time in perpetual need of scrutiny.

Perhaps the most compelling reason for not accepting Professor Klein's demurrer against attempting a reform in basic theory lies in the overwhelming power of the Zeitgeist itself. In the present climate of opinion, not to change the basic theory is simply to leave the reigning philosophy enthroned. This climate of opinion is not a matter of passing fashions or changing decades. It is an epochal climate of three centuries that has become the historical destiny of the West, with this latter now drawing the rest of the world in its wake. This climate, extending far beyond psychoanalysis, pervades every form of our social and scientific life, particularly in our own country, and rules all the more strongly where it is unconscious. How shall we name it? Looking at it historically, we can call it variously the Cartesian or the Cartesian-Newtonian epoch or, following Max Weber, the era of rationalization.

Descartes sketched the project for a new mode of human thinking, which Newton's extraordinary accomplishment in physics both fulfilled and entrenched. To say that this is the framework within which Western thinking still moves does not mean that those who cannot look beyond that framework have actually read Descartes or, if they did, would spontaneously recognize their thought as it is expressed in his terms. An epochal climate is a far more subtle, powerful, and fateful thing than that. Freud did not erect his theory of the psychic apparatus only because he had been under the early influence of Brücke, Meynert, and Helmholtz. This perspective for viewing him is much too narrow. The short span of Brücke and Helmholtz is itself held inescapably within the grip of the encompassing Cartesian epoch. Freud thought as he did because it was impossible for him to think any other way, impossible to find any ground of intelligibility or explanation beyond the Cartesian-Newtonian restrictions.* Psychoanalysis has remained mired within that framework to this very day, and unless we recognize the Cartesianism of our own epoch in its full manifestation and density we shall be unable to break new ground.

But before proceeding to that, let us repeat as forcefully as we can, that if psychoanalysis fails to attempt a reform of metapsychology and plunges instead into pure clinical observation and measurement, it will *de facto* leave entrenched the prevailing philosophy. Within the arena of contemporary psychology, psychoanalysts are constantly pressed by experimentalists and others who taunt them by insinuating that psychoanalysis is not "scientific." Under this pressure, they tend to borrow the presuppositions and even to imitate the methods of their critics. "Scientific" psychology, however, is itself one

---

* The sources of Freud's full range of thought are extraordinarily broad, extending far beyond his scientific interests. The point we are making here is that when Freud attempted to think within the mode of strict science—as he did in his metapsychology—his thought narrows to fit itself tightly within this frame.

of the most distinct contemporary descendants of Cartesianism. Such an assertion might seem far-fetched if applied to that most elusive of the behaviorists, Professor B. F. Skinner, who rejects all talk of mind, Cartesian or otherwise. Yet behaviorism insists on the primacy of the computable and calculable as the real reality for science, assigning all other experience to the merely "subjective"; from the very beginning this is a way of thinking that is dominated by the drastic Cartesian bifurcation of the world into subject and object. It is significant therefore that Professor Klein, rejecting the metapsychology, offers as his positive program for the improvement of psychoanalysis certain technical suggestions: the introduction of sound-recorders, cameras, possibly electronic equipment for recording brain impulses, etc., etc. The culmination of the Cartesian epoch is marked of course by the dominance of technique, or technology. When Descartes sketched out the project for a mathematical science of nature, he was laying the ground for the domination of nature by machines, although this project was not to emerge clearly until much later. It has continued with gradually accelerating force until it has now become the overriding fact in Western history. The contemporary frenzy about technology as the perpetual hope of solving all human problems descends from the same Cartesian thought that led Freud to his theory of the psychic apparatus. The trouble, we suspect, is that Professor Klein, while advancing a very incisive logical critique of the metapsychology, has failed to confront its historical roots in Cartesian thinking, and therefore is caught up in another branch that grows from the same root.

Historical Background

In the West, before the Renaissance and the birth of modern science, a coherent world view held sway for over eight long centuries. It is beautifully described by H. O. Taylor in his classic work, *The Medieval Mind*:

> . . . the peoples of western Europe, from the eighth to the thirteenth centuries, passed through a homogeneous

growth, and evolved a spirit different from that of any other period of history—a spirit which stood in awe before its monitors divine and human, and deemed that knowledge was to be drawn from the storehouse of the past; which seemed to rely on everything except its sin-crushed self, and trusted everything except its senses; which in the actual looked for the ideal, in the concrete saw the symbol, in the earthly Church beheld the heavenly, and in fleshly joys discerned the devil's lures; which lived in the unreconciled opposition between the lust and vain-glory of earth and the attainment of salvation; which felt life's terror and its pitifulness and its eternal hope; around which waved concrete infinitudes, and over which flamed the terror of darkness and the Judgment Day (p. 13).

Only against that medieval background, at once somber and luridly lighted, can we understand the full explosive impact of the revolution in thought capped by Galileo, Descartes, and Newton which marked the end of more than eight centuries of medievalism. It set the mold of the modern Western mind as it has existed ever since. The heritage of the great seventeenth century created modern science, undermined speculative philosophy, gave rise to modern technology, and, in conjunction with social and economic forces, led to the decline of religion as a dominant theme in daily life.

It would have been well if the dazzling triumphs of the New Sciences had been taken for the useful tools they were— if men had recognized that they were here furnished with a new set of abstractions of an amazing ingenuity, which permitted precise calculation of the behavior of certain restricted and artificial systems (like machines), or of certain inertial systems like the movements of the planets or of falling bodies, or generally of those material processes in nature that approximated to the abstractions themselves. These new abstractions provided a practical tool for engineering and technology, achievements so gigantic that they would ultimately transform the earth and man's relation to it. On the side of pure theory, the new discoveries brought with them a mathematics of inexhaustible intellectual delight and of unexampled fecundity for the discovery of new mathematical truths.

These glories would have been enough to celebrate a new epoch in human history. But revolutions have an unfortunate way of becoming total and blotting out all ideas except those that are inscribed on their own banners. So the dazzling triumphs within mathematical physics became codified into a total world-view. The abstractions of the Cartesian-Newtonian epoch, which had worked so well for certain systems, were taken as the ultimate concrete elements of reality in all realms of life. It began to seem "self-evident" that behind every apparency in nature or man the hidden and determining reality must be material forces, moving according to the mechanical laws described by the new physics. In the eighteenth and nineteenth centuries, the mathematical concepts of Newton, as Koyré has pointed out, were turned into a kind of reified solid geometry. (1965.) Whitehead sums up this new metaphysics born of the new physics most incisively:

> There persists (throughout the past three centuries) the fixed scientific cosmology which presupposes the ultimate fact of an irreducible brute matter, or material, spread throughout space in a flux of configurations. In itself, such a material is senseless, valueless, purposeless. It just does what it does do, falling into a fixed routine imposed by external relations which do not spring from its being. It is this assumption that I call "scientific materialism." (Whitehead, 1925, p. 23.)

Brilliant and incisive as is Whitehead's full analysis of the Cartesian legacy in his *Science and the Modern World*, particularly of its physical and metaphysical assumptions, he does not deal comprehensively with the human and epistemological consequences of Cartesianism. The reason may be that Whitehead was not a close reader of Kant, in whom these latter consequences are brought to full expression almost a century after the death of Descartes.

Kant had been an eager and diligent student of mathematical physics in his youth, and all his life he continued to reflect upon the significance and method of this science. Out of this reflection came the profoundest statement yet of what the revolution of the New Science really consisted in: namely, that the precision of the New Science derives from the imposition of human forms, that is, human concepts, upon nature. Mathematics, after all, was the instrument through which this precision came about; but mathematics was not to be found lying about in nature, it was clearly a construction of the human mind itself. The Greeks may have thought that the elements of geometry are perceptually given in nature, thence to be abstracted by the mind (if you draw the triangles and circles carefully enough in the sand you have only to look and think to derive the essential forms and relations). But when you come to the analytic geometry of Descartes, with it arbitrary correlations of numbers and magnitudes, and to the calculus of Newton, with its even more ingenious artifices of limits and integrals, it is clear that you are not dealing with simple abstractions from perceived nature but with man-made constructions—albeit constructions that prove extraordinarily fertile in helping us predict the behavior of certain systems. On the side of experiment, too, Kant saw that the power of the new method from Galileo through Torricelli was in the experimenter's imposing his own selected conditions upon phenomena. In this case, not only did the experimenter impose his man-made constructions or concepts but also man-made instruments and machinery in order to see how the phenomena measured up to these imposed forms.

Kant compresses all these thoughts in one remarkable passage in the preface to the *Critique of Pure Reason*:

When Galileo caused balls, the weights of which he himself had previously determined, to roll down an inclined plane; when Torricelli made the air carry a weight which he had calculated beforehand to be that of a definite column of water; or in more recent times, when Stahl changed metal into lime, and lime back into metal, by withdrawing something and then restoring it, a light broke upon all students of nature. They learned that *reason has insight only into that which it produces after a plan of its own,* and that it must not allow itself to be kept, as it were, in nature's leading strings, but must itself show the way . . . constraining nature to give answer to questions of reason's own determining. (P. 26.) (Our italics.)

With the insight of genius, Kant has here seen not only into the nature of the New Science of Galileo and Newton, but also into what this science has increasingly become in our own time —particularly in recent physics and information theory.

"Reason has insight only into that which it produces after a plan of its own." In modern parlance, this statement might read: An experiment is a programmed plan from which information can be read only within the framework of its programming. Here is a thinker whose depth of reflection is given practical validation a century and a half after his death. All of Kant's examples are drawn from the physical sciences; nevertheless, Kant's remarks are equally prophetic for the human sciences today, though this time in a negative sense, in respect to the quandary into which they have fallen. For if the experimenter has insight only in the light of the plan he himself has produced, then an inadequate and one-sided plan may prevent him from seeing all of his data. A good plan is an instrument of vision; conversely, a bad plan becomes not merely a deficiency, but a positive obstacle that causes distortion and blindness. What "plan of its own," to use Kant's words again, is the experimenter's "reason" going to impose upon the material? Such precisely is the quandary that has afflicted experimenters in the human sciences in our time. And this quandary underscores the need for an adequate basic theory, or metapsychology, without which meaningful and adequate plans of experimentation and investigation are not likely to be produced.

In pursuing his line of thought, Kant carried the subjectivism of Descartes rigorously through to the end. On the face of it, this Cartesian subjectivism is one of the most paradoxical aspects of his thought. For here is a mode of thought that seeks quantitative precision about nature, seeks above all to base itself upon the objectively calculable. But the method and the mathematical instrument that make such precise calculation possible are of the mind's own fabrication. Certainty and precision derive from consciousness, and it is from those ideas, begotten by consciousness itself, that material nature can be manipulated with clarity and distinctness. Here, then, is the enormous paradox in Cartesianism which launched the modern epoch! The

requirement of strict and calculable objectivity begets the extreme subjectivization of mind as knower.*

Descartes squirmed uneasily between the tension of these
opposing demands, but Kant resolutely accepted the consequences. If knowledge—that is, what can really claim to be
exact and cogent knowledge—results from the imposition of
human conditions upon the material of experience, it is foolish
to ask what things are in themselves. (Nietzsche was quite
right to see here a momentous, if unconscious, assertion of the
human will to power.)

Does this mean that psychologists and philosophers and all
the rest of us are professed Kantians? Such an assertion would
betray an oversimplified conception of the meaning of philosophy as a part of human history. The authentic history of
philosophy is not a succession of human opinions strung out
serially in time like clothes on a clothesline. The great philosophers are not spinners of more or less interesting speculations
out of thin air; rather, they bring to expression the half-hidden
assumptions of their time, which without them would exist only
as diffuse and unformulated thoughts and attitudes. But in
bringing this spirit of their time into the light they are also
prophetic of the themes that mankind in ensuing generations
and even centuries will have to play out within the sphere of
its scientific and social life. The movement of thought from
Descartes through the modern philosophers until, past Hegel,
it breaks out explosively in all the fragmented ideological fire-
works of the nineteenth century and our own, is not a sequence
that moves parallel to the movement of the rest of history in
this period; it is the light in which that process of history as a
whole is to be read.†
The Cartesian Revolution imposes a conceptual framework in

---

* Which is why Avery Weisman, for all of his searching inquiry into
the existential core of psychoanalysis, remains fixed within a Cartesian
frame.
† These claims for philosophy as authentic history may seem exaggerated in view of the fragmented and often inconsequential state of
philosophy (or should we say philosophies?) today. But may not that
fragmentation be precisely an expression of our present condition?
And when some philosophers today seriously put forward the most
hair-raising thoughts, judged from a human point of view, are they

the light of which the phenomena are to be selected and organized, and a selected physical arrangement or apparatus within whose setting the phenomena are to be produced and observed. These two types of conditions are not usually fortuitously concurrent; they often have to be manufactured artificially. The conditions (in the form of conceptual schemes) which man imposes upon the phenomena dictate the conditions (in the form of physical apparatuses) in which the phenomena will be elicited and observed. The relation may also go the other way: a newly invented apparatus may require the creation of a new conceptual scheme to be imposed upon the phenomena. An experimental genius like Rutherford, by contriving a new apparatus, created the necessity for a new and highly abstract theory of the atom. In our own day, the computer and even the telephone create new conceptual frameworks (rather than the other way around). In the historical development of chemistry and physics, there has been an ever-ascending complexity in the accompanying technology. Photographs of some of the original equipment in Rutherford's early laboratories look outlandishly naive and simple in comparison with the elaborate gadgets of physicists today—somewhat like the Wright brothers' first plane beside a modern jet. Nowadays, a university wishing to recruit even a moderately distinguished physicist for its faculty may have to promise him, in addition to a handsome salary, many hundreds and thousands of dollars in equipment.

In this connection there is the highly suggestive comment by Heidegger, which we put forward here without arguing, that technology was from the first the hidden essence of the New Science. True, technology does not seem to emerge until the Industrial Revolution a century after the Cartesian-Newtonian revolution; but it is only after planting and the passage of time that the acorn reveals that it was essentially directed toward the oak. If the New Science began at any single moment in time, it was when Galileo constructed the artificial condition for defining inertia: a ball set rolling on a frictionless plane will continue rolling in a straight line *ad infinitum*. In fact, we do

not being prophetic of a derangement of mind toward which our whole culture may be traveling? On the other hand, we believe that there are glimmerings here and there amid all the contemporary philosophic confusion that may light the dawn of a new epoch.

not find any frictionless planes or any infinite straight lines in nature. Galileo thus launches modern physics with a contrary-to-fact condition. Yet this supposition, which is not found in experience, has immense fertility for calculating certain effects within experience. Modern physics would thus begin as a theory of artificial systems, which whether constructed mentally or eventually realized approximately in some apparatus, would be, at least in part, a theory of technology.

Technology does not reside in a piece of equipment as a sheer chunk of matter. Children playing around an abandoned cyclotron are not using it as a technical apparatus. It does not even become a technical instrument in the hands of a single scientist; a whole team of scientists is needed to operate this machine, and only then does it become, properly speaking, a piece of technology. It is thus of the essence of technology that it requires, in addition to machines, the calculated organization of men. As the technology becomes more elaborate, there arise problems of capital outlays, disposition of resources, and assignment of personnel. Science becomes a form of management. Beyond the calculative thought that Descartes and Kant saw the creative scientist imposing on his material, there enters now the calculation of the planner managing a scientific program.

Inevitably, this predominance of complex organization and apparatus colors what we think science is or what scientific results should be. In the popular mind, the gigantic apparatus must itself produce something gigantic or sensational, or both. But it is not only the popular mind that succumbs to the sheer lure of technique. In the present climate of opinion it is harder to imagine the Nobel Prize for biology being awarded to a naturalist who studies life in the field than to scientists whose discoveries are produced in the laboratory. To make the point as specific as possible, compare Pavlov's studies of dogs with those of Konrad Lorenz. The Nobel Prize was awarded to Pavlov and is less likely to be awarded to Lorenz. Lorenz has studied dogs by living with them, breeding them, and, in short, letting the dogs be dogs. But does this not seem less "scientific" than the Pavlovian approach of strapping the dog in a man-made harness, subjecting him to man-made and mechanically produced signals, and measuring the quantity of saliva he exudes? As good Cartesian-Kantians, we must impose our human technological forms upon the dog. He is not to be let be a dog; before he can become a subject for science, he must be turned into a Cartesian object.

We have to add immediately that we are not in the least against the Pavlovian type of experiment. Quite the contrary. We wish only to show the intellectual ancestry of a certain prejudice for one and only one method in science (the experimental method), and at the same time to indicate the limits of that method. Suppose an intelligent creature from Mars, who had never seen a dog, were to arrive on earth. Wanting to learn about a dog, he is taken to a laboratory and shown a dog in harness being subjected to the stimulus of food and the sound of a gong. What would our Martian learn? That a dog is a creature capable of being conditioned by a stimulus—something that every dog owner knows, though somehow the master's whistle seems much less "scientific" than the mechanically produced sound of a bell. But what would the Martian not know about a dog? He would have no idea that this creature is capable of choosing a master, that it can be sensitive to the smallest movements and moods of the latter, and that it can in certain conditions learn things almost "on the spot" without persistent and routine conditioning. The Martian would have no idea of the long evolutionary bond between man and dog, or how the dog is related to other animal species, and what characteristics of the different breeds derive from those relationships. Above all, the Martian would not have the least idea that different dogs have distinct individual personalities of their own. Yet all these are quite crucial characteristics of dogs, and it is prejudicial to say they are not "scientifically" known simply because they are not the products of laboratory experiments.

This prejudice, indeed, is so endemic and unconscious that one can easily imagine that the great Darwin himself would not be given a Nobel Prize were he now alive. Darwin's originality was not as a general theorist; the idea of evolution was very much in the air, and even in the theory of natural selection he was anticipated by Wallace. The Darwinian genius lay in his great sensitivity as an observer in the field, the extraordinary range of his knowledge of flora and fauna as they are found in nature, and above all his imagination—which found not only links between different species but also the "purposes" of certain characteristics and behavior. For, contrary to the dogmatism that has prevailed since the seventeenth century that

science can only ask the question "How?" and never "Why?",
Darwin persistently asks "Why?" In this light we have to understand the force of his remark that "Aristotle was my real
master; in comparison with him, Linnaeus and the others were
mere schoolboys." Like Aristotle before him, Darwin was an
unabashed teleologist. Had he not been—had he not persistently
asked "Why?"—the theory of evolution would still be merely
a philosophical speculation. Darwin used no elaborate technical
apparatus, and he had no laboratory unless it was nature itself.

The prejudice, deriving from Cartesianism, in favor of measurement by mechanical devices over all other modes of knowing, pervades the most mundane aspects of our lives. Under
government Medicare regulations, for example, a physician may
charge no more than $10 for a diagnostic interview, but he
can change $15 for a laboratory test. Now, for the trained
internist, the diagnostic interview is the hardest part of his
job, just about the only part that totally resists mechanization.
Here is where his many years of training and experience come
into play in interpreting the precise nature of his patient's aches
and pains, and in skillfully drawing out the information he
needs for his diagnosis. The tests are important but they are
supplementary. Furthermore, in terms of his own time and
expense, they are negligible compared to the time and concentrated attention required by a skillful interview. But in the
formal institutionalizing of medical services, which accurately
reflects the value structure of the culture, it is the technological
side of his expertness that is more highly valued in dollars and
cents (and in other ways) than the direct human encounter
of the interview.

In our era of advancing technology, in which the Cartesian
epoch moves inexorably toward its culmination, it is perfectly
understandable that the behaviorists take the line they do.
Science, according to this view, consists, as Francis Bacon remarked, in putting nature on the rack: i.e., the scientist imposes his man-made conditions upon his material. The dog is
strapped in harness, the rat put in a man-made maze. (It would
be a much more troublesome business to let the rat run around
the household and observe him as a "free" agent, and besides
he would certainly gnaw at the furniture.) A peculiar difficulty,
however, arises when we come to human psychology. For if

science arises when man imposes his own conceptual forms upon his material, here man would be imposing the forms upon himself. But what kind of forms? Obviously, those of conceptual or calculative thinking. It is no wonder then that the material is assimilated to these formal conditions, for the latter will admit only what conforms to their requirements. Thus, technical man, as scientist, meets technical man as subject. The behaviorist savant finds himself on his own doorstep. It seems to us highly significant that the accomplishments of the behaviorists have been largely in matters of technique, in the construction of courses of programmed learning and the rest, precisely where man is involved as a calculating and technical being. Nor is it any wonder that behaviorists should have sensed in Freud their mortal enemy. For the paradox of Freud is that in this century of ever-accumulating technology, while hobbled by his own Cartesian-Newtonian preconceptions and even harboring in the concept of the psychic apparatus the image of a rather odd Victorian steam boiler, he nevertheless brings us into the world of Greek tragedy, i.e., of inherent human limitations. Such notions are alien to the world of technique and to the value systems of the behaviorist. For the behaviorist is often caught up by a prejudice against anything that smacks of an intransigent human nature; not only do such beliefs seem unscientific and not part of an enlightened, liberal, and modern mind, they also conjure up a retrogressive conservatism which suggests that there are limits to the process of manipulating man by manipulating the environment.

The proliferation of technique and the companion belief in the infinite malleability of nature are seen not only in science but in modern society as a whole. A good case could be made that the dominance of technology has now become the central fact of our era. It is technology that has shrunk the globe and made it one world at last, has brought about the increasing urbanization of mankind, and supports the ever-increasing numbers of human beings in the population explosion. These developments have changed man's relation to nature, since he comes to live more and more within the network of human contrivance; and, consequently, have changed man's relation to himself. The Cartesian era, which began with a theoretical bifurcation of man from nature, has now developed to the point where that bifurcation is becoming a *social* and *human* fact. Moreover, the advance of technology has an impetus of its own; no one can stop it and no one can readily be "against" it, for the lives of millions depend upon it; it is the movement of history in our time. This essay is not a social treatise, and we propose to halt at the frontiers of a sociology of Cartesianism. We do not have space even to indicate the extraordinary change that the Cartesian spirit has brought in man's relation to one of the most precious products of his culture—art. We have merely pointed to these vast historical and social processes to call attention to the fact that thought reflects our modes of living, and that the dominant thought of the era—the thinking of scientists included—is likely to be shaped by the dominant modes of life of the time.

Against the full historical context of Cartesianism, in all its concreteness, we cannot follow Professor Klein's advice that the fundamental reform of psychoanalysis must be mainly an improvement in technique. On the contrary: what the science of man now requires is some fundamental illumination that will make intelligible the very application of technique.

Psychoanalysis, then, we must conclude, cannot dispense with that philosophic scrutiny that Freud himself acknowledged as necessary. Moreover, such self-scrutiny—it should be equally evident by now—cannot be done in splendid isolation from other disciplines that figure in the background. Psychoanalysis is only part of a larger picture; its theoretical troubles, far from being unique, also afflict biology, psychology, sociology, and the other human sciences, where they currently produce the schisms of warring schools. In order to prepare the way for a reconstruction of psychoanalytic metapsychology, we must see its problems against the background of what has happened to scientific materialism as a philosophy of science since Freud's day (Chapter Twelve). Following that, we will take a look at the changed background in contemporary psychology as a whole (Chapter Thirteen). And then, we pass (in Chapters Fourteen and Fifteen) to those developments in contemporary philosophy that provide a source for a fresh start philosophically in the human sciences.

TWELVE

Scientific Materialism— and the Changed Background in Physics

It is one of the more striking paradoxes in the history of psychology that in seeking to establish a science of man on the model of physics, its older and more successful brother, psychology has been severely limited by its imitation, while physics itself has not let its own development be bound by such constrictions. As a result, a good many psychologists today sound as if they were living in the world of the older physics before any of the discoveries had been made in this century within quantum mechanics and nuclear physics generally.

Of course, specific developments within science do not necessarily dictate a change in philosophic outlook. Nevertheless, such developments do often serve to generate a new climate of opinion within which older concepts begin to look one-sided and oversimplified. Thus, today in psychology generally, and in psychoanalysis particularly, concepts which once sounded reasonable enough because they were modeled on physics now seem simplistic or even bizarre when viewed in the light of the changed background in contemporary science.

Our aim in this group of chapters is to prepare the ground for a philosophy that will be better suited than scientific materialism to psychoanalysis and to the human sciences generally. But to do this we must avoid taking any oversimplified view of scientific materialism, which in the light of contemporary discoveries has become a more complex position than might be supposed. Whatever other ideas may be embraced by the philosophy of scientific materialism, its doctrine has essentially to do with matter; but what is meant by matter has in recent years become increasingly problematic. The discoveries of science in quantum physics and in parts of biology like modern genetics redefine our conception of matter and hence carry large philosophical implications germane to our present concerns. We must, therefore, see what a contemporary and updated version of scientific materialism means for the human sciences. Do recent discoveries in science undermine the basic ways of thinking that are codified in scientific materialism? Or do some of these discoveries strengthen the stand of this philosophy? Unless we are able to place the problems of psychoanalysis (and the parallel ones that afflict academic psychology) against the background of contemporary natural science, we shall have less than a clear and total picture.

Let us begin by setting forth the assumptions that have had the most influence in shaping scientific materialism over its long history, both in the past and the present. Since we have made many references to this viewpoint in preceding chapters, we can dispense with a lengthy discussion of it here, and proceed instead to exhibit its bare bones devoid of dense qualification.

We start with that version of scientific materialism which prevailed through most of Freud's lifetime, up to the middle 1920's. Over a span of several centuries, the philosophy of science as influenced mainly by physics gradually developed its own strange picture of reality composed of the following assumptions:

First: of the traditional Cartesian categories, mind and matter, mind can be dispensed with and all reality, including mental phenomena, can be explained by physico-chemical processes (i.e., matter).

Second: matter itself can be reduced to discrete and analyzable elements having the property of simple location.

Third: the basic units or elements of matter are homogeneous in character.

Considered together, these three assumptions imply that whatever is real can be reduced to its material base and all forms of reality can ultimately be analyzed into combinations of nature's basic building-block, the elementary particle or atom. Before Rutherford, Bohr, and others did their work on the fine structure of the atom, this atomic unit was believed to be a small, hard, homogeneous, indivisible and unalterable element, often visualized in philosophical discussions (particularly in England) as a miniature billiard ball.

To complete this stripped-down version of reality, several other assumptions must be identified. A very important fourth assumption is the belief that atomic units of reality are additive. This is the doctrine that states that since all forms of matter, however complex, can be analyzed into their atomic components, the whole is reducible to the sum of its parts. We offer this innocent-sounding bit of "common sense," which in fact harbors the most outlandish metaphysical presuppositions, as an illustration of how old and familiar beliefs can come to sound like self-evident truths, easily passed over and rarely called into question. Indeed, analyzing wholes into their constituent parts has become such a common and acceptable activity in scientific circles that it is sometimes referred to simply as "scientific analysis." The belief that complex wholes, including living organisms, can be explained in terms of their parts was, until the advent of the gestalt point of view in this century, one of the key regulative principles of science.

A fifth assumption, historically important in crystallizing scientific materialism as a philosophy, holds that spatial relationships are the principal forms of relatedness obtaining among chunks of matter. This is one reason why motion has figured so prominently in science: motion, according to this assumption, is one of the few possible forms of change that can take place in the material world.

A sixth assumption maintains that material particles are combined in accordance with certain inexorable laws of nature such as the laws of gravity and motion.

This set of assumptions, considered jointly, has had a number of logical consequences which have been slowly elaborated over a very long period of time (from the seventeenth through the twentieth centuries). One such consequence is the doctrine that all events in nature can be explained by reference to their "causes" (i.e., the immediately preceding events interpreted in accordance with the laws of nature). Long ago, the French scientist, LaPlace, drew from this portrayal of nature the inescapable conclusion that it should be possible, in theory, to predict what would happen throughout all eternity by a correct understanding of what was happening at any one instant of time. *mechanism, determinism*

Another logical derivative of these assumptions is a belief in the unity of nature. If by nature we simply mean matter in its various forms; and if by matter, we mean combinations of atomic particles moving about in space, then the myriads of tiny atoms on earth, the great galaxies in the heavens, and the human world itself can all be "explained" by the same laws of the material world.

The most famous and controversial consequence of these premises is, of course, the belief in the total determinism of human behavior. Being an inherent part of nature, man is subject to its laws and his actions are, therefore, as fully determined as those of any other natural object. (It will be important later to recognize that these three doctrines—causality, the unity of nature, and determinism in man—are not themselves basic in character but are derivative from the more elementary premises of scientific materialism.)

These, then, are some of the assumptions of the philosophy of materialism as based on the physics that prevailed up to the 1920's. But remember that Whitehead used the phrase "scientific materialism," not just "materialism." The qualifier here is not an empty adjective. It conveys an additional set of assumptions relating mainly to how we know the material world by the use of scientific methods. Textbooks on scientific method often begin with a preface extolling the similarities of scientific method and common sense. Science, it is stated, is really "nothing more" than the familiar procedures of common sense, highly organized. Do we not in our day-to-day life have frequent occasion to observe, categorize, generalize, deduce, and even experiment? Well, then, science merely systematizes these steps and carries them out in a more orderly manner.

This analogy is, of course, grossly misleading. The daily life of mankind everywhere and throughout the centuries has been pretty much alike. Other cultures and other times are not marked by any lack of systematized common sense, including observation, categorization, generalization, etc. Yet, only in the West and truly only in the past three centuries has science as we know it today fully developed.

Science as it is actually practiced is nearly always at odds with common sense and textbook descriptions. For example, textbooks say that science always begins with observation. Yet, in practice, observation in science may be seriously scanted. The essence of the presently dominant epistemology in science lies in mathematical abstraction. But the relationship of mathematical abstraction to observation is curiously indirect. Since there are no perfect circles, numbers, factors, vacuums, or frictionless planes lying about in nature, mathematical abstraction is often contrary to fact. Indeed, its very usefulness tends to be proportional to its ability to exclude most of what one actually observes. A mathematical abstraction selects the most remote and general characteristics of what one is observing, excluding almost all of its dense and gritty reality. Therein lies both its strength and its most crippling limitation. For, when we describe the human world, what is excluded by mathematical abstraction is often precisely what is most wanted.

Our discussion of the Cartesian epoch further suggested that current forms of mathematical abstraction lead straight to technology; machines are made to embody its contrary-to-fact abstractions (i.e., artificial conditions not found in nature), and these include what might be called "thought machines" as well as physical ones. We refer here to the contemporary practice of thinking in terms of models and paradigms. These aids to thinking range from so-called "ideal experiments" carried out by scientists when they visualize what would happen if they had ideal instruments at their command, to a broad miscellany of contrary-to-fact statements, paradigms, and analogies that call attention to certain aspects of reality in the abstract.

To complete the picture we must, therefore, add some further assumptions of an epistemological character made by the scientific component of materialism. These maintain that

—We can arrive at scientific truths (hypotheses) by measuring phenomena through mathematical modes of abstraction;

—We can test these hypotheses by constructing contrary-to-fact experiments which embody these self-same abstractions; and

—We may even discover underlying reality by probing behind appearances with this same powerful tool. (Scientists often deny this latter assumption, but in practice it tends to prevail.)

It is these nine or so assumptions which, in combination, should be understood by the term "scientific materialism." To show their consequences, the chart on the facing page lists the answers scientific materialism gives to some of the most fundamental philosophical questions that have plagued men's minds for thousands of years.

From this chart, it will be immediately apparent that we are dealing with a total world view and not merely an accessory to empirical investigation. Scientific materialism does indeed claim to offer answers to what are and have always been the most fundamental philosophic questions: What is really real? (the question with which, in Plato, philosophy virtually begins). What is knowledge? What does valid explanation consist in? Why do things happen as they do? Is man as much a part of nature as the particles and the planets, or is he somehow a being distinct from the rest of nature? Does human freedom exist, or is all human thought and behavior merely the inevitable outcome of antecedent conditions?

A striking correspondence exists between these premises of scientific materialism and the premises of psychoanalytic metapsychology. That they virtually form a one-to-one relationship is shown in the second chart, where the relevant premises of the metapsychology are placed side by side with the corresponding premises of scientific materialism.

It is significant that the philosophy of scientific materialism has become increasingly problematic on its own home grounds —within physics itself. In the light of contemporary physics, one finds that the world of the subatomic particle can scarcely be rendered comprehensible by the heritage of Newton and Descartes. It is gradually becoming clear that the immense range

CHART 1	
Philosophical Question	*Assumption Made by Scientific Materialism*
I. What is *really real?*	The real is that which has the property of simple location.
II. Of what elements is reality composed?	Reality is made up of matter or energy in the form of elementary particles and physico-chemical processes. ~~ATOMIZATIO~~
III. How can we explain the nature of reality?	The whole of reality can be reduced to the sum of its parts. We explain it through "scientific analysis," i.e., breaking down objects into their constituent units and relationships so that they can be objectively measured: in physics the basic unit is the molecule or electron; in biology, the gene; in astronomy, the star; in behaviorism, the unconditioned reflex
IV. What is the relationship of the perceiving subject (the knower) to the perceived object (the known)?	The knower is related to the known through the causal theory of perception. The subject can never know the "true" nature of reality, but only what his senses and measuring devices tell him. External objective stimuli interact with the perceptual apparatus of the subject, "causing" the nervous system to respond.
V. Why do things happen?	Everything that happens is the expression of a few immutable laws of nature.
VI. Is man as much a part of nature as the particles and the planets?	There is homogeneous unity in nature. Man is nothing but a more complex form of organization of the same processes that dominate other aspects of nature; he obeys the same laws.
VII. Does human freedom exist?	Strict determinism prevails. Free will is an illusion. For every effect there is a necessary and sufficient cause.

CHART 2

Philosophical Question	Assumptions Made by Scientific Materialism	Assumptions Made by Freudian Metapsychology
I. What is *really real?*	The real is that which has the property of simple location.	The real is that which can be traced to body processes (i.e., the instinctual drives).
II. Of what elements is reality composed?	Reality is made up of matter or energy in the form of elementary particles and physico-chemical processes.	Psychic reality is made of quantities of instinctual energy. The psychic apparatus is a particular form of organization of these energies.
III. How can we explain the nature of reality?	The whole of reality can be reduced to the sum of its parts. We explain it through "scientific analysis," i.e., breaking down objects into their constituent units and relationships so that they can be objectively measured: in physics the basic unit is the molecule or electron; in biology, the gene; in astronomy, the star; in behaviorism, the unconditioned reflex.	The whole person can be reduced to the sum of his parts—ego, id, and superego. There is no such thing as a person apart from his ego, id, and superego. We explain him metapsychologically by analyzing the quantities of energy and their distribution in the service of the id or the ego.

IV. What is the relationship of the perceiving subject (the knower) to the perceived object (the known)?	The knower is related to the known through the causal theory of perception. The subject can never know the "true" nature of reality, but only what his senses and measuring devices tell him. External objective stimuli interact with the perceptual apparatus of the subject, "causing" the nervous system to respond.	The knower is related to the known by cathecting objects, i.e., by emitting and withdrawing small parcels of energy (including the body as object). The representations of the senses (*Vorstellung*) and the process of thinking itself can be defined in terms of small investments of energy (cathexes). Images are formed by the senses, which collect varying amounts of cathected energy.
V. Why do things happen?	Everything that happens is the expression of a few immutable laws of nature.	Everything that happens is the expression of two immutable laws of nature— Eros and Thanatos; life and death; attraction and repulsion; the urge to procreate versus the urge toward the inorganic. Clinically, these are represented by the instincts of sex and aggression.
VI. Is man as much a part of nature as the particles and the planets?	There is homogeneous unity in nature. Man is nothing but a more complex form of organization of the same processes that dominate other aspects of nature; he obeys the same laws.	There is homogeneous unity in nature. We have not yet been able to trace all psychic acts of man to their physico-chemical causes but this is due only to a lack of knowledge. It will come in time.
VII. Does human freedom exist?	Strict determinism prevails. Free will is an illusion. For every effect there is a necessary and sufficient cause.	Strict psychic determinism prevails. The feeling of freedom is an epi-phenomenon (the causes are merely unconscious).

of this great complex universe—from elementary particles to galaxies—cannot be reduced to the assumptions of a philosophy codified several hundred years ago. Today, Newtonian physics and the philosophy it reflects is seen as a special instance within a more general theory. This is well recognized within physics. But its broader implications have not been fully developed beyond physics because of a few missing links.

Whitehead has stated that he conceived his own philosophy of organism to counteract scientific materialism. Yet, with all deference to the great mathematician-philosopher, Whitehead's philosophy of organism when applied to the human world conveys a strangely dry, remote, and abstract flavor. Why this is so becomes clear when Whitehead tells us that his philosophy of organism did not originate in the study of man or animals but in his deductions from discoveries in physics that were just beginning to become evident in the late 1920's when he wrote his greatest philosophical work.

These discoveries, and more recent ones, cast an entirely new light on the nature of the atom. In the simpler world of earlier physics, the word "atom" meant what it did in the original Greek, an indivisible unit. In contemporary physics, however, the atom is far from being regarded as an elementary unit of matter. Indeed, it is scarcely an exaggeration to talk of the world of the atom, for what is meant by an atom refers to a bewildering variety of entities and processes: these include electrons, protons,* neutrons, mesons, etc. (not to speak of anti-electrons, anti-protons, anti-neutrons, and anti-mesons), all of which fall under the familiar heading of elementary particles as well as under the less familiar heading of antiparticles.

In addition to its particles, we must also include the electromagnetic forces of the atom—a mode of being about which we understand very little. Essentially, electromagnetism in the atom appears to be a form of attraction and repulsion enjoying a different ontological status than particles and not capable of being reduced to them. For very large objects, attraction and repulsion can often be explained in terms of mass and the laws of gravity. But gravity is negligible on the atomic scale and does not seem to account for its electromagnetic force.

Even this partial indication of the processes that comprise

the atom shows how far we have come from the days when the atom was considered indivisible. But we have only begun our inventory. What follows takes us even further away from the simple world of Newton. We must, of course, include the observation that launched quantum physics—the discovery that the atom's radiant energy is emitted in the form of discrete units or packets. This assumption of so-called quantum action is perhaps the most basic presupposition of atomic physics, probably even more fundamental to the subatomic world than the older assumption of simple location which defines its constituent particles. The central problem raised by Max Planck's concept of quantum action was that of describing how the transition process of an electron from one quantum state to another was effected. This difficulty plagued physicists for many years until the theories of De Broglie and Schrödinger identified a wavelike motion to account for subatomic processes. But being a wave is not the same as being a particle or being an electromagnetic force—giving us yet another category of subatomic activity.

We must add still another defining characteristic of the atom, namely the complex forms of inter-relatedness that forge its various elements into a total system. The system encompasses the electrons whirling around the nucleus, the protons and neutrons of the nucleus itself, the forces that hold these together, and the number and position of electrons. The number of electrons, of course, determines the qualitative characteristics of the material world (i.e., the carbon atom contains four electrons, the hydrogen atom one).

Thus, no adequate description of the building-block of matter itself, the atom, is possible without reference to a broad miscellany of elementary particles, electromagnetic forces, pilot waves, quantum action and complex patterns of interrelatedness. The tiny atom exhibits many of the characteristics of an organism with its essential emphasis on structure and form.

---

* Recent experiments suggest that even the proton may not be an elementary and indivisible particle, but possibly an "onionlike" entity with at least one soft outer layer and a harder inner core. (*Physical Review Letters*, A. Kerly, Krisch, *et al.*, November 1966.)

In this "inventory," only the elementary particles can be said to have the property of simple location and mass (and there is now some doubt on this point with respect to electrons). Its other characteristics, particularly that of quantum action, cannot be defined in terms of simple location in any traditional sense of the word. To exaggerate for the sake of making this important point vividly clear, it is as if a man existed in Boston, ceased to exist and then existed once again in New York—without having traveled in any conventional sense of the word from the one city to the other. Other equally "bizarre" characteristics (from a common-sense point of view) are also considered to be inherent aspects of matter—illustrating Whitehead's conclusion that simple location is a high abstraction, not a literal description of reality. In fact, we would do far better to refer to the atom's interrelationships, electromagnetic forces, wavelike motions, and particles as modes of being of the atom rather than as its parts. Referring to them as parts implies a concreteness and a locus that is unjustified, and obscures the crucial point that *all* of these terms are high abstractions.

The above-mentioned categories of mass, electrical charge, waveness, quantum action, relatedness and structure do not exhaust the description of even a single atom. They simply indicate some of the modes of being of an atom. In any such description (either of the atom or of human experience), we must keep in mind that we are always up to our neck in abstractions. All scientific analyses, all breakdowns, all explanations, all descriptions come in the form of abstractions.

Once we recognize this crucial fact, the way is open for what are often startling shifts in perspective. Thus, in classical physics, three master abstractions were presupposed: length, time, and mass. In quantum physics, it has recently been suggested that these might well be replaced since they do not refer to ultimate facts.

One of the new basic presuppositions would be the velocity of light in a vacuum; another would be the quantum constant "h," which governs all atomic phenomena. What the third independent unit should be is still in doubt. The logical candidate, Newton's gravitational constant, is questionable because of its unsuitability for explaining atomic and nuclear phenomena (and because it might not turn out to be a true constant). The physicist, George Gamow, speculates that the third constant, following a proposal by Russell and Heisenberg, might be the irreducibly small length separating two particles. Gamow then makes the highly significant point that if light propagated with infinite velocity instead of at 186,282 miles per second, if the quantum constant were zero instead of 6.77×10^{-27} (in the centimeter-gram-second unit system), and if the presumed elementary length of distance between two particles were zero instead of approximately 10^{-13} cm., then modern physics (including Einstein's relativity theory, Planck's quantum theory and Bohr's atomic theory) would indeed "reduce to the classical mechanics of Isaac Newton." (Gamow, 1966, p. 157.)

Gamow's observation implies several far-reaching conclusions:

1. That physical reality can never be fully described by completely general abstractions such as length, mass and time;
2. That there are precise boundaries to physical reality, or at least to our understanding of it (e.g., no velocity can exceed that of light, no distance can be shorter than an elementary length, no mechanical action can be smaller than quantum action);
3. That while vitally important aspects of physical reality can be well described by mathematical abstractions, these are always delimited by the highly specific and concrete behavior of the phenomena themselves; and
4. That the choice of fundamental presuppositions has a highly pragmatic aspect, depending upon one's purpose.

According to Gamow, any three independent units of measurement could, in theory, serve as basic presuppositions: their selection is governed mainly by considerations of utility and power of generalization. The constants proposed by Gamow point best, he believes, to just those aspects of the physical world that highlight the subject matter of physics. Obviously, other abstractions become more relevant and appropriate when one moves from atoms to people. In an earlier age, when physics was simpler, it may have sounded plausible to suggest that the human as well as the physical world could be reduced to a common substratum of matter, or its equivalent, energy. Today, it is unlikely that even the most thoroughgoing materialist would wish to describe human life in terms of the speed of light or quanta of action or minimal lengths separating particles.

Perhaps we may gain the clearest idea of what the new physics in general implies for the human sciences by resorting to a convenient paradigm: imagine some intelligent person from a culture uncontaminated by Western modes of thought (or by his own presuppositions) who has been thoroughly instructed in recent physics but has no knowledge of psychology, psychoanalysis, or any of the human sciences. Suppose we now ask him to go about setting up a science of man. What are the kinds of concepts he is likely to introduce insofar as he comes to a human subject matter with no other knowledge than a thorough background in the newer physics?

From his awareness of the degree of complexity in understanding the once indivisible unit, the atom, he would be likely to interpret the human person in terms of structural concepts. The atom, as we have indicated, has to be interpreted as a fairly complex structure—and, furthermore, as a structure that has to be understood by its many forms of interrelatedness, both internally and in respect to other structures. Thus, a background in the physics of the atom would suggest fundamental concepts of structure and relatedness as key tools in interpreting human beings.

A background in the new physics would also prepare our visitor to expect a large margin of indeterminacy in individual cases of human behavior. He would search for statistical arrays rather than seek the strict determinism of a simple machine. The mathematics he would expect to use would be current methods for dealing with stochastic processes. That is, he would expect to study human beings in the mass by methods of sampling and probability, rather than by hypothesizing some simple mechanism that supposedly lies behind the observed behavior of each individual person.

Our physics expert would also expect human nature not to be entirely plastic, but would look for some stubborn and in-

variant constants of human behavior—in analogy with the
constants that are basic to physics. Here we must emphasize a
special characteristic of two of these constants: the speed of
light, and the h, or Planck constant, of quantum action. These
constants are inescapable for the physicist because they form
the conditions for his measuring apparatus itself. They govern
the interaction of the apparatus with what it measures. Or to
put it another way: there is no reality to be measured independently of the measuring apparatus. If, now, one thinks of
the measuring apparatus as a means of perception, then we may
say that the lesson of modern physics is that subject (perceiving
apparatus) and object (the reality measured) form one seamless whole. Our visitor, with his background in modern physics,
is thus not likely to found the human sciences on a dichotomy
between subject and object. The kinds of concepts he will
choose for understanding human beings will be those that see
the human person as indissolubly one within his group, his
world, and within physical nature generally.

Our example, of course, need not be quite so hypothetical.
We can easily imagine that young American scientists, coming
to the problems of the human sciences from a background in
contemporary physics but bearing no burden of the history of
psychology, will take off in the direction we have just sketched.
But whatever method we evoke to dramatize the points above,
the conclusion remains the same, and it is a most remarkable
one: namely, that if one approaches the problems of the human
sciences from the discoveries of present-day physics, one will
be led to posit key concepts that are diametrically opposed to
those on which Freud, borrowing from the physics of his own
day, founded psychoanalysis, or with which the first experimentalists drawing directly upon nineteenth century physics
sought to establish psychology. History, here, seems to have
worked a rather neat irony.

The New Scientific Materialism

Earlier we implied that the new discoveries of science have had the paradoxical effect of simultaneously weakening and strengthening scientific materialism at the same time. We have seen how modern physics has rendered infinitely more complex the notion of matter itself, compromising the simplicity of the underlying philosophy. Some aspects of scientific materialism, however, have actually gained in momentum and prestige.

Many current theories of genetics, for example, take an out-and-out materialist approach. They propose that living organisms and their hereditary characteristics can be explained by a straightforward reduction: our chromosomes and genes can be broken down into component nucleic acids, which can then be analyzed into their component carbon-containing molecules. These can be further broken down into combinations of the five basic elements of life—hydrogen, oxygen, carbon, nitrogen and phosphorus—and finally, these can be explained by their atomic composition. In his discussion of the nature of protoplasm, the biologist Sinnott describes the dilemma which the contemporary version of materialism has created in modern biology:

> In protoplasm comes to focus sharply the significance of materialism as a philosophy. If whatever I am is closely dependent on the protoplasm of my cells, especially those of my brain, and if all the changes that go on in protoplasm are no different from the ones that occur in lifeless nature, then life is simply a chemical process and I am a chemical machine. It is very difficult to see how freedom and responsibility can be attributes of such a mechanism, or how man's ideals and aspirations can arise in it. On the other hand, it is hard to understand how the universality of natural law can be violated in a living thing. (Sinnott, p. 93, 1966.)

dilemma

We see, then, that while the discoveries of twentieth century science may have radically changed what the materialist means by physico-chemical processes, far from shaking his faith in the possibilities of carrying out the reduction of all reality to matter, these discoveries have reinforced them by making them more detailed and concrete. The new insights into genic codes which control inherited traits, the enhanced understanding of the chemical composition of cells and the electric nature of the nervous system, and many other discoveries in biology, are cited in support of the materialist's viewpoint.

Thus, while a far more subtle and elusive concept of matter separates the contemporary materialist from his nineteenth century counterpart, it does not at all change the core of his belief that only physico-chemical terms need be presupposed in explaining all forms of reality. In its contemporary version, mind and consciousness and purpose and will and indeed life itself are all held to be reducible to matter. Even evolution is accounted for by reference to patterns of random change in genic structure, without presupposing either life or purpose. Matter remains the sole category of "real reality" in the view of many, if not most, contemporary scientists.

There is, however, a grave difficulty in maintaining this view. True, the new scientific understanding of matter is most welcome, and it makes materialism a more plausible and useful philosophy. But the more we inspect matter, the more elusive it becomes as a basis for explaining reality. Our inventory of the atom showed how many items had to be accepted as primitive, i.e., terms that are incapable of being explained by reference to any others. Remember that the essence of materialism as a philosophy is the view that matter and matter alone is fundamental—it cannot be broken down and reduced to anything else. And the essence of scientific materialism—in both its earlier and later versions—is that when you have analyzed reality into its physico-chemical components by scientifically acceptable operations you have exhausted its meaning.

Yet, modern science implies that the word matter, far from referring to objects with simple location (like the English philosophers' miniature billiard balls) is simply a grand abstraction that covers a bewildering variety of processes. Among these, the elementary particles may conceivably belong in the old familiar category of matter, but quantum action, wave mechanics, the atom's electromagnetic forces and its various modes of interrelatedness belong in other categories that radically change what we mean by matter. These latter categories point to the variety of modes of being of the items found in nature. And the further physicists and geneticists probe into matter, the clearer it becomes that the term matter itself is shot through and through with ambiguity.

Is reference to matter even meaningful if this one word covers so many disparate activities? It has the serious disadvantage of excluding huge chunks of experience while no longer implying a common generic meaning to the processes it does subsume. It fails to describe many processes in experience entirely, and among those that are included it singles out selected aspects, arbitrarily ignoring others. Close inspection reveals, however, that when applied to the human world, the various aspects of matter (or if one prefers, physico-chemical processes) are often given a unifying meaning; they refer to characteristics that the human and physical world happen to share in common. This assumes, in effect, that we can reduce life to the domain of the inorganic if only we understand the latter well enough. But this procedure of taking an abstraction that highlights one aspect of reality, and then subsuming all others under it, is precisely the fallacy of reductionism that has become the target of criticism of so many contemporary philosophers. Indeed, it is no accident that the closer one comes to the human world, the larger the fallacy of reductionism looms as the dominant feature of scientific materialism.

Yet it would be an even worse error than reductionism to dismiss out of hand the claims of scientific materialism as a philosophy. We should recognize that this doctrine has proven extraordinarily fertile. Unquestionably, it groups in a powerful way a system of abstractions that highlights some vital aspects of reality, whatever others it may plunge into obscurity. We must be careful, therefore, to avoid the very trap followers of scientific materialism have fallen into: namely, proposing one dogmatic ideology to replace another. The history of science is not a sequence of "right" theories replacing "wrong" ones.

Most frequently, new scientific theories subsume older ones, showing that they erred mainly in exaggerating their level of generality. So it is here. Obviously, the human world has a material side, and our bodies are often the most important part of our human experience. But it is, we submit, more faithful to the density and richness of human experience to understand how physico-chemical part-processes fit into this experiential totality than to reverse the procedure by reducing the full range of human experience to an abstract version of one of its aspects.

In brief, then, those who have applied scientific materialism to the human world have compromised the valuable contribution it might have made because they have been guilty of a triple fallacy: mistaking a part for the whole, mistaking an abstraction for concrete reality, and then reducing the concrete whole to the partial abstraction. Skill in applying this triple fallacy accounts for a large proportion of the errors and half-truths afloat in the human sciences today.

Mathematical physics did not beget our era. Philosophy itself led the way by launching a certain project of construing nature in such a way that physics could develop. But there is no doubt that the dazzling triumphs of Newtonian physics were what really entrenched the metaphysics of scientific materialism as the basic model for all explanation. Hence, there is more than a modicum of poetic—or should we say, historical—justice in the fact that physics has been precisely the discipline that has done most to shake up the old ideology.

A remarkable comment on these new developments in physics was made by the late physicist, J. Robert Oppenheimer (1966, p. 39). He began by pointing out some of the great achievements of physics in this century: relativity theory, quantum mechanics, the many extraordinary discoveries in the physics of particles, Hubbel's discovery of a constant in nature such that an interval of ten billion years separates the time in which galaxies double their distance from one another—to name only a few. All of these discoveries show us a nature far more inexhaustible and complex than Newton's neat and tidy concepts had allowed. Above all, these newer developments shatter the postulate that made possible all the neatness of the Newtonian system: strict determinism. Oppenheimer writes: "The ineluctable element of chance introduced into 20th Century physics heralds the end of the Newtonian paradigm of certain predictions of the future from the knowledge of the present." (P. 41.) And he goes on to praise these new discoveries in words that do not seem to us exaggerated: "What has happened in this century in physics rivals in its technical and intellectual imagination of profundity what has happened at any time in human history." Yet Oppenheimer is disappointed in the consequences, or lack of them, that this extraordinary scientific flowering has had. He points out that these great achievements have had nothing like the far-reaching effects on the whole culture that were produced by the revolution triggered by the theories of Copernicus, the discoveries of Galileo, and the syntheses of Descartes and Newton.

Impressive as his testimony is, we have nevertheless to be circumspect about what ultimate cultural consequences Oppenheimer may have in mind. If the new physics is supposed to provide the basis of a new world-view, we shall merely be repeating the philosophical error of the last three centuries. Perhaps it is fortunate that the new findings in physics do not seem to lend themselves to any quick and easy philosophic systematization; they are too rich and diverse, and they suggest a pluralistic view of things rather than the monism of an overarching system. We do not imagine, moreover, that Oppenheimer would want us to base our belief in human freedom, as Eddington once did, on the indeterminate behavior of subatomic particles. It would be a poor kind of human freedom that depended on the erratic jump of a particle in the brain. Yet Oppenheimer is surely right that these newer discoveries in physics should have greater impact on the whole culture—mainly, the negative one of undoing the modes of thought that the older physics had entrenched. Physics itself now teaches that those older models of explanation, mechanical and deterministic, are not *a priori* necessities, universally binding for all subject matters, but merely convenient tools for certain restricted purposes. By undoing the old mystique, this negative effect of the new physics could have an enormously liberating effect if it were to penetrate the whole culture. At the same time, however, we are forewarned by the past not to attempt to build psychology positively on the basis of physics.

Yet there are more consequences stirring in the contemporary culture than Oppenheimer allows. On their own terrain, both psychology and philosophy in this century have been struggling to free themselves from the Cartesian straitjacket. Let us first see how psychology has grappled with the problem, and then turn to contemporary twentieth century philosophy.

[✿]

THIRTEEN

The Background
in Psychology:
Schisms and Satan

William James, throughout his twenties, suffered from a severe depression; the fear of moral impotence obsessed him; he lacked the will to act and he was unable to find a focus for his life. Then one day, at the age of twenty-eight, James had a sudden insight. In April 1870, he made the following entry in his diary:

> I think that yesterday was a crisis in my life. I finished the first part of Renouvier's second essay and see no reason why his definition of freedom—the sustaining of a thought because I choose to when I might have other thoughts— need be the definition of an illusion.

The entry ends in characteristic Jamesian fashion: "My first act of freedom shall be to believe in freedom." (James in Perry, 1948.)

Shortly after this episode, James's depression began to lift. He got married, started a correspondence with Renouvier, and launched his career as teacher, psychologist, and philosopher at Harvard. The abysmal years of misery and confusion were past.

Throughout the rest of his long life, James struggled to maintain his hard-won insight against the scientific determinism

of his day. In a world of contingency, he stressed human freedom. Against derisive opposition, he insisted upon believing
that naturalism and human spontaneity could live side by side
without contradiction, a point of view that collided head-on
with the most vigorous trends of his day. This was the age of
the great nineteenth century German physiologists, whose influence on Wundt as well as on Freud was as decisive for the
development of American academic psychology as for psychoanalysis.

In James's time, biology, mathematics, physics, and chemistry
as well as physiology were building a record of unparalleled
accomplishment. Their success won so much prestige that any
conception of man and his world other than that implied by
the natural sciences smacked of sentimentality or mysticism.
But James found repugnant the vision that appeared to be
inspired by the science of his day. It suggested an image of a
finished universe slowly petering out from heat-death and
peopled by automatons. The insight stimulated by reading
Renouvier had revealed what seemed to him to be a flaw in a
closed system. If man can exercise any choice whatever within
the inexorable conditions of his life, moral decisions are possible
and man's projects become meaningful. Somehow, he felt, determinism in science and freedom in man had to coexist. James's
response to Renouvier became the foundation of his mature
viewpoint that a belief in science need not contradict the possibility of believing in human freedom also.

A century later, in 1960, at the annual meeting of the American Psychological Association, the speaker was Henry Murray,
a Professor of Psychology who also came from Harvard. He is
a successor to James and he shares some of James's personal
charisma and unconventionality. He had chosen to talk to his
fellow psychologists about Satan and his influence on modern-
day psychology. Referring to the many indirect forms Satan
can assume, he ended his talk with these words:

> . . . here is where our psychology comes in with . . . its
> prevailing views of human personality, its images of man
> obviously in league with the objectives of the nihilist Sa-
> tanic spirit. Man is a computer, an animal, or an infant.

His destiny is completely determined by genes, instincts, accidents, early conditionings and reinforcements, cultural and social forces. Love is a secondary drive based on hunger and oral sensations or a reaction formation to an innate underlying hate . . . There are no provisions for creativity, no admitted margins of freedom for voluntary decisions, no fitting recognitions of the power of ideals, no bases for selfless actions, no ground at all for any hope that the human race can save itself from the fatality that now confronts it. *If we psychologists were all the time, consciously or unconsciously, intending out of malice to reduce the concept of human nature to its lowest common denominator, and were gloating over our successes in so doing, then we might have to admit that to this extent the Satanic spirit was alive within us.* (Murray, 1962.) (Our italics.)

The years that separate James's reading of Renouvier from Henry Murray's paper to the American Psychological Association cover the lifetime of psychology as a discipline independent of philosophy—from the establishment of Wundt's experimental laboratory in 1870 to the present. Note that James and Murray were concerned with the same issue: a plea for a belief in human freedom in a world dominated by the deterministic premises of natural science. Nothing much has changed in those many years to remove this unresolved problem within psychology. Both men were preoccupied with it; both rejected the notion that one can be faithful to the ideal of science only by denying man's freedom; and both faced unrelenting opposition from the dominant tradition of scientific psychology.

William James was well-loved by his students and colleagues. But the positivists of his time lumped him together with the nice old ladies of Cambridge as amiable souls who did not like to face up to the hard truths of science. Henry Murray is also well-regarded by several generations of students, but his colleague, B. F. Skinner, whose behaviorist psychology is based on scientific materialism to an even greater extent than was Freud's metapsychology, is probably Harvard's most influential psychologist.

Today, the continued success of science has strengthened the hold of scientific materialism, in an updated version, as an inherent part of the scientific outlook. In recent years, however, the assumption that this one philosophy of science must be valid for all sciences has come under more careful scrutiny. Koyré and others have observed that while such a philosophy has worked well for the physical sciences (at least up to the 1920's), it has proven to be a disaster for the human sciences, especially for psychology (Koyré, 1965). It is a sad fact, as the philosopher Michael Scriven has noted (1964), that the most basic philosophical issues of modern psychology, alive when Wundt and Freud were beginning their work, are still wholly unresolved today. The Murray-James concern with the freedom-determinism issue is but one example. In today's psychology, other equally basic and "elementary" questions are as unsettled now as they were almost a century ago, and our psychologists continue to be divided on fundamental questions such as:

—Whether the methods of the physical sciences truly apply to a psychological subject matter;

—Whether a belief in freedom need necessarily imply vitalism or mysticism or logical inconsistency with science;

—Whether human behavior can be studied without resorting to mentalistic concepts such as mind, consciousness, purpose, will, and other "inner" variables;

—Whether human behavior is governed by peripheral or by central processes;

—Whether the human organism is active or reactive, empty or full;

—Whether clinical insight is superior to quantitative measurements or vice versa;

—Whether the human mind is more like a computer or a switchboard or a map room—or none of these;

—Whether the suspect data of introspection are to be readmitted into psychology or whether only the objective correlatives of inner states are fit subjects for scientific investigation.

Psychology had divorced itself from philosophy precisely to avoid such sticky philosophic problems and to adopt pure scientific procedures. But the problems have refused to go away; they keep on reasserting themselves in one form or another. And their lack of resolution stands squarely in the way of progress.

Several times in the past century psychologists tried to settle their conceptual problems without confronting the underlying philosophical issues. Each time the settlement became unstuck, precipitating a crisis in fundamentals. In 1870 Wundt thought he had the answers when he began to apply experimental methods to the study of consciousness. In 1913 Watson challenged introspectionism, raising all the basic questions again and answering them with radical behaviorism. Soon thereafter behaviorism came to dominate American psychology. But almost from its beginning it too began to change, undergoing a process of progressive modification and attenuation. With neo-behaviorism liberalized, watered down, and challenged by other branches of psychology, these last few decades have once again seen all of the basic questions brought into the open. Today the American Psychological Association with its more than thirty divisions is split into many opposing camps, the behaviorists and clinical psychologists representing the largest groupings. Moreover, their sharpest disagreements are not so much psychological as philosophical.

Thoughtful psychologists are deeply distressed over these unresolved fundamentals; and rightly so, for their lack of resolution seriously enfeebles the psychological enterprise. This irresoluteness is made clear in almost every serious psychological work of note. Lest the reader think the quotation from Henry Murray is atypical, here is how other prominent psychologists who share Murray's general orientation express themselves on this same dilemma:

> [No other field] has ever been so harried by the shining success story of the older sciences . . . From the very beginning the psychologists' stipulation that psychology be adequate to science has outweighed its commitment that it be adequate to man. (Koch, 1964.)

So dominant is the positivist ideal that fields of psychology other than those which treat the human personality as a concatenation of reflexes and habits have come to be regarded as not quite reputable. Special aversion attaches to complex motives, high level integration, conscience, freedom, and selfhood. (Allport, 1955.)

. . [the advocates of a particular kind of psychology—a psychology-without-a-person—have been able to gain and maintain power through putting across the idea that they are representatives in psychology of *true* science] . . we have produced a whole generation of research psychologists who have never had occasion to look closely at one person, let alone themselves . . . Reading their papers you get a strange sense of the unreality of it all; the authors' conceptions of variables and processes seem a bit off; and then you realize that the authors have never looked at human experience; they went straight from the textbook or journal to the laboratory . . . *Our young psychological researchers do not know what goes on in human beings and their work shows it.* (Sanford, 1965.) (Our italics.)

There is no reason to believe that these open wounds in psychology will be healed unless the underlying philosophical dilemma is confronted and correctly resolved.

The main issues in academic psychology that have a philosophical basis polarize around three controversies. The first is how to define the ego or self (our central theme). The psychologists quoted above—Murray, Sanford, Allport, and Koch—are fearful that the human ego cannot be adequately conceived within the *a priori* structure of scientific psychology. In particular, they are concerned lest psychology fails to grasp aspects of the self that relate to (a) the individual's uniqueness, (b) the concreteness of his own special experience, (c) his wholeness as a person apart from part processes, (d) his growth and change within the context of an enduring identity, (e) his ethical reality and (f) his efforts at self-comprehension.

The second controversy relates to the appropriateness of applying the methods of the natural sciences to human experience. To psychologists this is perhaps the most divisive of all issues. It also has the most immediate and practical consequences in that how it is resolved shapes the subject matter to be studied and directs what is to be researched.

The third of the main issues is the age-old problem of freedom versus determinism which plagued James and Murray.

When we turn to our proposed reconstruction of psychoanalytic metapsychology in the final section we will come back to all three issues. In the present discussion let us look somewhat more closely at how the all-important issue of freedom versus determinism affects contemporary psychology. Perhaps no other issue exhibits more clearly the dilemma created in psychology by its failure to close with the inappropriateness of its philosophical foundations.

The Freedom-Determinism Issue

Whole libraries have been written on the subject of freedom versus determinism. Yet the central issue can be posed quite simply. If you believe in human freedom you maintain that for some of your actions you could have chosen to act otherwise. If, on the other hand, you are a determinist, you maintain that the *feeling* of freedom, of choice and of decision, is an illusion. All the causes of human behavior may not be known, but you maintain that theoretically they can become known, and when they are it will be apparent that choice and freedom never existed.

To those who believe in determinism, freedom implies lawlessness, natural disorder and unpredictability. Many psychologists do not believe that a nondeterminist science of man is possible; to most psychologists, freedom and choice are felt to lead irresistibly back to the animism, vitalism, and muddleheadedness of a prescientific era. As one philosopher of science put it, "If human behavior does not exhibit cause-effect sequences, then the scientific method is irrelevant to the elucidation of man, and both scientific psychology and the social sciences are permanently barred from achieving the status of a science." (Grunbaum, 1953.)

The psychologists we have quoted earlier in this chapter do

not share this conclusion. Those who believe in human freedom hold that if man's life is wholly determined by physical processes, then no meaning can be given to human responsibility, growth, courage, integrity, freedom, or purpose. If man is a machine, a robot, then life is stripped of meaning. Such determinism leads to a profound anti-humanism.

Nor is psychology the only arena for the issue of freedom versus determinism. The question pervades the entire domain of the natural sciences and the humanities as well. Indeed, Whitehead has claimed that our failure to resolve it has enfeebled our lives: "This radical inconsistency at the basis of modern thought," he states, "accounts for much that is half-hearted and wavering in our civilization." (Whitehead, 1925.)

In the middle of the last century the issue of freedom versus determinism came to a crisis that threatened the uneasy compromise between religion and science that had prevailed over the two preceding centuries. Determinism had been confined to the material world, and human action largely exempted from its inexorable laws. But the truce slowly disintegrated as secularism advanced along with the growth of science. Helmholtz, Darwin, Freud, and Marx—each a seminal thinker from his own vantage point—proposed a common theme: man is part and parcel of the unity of nature; he is subject to its iron laws; and these rather than the individual's own free choice determine man's behavior.

At the very end of the century a reaction set in. Doctrines that opposed this determinism were put forward: vitalism and "philosophy of life" were advanced by Dilthey in Germany, by James in this country, and by Bergson in France. In fact, the voice of protest against total determinism has never been stilled. But at least in the United States, the philosophy of scientific materialism, with determinism as one of its cardinal supports, has advanced despite opposition, until today it is the prevailing, and in some branches of psychology, the only official philosophy. This is also true for some branches of biology, medicine, and sociology. The ghost of Newton, having suffered at the hands of modern physicists, has taken full revenge within the sciences of man.

The freedom-determinism issue has little practical significance for the physical sciences. Physicists do not care about the behavior of a single electron or proton or even about a single atom; they are concerned, typically, with the behavior of large aggregates. But psychology must take the individual into account. In physics there can be disagreement on determinism (as there was between Bohr and Einstein) without unduly influencing the topics selected for research or the choice of research methods or even the subjects taught to students. In psychology, on the other hand, disagreement on how much free choice a man enjoys enters into most phases of the psychologist's work.

Many psychologists do not like to get entangled in philosophical arguments of this nature. They say, in effect, "Whatever side of the fence I settle on, it would make no difference to my everyday work." But this indifference is short-sighted, for when one is immersed in a doctrine it is not easy to think within any other framework or to see the implications of alternative points of view. Actually, the leading psychologists of each school fully realize the significance of the issue: between Skinner, Hebb, Miller, and Festinger on the one side, and Sanford, Maslow, Rogers, and Chein on the other, there is an unbridgeable world of difference in outlook. The two sides have tried to build bridges many times, but they just do not work and they will not so long as the basic philosophical issues are avoided.

Each of the major contemporary schools of psychology takes a different stand on determinism, but no American psychologist holds so extreme a view as that of Jean-Paul Sartre, who defines one end of a spectrum. Sartre has stated repeatedly that man's own decisions determine the nature of his being. Man makes himself; this is the import of Sartre's slogan that existence precedes essence. First man exists, and then he "decides" what he is to be. Here, indeed, is human freedom in its most radical form. Sartre, the author of an existentialist psychoanalysis, is aware of the discoveries of science; yet, his belief in radical freedom for man stands at the very center of his philosophy.

The extreme opposite point of view is represented by B. F. Skinner, whose behaviorism has evolved considerably from the early days of Watson. Koch distinguishes three periods of behaviorist psychology: classical behaviorism dominated by Watson from 1913 through the 1920's; neo-behaviorism, dominated by Hull, Stevens and Tolman in the thirties and forties; and neo-neo-behaviorism current today. (Koch, 1964.) Contemporary behaviorism is represented by many prominent psychologists, with Skinner leading the most extreme group and Hebb, Miller and others presenting a more moderate viewpoint.

For our purposes, we need not concern ourselves with the subtle shadings that distinguish the Skinner from the Hebb-Miller positions. Whatever their differences, all behaviorists share a belief in a thoroughgoing determinism. Skinner wavers between a pragmatic justification for determinism (as a mere working hypothesis) and a metaphysical justification. In his book, *Science and Human Behavior* (1953), Skinner raises the problem in the very first pages. He points out that scientific materialism had a liberating effect on the physical sciences in the seventeenth, eighteenth and nineteenth centuries. He quotes a seventeenth century scientist as saying that ships lighter than air cannot work since "God will never suffer this invention to take effect because of the many consequences which may disturb the civil government of man." Skinner remarks dryly, "Contrary to his expectation, God *has* suffered this invention to take effect." Skinner expects that scientific determinism will have as liberating an effect on the human sciences of our own day as it had on the physical sciences in the past.

Skinner represents one extreme version of a classic American tradition, symbolized by John Dewey, whose faith in a beneficent science he shares. Like Dewey, he holds that science has got us into our current mess and only more science can get us out. And for Skinner, like Dewey, science unequivocally means behaviorism. "If we are to enjoy the advantages of science in human affairs," he states, "we must be prepared to adopt the working model of behaviorism *to which science will inevitably lead.*" (1953.) (Our italics.) In his book, *Walden II*, Skinner carries these methodological convictions about science and behaviorism over to his social philosophy. Here he offers us a fresh version of a scientific utopia supposed to be benign but which is almost as terrifying as the ones that Orwell and Huxley and others have so vigorously attacked. The Skinnerian position leads to the view that only by conceiving man as wholly moved by forces outside of himself, controlled and manipulated for his benefit, can we hope to arrive at a new level of humanism.

Although he reaches conclusions about determinism that are diametrically opposed to those of philosophers such as Sartre and Whitehead, Skinner agrees that the issue has crucial significance. "A scientific conception of human behavior," he states, "dictates one practice, a philosophy of personal freedom another." And he adds, almost echoing Whitehead's words, "The present unhappy condition of the world may, in large measure, be traced to our vacillation on this issue." (1953.) Thus, as often happens, those who represent the extreme-opposite positions nonetheless agree fully on the significance of the question over which they are divided.

As a working psychologist, Skinner states that a scientific approach to man demands leaving out of psychology concepts of mind, consciousness, purpose, freedom, will, and decision as explanations of human action. This is in the classic tradition of behaviorism. The more moderate behaviorists do not go so far as Skinner. In fact, George Miller, a colleague of Skinner's, scores the doctrinaire character of behaviorism's positivist philosophy. "It is curious," he writes, "to see how easily positivism, which began in violent opposition to any metaphysical dogma whatsoever, slips over into this kind of materialism—into the metaphysical dogma that true existence is reserved exclusively for physical and chemical objects." (Miller, 1962.) But Miller himself is willing to admit the concept of choice and purpose into the study of man only to the extent that something like human purpose can be built into the programs of computers. (Miller, 1960.)

The logic of the behaviorist position can be best shown by an example taken from outside of the emotionally laden subject of human decisions. There is known to medicine a dread disease called lupus. Lupus results from a dysfunction of one of the major defensive systems of the body, the reticular activating system. By some apparent misreading of the chemical coding in the system, antibodies are manufactured which attack the protein thrown off by kidney cells, forming new virulent cells. The body, in effect, attacks and destroys its own healthy substance.

Lupus presents us with an example of a response by a living organism that does not require either cognition or consciousness. It shows a swift, regulatory response on the part of the organism—made vivid by its destructiveness—which does not involve the suspect concepts of purpose, freedom, or will. The process is purely automatic, and it contains all that is needed in the behaviorist model. There is a living organism, represented by the reticular activating system. There is an environment, represented by the body tissues. The organism responds to changes in the environment in a complex fashion, but without requiring us to postulate any mental process whatsoever, No discussion of free choice, will, or decision need cloud the issue. A stimulus in the form of the kidney's protein provides the necessary and sufficient conditions to bring about the response. The entire process can be expressed in physicalistic language, can be translated into "operational definitions," and is explicable in terms of measurable chemical processes.

The most stringent behaviorists maintain that this model can be applied to all human actions—at least to those that represent the proper domain of a scientific psychology. The more moderate behaviorists no longer go that far. Increasingly, they admit terms that conjure up the philosophical bogeyman associated with mind, consciousness, purpose, and freedom—although they do not use those words. Processes that interfere with a total and automatic correlation between stimulus and response are called "intervening variables." Gibson has listed some forty different "intervening variables" that behaviorists use to describe processes such as attention, purpose and insight. (1941.) Examples of these are given below. These same psychologists have not, however, adjusted their theories to take these processes into account. To do so would compromise their philosophy of determinism too greatly.

The words Gibson and others use—expectancy, hypothesis, intention, preconception, need—clearly suggest that human responses are determined by something more than the immediately preceding sensory stimulation. This concession represents a long-awaited expansion of the behaviorist viewpoint. Behaviorism is usually referred to as S-R psychology, standing for Stimulus-Response. One psychologist has noted that behaviorism is increasingly becoming the study of the hyphen between the S and the R. The noted behaviorist Hebb, for example, stresses the importance of what he calls "the autonomous central process." He justifies this departure from classical behaviorism by reference to recent physiological discoveries. Grounding his work in physiology enables him, he states, to maintain the purity of a belief in "a mechanical process of cause and effect" and avoid the "mysticism" associated with a belief in human freedom:

> The role of the psychologist [is] to reduce the vagaries of thought to a mechanical process of cause and effect . . . One cannot logically be a determinist in physics, chemistry and biology and a mystic in psychology . . . Modern psychology takes completely for granted that behavior and neural functions are perfectly correlated, that one is completely caused by the other. There is not a separate soul or life force to stick a finger in the brain now and then and make neural cells do what they would not otherwise. If one is to be consistent . . . there is no room for a mysterious agent that is defined as not physical and yet has physical effects. (Hebb, 1949.)

Note that Hebb's belief in materialism is not based on empirical evidence but on an *a priori* philosophical conviction. Hebb simply cannot get around the metaphysical dilemma of Cartesianism, and so his deepest convictions on the nature of what a scientific psychology should be are dictated by philosophy— as are those of all behaviorists. Like Skinner, Hebb wavers between a pragmatic justification of determinism and a metaphysical one. He says, "Actually of course, this belief (in material determinism) is a working assumption only . . . It is quite conceivable that some day the assumption will have to be rejected." (Hebb, 1949.) But he quickly adds that "the working assumption is a necessary one and there is no real evidence opposed to it."

Hebb's point, that there is no real evidence opposed to the doctrine of scientific determinism, reveals how a closed system of thought operates. Suppose, for example, in reviewing American political history, you perceive the late President Kennedy's decisions in the second Cuban crisis as an act of political courage. Further, you state that you do not see how this act can be usefully explained in terms of adrenalin secretions, muscular responses, or as an example of trial-and-error learning in response to the "punishment" of the first Cuban crisis. The behaviorist answer tends to be that psychology is a young science, that we must begin with the simplest units of behavior and gradually build these into the complex patterns of higher human response, and that Kennedy's decision is theoretically explicable in behaviorist stimulus-response terms. By definition, if reductionism is wielded with skill, no real evidence can ever be cited in opposition to such a closed system. The determinist makes evidence against his system impossible by appealing to unknown factors. And he further implies that these unknown factors are not truly unknown but merely unmeasured. He assumes that if one were able to measure them, one would find that they are reducible to physico-chemical processes—perhaps very complex processes, but nonetheless quantitatively determinable. It should be recognized, however, that this system of assumptions has little empirical evidence to support it.

Thus, we see that for the more moderate Hebb, as well as for the more extreme Skinner, human freedom and scientific lawfulness are held to be incompatible. They both believe that if one is to be a scientist, one has no choice but to be a thoroughgoing determinist.

The Third Force

There is a group of psychologists who refer to themselves as a "third force." As the name implies, they are defined as much by their opposition to the other two forces in American psychology—behaviorism and psychoanalysis—as by the positive views they hold in common. Apart from their opposition to these common foes, as a group they are committed to the classic humanist values of the Graeco-Hebraic tradition and the worth it places on the uniqueness of the individual. Their main concern is with how to adapt scientific method to fit the study of people, rather than distorting their subject to fit *a priori* conceptions of scientific method—an accusation they level at the behaviorists. They take a far more flexible stand on the freedom-determinism issue than the behaviorists and the psychoanalysts, and they have devoted a good deal of attention to the nature of the self.

These and similar beliefs give the "third force" a common rallying ground, but they form a less cohesive group than the other two schools of psychological thought. One can better think of them as a widely scattered group of gifted individuals who share a grievance and some values in common than as advocates of a closely knit doctrine or method or philosophy. Leaders of this "third force" include the late Gordon Allport, A. A. Maslow, Carl Rogers, Nevitt Sanford, and Isidor Chein. Because of the large differences that exist even among these few psychologists, we cannot take the thought of any one of them as representative of the third force movement. However, the most philosophical of these psychologists is probably Professor Isidor Chein of New York University. A brief mention of Chein's stand on determinism will serve our present purposes. He sees the freedom-determinism issue as central to the problem of what psychology shall assume as its working hypothesis. The choice, he states, is between an image of man as an active responsible agent versus a helpless, powerless reagent. Chein believes that behaviorism is guilty of a dogmatic reductionism leading to the latter conception. He states that he is not opposed in principle to seeing how much of human behavior can be subsumed under physiology or physics, but he is opposed to the habit of assuming in advance that human behavior must, *a priori*, be reduced to physicalistic causes.

Chein has come to some fundamental conclusions about determinism. He holds that a belief in human freedom rests on only three premises—volitions (drives, motivations, wishes) exist; they have behavioral consequences; and they are not reducible to variables of the physical environment or physiological process. (These are precisely the premises Hebb would not allow.) And he holds that he is himself a determinist—who also happens to believe in freedom, a dual conviction he shares with William James. He agrees with the behaviorists that determinism is a basic working hypothesis of scientific method. (Concerning any given class of events, the scientist has the right to ask, "What are its necessary and sufficient conditions?".) But he also agrees with those of his fellow psychologists who believe in human freedom.

Chein reconciles his belief that determinism and freedom are logically compatible by stating that behaviorists who oppose the two are guilty of confused semantics: they have mistaken, he states, the distinction between freedom and necessity for the distinction between chance and necessity. A belief in freedom does not imply chance, disorderliness, or unpredictability. A belief that the individual is self-determining does not, in Chein's view, violate a belief in an order of nature, nor does it imply mysticism, animism, or regression to prescientific modes of thought. He points out that when we find the ultimate laws of the universe they will not themselves be determined; they will just be. Chein does not claim as much freedom for man as Jean-Paul Sartre. But of all American academic psychologists, he perhaps goes farthest toward the Sartre end of the freedom-determinism spectrum.

We shall come back to Chein's position on determinism later; it is mentioned here in passing in order to set before the reader an example of the debates taking place in modern psychology on this and other basic philosophical issues. To claim that all of the varied conceptual troubles besetting modern psychology can be traced to the same philosophical neurosis as that which affects psychoanalysis would perhaps overstate the case. But it should be clear by now that the central difficulties—those concerned with the nature of the human self, with the appropriateness of scientific methods for studying people, and with the crucial issue of whether human freedom exists—flow directly from the same philosophical sources as those which beset psychoanalytic theory. For academic psychology as well as psychoanalysis has been obliged to stake out its position within a Cartesian framework. Working in the Cartesian legacy with its dichotomies of mind versus body and subject versus object, psychology has but three alternatives: either it can reduce the study of the mind to the body (i.e., to physiology and chemistry) or to overt physical behavior; or it can posit a rich, phenomenal world of thought, action, human purpose, and mind, which coexists in some mysterious fashion with the body; or it can virtually forget about the physical-behavioral side of man's existence and ground itself on the religious-humanist-

idealist tradition in Western thought, even though this is unacceptable to most scientists as a basis for a scientific discipline.
Psychology has done all three; the various contemporary schools
of psychology tend to fall into one or a combination of these
categories. The behaviorists, along with their philosophical
mentors, the logical positivists, have chosen the first alternative;
contemporary ego psychoanalysts, the second; and the third
force has drawn deeply from the Christian-Hebraic conception
of man (with some of the more overt religious aspects muted).
Other parts of psychology pick and choose among the three
alternatives, combining them in various ways but not departing
from the framework itself. Since no one of these three alternatives seem wholly faithful both to the ideals of science and to
the subject of the human person, the dilemma of Cartesianism
continues to have its crippling effect.

The only way out for psychology is to break through the
outmoded rigidities of Cartesianism, and this, precisely, is what
contemporary philosophy may at long last have succeeded in
doing. The motive for this struggle has not come principally
from science, except perhaps in the case of Whitehead. Twentieth century philosophers have worked with their own materials
and their own methods; and this independence of any special
results of the sciences is a good thing, for philosophies built
chiefly upon such results usually produce a Procrustean bed for
chopping off other parts of experience.

These anti-Cartesian strivings of contemporary philosophy
are cast in very different molds. Critics of philosophy today
make much of its fragmented and anarchic condition, but in
fact it is extraordinarily encouraging that the various schools
of philosophy, taking off from many very different points of
view, nevertheless have all been struggling to get beyond the
Cartesian framework. As an effort running parallel to the new
physics, and yet independent of science, these philosophic movements, to which we turn next, open up a new chapter in the
intellectual history of mankind, and they provide us with new
and highly appropriate materials for a reconstruction of the
sciences of man.

FOURTEEN

The Changed Background in Philosophy

If physics has not stood still in our century, neither has philosophy. Yet psychoanalysts seem to have taken as little note of the one as of the other in their formal theorizing. Philosophers, for their part, have not paid attention to the newer developments in psychoanalysis, but instead confined themselves to shooting semantic holes in the older and more rigid theory. So far there has been a great opportunity lost for profitable dialogue. For at the juncture where philosophy and psychoanalysis meet, their problems converge in a most remarkable fashion. The insights of post-Freudian psychoanalysts such as Erikson, Kris, Rapaport, and Weisman, as they trace the development of the ego and its cognitive processes, have a great deal to contribute to philosophy; and although modern philosophers, with few exceptions, have had little to do with psychoanalysis, their central preoccupation—seeking a way out of the Cartesian impasse—urgently and directly concerns psychoanalysis and psychology in general.

In the present epoch, after more than two hundred and fifty years, there are signs that philosophy may be finding its way out of the dead-end. There is common understanding in many quarters of the need for thinking beyond the Cartesian tradition of Western philosophy, that is to say beyond scientific materialism—the most enduring offshoot of Cartesianism. In this century, a few philosophers from a wide variety of traditions have finally succeeded in breaking through the framework in which they had been trained. Philosophers who are generally regarded as having little in common—Wittgenstein, William James, Whitehead, Austin, Husserl, and Heidegger, among others—have reached a partial consensus on a few fundamentals. Our point of departure, therefore, shall be the testimony of some of the most original philosophers of this century and the common ground on which they stand.

We have alluded to Alfred North Whitehead so frequently that perhaps we had best begin with him, if only to bind together the particular points in his thought of which we want to make systematic use. Trained in mathematics and physics, Whitehead's early outlook was molded during the high point of nineteenth century determinism and mechanism. Technically equipped to follow at first hand the new discoveries of relativity and quantum physics, he was able to experience the shattering impact of these discoveries upon the world-view that was implied by scientific materialism. Gone for good were the simplicities of Newton's absolute space and time in which particles—bits of stuff in space—were concretely located and thus formed the ultimate building-blocks of a thoroughly calculable universe. Instead, physics now offered a picture of radical discontinuities, of space and time not as simple containers but as highly abstract relations between events that could, at best, be statistically ordered. Out of the ruins of the view that had been taught him as unshakeable dogma, Whitehead felt called on to construct a quite different philosophy. He was the first thinker of stature to grasp the philosophical challenge posed by the new mathematics and physics, and he was the first to construct on the new insights a positive world-view which he called his philosophy of organism.

Whitehead's critique of the old philosophy, however, is more relevant to our purposes than his specific philosophy of organism. For though this philosophy was intended to have universal applicability, its basic postulates were mainly inspired by mathematics and the natural sciences. In an earlier chapter, we spoke of a visitor from another culture who had constructed a meta-theory of human experience solely from the vantage point of modern physics. Whitehead's philosophy of organism accomplishes this, standing forth as a truly original contribution. But human experience cannot be understood within a framework derived from physics and mathematics, however enlightened it may be. As the physicist Werner Heisenberg observed, any truly distinct field of inquiry calls for its own basic postulates which can never be borrowed from another field.

We must, however, briefly summarize a central insight Whitehead gained from his critique of the old philosophy in the light of the revolution in modern physics and mathematics. He confronts the old physics and philosophy on two levels. As great an achievement as Newtonian physics was, strictly as a system of physics it was limited (as any scientific theory must be), and with scientific progress it had to be revised and fundamentally altered. But Newtonism as a more general mode of thought had been diffused generally through the intellectual culture and had vexed the thinking of philosophers. Whitehead defines the Newtonian mode of thought in terms of two fundamental errors: the fallacy of misplaced concreteness, and the fallacy of simple location.

The fallacy of misplaced concreteness occurs when we make the mistake of taking high-level abstractions as ultimately concrete entities. A particularly disastrous example is what happens to the Newtonian concept of mass when taken out of its properly abstract context. Consider the table across the room: a familiar cluster of qualities, oaken brown, nicked in spots but still dully handsome, cool and reassuringly solid to the touch. If we try to move it, we find it heavy. On the surface of the moon, it would not be so heavy. For certain purposes of physics, however, we might want to speak of it as unchanged despite the change of gravitational field. So the concept of *mass* (a very far cry from the felt heaviness of the table) is defined as a certain function that remains invariant despite changes of gravitational field.

Obviously, the notion of mass is already a high-level abstraction. When relativity physics enters the picture, with its considerations of various conditions for transformations of mass, the concept becomes even more abstract and complex.

What happens, then, when we mistakenly think of the mass of an object as the residual and concrete substance that underlies all the surface qualities of the table? It is now somehow a qualityless stuff that has extension—viz., fills space. As the "real reality" behind the apparent table, it now presents us with the acute difficulty of understanding how we can pass from it to the table we experience. Thus results, in Whitehead's phrase, "the bifurcation of nature" into two spheres: the quantitative but qualityless facts of mass, and the familiar qualitative features of the table, which are now not quite objectively real. And this bifurcation has taken place through the fallacy of misplaced concreteness: an abstract concept, mass, which was originally devised to explain certain aspects of the very familiar table, has been converted into the ultimately concrete, "really real" reality, that displaces the familiar table altogether.

This fallacy is not confined to examples from physics; the history of psychology affords us other cases of its application. With Wundt, psychology was founded on the notion of "elementary sense-data"; and many psychologists still go on thinking in this way without taking note of the voluminousness of the concrete context within which we can, if at all, speak meaningfully of such atomistic chunks of experience. How very complex an abstraction is the notion of "libidinal cathexis," which nevertheless psychoanalysts continue to speak of as if it were a concrete motor force (almost like the gasoline of a motor car) that drives certain of our actions.

The companion fallacy of simple location, identified by Whitehead, is the attempt to circumscribe the place of any phenomenon in an oversimple and absolute way. With this fallacy goes the tendency to assign a more basic status in reality to those phenomena that seem to offer the possibility of such simple location—e.g., to particles or to locatable physico-chemical processes.

Here again, relativity physics has made us aware that the location of any object must always involve some chosen framework or other, and apart from some such contextual whole the object cannot, strictly speaking, be said to be anywhere.

But the habit of mind represented by this fallacy is not confined to the problem of locating a physical body. Among behaviorist psychologists, for example, this fallacy flourishes in the form of an habitual prejudice for data of simple peripheral movement, which, so it can be said, can be described without any "subjective" interpretive component on the part of the observer. Thus, a man tells us he is feeling angry; and his anger on this occasion, he further specifies, is directed at the current state of the world: at the follies and crimes of man unable to deal with human affairs. If we know him well, we may have reason to believe that his anger flows from many sources—from his responses to the state of the world just as he claims, but also from an aggravated domestic situation, a tendency to lash out angrily at any affront, and a generalized insecurity that often expresses itself in aggressive acts. The meaning of his anger—whether we trace it back to its early developmental roots, describe it phenomenologically, rationalize it objectively, or discuss its psycho-dynamic implications—is not a simply locatable phenomenon. Its reality is not captured by reference to twitching eyebrows, grumbling noises, jerky gestures of the hand, harsh words and actions or adrenalin secretions. It is not a coincidence that those psychologists who are most passionately concerned with elevating the study of man to the status of rigorous science are most prone to assume that what is real has the property of simple location.

In Whitehead's view, these two fallacies stem from, and are reinforced by, the Cartesian doctrine of "clear and distinct" ideas. Descartes' answer to the question "What is knowledge?" was that it consisted in the reductive analysis of complex states of affairs into simpler components, and ultimately into the simplest components that would be altogether clear and distinct. Only the clarity and distinctness of these ultimate components could guarantee the absolute certainty without which knowledge would not be truly knowledge. This view is further reinforced by "common sense." Our most clear and distinct perceptions are of concrete physical objects that occupy a locatable and stable region of space, i.e., our bodies, the ground beneath our feet, and the solid bric-a-brac amid which we spend our lives.

What we have here, then, is a single ideal model of knowledge (which, paradoxically, Descartes had generalized from his experience specifically within mathematics) that is to be imposed upon every field of research—a Platonic archetype of knowledge that must be approximated by any discipline that aspires to be truly "scientific." Psychologists are easily caught up in this Cartesian quest for certainty.

The Pragmatists:
James and Dewey

William James was at different times both a professional psychologist and a professional philosopher, but in fact the two roles were never separated in his thinking. Indeed, a good case could be made for the contention that his *Principles of Psychology* (1890), where he professed to write as an avowed scientific psychologist, happens also to be his major philosophical work. In any event, the fact that he functioned as both philosopher and psychologist should make this work, old-fashioned as it may seem to many contemporary psychologists, a primary text for anyone who seeks a more adequate theoretical grounding for psychology.

James's avowed intention in this work was to advance the cause of psychology as a "natural science"—that is, to help its development as a laboratory science along the lines in which it had only recently been set up on the European continent. At the time, brain physiology was very much to the fore, and the task of psychology was conceived in this light. The ideal goal of psychology, conceived as a "natural science," is, as James puts it, to establish laws of correlation between brain states and states of consciousness. Accordingly, James begins with the assumption of a working, or scientific "dualism": there are, on the one hand, brain states, and, on the other hand, corresponding states of consciousness; the task of the psychologist is to establish lawful correlations between these two separate sets of entities. And in this project James insists that he is proceeding as a practical scientist wishing to steer clear of all philosophical speculation. Yet he was also candid enough later to acknowledge that into this whole structure "the waters of metaphysics leak at every seam"; and indeed, as the argument of his *Principles* proceeds, these leaks turn into a small flood.

The first difficulty arises when we seek to identify the conscious states with which we would like to correlate corresponding brain states. For conscious states have to be identified by the objects they are conscious of: such and such a mental state, say, we identify as the perception of blue. Conscious states are thus not self-enclosed entities, but always point beyond themselves to the objects which they intend or are conscious of. We have, therefore, to add to our two original sets of entities —brain states and conscious states—a third: namely, those entities of which mental states are conscious, and without which such mental states could not even be identified.

But the trouble does not stop there. You cannot add this third set of objects (viz., the objects of consciousness) without altering the whole theoretical set-up. Not all objects of consciousness are simple patches of blue; psychology has to deal with the whole rich and varied welter of experience, which includes such complex states of mind as fantasies, delusions, and obscure feelings about the self. How do we distinguish a fantasy from an ordinary perception? The object of the former, we say, is not real. And James is thus forced to posit a whole "world of practical realities" (the real world as distinguished from delusions) within which we can identify conscious states, and without which those states would have little meaning. (This "world of practical realities," as we shall see shortly, is exactly identical with what Husserl was later to call the *Lebenswelt*, or life-world.) When we come to the various complex feelings about the self, we are pushed beyond isolated and self-enclosed states of consciousness into a whole network of human and object relations with this practical world, apart from which the human ego could not be understood.

Thus, the cardinal lesson of the *Principles* is that James was forced by what he called "the stubborn and irreducible facts" to renounce his initial dualism and to posit the concrete everyday world as the matrix within which all meanings are developed, and the context in which experiments are set up and communication between fellow scientists takes place.

This conclusion, forced upon James the psychologist, provides the key to his later philosophy. James's variety of pragmatism was not merely an adherence to the pragmatic principle of verification (namely, that any idea is to be tested by its consequences in action). The pragmatic principle itself becomes a kind of appeal to turn our attention to the concrete, every-

day human world as the constant in which all thinking is
grounded. Indeed, instead of "pragmatism" he is more likely
to call his thought in its later phases by the names "radical
empiricism" or "radical pluralism"—terms intended to emphasize the sheer diversity and variety of the items within experience. James's own answer to the question "What is really
real?" is that the life-world in all its concreteness and fullness
—"the world of practical realities"—is the reality with which
thinking must always start and to which it has always to return.

This answer gives rise, in turn, to a corresponding theory
about the nature of knowledge. In our desire for explanation,
James acknowledges, we have of course to collect and classify
facts, and thus at some points neglect the diversity and concreteness of experience. But at the same time, he warns us that
this desire for explanation can become self-defeating if it proceeds by replacing the concreteness of experience with some
empty and all-embracing monism (such as, in our time, the
reduction of experience to units of sensation, or stimulus-
response bonds, or instinctual drives seeking release). Human
reason is not a faculty that enables us to penetrate to some
absolute scheme of reality that lies above or behind what we
actually observe in experience. Rather, our ability to reason,
perceive, and analyze is a kind of activity arising within past
and present experience and directed to future experience. This
activity arises out of some discordance or irritant within experience and orients us toward the removal of that irritant in order
to assure a stable expectation about the future. All matters of
theory and explanation are thus ultimately activities of man
functioning within his own life-world, and not those of the
analyst-observer standing outside of this world.

The pragmatism of John Dewey presents many contrasts and
similarities with James's thinking; but for our purposes the
Dewey we wish to draw upon is the philosopher in what may
be called his late-middle period, particularly as brought to expression in one book, *The Quest for Certainty* (1929). Dewey's
central theme here takes off from an interpretation of Cartesianism as a philosophy dominated by the search for absolute
certainty. (Heidegger's interpretation of Descartes also insists
that the latter's thought has to be construed from this basic

motif of the search for unshakeable certainty. This search for absolute certainty leads the thinker far away from the rough-and-ready world of human affairs, in which at best only more or less reliable probabilities are attainable. Instead, the strict Cartesian fastens upon some *a priori* scheme of entities—clear and distinct ideas, atomistic bits of experience, etc.—and seeks to impose this scheme rigidly on the changing and shifting facts of our experienced world. There then arises a distrust of the day-to-day world of human affairs and of the knowledge that can be gained about it. Basically, such distrust casts doubt on the capacity of our ordinary day-to-day experience to generate its own standards for gaining true "scientific" knowledge of human affairs. The appeal is always to something more certain —more "really real"—that lies above or behind this day-to-day prosaic experience.

Dewey, of course, is very much limited by the historical conditions in which he grew up. Since he wrote his major work, scientific psychology has greatly expanded in influence, and were Dewey alive today, he might well be troubled by the many ways in which the quest for certainty has led academic psychologists away from pressing, substantive issues into an ever-increasing formalism and preoccupation with methodology, especially on its mathematical side. But in his formative years—a time dominated by transcendental and religious philosophy—a generous dose of behaviorism and experimentalism was a welcome transfusion into the intellectual bloodstream. The shoe is now on the other foot.

As for his views on psychology as a science, Dewey inclined to a rather ambivalent, loosely phrased, but suggestive version of behaviorism. Nevertheless, his basic contention, moving in the opposite direction to behaviorism, seems to us very relevant to the needs of the human sciences today: namely, that they will advance only by allowing "experience itself to generate its own regulative standards" for knowing, rather than by clamping down some absolute and *a priori* models of "scientific" knowledge that happen to work well for unrelated disciplines.

British Analytic Philosophy: Moore and Wittgenstein

British philosophy speaks with a very different tone of voice from that of American pragmatism; its tradition, terminology, and methods of procedure are all distinctly its own. Yet British philosophers in this century have carried on much the same kind of struggle against the entrenched modes of Cartesian thought.

The innovator in this struggle was G. E. Moore, who described his work as a "philosophy of common sense." Here common sense is not meant as the popular amalgam of values, folk wisdom and familiar truisms. Rather, Moore, like Dewey and James, is concerned with defending the world of our ordinary experience and the truths we can have within and about that world as reliable, against any attempt to reduce this ordinary world to an illusory appearance of some other reality, alleged to be more basic.

The force of Moore's position can be best gauged in terms of his opposition to Bertrand Russell. If the exception is needed to prove the rule, then Russell might be cited as the perfect Cartesian exception to prove that the dominant tendency of contemporary philosophy has been anti-Cartesian. For Russell has persisted throughout his long career as the one uncompromising Cartesian of our century.* In his usual witty and incisive fashion, Russell has summed up his Cartesianism in the form of a concise logical dilemma:

If physics is true, then common sense is false.
[Physics reveals a world of atoms and electrons that is

---

* Still, even Russell has had his waverings. In the period of his Neutral Monism he was concerned with overcoming the basic Cartesian dualism of matter and mind. However, his method of attempting this was still fundamentally Cartesian in outlook.

altogether different from the world as we commonly perceive it.]

But if common sense is true, then physics is true.
[On the basis of our ordinary perceptions, we can confirm the theories of physics.]

Hence, in any case, common sense is false.
[It leads to its own undoing by leading us beyond itself to another and very different world that is more really real than it.]

One could scarcely have a more pointed expression of the Cartesian dualism between the human world ("common sense") and the world of physics. And, just as typically, the world of physics is accorded a primary status in reality.

The gist of Moore's philosophy might be summed up by his response to Russell's dilemma. Moore takes this dilemma by the horns: if common sense were not true (at least in some part), how could we ever derive physics from it—and curiously enough, a physics that is supposed to refute it?

Moore is particularly revealing in his discussion of one of the most perplexing problems we have inherited with Descartes' legacy—the so-called Problem of Other Minds. We see other people from the outside, hear their voices, and watch their movements; but we never directly perceive their minds. Can we ever, then, be absolutely certain that they have minds like our own? (Or even that they have minds at all, since we never directly experience those minds?) On the face of it, this might seem one of those problems that are the silly games of the academic recluse and have no bearing upon practical matters —certainly not upon the concrete research of psychology. But the question of whether other minds are accessible to the psychologist has a considerable bearing upon how he proceeds to build up his science. Many behaviorists, for example, have decided both on philosophical and practical grounds that other minds are, in principle, inaccessible, and they therefore restrict their data to externally observable behavior. Moore, on the other hand, sides with common sense in holding that other people most assuredly have minds and that we do in fact know (under certain circumstances) what is going on in them. It is simply a case, he states, of a misplaced Cartesian search for absolute certainty, to demand some immediate and indubitable proof of the content of other people's minds before we are willing to say that these minds are accessible to us. (Perhaps the most disastrous assumption made by the strict behaviorist is that his experimental and operational "proofs" are somehow more certain and indisputable than those which attempt to gauge men's thoughts and feelings more directly.) The persistent direction of all Moore's arguments is to establish the world of our ordinary experience—which is also the world of our ordinary language—as the basic matrix from which all thinking, certainly the philosopher's, has to proceed.

Moore emphasized ordinary language, but Ludwig Wittgenstein carried the idea much further. Wittgenstein has become the strongest influence in British philosophy today, and probably in American philosophy as well. His thinking is divided into two very different periods, which are commonly labeled Wittgenstein I and Wittgenstein II. This development from the earlier to the later Wittgenstein seems to us one of the most instructive lessons provided by contemporary philosophy, and one that is particularly relevant to our present task of seeking some more adequate foundations for psychoanalysis.

Wittgenstein I is a visionary who found his vision of the one ideal and paradigmatic language in Russell and Whitehead's *Principia Mathematica,* a work which attempted to express the whole of mathematics as a part of pure logic. This logical language would thus be basic to all forms of human discourse that made any claim to rigor or cogency. Indeed, it would be a kind of Platonic archetype, to which other forms of language must approximate to the degree that they can be said to be precise. Thus an antecedent standard of rigor is laid down *a priori* for any discipline, quite apart from its own particular subject matter or needs. Moreover, this ideal language of the *Principia* analyzed expressions into complex and simple —molecular and atomic—statements. Since there are atomic statements—so Wittgenstein reasoned in quite Platonic fashion from the character of language to the character of reality— there must be atomic facts corresponding to those statements. What we call the world is ultimately nothing but the totality of atomic facts, all of them externally related. Here is the most austere and thoroughgoing philosophic reductionism that contemporary thought has produced. If science were to become ultimately complete, it would be no more than a systematic catalogue of the atomic facts.

The early Wittgenstein may thus be summed up in three points:

1. Linguistic monism: there is one ideal language that furnishes the standard for all other forms of discourse;
2. Logical atomism: the world is simply the aggregate of atomic facts;
3. Reductive and prescriptive analysis: one language should be prescribed as the standard for discourse in all fields, and all discourse should be reduced to the ideal form.

On all these points Wittgenstein II took a radically opposed position. He became a linguistic pluralist rather than a monist. There is no longer, he maintained, a single ideal language whose standards must be prescribed as binding for all other modes of discourse. Instead, there are plural fields of discourse—"language games," as he called them—which must be played, as we do in games, according to their own specific rules. Gone too is the notion of language as a one-to-one picturing of facts; and, consequently, the attendant notion that there are atomic facts to be pictured. The meaning of any word is not a compact mental concept lodged somewhere in a container mind. Meaning is always contextual—given to us in the activity of using language. The context of language, moreover, is never closed, but open-ended: "The meaning of the expression depends entirely on how we *go on* using it." (Our italics.) Ultimately, this context of language and meaning cannot be bounded anywhere short of its being total: "A word has meaning within the stream of life."

The later Wittgenstein still maintains continuity with his earlier period by claiming that what he is doing is merely analyzing linguistic usage. Our intellectual puzzles, he tells us, arise from our snarls in language. We take one expression to be the same as another because they are superficially similar, and we therefore fail to note that in their meanings and usage the two expressions are of very different kinds. When this snarl of language is untangled, our intellectual cramp (the puzzlement at the original problem) disappears. But, in fact, the linguistic analysis employed by the later Wittgenstein is much more than talk about words; for the process of linguistic disentanglement has to be guided throughout by the persistent scrutiny of the typical situations in life where we use language. The later Wittgenstein is talking about the world of reality as much as about language. (In the philosophic jargon, he is talking in the material mode as much as in the formal mode; and indeed, it would be more accurate to say that he has passed beyond the dualism of these two modes.)

In what has now become a famous imperative from his *Philosophic Investigations* (1953) Wittgenstein tells us: "Don't think, look!" What can such an apparently paradoxical exhortation mean, coming from a philosopher, when philosophers are supposed to be people who spend all their time "thinking"? Wittgenstein's words here—granted all the differences of method, terminology, and background—have the same intent as did Husserl's famous rallying cry to his phenomenological disciples: "To the things themselves!" We are not to let our own preconceived abstractions obscure what is there to be looked at. And what is it that is there to be looked at? The world that is open and accessible to our common human experience—the world from which thinking starts and to which it must always return. "The facts that concern us," Wittgenstein tells us in a memorable sentence, "lie open before us." And in case there should be any doubt how far his notion of analyzing language has departed from his earlier reductive and legislative positivism, there is the even more memorable sentence (which ought perhaps to be emblazoned as a banner for psychologists): "It can never be our job to reduce anything to anything." What remains then as the job of philosophy? "Philosophy," he states, "really *is* 'purely descriptive.'" We seem here to have arrived, by a very different route, at the same goal of philosophy as pure description that the phenomenologists aspire to.

Wittgenstein never developed his thought in its full historical context as an encounter with the dominant conceptions of the Cartesian epoch. Such an explicit confrontation is carried out by his follower, Gilbert Ryle, in his valuable book, *The Concept of Mind*. (1949.) Ryle sets out explicitly to demolish the

Cartesian concept of mind as the myth of "The Ghost in the Machine." The phrase is so apt for portraying the Cartesian dualism of mind and body, and has become so current in the literature, that we shall henceforth make use of it where convenient. For Descartes, the human body as pure extended substance (*res extensa*) is a machine inside which is located a radically different kind of entity—the "immaterial" entity of mind—that somehow interacts with the machine. Most of Ryle's book is devoted to expelling the myth of the ghost; and he does so cogently. But when we have expelled the ghost, are we to be left only with the machine? Are we back to the early materialist conception of a narrow mechanism as an adequate account of the conscious human person? Ryle indicates his rejection of such an alternative; but he is able to approach the question only at the end of his book (it takes so many pages to drive "the ghost" out), and so his answer to mechanistic behaviorism seems not nearly satisfactory enough.

A more satisfactory answer, or at least the basis of such, is provided by one of the most austere and respected English philosophers, John Austin, in a paper on "Other Minds." It is regrettable that Professor Austin's premature death did not permit him to pursue the clues to this question that he planted in his essay of 1948. In his basic contention Austin merely reaffirms the position of G. E. Moore on the problem of other minds: of course, we do know that other minds exist, and of course, we do know, in certain situations, what goes on in other people's minds—for example, whether another person is angry, dejected, or whatever. Austin's originality consists in the abundant detail by means of which he energetically brings forward our ordinary experience and our ordinary language as the indispensable context that cannot be brushed aside without destroying the possibility of sense and meaning altogether.

The most searching part of Austin's essay occurs toward the end, and it seems almost incidental. He asks what leads people to raise questions about other minds in the first place. Let us say that in a certain situation we ask ourselves why we believe a person when he tells us he is angry. We go on, then, to the more basic question: "Why ever believe him at all?"

The question, pushed further, becomes a challenge to the very possibility of "believing another man," in its or-

dinarily accepted sense, at all. What justification is there
for supposing that there is another mind communicating
with you at all? How can you know what it would be
like for another mind to feel anything, and so how can
you understand it? It is then that we are tempted to say
that we only mean by "believing him" that we take
certain vocal noises as signs of impending behavior, and
that "other minds" are no more really real than unconscious desires.

This, however, is distortion. It seems, rather, that believing
in other persons . . . is an essential part of the act of
communicating, an act which we all constantly perform.
*It is as much an irreducible part of our experience as . . .
sensing colored patches.* (P. 820.) (Our italics.)

It is unfortunate that Austin ended with this observation
instead of beginning with it. It is not so much a conclusion to
the problem of Other Minds as a point of departure. For all
such questions presuppose a common world of meaning—and
language—within which the discussion takes place. Indeed,
wherever you start investigating human experience you are
already immersed in meaning as well as language.

Consider the infant. Very early in his life he and mother and
mother's breast become part of an inextricable world of meanings that is not exhausted by simple location or subject-object
differentiations. The meaning of mother's breast is hardly the
same as or coextensive with a mass of tissue; it includes mother-
and-infant and the structures of basic trust, warmth, satisfaction, relief from frustration and sensory stimulation—all as
parts of a total context of meaning. From his very earliest
moments, the infant develops within a world of signs and
meaning; he is never outside of it. "Language," in the broadest
sense, signifies his ability to express himself, to respond to
meanings and to communicate—language in this sense, of
course, develops before the child actually learns to speak. A
disbelief in the existence of other minds (if such a disbelief
could even be entertained) would also be a disbelief in meaning
and language. In language we are already beyond ourselves
within a world whose meanings derive from and are shared

with other people. To cut myself off from that world would be to cut myself off from any possibility of meaning whatsoever. For language, as communication, is the activity in which that old absolute dichotomy between "inner" states of mind and "outer" peripheral body movements has already been transcended. Or, to put it another way, language is a witness of the one world in which the so-called "inner" and "outer" realities are equally at home. And, if we take language and signification seriously, the Cartesian abstractions are seen vividly as being too narrow, one-sided, and indeed—irrelevant.

The Phenomenologist:
Edmund Husserl

That most European of philosophers, Edmund Husserl, the founder of phenomenology, acknowledged the American William James as one of the main sources for his own conceptions of consciousness and its essential connections with the life-world. Yet his thought grows indigenously out of his own situation within German philosophy. At the end of the nineteenth century there was in Germany as well as elsewhere a deadly impasse in philosophy between idealism and materialism —an impasse that stemmed from the original Cartesian dualism between mind and matter. Where, then, was philosophy to turn, and what was to be done to break out of its futile and demoralizing paralysis?

Husserl, who pondered this problem at length, proposed a strategy of starting all over again with a new point of departure. There lies ahead for philosophy, he said, an immense task of pure description. Before we can resolve the puzzles that so confound us we must return "to the things themselves," and study what is given in experience directly, without the obscuring abstractions and distorting preconceptions that have been allowed to creep into philosophy. To this discipline of pure description—this strict method for approaching experience free of *a priori* presuppositions—Husserl gave the name phenomenology. Its fulfillment he conceived to be a joint task shared by many philosophers working together.

To prepare philosophy for its new task of pure description, certain prefatory steps were necessary. First of all, the reality question ("What is really real?") is to be provisionally set aside so as not to intrude in the work of description. When we turn to look at the objects around us, such as the ordinary things in a room, these objects present themselves in varying modes of shape, color, changing perspectives, temporal and spatial variations. We must try to describe and place these manifestations in context, but we must not take the leap beyond the phenomena as they are given in order to speculate whether they belong to the category of "matter" or of "mind." It is not the task of phenomenology, as a descriptive discipline, to make metaphysical speculations about what lies behind what is presented in experience.

Secondly, one has to get rid of the distorting notion of consciousness as a container filled with contents. This metaphor of the mind as a container has had a peculiar dominance not only within philosophy but within everyday language as well. The phrase "in the mind" is one of our commonest locutions, and as such it seems to be understood by everybody and therefore to be perfectly harmless. "What do you have in mind?" we ask another person; and the question seems perfectly clear and understandable (as it is, in fact, but on a higher level of abstraction than might first appear to be obvious). The phrase "in the mind" gives rise to the habit of thinking of the mind as a peculiar kind of cabinet that contains special kinds of contents: "mental contents," which as mental, of course, must be very different in their nature from the material objects around us. And so we are trapped again in the dualistic puzzle. On the contrary, Husserl insists, nothing is, literally speaking, "in the mind": it is the very nature of consciousness to point beyond itself. This is the doctrine of the "intentionality" of consciousness: consciousness always intends, refers, or points toward something other than itself. Consciousness is always consciousness *of*. Only because consciousness always points beyond itself is genuine communication possible, and it is the world we experience in common that makes other people's minds accessible to our own experience.

To describe the field of phenomenology we need one additional notion—Husserl's concept of the life-world (*Lebenswelt*) as the enveloping context within which all our meanings, theoretical as well as practical, have ultimately to be grounded. Intentions, or meanings, do not come to us in isolated atomistic fragments; they are always interwoven with other intentions and meanings that lead on to an ever-broadening context. This total context, with its interlinked meanings, is the world in which we live, the human world and not the abstract world depicted by the physical sciences. All scientific abstractions are developed and assume their ultimate meaning within this concrete life-world; such abstractions help us to connect parts of this experiential world and see their interrelationships; but these abstractions can never be used to substitute for the concrete world of human life. The mistake of scientific materialism is to confuse what is derivative with what is basic, i.e., to take the abstractions of physics as the ultimately concrete—the really real—realities behind the everyday world rather than the other way around.

A paradoxical aspect of Husserl's thought is that, though he set out to knife through a philosophic obstacle originally created by the dualism of Descartes, he nevertheless continued to the very end of his life to consider his own theory as a purified and corrected form of Cartesianism. It would be a Cartesianism more rigorous than that of Descartes and without the presuppositions the latter carried over from medieval metaphysics, but it would stay faithful to the Cartesian tradition.

It remained for Husserl's disciple and successor, Martin Heidegger, to throw off the Cartesian trammels thoroughly and decisively from phenomenology.

The Existentialist:
Martin Heidegger

Heidegger pushed Husserl's notion of the intentionality of consciousness to its logical conclusion. All traces of consciousness as a subject-container of experiences are now gone for good. Consciousness does not reside in a cabinet from which it goes out into the world to bring back the booty of experiences that it then stores within the cabinet. On the contrary, man is always and everywhere beyond himself within a world of objects, people, and meanings. We can "intend" any object—for example, the simple business of pointing to the chair across the room—only within a whole; and ultimately the whole is the concrete totality of our world. Thus, it is only because man is essentially a being within the world that anything like the intentionality of consciousness—i.e., consciousness as a bearer of meanings—is even possible.

Heidegger, in fact, carries on an elaborate and very subtle description of human existence without using the term "consciousness" at all. But he does not accomplish this description by a behavioristic reduction that would confine itself only to elementary peripheral or so-called "outer" data. Here Heidegger's example can be extraordinarily helpful to psychologists who have long been hung up on the dispute over whether so-called "introspective" data are scientifically permissible, or whether the really scientific psychologist must confine himself to reporting external behavior that can be observed without any elements of "interpretation" on his part. Behind this debate there has lurked the unexpunged dualism between physical behavior, which is taken to be public and accessible, and mental states, which are hidden away in the supposedly private and inaccessible container called mind. Heidegger shows us that so-called "introspective" data—including the most intimate and subtle of moods and feelings—are modes of being in which we are attuned in one way or another to the world. Hence they are in principle accessible to mutual and common understanding.

For Heidegger, the world is not merely a matter of concepts and states of mind within which we move as thinkers or knowers; it is, more basically, the whole field of our human cares and concerns in the most ordinary as well as most extreme situations of life. Man is a tinkerer-about-the-home as well as a heroic or cowardly facer-of-death. Man is a radically finite and time-bound creature, exposed to the possibilities of death, anxiety, guilt, and responsibility, the loss of or the establishing of the self—a creature capable of losing himself in inauthenticity, or measuring up in lucid resolve to his potentialities. And, among all the potentialities that make man's being what it is, the most central and dramatic is the promise of finding meaning for ourselves. The world, as we know it most urgently and intimately, is the total structure of all such promises and possibilities; and only within that structure are we able to win what meaning we can for our lives.

The highly dramatic character of many of Heidegger's analyses has obscured for some readers his central views on the nature of truth and language, which while less flamboyant, are perhaps more valuable for our present purposes. Truth, as traditionally understood, consists in the correspondence between a mental state (a judgment) and the fact that the mental state somehow "represents." But what does such a correspondence mean? We can match up one half-dollar with another, and say they correspond (i.e., they coincide in size and shape, resemble each other in color, hardness, etc.). But we do not go around matching up mental states with facts in any such literal sense. The statements of language do not designate isolated mental states (present in the mental cabinet) that are then to be paired off with things external to the mind. The farmer, squinting at the sky, says: "Those clouds mean rain." Things connect and link up with one another within the world; and as we move within that open world of meanings, we exist within a universe of signs and language. Language is not, essentially, a series of sounds that are supposed to "represent" mental states, which in turn somehow "represent" things external to the mind. Sounds become meaningful language only because man exists within a world of stable and lawful events,

interconnections and meanings. Thus, any concept of proposi-
tional truth must presuppose the prior concept of truth as un-
concealment (*a-leitheia*): that the world of persons, clouds and
rain already to some degree lies open and accessible to us. We
"know" this world before we formulate propositions about it,
and we presuppose it whenever we deliberately fabricate language and meaning.

This view of truth and language has a very useful implication in that it suggests a way of taking into account the many
different modalities of truth with which the sciences of man
have to be concerned. If truth occurs in the activity of disclosing or bringing into the open, then our idea of truth must
encompass many different modes of disclosing besides those of
straightforward and baldly factual statements, to be verified
by a series of "operations." A poem does not disclose in the
same way as a proposition or a theory in physics or a psychotic
delusion or an executive's ambitions for his company. Nor
need we confine disclosure merely to the use of verbal language;
a painting or a political action or a painful back may all disclose to us the truth of some portion of the world and human
existence within it. Obviously, any worker in the human
sciences has to be aware of the diverse ways in which human
beings come to reveal themselves, and must develop sensible
and relevant standards for using and evaluating these different
modes.

We started this discussion with Whitehead and we will end
it with Heidegger. Since these two are the most explicitly
anti-Cartesian of modern philosophers, it is revealing to observe
their strikingly different approaches to the same theme. Whitehead, trained in mathematics and natural science, comes to
these questions via the convulsive discoveries in modern physics
that have shaken up the older tenets of scientific materialism.
His method, accordingly, is logical and analytic as he seeks
to identify the fallacies that lie beneath the Cartesian assumptions. Heidegger, on the other hand, as the heir of the great
German philosophic tradition, relies more heavily on an interpretive reconstruction of the history of philosophy. He raises
and answers the question of how the views contained in the

Cartesian dualism arose, and where, at their very source in the Western tradition, they arose.

Just as we borrowed from the critical side of Whitehead's thought without calling upon his positive philosophy of organism, we shall borrow from Heidegger's superb insight into the history of philosophy without bringing in his highly charged and ambiguous existentialism. For whatever reservations there may be about Heidegger's positive philosophy, his historical grasp of the origins of Cartesianism is sweeping and profound. It is well worth citing here, even in compressed form, because it lays bare in a single flash of insight the whole vista of our Western intellectual history of which Cartesianism became the essential, not merely peripheral, development.

For Heidegger, the modern European tradition in philosophy, from Descartes through Kant and the post-Kantians, is the culmination of a long-established line of thought built on a false foundation. Logic-minded philosophers working in this tradition have done a superb job in drawing forth the implications of the premises which they inherited. But it is the premises themselves which are to be questioned; and these roots Heidegger traces back to fateful decisions made several thousand years ago by Plato and Aristotle. These are not, of course, mere factual errors or logical fallacies gone undetected for over twenty-five hundred years. Rather, for Heidegger, they are partial and derivative truths that illuminate with stark clarity one aspect of reality, but plunge others into obscurity. These decisions helped to create the physical sciences—the supreme and unique achievement of the West. At the same time, however, they built a false base for the understanding of man's nature.

In Heidegger's reconstruction, it is Plato's and Aristotle's theories of the nature of being, truth and reality that ultimately culminated in the one-sided truths of modern philosophy. The very core of the problem is to be discovered by putting together Plato's doctrine of Universals with Aristotle's doctrine of Being.

Plato turned the pre-Socratic question of the nature of Being into his own theory of the nature of reality. And reality for Plato most emphatically did not mean the common, everyday world experienced by the senses of man, which he felt was evanescent, corrupt and shot through and through with error. In his famous metaphor of the shadows in the cave he equates the shadows with the mistaken impression of reality we get when we rely on our ordinary sense perception. For Plato, the "really real" lies rather in an abstract structure of universal Ideas. Heidegger's interpretation of Plato is that in denying to the senses the ability to grasp truth and in awarding this vision solely to the rational intellect, Plato reified the domain of abstractions and located truth in the subjectivity of the reasoning mind. He thereby identified reality not with a world we can see or hear or feel but with purely rational (i.e., logically analyzable) perspectives. Plato's reality is thus the abstract "object" of the reasoning intellect—the silent, static, eternal world of Essences.

In cleaving reality into two worlds—the intelligible and sensory—Plato also changed the very meaning of truth. And this shift in the meaning of truth, according to Heidegger, was a momentous step for Western civilization as a whole. For the earlier Greeks, truth was realized by any actions or words that served to reveal things or beings in the world around us. Thus, the miming gesture of a dancer could show in a sudden flash all the nuances of a character type. The speech of a statesman could disclose to his people the full meaning of their life together within the city-state. The Homeric chant, in its majestic rise and fall, could show the brief transience of the hero's glory and the bitter pathos of man's brief days upon this earth. All of these and many more were equally modes of truth; all served to bring forth into the open what may have been virtually known but was never seen so clearly. With Plato, however, these plural modes of knowing are narrowed into a monolithic ideal: truth exists in the intellect, and only in the intellect, and consists in the correctness or rigor (*orthotes*) of its concepts. Behind this shift lies the priority that Plato accords to mathematics among all the human sciences. Here we are but a step from, if indeed we are not already arrived at, the position that every discipline becomes really scientific only to the degree that it approximates the model of mathematics. Later, Descartes and Kant are only carrying out the Platonic emphasis when they declare that the mind will attain absolute certainty only when it imposes its own constructs upon the world.

Heidegger elucidates his Platonic shift of truth strictly within the context of the history of philosophy; but the point has a special and profound relevance for the human sciences. For it is precisely in dealing with the human person that we must be prepared, as Weisman sensed, to countenance plural modes of knowing: different ways and means of bringing into the open what human beings are and what they experience.

The dualism Plato introduced between the world of intellect and the world of the senses led eventually to the Cartesian split between subject and object. The post-Cartesian idealists took over the subjective side of Plato; the empirical realists rejected Plato's Universals as mere empty abstractions. They assigned reality instead to the material objects of the senses, and later to operations performed by measuring devices. In so doing, they were in fact retaining the framework of Plato's basic dualism, while merely altering the terms that function within that framework.

Partly building on Plato's thought and partly reacting against it, Aristotle made a second fateful move. In his introductory work on logic, *The Categories*, Aristotle developed an analysis of Being in terms of ten categories—substance, quantity, quality, relation, place, time, position, action, passion, habit. He uses a language and a metaphysics less appropriate to the study of human experience than to physical objects—their spatiality, their material composition, and their qualities. In Aristotle's analysis of the physical world, any unique characteristic of man such as the sheer temporality of man's being—for Heidegger the crucial category of human existence—somehow recedes into the background. If the world of Plato is timeless in the sense of being out-of-time altogether, the categories of Aristotle imply the kind of existence in time experienced solely by a physical object —a material substratum with qualities inhering in it—whose identity does not change in time in the same sense in which a man's identity will become transformed over the course of his life.

Aristotle's categories, therefore, set the pattern for human experience to be analyzed within a framework more appropriate to solid physical objects than to the human experience. In Aristotle, however, the concept of what an object is still remains a very broad one. In Aristotle's world of objects, birth and death are meaningful concepts; and purpose, direction, and fulfillment are possible for all forms of organic being, even plants and trees. Each object under the sun has its own *dynamis* (potentiality)—its opportunities for purposeful growth.

Descartes inherited the Aristotelian orthodoxies of the Middle Ages at a time when Galileo's revolution had begun to strip objects of their rich qualitative characteristics. (Newton's revolution ultimately reduced the world of objects to aggregates of bits of matter moving about in otherwise empty space.) In Descartes' hands, material objects come to lose their concrete and specific character: the vital world of Aristotelian objects is transformed into an inert world of abstract matter whose defining characteristic is extension in space. Descartes reserved purpose and becoming to the thinking self, the Cartesian ego. But even the Cartesian ego is modeled on the world of objects. Ideas are in it in the same metaphysical way color, for instance, is in physical objects. This nonmaterial object, the thinking ego, is locked up in the physical body. In Ryle's phrase, it is the "ghost in the machine."

We cannot, then, says Heidegger, blame Descartes for Cartesianism. When Aristotelian logic became the chief conceptual tool of the Middle Ages, the metaphysical equation of reality with the world of objects was already built into the very structure of Western thought and language. Descartes, usually considered the villain, did not invent this usage; he simply took it over from his medieval predecessors. His own contribution was to narrow the definition of what a material object is: the Cartesian world of matter became quality-less and abstract, reflecting the new physics of his day.

Within the historical context sketched by Heidegger, we can perhaps more readily understand why the struggle against Cartesianism is so stubborn and why the thought of philosophers so diverse in temperament as well as national tradition must move toward closing with this central issue in our Western intellectual heritage. We begin to see that whether we stand within our own native tradition of American pragmatism, or a philosophy of science based, as with Whitehead, on modern mathematics and physics, or within the "ordinary language" school of British philosophy of Wittgenstein and Austin, or the tradition of phenomenology and existentialism, we find a common thrust, at long last, toward breaking out of the Cartesian bonds. We also find the common conclusion that reducing the world as we experience it to indirect and abstract forms of "reality" which we do not experience is a false and unrewarding procedure.

The new philosophical consensus opens a gaping hole in what once seemed to be the logically unassailable structure of determinism, materialism and the causal theory of perception—the structure within which the theory and practice of psychoanalysis, experimental psychology, sociology, and the other sciences of man continue to exist.

FIFTEEN

The Lessons of the "Consensus"

For our purposes the philosophical "consensus" may be represented as an agreement on three points: first: Cartesianism is fundamentally wrong—in its conception of mind as matter *manqué*, in its locus of certainty in the knowing subject, and in its dichotomies of mind versus matter and subject versus object. Second: the Cartesian mind and matter are not the ultimate items of reality but high-level abstractions, useful in some contexts but misleading in others, but in no case providing us a presuppositionless and concrete description of reality. And third: the reality that underlies these abstractions has, in some way or another, to do with common everyday prescientific experience. This version of reality is what Wittgenstein means when he states that the facts which concern us lie spread out before us; it is what William James means by radical empiricism, what John Dewey means by his emphasis on common experience, what G. E. Moore means by his particular concept of "common sense," what Husserl means by the *Lebenswelt*, and it is what, with some qualifications, Heidegger means by his concept of being-in-the-world.

The consensus is a notable achievement of twentieth century philosophy. But it is clearly only a beginning. For our purposes let us assume that its negative side has been well documented and let us proceed to its positive contribution—its appeal to common human experience. For here we may find a point of departure for developing an alternative philosophy that will work better for the human sciences.

The first of the philosophical questions for which we will seek a new answer is the ancient Platonic one, "What is really real?" Scientific materialism answers this question by reserving the status of reality to entities that enjoy the property of simple location. In the metapsychology, it is the instinctual energies rooted in the bodily processes that are "really real." The Freudian concept of the psychic apparatus mirrors the Cartesian definition of mind as a nonmaterial substance, i.e., it is conceived in analogy with a physical object even though it lacks the defining characteristics of a physical object.

How one answers this curious philosophical question dictates everyday scientific practice and everyday therapy to an extraordinary degree. Certainly it bears on two crucial decisions psychologists are constantly called upon to make—where to begin their investigations and how to explain human experience. If a psychologist starts from the old tradition—Cartesianism as elaborated by Locke and Hume—he will show his philosophical commitment in three ways: he will tend to begin with some atomistic unit (a unit of energy, a need, a drive, an instinct, a sensation, a perception, a stimulus-response bond, etc.); he will seek to ground this unit of experience on indisputably certain data (i.e., data having the "real reality" of simple location such as overt behavior, measurable sensations, bodily processes, etc.); and he will look behind experience in order to find an explanation of it (e.g., to the energies of the psychic apparatus, to the drives, to operant conditioning, etc.). — *mechanism*

It is not easy for most psychologists, if they have been scientifically trained, to proceed in any other way. No other way appeals to what has become, after centuries, a heritage of scientific common sense. The human sciences have let themselves be boxed in.

A viable alternative must develop a full understanding of why one should not take any of these three steps: why one should not start with an atomic unit of experience, or identify psychic reality with what can be established with absolute theoretical certainty, or look to the world behind the world as an explanation of it on the grounds that somehow this concealed world is the more real one.

Merleau-Ponty, the outstanding French interpreter of phenomenology, makes the point that even in Europe where phenomenology is far more popular and better known than in this country, the question of what it is remains largely unanswered —and this despite the more than a half century that has passed since Husserl's work first appeared. Merleau-Ponty marvels at the favorable reaction so many readers have to their first encounter with Husserl, and to his successor Heidegger, without necessarily understanding what they are responding to. "People," he says, "have the experience not so much of encountering a new philosophy as of recognizing what they have been waiting for." (Merleau-Ponty, 1962, p. *viii.*)

The words are apt. Workers in the human sciences constantly experience dissatisfaction, a sense of uneasiness, a vague feeling that something is basically wrong. When some encounter phenomenology, they sense that here is a theory which seizes upon and correctly diagnoses a fundamental flaw in our scientific approach to human experience. Phenomenology offers compelling reasons why these sciences seem so frequently to remain on the surface of human life—swarming all over the subject without ever truly coming to grips with it. A psychoanalyst tells a revealing anecdote. Planning for a long European trip, he transferred one of his patients to a colleague. He gave his colleague his files and a thorough briefing, including a massive written description of the case with details of dreams, associations, important experiences of his patient's early life, a medical work-up, information about the man's family, his work, etc., etc. After all these materials and the elaborate description of the case, his colleague turned to him and said: "That's all fine. But tell me, what's the man really like?"

Somehow the promise implied by phenomenology is that it is going to reveal "what the man is really like." It hints that it is moving directly to the heart of the matter, cutting through the abstractions and the formal conceptual machinery and the test results and all the obscuring scientific paraphernalia. It further implies that when we find out what the man is really like, the revelation will not be "scientific" but it will, nonetheless, help to make science more meaningful.

Does Husserl's phenomenology fulfill this promise for us? As it exists today, probably not. Husserl's work is too overladen with the preoccupations of another tradition to be directly transportable to the practical and pragmatic American scene. Further, in our judgment, it is full of one-sided and arbitrary assumptions alongside its valid insights. But it is immensely provocative, and if we follow the clues it gives us, there may truly be something we have been waiting for—a foothold, a place to stand, a place to begin.

It is likely that Husserl will play in our era the role that Descartes played in his own time, and for similar reasons. Husserl sought the same philosophical will-of-the-wisp as Descartes —an absolute foundation for certain and indisputable knowledge through philosophical reflection. Like Descartes, Husserl used the method of questioning all assumptions in order to arrive at what he believed to be a bedrock base of certain knowledge. And like Descartes, Husserl has left us with serious and far-reaching puzzles. Yet philosophers for several centuries have had to begin their work with Descartes; it was he who raised the most basic and perplexing questions, and it was he who established the framework within which these problems were to be examined.

And so it is with Husserl today. Husserl's work is full of difficulties, and his accomplishment is rendered ambiguous because he failed to achieve most of the objectives he set for himself. He failed to find a method for arriving at certain and indisputable knowledge through philosophical reflection; he failed to escape from the cage of subjectivity; he failed to establish philosophy as an exact science (even in the larger German meaning of science as *Geisteswissenschaft*); and most seriously of all, he failed to break out of the Cartesian impasse since he began as a Cartesian and remained one to the end. On the sociological side, he further widened the gulf between the "two cultures" by setting up a sharp opposition between science and philosophy, thereby reinforcing the prejudices of both.

But what he did accomplish may well count for more than any of these failures. In our earlier discussion of the consensus, we saw that Husserl proposed, initially as a matter of tactics, that we suspend our assumptions in order to go back "to the things themselves." Significantly, what started out as a mere tactic gradually took on an importance of its own. As Husserl looked more closely at the "things themselves" he became entranced with what he saw. In his later years the concept of the *Lebenswelt*—the world of everyday human experience as presented to us without an *a priori* interpretive framework— became his master concept.

But Husserl ran into difficulties with the *Lebenswelt* almost immediately. He himself had to conclude that an attempt to bracket all assumptions was doomed to failure because it was impossible to achieve. When he did attempt to carry it out rigorously, he ended up exactly where he started—with a Cartesian separation of experience into a highly subjective and abstract "inner" consciousness on the one side and the world of "outer" things on the other. Though he was on to something of major philosophical significance, he failed, in part, because he was looking in the wrong direction and because he was not able to suspend his own Cartesian assumptions.

Husserl set himself the task of establishing philosophy as a rigorous science that would lead to certain and indisputable knowledge. The method he proposed centered on a set of conceptual devices for getting behind both science and philosophy to their common ground in ordinary human experience. Disciplined philosophical reflection, he assumed, would lead to insights into the essential structure of a reality free of all presuppositions. To clarify his method, he contrasted his own concept of reflective perception ("eidetic insight") with ordinary sense perception. Originally trained as a mathematician, he was here applying mathematical modes of abstracting essences to an empirical subject matter. It was his belief that once the preconceptions of ordinary sense perception were removed, the essence of an object would appear as self-evident and would display its inherent rational structure.

There are, we submit, formidable difficulties in this procedure. It mixes together a number of problems and issues that are very different from each other and should be considered separately: the issue of how to describe reality should not be confused with the issue of how to establish a principle of certainty or with the objective of defining the specialized capabilities of the various modes of knowing, or with the question of whether presuppositionless perception is possible. To unravel these various threads will clarify matters considerably.

First of all, as Husserl himself rediscovered from Kant, one cannot perform acts of perception without some presuppositions. To get behind the abstractions given in any one set of perceptions you need to use other abstractions, and to get behind these you need still others, leading to an infinite regress.

Some years ago (1932), Von Senden conducted research on a number of people who had been born blind and had had their cataracts removed and their sight restored. Surprisingly, the experience proved to be a very distressing one to those who had been blind. It took them months and years to learn to see, although technically they had had *vision* as soon as they recovered from their operations. Without sight they had built up their own world of meanings based on the evidence of the other senses, plus their reasoning and imagination. The restoration of their visual sense ravaged this world of meanings, and sent them into tailspins of nausea and confusion. It is almost impossible to exaggerate the enormity of the task required here to reorganize experience and to reorient oneself within an altogether new world of meanings.

More recent experiments by perception psychologists vividly describe how persons adjust to a special headgear mechanism which causes them to see the world upside down. After an initial period of painful confusion, the subjects orient themselves to this new mode of seeing—only to reexperience distress and confusion when the apparatus is removed and the world appears once again right side up.

These examples, and they can be multiplied, bear indirectly on Husserl's theories and directly on the well-established principle that sense perception is never a literal replication of concrete reality (as represented by the doctrine of naive realism) but is shot through and through with judgment, interpretation and creativity. Perception in any of its forms is a highly creative act, whether the perception be that of a single sense modality (sight), or of the entire sensorium, or of the senses modified and corrected by reflection of the Husserlian type. The traditional philosophical distinction between sensory perception and reasoning is itself highly artificial. Here, again, we have an example of an abstraction mistaken for a concrete reality. In practice, the various modes of knowing (sense perception, reasoning, and insight) interpenetrate one another and function conjointly. While it may be useful to abstract one or the other for analytical purposes, it is misleading to consider them as separate, independent—and even opposed—modes of mental functioning.

Long before the days of modern perception experiments, there was widespread awareness of optical illusions, delusions and other distortions of perception. Such knowledge has always been cited to negate naive realism, to cast doubt on the reliability of sense perception as a certain and indisputable mirror-image of the real.

The problem posed by the fallibility of our perceptions should not be minimized: it is extraordinarily difficult and it has haunted philosophy for centuries. The notion of sense data—the favorite atomic unit of perception philosophers—is a high abstraction. When you look at a table you do not see a bundle of sense data, you see a table. Yet, at the same time, your perception of the table cannot be considered as an irreducible and indivisible percept, but as a highly creative construct loaded with interpretation. How does one get around this well-grounded fact in order to establish a base of certain knowledge?

The answer is to be found in the way the problem is formulated: in its customary form, it contains the assumption that a necessary connection exists among three diverse elements: the various modes of knowing such as reasoning or sense perception; a theoretical base for indisputable knowledge; and presuppositionless perception.

However, when these elements are considered separately, the problem shows a very different aspect. In the first place, the issue of separating perceptions from presuppositions is a matter of detailed empirical investigation, not a philosophical puzzle; i.e., the descriptive act, tracing how interpretations and meanings get built up, should not be mistaken for an *a priori* logical principle of exclusion to be introduced in advance of inquiry. Consider the blind persons to whom sight has been restored. Careful empirical investigation could chart precisely the process of destroying old networks of meaning and building up new ones. There is no fundamental philosophical problem here. The starting point is the world of meanings as it is experienced by the individual—blind, deaf, dumb, or in full possession of his senses. We may wish at some stage to analyze this world of meanings more finely, but on the decisive question of what is really real, the lesson the consensus points to is that we must start by considering as real the world as it presents itself to human experience—the abstract *and* the concrete together, truth *and* error, sense perception *and* interpretation, delusion *and* true perception—all jumbled together, more or less organized, more or less coherent.

Second, we must separate the individual modes of knowing from the problem of establishing a principle of certainty. There is no necessary relationship between them. Moreover, their arbitrary connection has confused the issue to an unbelievable degree. As Dewey observed, it is the passion for absolute certainty that more than any other lure has led philosophy down the garden path. Since Plato, the dream that the individual could arrive at certain and indisputable knowledge by intellectual reflection of one form or another has haunted men's minds. It is an ideal born of some deep-rooted need; it is a noble ideal and life may be poorer if it cannot be achieved. But over the course of the centuries, it has received one disheartening blow after another. For example, the problem of induction, which is so famous in the history of philosophy centers on the presumption that there is no certain reason why the future can be predicted from the past. Some broad features of nature are quite likely to recur, but there is no inherent reason that tomorrow should be predictable today. For another example, the central problem that preoccupied Kant was the possibility of discovering so-called synthetic *a priori* truths, indisputable truths about the world that could be known without recourse to empirical investigation and which depended solely on the process of reasoning. For Kant, mathematics afforded the prime illustration of this kind of truth. But the development of non-Euclidean geometry and the discoveries of the great nineteenth century mathematicians—Riemann, Gauss, and Lobachevski—were to destroy this one crucial paradigm by demonstrating that *a priori* mathematical postulates need have no necessary relation to the world as it exists.

There is, perhaps, no aspect of philosophy more compelling in its implications than the history of logic and the progressive narrowing down of the scope of what logic by itself can accomplish. The lesson this history tells can be summed up in a simple flat statement: logic is unrelated to existence. In mathematical logic, an existence premise ("x exists") must be inserted before a proof can proceed to establish any consistent formulation about existence. In other words, to prove the world you have to assume it in the first place. Logic is the exercise of reason formalized and systematized. The recent recognition of its harsh limitations has scotched the hope that abstract reasoning by itself can establish indisputably certain truths about the world. In parallel fashion, the history of philosophy and science, considered apart from logic, presents a persuasive case against the possibility that individual sensory perception—or any assemblage of such perceptions—can ever become a sound theoretical basis for indisputable knowledge. Therefore, both logic and sense perception, the *a priori* form and the empirical matter, if allowed to go their separate ways, fail to produce the philosopher's stone.

We should distinguish among the emotional desire for certainty, the theoretical possibility of certainty, and the practical possibility of certainty. If we do so, we shall see that a good many philosophers have been looking in the wrong direction. Theoretical certainty about the world, i.e., a logically self-evident answer to the skeptic's question, "how do you know?" is impossible to establish. But practical certainty is not. Establishing practical certainty is, in fact, the major contribution science makes to modern knowledge. Outside of scientific circles, it is a little-understood fact that the power of science as a systematic method lies more in its ability to prove than to discover. The scientific processes of discovery tend to be far less organized than verification procedures. It is an open secret that many scientific papers neaten up the history of discovery with considerable "poetic license." Typically, after a scientist has arrived at some insight or discovery in anything but a systematic fashion, he writes a paper which, in "systematically" reconstructing the event, also distorts it. In their autobiographies, scientists—especially the great ones—are much more honest, and there they recount what Whitehead has aptly described as "the state of muddled suspension" that generally precedes successful scientific discovery.*

Today, the great power of organized science comes into play mainly in the form of the elaborate methods and mechanisms developed to establish formal empirical verification. The methods of scientific verification are the glory of science and modern man's outstanding achievement. They are extraordinarily subtle and complex. They combine (1) formal methods of measurement, (2) rigid experimental and statistical controls, (3) informal but strictly observed canons regarding full disclosure of results, (4) replicability of experiments, (5) highly organized areas of specialization, and above all (6) well-institutionalized values. These values include a strong belief in scientific integrity, in the full specification of operations and evidence, in the value of esteem from one's peers, in the willingness to work within the frame of some specific well-established paradigm, and in many cases, in the dedication to a lifetime of arduous and even routine mop-up operations. We mention these aspects of the scientific enterprise in passing here in order to show the massive cooperative effort, supported by a powerful ideology, required to establish even practical certainty.

Whatever contributions the ancient discipline of philosophy can make to modern life—and they are too important to be minimized—establishing a base of certain knowledge by the method of reflection is not among them. There are people in whom the need for certainty overrides all others—and the need can take on a passionate intensity; philosophy is not the place to fulfill it.

What we wish to insist on firmly here is that the question "What is really real?" is independent—both logically and practically—of the ancient and haunting questions, "How can we establish a theoretical base for certainty?" "How do we know

---

* We do not wish to draw too rigid a distinction between discovery and proof. In practice, the two go together, since it is easier to discover something when one can build on a body of verified knowledge and then purposefully select problems for investigation that lend themselves to experimentation and proof. But with this qualification, the processes of hypothesis formation (discovery) and formal verification (proof) can be analytically separated.

we know?" and "What modes of knowing tell us most about the nature of the real?" Such questions about knowledge must, of course, be considered; but only after the logically prior question of the nature of the subject matter itself has been answered. What modes of knowing we are to employ will depend, after all, on what kinds of things there are to be known.

To put the cart before the horse and make the quest for certainty primary, has usually led in the history of human thought to the replacement of everyday reality by a hidden reality that is more remote from experience. Ordinary experience becomes mere appearance, while reality is something very different. In the philosophic tradition of Descartes-Locke this dichotomy was focused mainly on perception and the problem of perception. The table I perceive does not resemble the "real" table; its colors, texture and solidity—its so-called secondary qualities—do not belong to the particles in space that make up the real table.

Worse than that; this real table (the table of physics) is somehow the cause, as its particles impinge upon me, of the table I perceive, which is so utterly unlike it. Thus arises the famous "causal theory of perception," with whose difficulties philosophers are still struggling today.

It is beside our purpose here to go into the intricate difficulties of the causal theory of perception. We wish rather to call attention to the long-entrenched habit of thought that true causal explanation must refer to causal agents that do not resemble the facts of experience they are supposed to explain. This habit of thought, in the centuries after Descartes, expanded beyond the confines of perception; it was felt that all facts of experience, to be properly explained, must drop out of the ultimate explanation and be replaced by other, allegedly more basic realities that are not and can never be directly experienced. The causal relations one might expect within experience become replaced by a supposedly truer "scientific" causality that can only hold between the realities hidden behind experience. And indeed, this conclusion follows inevitably from its initial assumption. If you assume that large chunks of experience are not really real, then the only truly "scientific" explanation of them must lead in the direction of explaining experience by reference to something other than what is actually perceived.

A few examples, ranging from ancient to contemporary, may illustrate this curious slighting of "appearance" for "reality":

The figures on the wall of the cave are not really real. (Plato's example.)   FORMISM

The color of the flowers does not really exist in the flowers themselves. (Locke's example.)

What is real about the fire is not its warmth and its glow, but the agitation of molecules and the processes of oxygenation. (Whitehead's example.)   Mechanism

Some of the stars we see in the sky are not really there—viz., when we are seeing a star thousands of light years away. (Russell, *et al.*)

Freedom does not really exist; it is an illusion, an epiphenomenon. (Freud's example.)

In each of these propositions what we experience immediately and directly—shadows, flowers, stars, warmth and freedom—is explained away as less real than some causal agent not directly experienced.

Coming closer to the present, we find the metapsychology speaking in the same fashion:

The anxiety we experience is really converted libidinal energy. (Early psychoanalytic version)

The anxiety we experience is really a signal of unpleasure regulated by the pleasure principle. (Later psychoanalytic version)

A feeling of being better loved is really a heightened level of libidinal cathexis of the self.

The gist of the philosophical consensus is that something is terribly wrong about this way of approaching data, since these are examples of abstractions being mistaken for concrete reality. What does the word "abstraction" mean? One of its meanings is that part of the truth or reality is always left out, and the danger exists that one may draw a false conclusion by not taking what is omitted into account. In describing human experience, abstractions about what is real will tend to be misused if the description of the experience and the explanation of it are so sharply different that the explanatory items never appear in the description—but are nonetheless assumed to be the cause of it. (This is what is implied by the causal theory of perception.)

The insight which has simultaneously come to philosophers of many different schools is that you cannot begin an explanation of human experience by saying that some parts of our experience are not really real, but merely an appearance or screen for what is really real. You cannot pick and choose among the data in this way. You cannot say that some of it has no right really to be there—all of it is already there and manifest within experience.

Such a fundamental insight is a lesson finally learned from three centuries of intellectual embarrassment before the Cartesian-Newtonian doctrine of primary and secondary qualities. The primary are the physical qualities: mass, extension, solidity, the configuration and number of parts. They are assumed to be the real and causally efficacious qualities. The secondary qualities are colors, tones, odors, tastes, and the rest—all those attributes that make up the rich texture of the world in which we live. Yet these latter qualities are given only a peripheral status in reality. They are not real outside the mind, but are somehow produced or created by mind. How the mind creates these qualities out of a world which contains nothing like them remains the abysmal mystery in this doctrine. There is the equally abysmal paradox that the mind, which is here supposed to be accorded only a peripheral reality, turns out to be endowed with a miraculous creative power. It is a curious arrangement, Whitehead dryly comments, that we should see so many things which are not really there.

The conclusion is forced upon us that we can never fit the secondary qualities (e.g., the glow and warmth of the fire) into a theory unless we begin by taking them as being already there with the rest of the data. We cannot get to anything like the world in which we live except by taking off from it.

We have been considering Plato's master question, "What is really real?" We have shown that the answer scientific materialism gives is to limit reality to aspects of matter, however matter is defined. We therefore opt for a radically different philosophy for the human sciences than an up-to-date scientific materialism: even though the latter is mercifully free of the cruder features of Newtonism, it nonetheless remains one vast metaphor, illuminating only those aspects of the human condition that our experience shares with the world of objects.

The compelling philosophical consensus developed in this century, which we have pointed to earlier, holds that such a viewpoint is a piece of dogmatic and arbitrary metaphysics based on mistaking abstractions for concrete reality, a map for a countryside it describes in some respects and not in others. The countryside itself is more thickly populated. It contains more than atomic bits of matter or units of energy moving in otherwise empty space. For the human sciences, it contains all the rich items in man's everyday experience. The cardinal point here is that a religious experience, a delusion, a friendship, a rock, a worm, defecating, being born, feeling crowded, loyalty, automobiles, making love, taking a walk, dying, being depressed, going to the laundry, smelling a rose, moral exaltation, murder, loneliness, saying hello, questing for certainty, coveting your neighbor's wife, mountains, TV sets, being a comedian, waging war—all have exactly the same ontological status. No one is more real or less real than any other—all are really real. No one item can *a priori* be reduced to any other item. And none can be explained *a priori* by psychic apparati and quantities of instinctual energy that lurk behind them.

What does all this mean for psychoanalysis? We will discuss its detailed implications in the section that immediately follows. But for the sake of clarity we should briefly illustrate here one implication of this first counterproposal to scientific materialism.

Consider religious experience. Experiences of a kind that are called religious do occur; they are a fact, and the psychoanalyst must therefore take account of them. Loyal as he may be to the master, the analyst has nevertheless to recognize that Freud's summary statement of his views on religion, *Future of an Illusion,* is pure pre-Kantian dogmatism. It is a declaration of Freud's own personal ideology; it is not Freud speaking as a scientist. Science is agnostic; it makes no assertions, for or against, objects that lie beyond possible experience. The psychoanalyst may encounter experiences that are called religious among his patients. Some of these may be bogus and quite clearly neurotic disguises for something else. But there is no *a priori* reason for asserting that all such experiences must be fakes, especially since there is a considerable body of testimony to confirm that some such experiences, however difficult it may be to interpret them, play a genuinely constructive role in the believer's life. The psychoanalyst cannot throw them away; they too are data. And he must make the difficult effort of taking these seriously as what they are even when he, personally as well as scientifically, is an agnostic who cannot enter into those experiences. If he is sensitive and unbiased, he will stand in a delicate position; he has to take stock of attitudes and emotions in the patient into which he himself cannot directly enter. What criteria can he use? He can only measure the patient's religious attitudes against the totality of the patient's experience. Do those attitudes produce any fanatical distortions of consciousness? Do they unify rather than fragment his experience? Do they enhance his energies and give a purpose and meaning to his life that are not in conflict with normal social duties? If the analyst takes the automatic stance that the experience must be reduced to something else (a sexual substitute or what not), he is speaking for an ideology—and a rather timid and dreary one at that—rather than as an empirical scientist. Moreover, he may be causing actual harm to the patient, destroying a positive adjustment and creating havoc and confusion in the patient's life.

Consider a more mundane example. A psychoanalyst encounters a patient who is excessively neat and orderly in his ways and whose attitudes toward money and toward his intimates betray features analysts classically associate with the so-called anal character structure. The temptation to reduce these various modes of individual experience to their "cause" in early toilet training is, for many analysts, irresistible. But the temptation to so reduce them *a priori* must be avoided, as must the temptation to reduce moral dilemmas to a superego subject-substance hidden behind the appearance of the moral dilemma, or to reduce curiosity to repressed libidinal impulse, or courage to reaction formation. This does not deny the unconscious roots of these experiences or their intimate association with earlier modes of relatedness (e.g., the association of certain forms of play with sexual curiosity). It does deny that they can be reduced to these earlier experiences. Psychoanalysis might do well to inscribe on its banner Wittgenstein's warning to philosophers: "It can never be our job to reduce anything to anything."

Thus, to the question, "What is the really real?" we propose an answer that locates reality in the raw experiential world of the individual, to be comprehended without *a priori* judgments as to what is primary or secondary, truth or delusion, concrete or abstract, cause or effect. In short, the phenomenally given world, the world in which we live, is the root of whatever meaning and intelligibility human beings can attain to. Skipping over it is the source of most of the false reductionism, irrelevancy, and distortion that prevail today in the human sciences.

With the Newtonian element out of the way, certain principles now implicit in the clinical theory can be generalized to the level of meta-theory. Such generalization will be a move toward replacing an inert theory with a working one—a theory that will stimulate research, relate psychoanalysis to other disciplines, and do all the things a meta-theory should do.

We illustrate how this process might work by considering the concept of meaning in relation to the present theory of energies and forces.

Freud's work shows two separate theories of psychic structure-formation, one of which belongs to the clinical side of psychoanalysis and the other to the metapsychology: the first is a theory of meanings; the second, a theory of forces. The theory of meanings showed itself in the first case history we discussed, that of Miss Lucy. We saw how Freud analyzed the structure of her neurosis by tracking down the meaning of Miss Lucy's symptom of being pursued by the smell of burned pudding. Freud's masterpiece, his *Interpretation of Dreams*, which followed closely on his early case histories, is mainly a brilliant unlocking of the various kinds of meanings dreams can have. About his work on dreams, Freud stated: "Insight like this is vouchsafed but once in a lifetime." Most knowledgeable commentators on Freud's work would agree, for he showed how dreams, jokes, slips of the tongue, neurotic symptoms, and play

—phenomena which theretofore had not been regarded as having anything in common—actually formed similar structures of meaning.

The theory of meaning outlined in Freud's work on dreams embraces both the primary and secondary processes and also the so-called genetic method of reconstructing early experiences, which is the main support of psychoanalytic therapy. The technique of free association—a method of eliciting meanings—was evolved by Freud only after first experimenting with suggestion, hypnosis, and the laying on of hands. These latter methods are not concerned with eliciting meanings but with inducing change directly by treating the human person as an object to be manipulated. Unfortunately, the full implications of this decisive shift—from manipulating the patient as an object to exploring structures of meanings with him—have never been carried over to the metapsychology.

In his earliest work, Freud was under the influence of the associative psychologies of his day. His analysis of meaning in the Lucy case and other early cases shows his debt to these theories. The major principle of nineteenth century associative psychologies is meanings formed by contiguity: a bond of meaning is established when events are contiguous in time or space or when they share common attributes. Lucy's cigar smoke phobia was traceable to the incidental occurrence of cigar smoking on the occasion that reminded her of her disappointment (contiguity in time). Lucy also associated cigar smoking with the children's father (contiguity in space). And even the connection between the smell of burned pudding and the smell of cigar smoking can be accounted for in terms of the old association psychology, linking together two similar odors (sharing of common attributes). As Freud continued to dig away at the meanings of symptoms and dreams in later cases, he uncovered a world of symbolic processes scarcely imagined by the old association psychology. The split-off of the symbol from the affect that accompanies it; repression of the affect; displacement of the original symbol by symbols having the same emotional referent; piling up of meanings one on top of the other, all condensed into a single symbol; mutilation, censorship, and repression of meanings in dreams; various levels of meaning, overt and latent, connecting adult theorist may be that he carries out this futile exercise with such Germanic thoroughness.)

Freud's reluctance to drop either the theory of forces or the theory of meanings reflected his belief that each got at an aspect of reality missed by the other. As George Klein has pointed out, Freud's commitment to a scientific ethos that equates scientific explanation with energies and forces would tend to make him give greater weight to a theory of forces as an ultimate explanation. But it would be grossly unfair to Freud to suggest that his theoretical commitments caused him to be insensitive to what was going on in his patients. He was, as usual, digging away at something quite important; and each theory helped him get at a different aspect of it. The theory of meanings helped him to interpret symbolic processes; the theory of forces was a handy device for explaining, or appearing to explain, the selective character of learning—on the tried and simple principle that the burned child dreads the fire. The stronger charge of energy, negative or positive, on any experience creates a greater force for shunning or seeking that experience in the future. (The reader will recall that Freud's final theory of anxiety explains how the pleasure principle is invoked to keep the person away from experiences that caused him to be overwhelmed with tension in childhood.) Any substitute for the theory of forces must, therefore, account for this latter phenomenon.

Eliminating the specifically Newtonian theory of forces, and distinguishing generally any theory of forces from a theory of meanings, we are able at last to see clearly what must be done to fill the void that the elimination has created: an analysis not of elements but the relations between elements, not of isolated drives but the structures within which drives have the particular meaning they do for human beings.

PART FOUR

TOWARD

RECONSTRUCTION

[✳]

SIXTEEN

Requirements for a Metapsychology: What It Can and Cannot Do

We have maintained that bringing philosophy and psychoanalysis together in a more formal fashion might help to resolve a philosophic neurosis that lies at the core of the human sciences, and also pervades American culture in general. Although philosophers, with few exceptions, have shown an odd distaste for psychoanalysis (if not for Freud himself), and although psychoanalysts, with few exceptions, have remained indifferent to the issues thought to be vital by modern philosophers, the two professions have an essential contribution to make to each other.

The first three parts of this work have prepared the ground for a new approach to psychoanalytic metapsychology in the light of recent philosophical trends. Parts I and II were mainly concerned with showing how the current interest of Freud's heirs in ego development and identity has caused psychoanalytic theory to outstrip its old philosophical foundations, leading it to a crisis in fundamentals. Part III described the efforts of certain twentieth century philosophers in breaking through the Cartesianism which has severely hampered the development of psychoanalytic theory. Now we must bring together these various themes to see whether they do, in fact, lead to a new synthesis. For while we have assumed that a fresh philosophy will liberate psychoanalytic theory we have yet to prove it; it is easier to formulate a broad claim of this sort than to fix precisely where it does and does not apply. If the line of reasoning suggested by the new philosophy is to contribute more than mere logical clarification, if it is to become an inherent part of how the psychoanalyst thinks about his subject, then it must pass the pragmatist's test of having practical and demonstrable consequences. It must answer the difficult question, "What difference to the theory and practice of psychoanalysis does any philosophy make—new or old?"

Few psychoanalysts will acknowledge the influence of philosophy, either when it is overtly labeled as such or in its disguised form as metapsychology. Among the psychoanalytic thinkers we have discussed, Erikson has put such theoretical matters behind him, and Klein has argued for a total, even brutal, separation of psychoanalysis from any philosophical moorings whatever. Most practitioners bypass the metapsychology if they can.

At issue is the always confusing question of how a specialized discipline fits into a broader context. The metapsychology is, as the prefix implies, a *meta*theory; i.e., a theory that goes beyond its subject (the neuroses) to generalize about man's place in nature. Even though practitioners pay it little conscious heed, the metapsychology does exert a compelling, if unwitting, influence on them, an influence we shall now examine more closely.

As we have seen, Freud relied on the metapsychology to meet a need that could not, he felt, be filled by his clinical case descriptions. The metapsychology was supposed to explain his clinical findings and, in so doing, to place them in the broader context of a general theory of human nature. But in practice this intention worked out poorly. For while Freud's clinical descriptions presented the world with fresh, vivid, insightful and scrupulously honest portrayals of human problems, the "explanations" turned out to be mere exercises in a kind of semantic game Freud played on himself. The rules of the game required Freud to translate his case histories from concrete descriptive language into the abstract "scientific" language of energy systems seeking to maintain equilibrium. A great deal was lost in the translation.

Unfortunately, psychoanalysts have continued to follow Freud in this procedure of semantic double bookkeeping. There are, in effect, two psychoanalytic languages; one clinical and descriptive, the other a supposedly explanatory metalanguage derived from the metapsychology. When psychoanalysts write their formal papers they use both. Here are three brief examples from recent psychoanalytic writings showing how both languages are employed in the very same sentences. In each of the examples we have italicized the metalanguage:

Example 1: "The analysis of resistance must take into account aspects which are adaptive, i.e., *which do not utilize counter-cathectic energy*." (Gertrude Blanck, 1966.)

Example 2: " 'There are two techniques of restoring a feeling of being loved (*of increasing the libidinal cathexis of the self*).' " (J. J. Sandler quoted by H. J. Home.)

The British analyst and philosopher, H. J. Home, comments: "The first part of this sentence seems to me perfectly comprehensible; the second part is, I believe, meaningless."

The third example is an item on a checklist developed by Anna Freud to serve as a metapsychological profile:

Example 3: One must determine "whether *the self is cathected as well as the object world and whether there is sufficient narcissism (primary and secondary) invested in the body, the ego or the superego* to ensure self-regard, a sense of well-being without leading to overestimation of the self or undue independence of the object . . ." (Freud, A., 1965, p. 141.)

Each one of these three sentences uses either ordinary or clinical language to describe some aspect of common psychoanalytic experience; but then falls back on the metalanguage to designate the process that purportedly underlies—and explains—the experience. The examples are atypical only in that the authors use both sets of language with roughly equal emphasis. More typically, the analyst will emphasize either clinical language if he is mainly a practitioner, or the metalanguage if he is mainly a theorist. (However—and the fact is most revealing—not even the most theoretically minded psychoanalysts will use metapsychological terms to explain to their patients what is going on in their therapy.)

Note that each one of the three examples describes some important and familiar aspect of human experience. Dr. Blanck refers to psychological resistances which serve a positive as well as a destructive purpose (e.g., a writer's intellectualism may act as a harmful defense mechanism in his marriage but be an indispensable asset to his work). Although her clinical language is abstract, all practicing psychoanalysts will readily understand Dr. Blanck's references and will be able to summon up instances of the same. The language of Sandler and Anna Freud is less abstract: Sandler refers to how a person goes about restoring a feeling of being loved, and Anna Freud describes how people maintain their self-regard and sense of well-being.

In each instance, the metapsychological translation suggests that the underlying process is a form of energy transformation. We believe that Home is overstating the case when he says that the metapsychological translation of Sandler's phrase is meaningless. Rather, it has too many meanings. One meaning derives from the ordinary language in the sentence and is simply a restatement of it in more arcane terms. But over and above the restatement, a meaning is added that presents the psychological processes at issue in a very odd fashion (i.e., restoring the feeling of being loved is assumed to involve the process of pumping up a fresh supply of libidinal energy). The issue is not whether the energy transmission process has any meaning but whether its meaning is relevant: is it, in truth, a valid description of how an individual goes about restoring the feeling of being loved?

On a recent occasion a literal-minded use of the energy model by one of his colleagues caused Hartmann to remark bitingly that there are some naive psychoanalysts who want to see, feel, touch, smell, or measure the cathexes. "Don't they realize that we are talking about *concepts not things?*" But concepts have referents; and the simple-minded desire to see, touch, smell, or measure the cathexes may be a sounder impulse than Hartmann's insistence that they cannot be seen, touched, smelled, or measured because they are concepts.

Consider the following statement: "I am moving to the West Coast and I have begun to *decathect* persons and places here in New York." What does *decathect* mean in this context? It has at least two possible meanings: the literal one is that I have begun to withdraw the packets of psychic energy that I had previously emitted onto persons and places in New York in order to carry them to the West Coast where I will, presumably, emit them once again onto a new set of persons and places. The other meaning refers to a complex process of decreased emotional involvement that takes place as I prepare to separate myself from my New York world and all that it means to me. At a phenomenal level it is desirable to have an adequate descriptive language to depict the process of emotional disengagement. At a theoretical level it is even more desirable—indeed, it is essential—to be able to describe *how* emotional disengagement takes places. Whatever these processes may be, we can be sure that they do not involve an in-gathering of packets of energy in preparation for their re-emission.

These three examples, which could be multiplied at will, show how the metapsychology actually interferes with the description and explanation of clinical processes. In each instance there has been a step backward in understanding; moving from a description of human experience in clinical or ordinary language to its "explanation" in the metalanguage adds up to a net loss.

Freud, too, used the metapsychology as a deductive theory; that is, he assumed that certain consequences would follow from the energy model, which he could then apply to his clinical practice. Unfortunately, whenever he worked downwards in this fashion—deducing from the metapsychology to a clinical interpretation—he created an even worse impasse for himself and his followers than when he used the metapsychology as an explanatory device. Metapsychological "explanations," though they explain nothing, may often be suggestive as metaphors; at worst they are merely tautological. But the practice of deducing consequences from the metapsychology is a more serious failing, for it misdirects the attention of psychoanalysts, sensitizing them to one-sided phenomena and drawing their attention away from important aspects of their patients' lives. And because the metapsychology is a closed system, there is no way of detecting and eliminating misleading conclusions arrived at in this fashion. In its everyday practice, psychoanalysis has a built-in resource for correcting far-fetched clinical theories: the frequent encounters between therapist and patient keep clinical formulations close to observed behavior. But when the metapsychology is the source of the interpretations, psychoanalysts lack the logical devices for criticizing them.

Consider, as an example of how deduction from the metapsychology can be misleading, the concept of the therapeutic alliance—the real relationship between patient and therapist. As Erikson points out in "The First Psychoanalyst" (1964a), Freud discovered the importance of the therapeutic alliance at the beginning of his psychoanalytic career. In his early cases of female hysteria, he found (to his surprise) that many of the women he treated were intelligent and sensitive persons, far removed from the "degenerate minds" associated in that day with mental or emotional disorder. In following the rule of free association (a strange rule for a physician of that era to impose), these women patients put aside the reticences of their private lives and placed themselves trustingly in Freud's hands. Each woman made an implicit bargain with Freud: she entrusted vulnerable aspects of her emotions to him while he, leaning heavily on her trust, called upon her to make a number of painful decisions—decisions presupposing considerable ego strength on her part.

Nowadays this therapeutic alliance between patient and analyst is held to be a necessary precondition to successful therapy. In fact, where the transference relationship cannot be fully developed, as in some ego disorders, the therapeutic alliance becomes the active agent in creating change in the patient. Yet for many years Freud underemphasized the significance of his own early insight. He was too firmly committed to total psychic determinism (a cornerstone of the metapsychology) to pay attention to a relationship that depended so much on the individual's ability to become a free partner in the work of therapy. For almost three decades the therapeutic alliance was all but forgotten, and had to be rediscovered all over again.

Freud's theory of the psychoses as a regression to narcissism is another—and far more serious—instance of how the metapsychology miscarried as a deductive system. Reasoning from the energy model, Freud deduced that the psychotic patient had to be incapable of forming a transference relationship—a conclusion that bears directly on the choice of method for conducting therapy with psychotics. Reasoning from the energy model, Freud assumed that the infant starts out life in a state of "primary narcissism" (i.e., all of his psychic energy is contained within himself in the same sense in which a battery contains an electric charge). As he grows older the health of the infant's ego depends on his ability to differentiate between himself and external objects. But such differentiation, it is held, depends in turn on the infant's ability to abandon his total narcissism so that he can emit some of his energy onto objects. To oversimplify from this process to the psychoses: when a patient regresses to schizophrenia it is assumed either that his vital energy is withdrawn from the environment and pulled back into the self, or else that the differentiation between self and object never took place at the proper stage of development. Thus, the conclusion that schizophrenic withdrawal (as in catatonia) corresponds to a withdrawal of cathexes of energy from the rest of the world into the self is a pure instance of deduction from the metapsychology. Yet in this case the deduction does not square with observed facts, as the English psychoanalyst Brandshaft has observed:

> This view of schizophrenia, that it involves a regression to an infantile state in which the psychic organization is narcissistic, in which there has been a loss of differentiation between ego and objects and objects have been decathected, and in which *no transference can take place*, is in accord with the view Freud put forward. It is still widely adhered to . . . *in spite of the violence it does to observational data.* (Our italics.)

Recent work with psychotics, such as that of Rosenfeld and others, amplifies Brandshaft's conclusion that Freud's metapsychology applied to the psychoses violates the observational data. Indeed, contemporary experience with psychotics leads to the very opposite of Freud's deduction. Apparently one of the greatest obstacles to helping psychotics is that the relationship between therapist and patient becomes dominated by the transference. In working with patients who are not psychotic, successful therapy depends on the patient's ability to maintain a good balance between transference and reality: i.e., the patient must always be able to distinguish between reacting to the analyst as if he were his parent (and the patient were still a small child) and reacting to the analyst as a professional physician participating in a joint therapeutic endeavor. Working with the transference presupposes that the patient will never lose his clear grip on reality. Otherwise, he would be unable to distinguish, when pointed out to him, how his transference reactions to the analyst—a form of reliving old childhood experiences—may be totally inappropriate to his present situation. The psychotic patient is far from being incapable of forming a transference relationship; rather, the transference is there in all too great abundance, but the patient is unable to maintain the reality of the doctor-patient relationship. Freud's conception of the psychoses, which is still all too influential, was not based on his clinical observations but was a pure and simple deduction from the energy theory applied to narcissism and object relations.

Yet another unfortunate instance of the metapsychology used as a deductive system is provided by Freud's theories of anxiety. It was a deduction from the metapsychology that first led him to conceive of anxiety as converted libidinal energy (reflecting the doctrine of the conservation of energy). Freud himself ultimately came to regard this view of anxiety as one of his major mistakes. But it is significant that the current formulation of anxiety, as a signal of distress issued by the ego to mobilize the "all but omnipotent pleasure principle," may be just as unsatisfactory. For it, too, is expressed in terms of the metapsychology—not as a direct deduction from it but as a translation of clinical observations into metapsychological language. Unfortunately, as in the earlier examples, the translation adds some questionable elements. Dragging in the pleasure principle and the ego-id dichotomy superimposes on the clinical descriptions of anxiety several dubious assumptions about the processes involved and about the psychological purpose served by anxiety.

Countless other examples could be cited to show how deductions from the metapsychology influence, and usually harm, clinical theory. A similar deductive line of reasoning may well have caused Freud to emphasize certain ego functions, such as delay (i.e., preventing energy from being discharged), and to de-emphasize those not so readily conceptualized in terms of energy storage and release. The constraints of the metapsychology almost certainly led him to de-emphasize or to deny the Jung-Erikson-Heidegger notion of a life-task. These same constraints led him and his followers to strained and artificial formulations of trust, freedom, hope, human growth, and maturity; the concepts of ego, reality principle, and psychic energy had to be twisted, pretzel-like, to accommodate these facts of ordinary human experience. And today, some sophisticated psychoanalysts are even having trouble in coping, within the orthodox framework, with the clinical facts of hysteria. The old theory focused on hysterical symptoms that can be described in the language of energy; newer and fresher descriptions call attention to the character traits associated with the hysterical personality and, perhaps most rewarding of all, to the quality of the hysteric's experience as he uses people and objects to create a characteristic emotion-charged mood.

These two uses of the metapsychology—as an explanatory language and as a deductive theory—are the main ones that influence the psychoanalyst's professional practice. There are, in addition, other uses, which have had a major influence on research and on the status of psychoanalysis as science.

The metapsychology makes the task of conducting research on psychoanalytic materials almost impossible; and what research does exist barely begins to draw from the incredibly rich storehouse of facts and insights collected by analysts. All of this irreplaceable experience lies untapped in the minds of a few thousand individuals. Those who try to carry out research within the framework of the metapsychology find that its defining concepts do not lead to hypotheses that can be verified, quantified, or even disallowed by orderly research procedures. The logician, Ernest Nagel (see Hook, 1959), has taken psychoanalysis to task on its logical status as a scientific theory. The metapsychology, he states, presents itself as a scientific theory in the same sense that the molecular theory of gases or the gene theory of heredity are scientific theories—sets of assumptions which systematize, explain, and predict observable phenomena. He urges that it should, therefore, be judged in the same way as other scientific theories. By such a standard, he concludes, the logical structure of the metapsychology does not satisfy the two minimum requirements for empirical validation: one cannot deduce from it consequences that are testable; and one cannot tie down its theoretical notions to concrete observations. Along with other critics, Nagel also notes that psychic energies endowed with causal efficacy is yet another form of the ghost-in-the-machine mystique—the postulating of a mysterious and invisible force that does work that a biologically oriented psychology might assign to the body.

Nagel, who has never been sympathetic to psychoanalysis, aimed these blows not at Freud but at an up-to-date version of the metapsychology presented by Heinz Hartmann (Hartmann, 1959). It is true that Nagel may have judged the metapsychology against a too-narrow standard, but it was Hartmann who put the ax in his hands. Despite Hartmann's careful qualifications, he left himself and the metapsychology all too vulnerable on the issue of presenting psychic phenomena in terms of energies and forces. Describing mental events in this fashion leads to the sort of statement positivists most enjoy pouncing on as evidence of "meaningless metaphysics," and Nagel pounced with great vigor. As he points out, if one accepts the metapsychology one might as well be a thoroughgoing materialist, since if we are going to invoke a theory of forces it makes more sense to reduce psychology completely to physico-chemical processes.

In fact, once the metapsychology in its present form is out of the way, it will be seen that the clinical theory—that is, the theory implicit in the general body of knowledge gained from clinical practice—is capable of meeting both of Nagel's requirements for a scientific theory—having testable consequences and tying down some of its theoretical notions to specific observables. For example, while there may be difficulties in testing the hypothesis that a person's defenses may also serve a constructive purpose, the proposition is nevertheless testable. So long as we do not make the simple-minded error of assuming that verification must be confined to the laboratory, there are many practical ways this hypothesis can be tested. And once the explanatory function in psychoanalysis is performed directly by the clinical theory, freed of the old metapsychological premises and divested of the old metalanguage, it is far easier to see what its testable consequences are and what research designs are required for testing them.

The metatheory should not attempt to "explain" the clinical theory, but it must perform several crucial functions: (1) correct distortion and reductionism inevitable in a discipline that studies only one aspect of human experience without a more general framework; (2) build a bridge between psychoanalysis and the disciplines closely related to it; and (3) satisfy certain scientific and philosophical requirements that will lead to a sounder theory. We are suggesting that instead of doing poorly what the clinical theory does well, describing and explaining the neuroses, the metapsychology be used for purposes that cannot possibly be met by a specialized scientific theory; i.e., for purposes that are properly philosophical.

Correcting Distortion

The clinical theory of psychoanalysis is responsive to the neurotic in man but it has the greatest difficulty in illuminating the whole person and in doing justice to the real human events in which the neurosis is situated. These shortcomings result in gross distortion, as vividly illustrated by the Freud-Bullitt book on President Wilson (1966). This posthumous volume embarrasses many psychoanalysts because the flaws in the psychoanalytic approach are magnified out of proportion to its virtues. The very exaggeration, however, dramatizes problems in interpretation that psychoanalysts must face every day of their working lives.

In reviewing the Freud-Bullitt work, the historian Barbara Tuchman has nothing but praise for Freud's acumen as a psychologist and for the illumination he brings to Wilson's personal characteristics. She feels that Freud's analysis makes the contradictions in Wilson's behavior fall sharply into place. But she adds the negative judgment, echoed by others, that once Wilson's neuroses are no longer the subject of discussion, Freud's analysis loses its relevance: "as an overall assessment of the whole man, it is lamentable and as an interpretation of events, it falls to pieces."

She notes, for example, that the book's authors state that for a period of months (from October 1915, to May 1916) Wilson's supreme desire was to lead the United States into war, and that he did everything he could to bring this desire to fruition (" 'the combined lure of being leader in war and arbiter of peace was irresistible to Wilson because the first would release his hostility to his father and the second would satisfy the superego's demand to become saviour of the world' "). Mrs. Tuchman points out that whatever Wilson's subconscious desires may have been, "the historical fact is that his conscious determination to stay neutral maintained control."

She adds that from an historical point of view the most gaping hole in the authors' argument is their assumption that in the aftermath of the armistice Wilson had the power to dictate a just peace and failed to do so because of neurotic weaknesses in his personality. Freud and Bullitt claim that if Wilson had shown a little more masculinity vis-à-vis Clemenceau and Lloyd George, he would have had no great difficulty in imposing a just peace and in solving the incredibly complex problems of postwar Europe. This conclusion more than any other arouses the irate historian in Mrs. Tuchman, and she inventories a few dozen of the factors she claims the authors have left out of account (such as the personalities of Lloyd George and Clemenceau). Her conclusion about the relevance of psychoanalysis to history is that it can do much as an instrument of illumination, but she adds in anguish, "Let it, for God's sake, be applied by a responsible historian."

Mrs. Tuchman's assumption that the historians have licked the problem of perspective better than the psychoanalysts may be questioned, but she is surely correct in pointing out how treacherous it is to generalize from Wilson's neurosis (however brilliant the analysis) to Wilson the man and political leader and from Wilson the man to the complex historical events in which he participated. We are not concerned here with supporting Mrs. Tuchman's case against Freud, but only with exhibiting why a general scheme of ideas is needed to correct distortion if psychoanalysis, basing itself so heavily upon the events of childhood, is to generalize about mature people moving in the historical theater of events.

This strange work on Wilson should not embarrass psychoanalysts so much as it does: it is in many ways a reminder of Freud's stunning gifts. His insight into the contradictions of Wilson's personality is clear and lucid, and his formulation of Wilson's personal problem undoubtedly has relevance, if only one knew how to generalize from it. It is the double leap from the neurosis to the man and from the man to the historical event that causes the mischief. We can, if we wish, dismiss this work as the momentary aberration of a great man indulging his prejudices (Freud admits that he loathed Wilson); and, in this respect, the example may be an unfair one to insert here. Our purpose in citing it is not to put psychoanalysis in a bad light, but to show how and why its great strengths are being compromised by a missing part—one that is a necessary precondition to successful generalization.

Unless the missing part is provided, psychoanalysis can hardly function as a general psychology and can hardly fail to avoid distortion and reductionism when discussing how a neurosis functions in a person's whole life. For what the authors do in the Wilson book is done less flamboyantly by psychoanalysts every day in their practice. True, their subject is not a famous historical figure, but some ordinary middle-class housewife, businessman, professor, architect, or student suffering from some ordinary middle-class neurotic misery. The average psychoanalyst does not have Freud's gifts—but neither is he the crude and insensitive Dr. Blauberman, a psychoanalyst of obtuse vulgarity caricatured by Lillian Ross in her novel *Horizontal and Vertical*. He is likely to be an intelligent, intuitive, and skilled physician, sensitive to the tensions of his patient's childhood but less responsive to the problems of the individual's current life if they do not involve the neurosis he is tracking. It could hardly be otherwise, for the psychoanalyst is not professionally concerned with all of his patient's problems; his task is to help his patient reduce the ravages of an outmoded adaptation with specific roots in the past. Since his sensitivities must be highly selective, that is all the more reason for him to maintain some sort of perspective on the whole person, apart from the latter's neurosis.

Lacking a viable metatheory the psychoanalyst cannot prevent himself from going about his task backwards. He sees the patient in the framework of his neurosis rather than the other way around. But the patient is not reducible to his neurosis; in fact, to understand the neurosis, you must understand the patient as a whole person enmeshed in his society, in history, and in the human condition. To do otherwise is to slip inevitably into distortion and reductionism. Fortunately, we have left behind the dreary era of the recent past when psychoanalysts interpreted all manifestations of the human spirit as expressions of psychopathology. The days when Bergler could interpret human love as a pathological defense against hate (without arousing much protest from his colleagues) belong mercifully to the past. But the distortion persists nonetheless, although the form is less crude. And it persists because there is no alternative perspective to replace the old one.

Most psychoanalysts make a great personal effort to avoid reductionism. Those endowed with common sense and mature judgment manage to escape its grosser forms by constant vigilance. Though the Blaubermans, the purveyors of machine-made formulae, are still among us, they survive in greatly diminished numbers. But common sense and maturity of judgment can go only so far in compensating for a missing part of the theory that could positively guide their interpretations when they move from one area of experience, childhood conflicts, to another quite different area—the adult person functioning in his contemporary world.

It is curious that psychoanalysts assume that the fault lies in themselves, and seek to overcome it by unremitting personal cultivation. Most of them are well aware of the desirability of knowing more—more biology, more social science, more psychology, more history, more philosophy. They search out insights into the human condition won by the great artists, poets, playwrights and novelists. And, most important of all, the best of them develop humility in the presence of man's intractable nature and of the harsh limitations in our knowledge of people.

Recognizing the relevance of fields other than their own, they make a personal effort (when not too exhausted after a ten- or twelve-hour day) to dip into these related fields. Some even try to become the Renaissance man, all-knowing in all fields; but, of course, in this epoch they cannot succeed. The attempt is laudable, but personal diligence and self-cultivation, necessary and useful as they are, cannot compensate for what is lacking in the formal structure of their own theory.

If you are studying the psychoneuroses you must have somewhere in the background a conception, however vague or ill-defined, of the subject whose pathological condition you are investigating. You must have, explicit or otherwise, a general theory of human nature and culture as a silent standard against which pathology is determined. Otherwise, you do not even know what is meant by such terms as "mental health," "the goals of psychotherapy," "ego strength," "normal human behavior," "pathology," or even "neurosis." The very concept of neurosis implies someone whose neurosis it is. Without a conception of that someone you end up with a kind of rootless empiricism—a miscellaneous heap of information impossible to interpret, to generalize, or even to coordinate.

Links to Related Subjects

The second purpose of a revised metapsychology is to link clinical psychoanalysis to the closely related sciences, psychology, ethology, sociology, anthropology, biology, and behavioral genetics. This linking is important to psychoanalysis, because psychopathology cannot be studied in isolation; it is important to the other sciences because psychoanalysis throws light on crucial aspects of their own subject areas.

At an early stage in their training psychoanalysts are told that abnormal psychological states are not qualitatively different from normal states. They are led to believe that their study of dysfunction will reveal all they need to know about normal function. This belief is a good example of one of those bland and unexamined half-truths that can sidetrack a discipline for decades. As recent psychoanalytic studies of normal children show, one cannot get an accurate picture of the potential resources of children solely from studying disturbed children. Psychoanalysts recognize today that the study of normal childhood development provides the study of adult neurosis with an indispensable perspective. Normal growth is not the mere absence of dysfunction; mental health is qualitatively different from mental disease.

On an even more general level, the psychoanalyst cannot acquire a proper understanding of the instinctual side of life solely by studying the neuroses of one socioeconomic class in one culture in one species. He cannot properly understand normal ego function—or dysfunction either—without understanding how ego processes develop in the species as a whole in relation to self, to others, and to society; nor can he understand the symbolic meaning of a neurosis unless he also understands what role meaning and learning play in the psychic life of the individual and of the society. Finally, he cannot even define the goals and limits of therapy unless he also understands the role played by the culture and by practical circumstances in a person's life. The psychoanalyst's subject-matter is inextricably related to the varying perspectives of sociology, general psychology, anthropology, and even history.

Psychoanalysis has selected for its subject an aspect of man's life that lies at the very core of his being. Studying neurotic behavior is not some isolated medical specialty like ophthalmology. At its broadest it is the investigation of nothing less than the ills to which the human spirit is prey; even at its narrowest, it has to do with the individual's full emotional development. Because of its great breadth, it is drastically in need of information from disciplines psychoanalysts do not study directly.

Its clinical theory comprises a small number of master concepts (e.g., the concept of the instinctual drives). Such concepts derive at least in part from other sciences. To define fully just the one concept of the instinctual drives, psychoanalysis must draw upon at least three other sciences—ethology, the study of instinct in other species; cultural anthropology, the study of the cultural patterning of instinctual expression; and behavioral genetics, the study of the transmission of inherited characteristics. Only in the light of these latter disciplines can instinct be described satisfactorily. The integrity of psychoanalysis depends, therefore, on ending its not-so-splendid isolation from the other disciplines in whose domain its master concepts are rooted.

Formal and systematic links with other disciplines are mostly absent from the physical sciences, but vital to psychoanalysis, because of the nature of the subject matter. "Specializing," for example, does not have the same meaning for the human sciences as for the physical sciences. It is true that success in science is always closely tied to the ability to specialize: within each science a worker will carve out some relatively narrow province for himself, subjecting his area of specialization to detailed inquiry. If his specialty is conceived too broadly or too narrowly, or if the scientist is unable to abstract his specialized subject from the matrix of the whole in which it is embedded, many years of futile effort can follow. In the physical sciences, up to recent times, it has not been found necessary to build up formal conceptual bonds linking each area of specialization to all of its most closely related disciplines. Still, in the more advanced sciences, such as physics and chemistry, the organic relatedness of the various subspecialties has recently received much attention. The history of such sciences is one of discovering relationships among parts previously thought to be unrelated. The modern trend toward fused sciences (e.g., biophysics) reflects a recognition of the unity of science. It has become a truism that the most fruitful work in science today is being done at the interface of various disciplines connecting previously isolated areas of specialization.

However unified the physical sciences become, the human sciences must be even more so. The phenomena studied by the physical sciences tend, in the language of mathematics, to be "loosely coupled," while the phenomena studied by the human sciences are "closely coupled." In other words, while there is unity among the subjects studied by the physical scientists, the "parts" are loosely enough coupled so that they lend themselves to being segregated for separate study far more readily than do subjects covered by the human sciences. Of all possible subjects, human experience suffers most when arbitrarily divided up into its social, biological, psychological, and historical parts. When sociology, for example, attempts to study society without understanding individual human experience or without a sense of history, it ends up incapable of answering the most important questions about the social process. So it is with psychoanalysis. The very nature of the human condition—the subject, after all, of the human sciences—shows man to be so enmeshed in the larger context of his cultural, historical, and biological setting that isolated treatment of the neuroses is not practical.

We would like, without laboring the point, to distinguish between dividing a subject into its component parts and studying its varying aspects. If physical nature is the subject, breaking it down into the galaxies, the earth's crust, the elements, marine life, etc., is not analogous to dividing human experience into its historical, archaeological, sociological, anthropological, psychological, and biological aspects. (The distinction is blurred because the physical world is also a unified whole and cannot readily be chopped into separate parts, but aspects of physical nature are more readily segregated for specialized study than aspects of human life.) Man-in-culture, man-in-society, man-in-nature—these are indivisible subjects. Some specialization is demanded by science, but there must also be some counterbalancing perspective to show how the specialized aspects relate to the whole. When workers in the human sciences lose their blind idolatry of the physical sciences and look at human experience with a fresh eye, we predict that it. will be unthinkable for a specialized theory (e.g., child psychology, the sociology of the family, cultural anthropology, the clinical theory of psychoanalysis) not to have a formal metatheory placing it in correct relationship to the whole.

We are not suggesting that the metapsychology become either a general philosophy of human nature or the sum of all the other human sciences, but simply that it tie psychoanalysis to its sister disciplines at those strategic points needed to preserve the integrity of the clinical theory—which means to preserve the integrity of the human person. This point is vital, for it implies that each of the human sciences should have its own formal metatheory and that each such conceptual structure should be somewhat different from all the others, although they will have a family resemblance.

In subsequent sections we shall stress the similarity of theories to maps.* Let us, therefore, utilize a map analogy here. A map

---

* No analogy is ever perfect. There are many respects in which a theory may differ from a map. For one, there need not be a one-to-one correspondence of every element in the theory with a corresponding

showing how Cape Cod relates to the whole of the United States will not be the same as a map that shows how South America is related to the United States, although they will share some common features. In the first map, Cape Cod will be shown in great detail, Massachusetts and New England will be clear but less detailed, and the rest of the country will be seen in broad contour. If the map is correct, one will have a sense of where in the United States Cape Cod is located, how big it is in relation to the rest of the country, and how one might travel from the Cape to other parts of the country. Such a map will not "explain" the Cape in the same sense as might a history or sociology of the region, but it will locate it and define its relationships to other regions (which is what we are proposing the metapsychology do for psychoanalysis). In the map showing the relationship of South America to the United States, the broad contours of the United States will be the same but different characteristics will be stressed (in the second map, Cape Cod will barely be visible).

Psychoanalysis up to now has been like a map of Cape Cod standing alone without showing where it fits in the scheme of geography. And, like some residents of Cape Cod, psychoanalysts, lacking a proper map of the whole, somehow see all other aspects of man's life-space as peripheral appendages to their area of specialization. The reader may remember those humorous maps of New England which show the Midwest, California, Texas and the rest of the country as tiny territories somewhere off the Connecticut border. When a psychoanalyst looks at his patient's childhood conflicts, somehow the patient's contemporary reality recedes vaguely into the background: the years of growth and development intervening between childhood and adulthood almost escape attention and the world of the patient where it is not implicated in his neurosis seems to shrink into insignificance.

A revised metapsychology, then, should serve as a conceptual map placing psychoanalysis in proper perspective. A person's

---

element in reality. Also, a theory has a *functional* aspect of organizing past experience and pointing toward future experience. (The point here is fundamental in the transition from Wittgenstein I to Wittgenstein II.) Nevertheless, the map anology still serves a useful purpose.

childhood family drama is important, but so is his adult life, his economic and political interests, his institutions, his culture, his past history, and his relations with others and with nature itself. We need not understand all of these facets of his life in detail to understand his neuroses, but if we do not see where they fit in some general way, the most drastic distortions take place. Conversely, the neuroses play a role—sometimes a surprisingly large one—in human affairs outside of the psychoanalyst's office. But unless there are specific mediating concepts linking psychoanalysis to the other human sciences, psychoanalysis will not be truly accessible for use by others and will not be able to generalize beyond—or even within—its own boundaries.

As matters now stand, psychoanalysts who generalize from their clinical practice to broad social issues—international relations, peace, delinquency and crime, poverty, politics, etc.—are almost a menace to the public safety. And yet, they should have a great contribution to make to such subjects. But a huge piece of the puzzle is missing . . . or more accurately, the psychoanalysts themselves have the missing piece: it is the rest of the puzzle they lack.

Relation to Science and to Philosophy

The third function of a new metapsychology will be to resolve the dispute science and philosophy both have with psychoanalysis. The present glories of psychoanalysis are its data base, its clinical theory (freed from the metapsychology), and the personal skills of certain gifted individuals in blending theory with experience. Some of its most glaring weaknesses come from its problematic relation to science and to philosophy.

Its argument with science centers on two issues. The first is the equivocal stand taken by psychoanalysts on the issue of verification. Can the propositions of psychoanalysis be formulated so that they *can* be verified or disproven? (Professor

Nagel's claim is that they cannot.) If so, what would constitute verification? Must psychoanalysis rely exclusively on laboratory experimentation to verify its main propositions? On this latter question, Sears's survey of experimental psychoanalysis, recently updated, reveals a sad story of misunderstanding and failure to achieve even a common definition of terms. For example, psychologists have tried to prove under laboratory conditions that regression does occur; and psychoanalysts have criticized the research, stating that due to an artificial setting the experimenters are not actually testing regression. Yet, if laboratory experimentation falsifies the phenomena by forcing artificial conditions on them, as it often does, what about other approaches to verification? What about the opportunities to verify psychoanalytic propositions in the setting of so many thousands of ongoing therapeutic situations?

There is no methodological justification for the dearth of well-designed psychoanalytic studies. Their absence reflects a lack of interest in, and a lack of concern with, this classic mode of scientific knowing. Many psychoanalysts simply do not see what value can be added to their clinical experience by laborious formal documentation. And nowhere has psychoanalysis compromised its future as a science more than in its refusal to subject psychoanalytic propositions to formal verification. It is, however, the essence of modern science to regard discovery without verification as imperfect knowledge, knowledge that is not "scientific" in the true sense of the term. If psychoanalysis has any claim to scientific status—and it does and should have—then it must become more serious about verification and it must look to a revised metapsychology to define the nature of proof appropriate to a human subject matter. There is no reason why verification should have the same meaning in the human sciences as in the physical sciences.

The other scientific limitation of psychoanalysis is its weakness in describing process—showing how things work. American scientists, in particular, look to the how of a subject more than to the what or to the why. How does identification work? How does regression work? How does secondary autonomy evolve? How does emotional disengagement take place? When psychoanalysts answer such questions by talking about cathexes being withdrawn, about energies being neutralized, about objects being introjected, about libido being invested and then pulled back again—from a strictly scientific point of view they seem to be either speaking in literary metaphors or speaking nonsense. A new metapsychology must clarify the description of process so as to make it more meaningful—and more measurable (though not necessarily by means of numerical values).

The strained relationship of psychoanalysis to philosophy, less widely bruited, is even more problematic. The philosopher's argument with psychoanalysis centers on its horrendous logical state—its internal contradictions, unjustified reductionism, use of the same key technical terms for multiple and conflicting meanings, assumptions not made explicit, assumptions unseparated from fact; its utter oblivion to more than two hundred years of philosophical reflection on the Cartesian dilemma and philosophical attempts to avoid its pitfalls; its blind faith in scientific materialism as a suitable philosophy for studying man's nature; the "psychologism" of its treatment of vital ethical problems; and its truly sweeping oversimplification of the ontological question—the nature of man's being.

Notice that all of these compelling—and quite legitimate— complaints about psychoanalysis, both from a scientific and a philosophical point of view, converge on the metapsychology, not on the observations and insights of clinical theory or of therapeutic practice. Unfortunately, it is the metapsychology that represents psychoanalysis to the scientific and philosophical communities. Some of the most serious criticisms made above apply sharply to the metapsychology but become blunted when applied to other aspects of psychoanalysis. If psychoanalytic clinical theory and practice were the target of the criticisms instead of the metapsychology, we would find (1) that the issue of verification, though difficult in practice, is less problematic in theory—it becomes a technical matter of research tactics rather than a theoretical matter of intrinsic unverifiability; (2) that psychic processes, such as identification, involvement, defense, and so on, can be well described without reference to forces and energies; (3) that the worst of the logical flaws, such as the internal contradictions, are less glaring; (4) that Cartesianism and scientific materialism are not central issues; (5) that ethics and values are less oversimplified;

and (6) that glib and ready answers about man's inherent nature are less in evidence.

It is this paradox—that its critics are talking about the metapsychology while psychoanalysts themselves are talking about something else—that makes the dialogue between psychoanalysts and others so prone to confusion. Psychoanalysts feel, with justification, that they are unfairly criticized, and that their subtle and powerful discipline is being attacked by know-nothing critics who perhaps ought, each and every one, to be psychoanalyzed (in part as punishment for their criticism). The critics, however justified they may be, do seem to pounce all too enthusiastically on the wrong target. At the very least, a revised metapsychology should lead psychoanalysts and their scientific/philosophical critics to focus on the same subject.

SEVENTEEN

The Core of Reconstruction

The task of defining a new metatheory for psychoanalysis takes us beyond psychoanalysis itself. The philosophical breadth of the issues raised is suggested by the debate that has been going on in France for the last two decades between Jean-Paul Sartre, the philosopher, and Claude Lévi-Strauss, the anthropologist. The subject of the debate, at a typical Gallic level of abstraction, is the very nature of man, his freedom (or lack of it), his history, and the nature of the human sciences.

There might seem to be some disadvantages in turning, however briefly, to the French intellectual scene. In the human sciences the French can scarcely marshal the resources or number of researchers in the field that we in this country can. Moreover, bound tightly within their own tradition, the French were for a number of years cut off from external developments in these sciences. Nevertheless, this tight-knit unity brings one great advantage: where intellectual polemic is prompt and constant and where intensely theoretical matters may be debated in the daily press, there is always a greater chance that problems can be pared down to their core issues. The French are thus expert (sometimes too expert) at the *mise à point*—a particularly untranslatable expression that might be described as the trimming off of the fat till the bare bones—the key concepts —are exposed.

In the present controversy these key concepts are nature, history (or culture), and freedom—or, to make the dialectical opposition explicit, *history*, which is assumed by Sartre to presuppose total freedom for man, is contrasted with *nature*, which is assumed by Lévi-Strauss to presuppose total determinism. Both thinkers thus place the freedom-determinism controversy within the more general context (where it properly belongs) of man's nature in relation to his culture and his history. Sartre, the existentialist, advances a theory of radical freedom leading to the conclusion that man has no inherent nature but only a history. Sartre thereby places himself squarely within the tradition that emphasizes man's environment instead of his inherent nature, a tradition that includes most American social scientists. Man differs from all the other animals in that he can, by manipulating his environment, transform the conditions of his existence, and hence transform his own being virtually at will. The raw material of human nature is thus endlessly plastic before the possibilities of historical change that man himself creates and can control, at least in principle, if he sets his will and intelligence to the task. The goal of history, as it were, is to enable man to abolish nature, and any so-called *human* nature. One recognizes here a secular transformation of the old Leibnitzian dichotomy of the kingdom of grace and the kingdom of nature. The kingdom of grace (which for older theologians was also the kingdom of freedom) now becomes the thoroughly humanized world that will eventually be shaped and controlled by man's own hands.

It is worth noting in passing that the first significant protest against this doctrine in French intellectual circles was launched from the point of view of the poet and artist. It came from Albert Camus after he broke with Sartre. Art, for Camus, does not merely reveal man to himself in his actual social and historical conditions, as in the case of social realism. Art also brings us before the immemorial aspects of human experience. Our modern sensibility rejects the once popular dichotomy between the art of civilized man and the primitive: civilized art—where it really succeeds in being art—leads us back to the human and natural terrain where the art of the primitive is also rooted. Camus' critique suggests that Sartre's view could end by making man a prisoner of his history: a creature who, in the name of a limitless liberty, would in fact become caged in his own glass and steel labyrinths, cut off from the elemental poetic resources of nature.

Moving as this poetic revolt was, Camus did not get to the heart of the matter beyond his simple assertion that, contrary to the prevailing fashion (particularly, of course, in the climate of Sartrian existentialism), he did believe that there was an inherent human nature with definite limiting qualities. It was left for Lévi-Strauss, perhaps the most brilliant anthropologist of our time, to bring the controversy into sharp theoretical focus, especially so far as the human sciences are concerned. As a scientist he set himself up as a strict determinist against Sartre, the philosopher of freedom. In Lévi-Strauss's judgment, Sartre's theory suffers from a false distinction between so-called historical societies, such as our own, and primitive cultures. As he sees it, our claims of pure historical development are often "fraudulent."

According to Lévi-Strauss, man in his society today—whether in a primitive or an advanced culture—is caught in an "inertial system" from which he cannot escape. Observing primitive cultures in the field, Lévi-Strauss has been depressed by the fact that the primitive seems to absorb the waste-products of supposedly higher civilizations. We export our garbage, our inferior products, to the native. This image of advanced civilization as a secreter of waste-products was built up in Lévi-Strauss's mind until it found theoretical expression in the Second Law of Thermodynamics, according to which all complexes of energy dissipate themselves and peter out:

> Man's role is itself a machine, brought perhaps to a greater point of perfection than any other, whose activity hastens the disintegration of an initial order and precipitates a powerfully organized matter towards a condition of in-ertia which grows even greater, and will one day prove definitive. (1964, p. 397.)

We are brought back once again, by a different route to be sure, to that same controversial concept that so haunted Freud —the belief in a Death Instinct in nature and in man based on the principle of entropy—the ultimate disintegration of all energy-structures. And on this subject of entropy Lévi-Strauss grows positively lyrical in his melancholy:

> No doubt he [man] has built cities and brought the soil to fruition; but if we examine these activities closely we

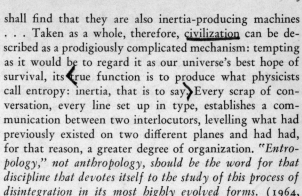

shall find that they are also inertia-producing machines
. . . Taken as a whole, therefore, civilization can be described as a prodigiously complicated mechanism: tempting
as it would be to regard it as our universe's best hope of
survival, its true function is to produce what physicists
call entropy: inertia, that is to say. Every scrap of conversation, every line set up in type, establishes a communication between two interlocutors, levelling what had
previously existed on two different planes and had had,
for that reason, a greater degree of organization. *"Entro-
pology," not anthropology, should be the word for that
discipline that devotes itself to the study of this process of
disintegration in its most highly evolved forms.* (1964,
p. 397.) (Our italics.)

It is a sad fact that anthropology is often the study of
societies on the way to becoming extinct. The anthropologist is
himself the harbinger of an encroaching civilization that threatens the primitive culture with disintegration. But Lévi-Strauss
wishes to elevate this historical circumstance into a principle of
cosmic process. Moreover, he would make this principle binding,
not merely for anthropology but for all the other sciences of
man. One could scarcely find a more sweeping assertion of
mechanism as a basic postulate for the human sciences.

Thus, the battle-line between these two French thinkers is
drawn sharply. On the one side, Sartre espouses a radical and
absolute freedom for man based on a remarkable presumption
that man's history is solely the product of his own existential
decisions, not bound in any important way by an inherent,
biologically rooted human nature. On the other side, Lévi-
Strauss advocates an inexorable determinism that portrays man
as petering out in the death-heat of the planet. He makes the
equally remarkable assumption that the thrust of evolution, as
it carries over into human culture, moves inexorably toward
decay: man, subject to the iron laws of entropy, can exert no
meaningful effect on his own destiny.

We would seem to have here, then, yet another variation of
the theme of that conflict that has raged within Western
thought for the past three centuries. Yet there is a significant
difference in this particular variation. While the question of
freedom versus determinism has been treated in philosophy

mainly as it concerns the individual and his autonomous moral life, in the present case this issue is raised apropos of securing a foundation for the human sciences. The key concepts—history,* nature, freedom, and their relative roles for the understanding of man—pose basic questions that have to be answered by any scientific theory of man's nature. These questions turn about the classical nature-nurture controversy: what are the relative roles of environment and heredity in shaping human beings? Or, perhaps more generally, how is culture related to nature in man? The relevance of man's freedom to these questions is summed up by Sartre in a single incisive sentence: "What we call freedom is the irreducibility of the cultural order to the natural order."

The modern scientific perspective calls into serious doubt this formulation of Sartre's. History and nature do not exist as separate and distinct categories. These concepts are high intellectual abstractions; man-in-his-historical-environment should be a single term referring to an indivisible, unified whole. Despite its rhetorical incisiveness, Sartre's claim that the cultural is not reducible to the natural is, as formulated, more cryptic than meaningful. Moreover, his further assumption that the biological side of man's life is fixed and unchangeable while his history is infinitely malleable—a testimony to man's freedom—is highly questionable. Ours is the age of drugs, X-rays, radiation, and other genetic interventions in man's biological make-up; we may be unable to control their consequences, but we are ferociously engaged in bringing about biological changes. Conversely, as every psychiatrist knows, modifying the effects of an individual's early interpersonal relationships (an aspect of his history) is often impossible. We cannot assume *a priori* that all biological aspects of man's life are more fixed and rigidly determined than all cultural aspects; the matter calls for detailed empirical inquiry.

As both Lévi-Strauss and most modern social scientists insist, there can be no hard and fast dualism between the natural and

---

* In this context, we are using the terms history and culture interchangeably. History emphasizes the time dimension; culture emphasizes the patterning of social institutions. But both concepts refer mainly to the social environment in which we live.

the cultural. We do not discover natural man hidden under the trappings of social man, as Rousseau did. In one of his most pregnant statements Lévi-Strauss observes: "Whoever says 'Man' says 'Language,' and whoever says 'Language' says 'Society.'" (1964, p. 389.) Human cultures arise from a natural basis and seek some integration into the natural environment. As we shall put it later, culture is evolution carried on by other means. But, it must be insisted, these means are "other" —that is, distinctly human means—and they bring before us specific types of structures that are not reducible to those of the natural sciences. Lévi-Strauss is entirely right in claiming that the vocal structures that find their completion in language are as much part of the inherent nature of man as the muscular structure that is fulfilled in walking.

Against Sartre, therefore, Lévi-Strauss is right in claiming that the former inflates the degree of freedom in human history. This freedom has brakes and resistances—well illustrated by the curious ironies of contemporary history. The dizzy rate of historical change, which moves like an exponential curve, has brought us back to problems that are always in the foreground for primitive cultures: pollution of the environment, depletion of resources, limitations upon the human numbers of the culture, and generally the erosion of those institutions (the word here understood in its most inclusive sense) that keep the culture going. Indeed, just because of this rapid historical change, contemporary societies may be caught up in a peculiarly dizzy inertial system spinning wildly out of control.

Nevertheless, history does exist. Lévi-Strauss cannot get around this fact, despite all his subtle reminders of how fragile and ambiguous historical development may be. For if language is part of the nature of man, what in turn is the nature of language? Is language ultimately reducible, as Lévi-Strauss holds, to the mechanisms of information systems? Does not language bring man into the world of historical significances and meanings, the world within which William James discovered for himself the possibility of human freedom?

Indeed, as Sartre points out, Lévi-Strauss cannot avoid acknowledging the fact of freedom for himself. In the very section in which he sings the funeral-dirge of freedom, this arch determinist is pulled into the familiar paradox of speaking of

human choice and the difference that decisive commitment
makes. Torn between the relentless mechanism of his views as
a scientist and his need, as a man, to participate in the politics
of his own time, he proclaims his decision for socialism:

> And if, in the end, I *opt* for "ourselves" . . . there is
> really only one *choice* to be made . . . But no sooner
> have I *chosen* than, by that very *choice*, I *take on myself*,
> unreservedly, my condition as a man. Thus *liberated* from
> an intellectual pride whose futility is only equalled by
> that of its object, I also agree to subordinate its claims
> to the objective *will-to-emancipation* of those who are
> still denied the means of *choosing* their own destiny.
> (1964, p. 398.) (Italics ours.)

Notice the dense reverberation of words having to do with
decision, will, liberation for freedom of choice. Someone might
say that here only the man, not the scientist, is speaking. But
that is precisely the point: what he gives in this passage is a
true description of himself and his behavior within the human
life-world, a truth that must enter as a datum within the
human sciences. As we have repeatedly insisted throughout this
book, there cannot be two truths: one that holds within the
life-world, and another and canceling truth within the constructed world of science. If Lévi-Strauss is "liberated from an
intellectual pride" of the scientist in the existential world of
men, then the scientist must bend back upon himself and take
this liberation into his ken.

Sartre has a point when he accuses Lévi-Strauss of aspiring
as a scientist to study mankind as if it were a society of ants.
Lévi-Strauss cheerfully accepts the criticism with the sly dis-
claimer that his aspiration seems to him to be "just the attitude
of any scientist who is an agnostic." As a plea for the values
of objectivity and dispassion on the part of the human scientist,
the claim may hold. But the first conclusion a comparison of
ants and men ought to reveal is that the two creatures are
different (however hivelike our human cities have become).
Human possibilities of action and choice are simply not open
to ants.

The debate goes on, riposte following riposte, in an endless
rally that always sends the ball back across the net but never

brings the game to any decisive conclusion. What, then, is one to say about this confrontation between two of the most gifted and representative minds of our time? Our answer is that the controversy is pointless so long as the premises on which it is based are invalid. The views of Sartre and Lévi-Strauss present us with a drastic either-or: history, on the one hand, as the play of human freedom creating itself in a void without the constraining limitations of human nature or the harsh imperatives of the natural environment; on the other hand, nature—which in fact becomes merely another name for the relentless, inflexible, and irreversible mechanisms expressed by the Second Law of Thermodynamics.* This violent bifurcation leaves us with a Sartrean conception of freedom that does not take human limits into account, and Lévi-Strauss's conception of a nature whose richness and complexity are reduced to a mere energy-dissipating mechanism. (Whatever role entropy may play in nature or in human affairs, it must be understood within the broader context of the evolutionary thrust in quite the opposite direction: toward more complex forms of organic organization; only within such a context is it meaningful to talk of entropy and decay.)

To replace this unsatisfactory either-or, we are emphatically not proposing a both-and. One cannot find truth by the bland eclecticism of adding together two disparate views.

We can, however, locate our position in relation to the Lévi-Strauss-Sartre controversy; the key terms of any proposed philosophy of the human condition must be the same ones that

---

* Lévi-Strauss qualifies his application of entropy by the clever ploy of distinguishing between "cool" and "hot" societies—thus locating the problem once again within the context of a thermodynamic metaphor. "Cool" cultures, like those of the primitives, seek to cool off those internal processes that would disturb the initial equilibrium. "Hot" cultures, like the historical civilizations, heat up the energies that are leading to change. Thus, we would seem to be presented with a distinction only between two different inertial systems—one in stable equilibrium, the other in unstable disequilibrium. But this metaphor simply will not work. Whatever the contradictory forces that may have led to the disintegration of historical civilizations, the emergence of modern history has broken through the closed cycle of life of the primitives to create new forms of culture.

have figured most prominently in their debate. Such a philosophy must define its stand (a) on nature: how our biological evolution enters into the formation of personality and the shaping of needs, motives, values, conflicts, etc.; (b) on culture: what role our human history and social institutions play in relation to biological nature; (c) on freedom: whether our own existential decisions are merely epiphenomena or exert some influence within the limits imposed by nature and culture; and finally (d) on human science: what modes of knowing are best designed to help us acquire valid knowledge about the human person in his human world.

Since our aim is not to advance a systematic philosophy of man in the abstract (even supposing that this were possible), the position we adopt here on these great topics will be developed only insofar as they bear on the task of finding a better ground for psychoanalysis.

New Philosophical Premises

Psychoanalytic metapsychology is presently made up of random statements scattered throughout the psychoanalytic literature describing the psychic apparatus from various points of view —the topographic, the economic, the dynamic, the genetic, the structural, and the adaptive. Apart from a recent systematizing effort by Rapaport, there exists no one body of statements presenting the full metapsychology nor any strict method for distinguishing between a clinical and a metapsychological statement. The best clue to a statement's being metapsychological is that its language refers to cathexes, forces, and mechanisms.

We propose a number of changes both in form and content. With respect to form, instead of the customary six points of view, a revised metapsychology might be simplified so as to comprise only two types of propositions, corresponding to Kant's distinction between constitutive and regulatory principles. Constitutive principles describe the inherent nature of the subject; regulatory principles are what Peirce called leading principles—guideposts telling us how to use concepts, theories, abstractions and scientific methods in relation to the subject content.

Constitutive principles will make explicit the psychoanalytic premises about human nature, culture, and freedom as a context for the clinical theory. This body of doctrine will form the *ontological* side of the metapsychology.

Regulatory principles will concern the relationship of the metapsychology to the clinical theory to the raw data of psychoanalysis, to the other human sciences, to scientific method in general, and to other methods of acquiring knowledge about human experience. This is the *epistemological* side of the metapsychology, dealing with the vastly troubled questions of how to gain, use, and verify knowledge about human beings. (The terms "constitutive" and "ontological" will be roughly synonymous, as will the terms "regulatory" and "epistemological." Usage will depend upon context.)

Should we start with regulatory or with constitutive principles, that is, should we begin with methodological strategies for studying the subject or with a description of content? The question of priority, though it sounds like empty formalism, is fundamental. The modern emphasis in philosophy since Descartes has been mainly on man as knower—an emphasis Avery Weisman has introduced into psychoanalysis. Even today, philosophy favors purely methodological approaches which say little or nothing about the subject, leaving this latter task to the empirical sciences. Despite its influence on existentialism, phenomenology (at least in its Husserlian mode) is mainly regulatory. So is the Oxford school of ordinary language philosophy.

Yet, thanks to the philosophic consensus, we are able to reverse the traditional emphasis on method and to start instead on the constitutive side—with what Heidegger calls fundamental ontology, in which the subject itself will suggest its own regulatory principles. We shall follow the maxim that ontology dictates epistemology. This approach is, by far, the sounder and the more practical one, since epistemology discussed in a vacuum gets one nowhere. For example, if by its very nature a subject lends itself to logical dissection, then its epistemology will be different from one appropriate to a subject that must be experienced directly before knowledge of it can be won; e.g., understanding great music is hardly the same as understanding the logistics of a military operation. Our point of departure, therefore, will not be with man as knower but with those fundamental aspects of human experience that are most relevant to psychoanalysis.

The principles that follow do not claim to be a rigorous and exhaustive list, a table of ultimately irreducible categories. On the contrary, in a good many places they will overlap. Such overlapping, in fact, follows necessarily from the nature of the subject that they aim to structure, since human experience cannot be cut up into neat and mutually exclusive segments. The listing is purely a matter of convenience in order to outline the philosophical core for the new metapsychology that the rest of this book will be elaborating in greater depth.

Constitutive Principles

We are so accustomed to analyzing human experience with a logic appropriate to physical objects that our formal theories contain almost no terms to refer to the unique aspects of human experience, however commonplace they may be. Our first two constitutive principles call attention to several prominent—and essential—features of human experience. Such is the power of our traditional metaphysics, however, that these features elude the present metapsychology—despite the fact that one cannot describe human experience without taking them into account.

1. THE CREATION OF NEW FORMS OF RELATEDNESS

There must in the human sciences be ways of describing and identifying relationships other than by spatiality and aggregation. Two people joined by love or friendship are not the same as two people joined by space, as on a subway seat. A trait of character is not the same as a physical attribute. The coming

together of persons, events, and experiences will often create
what Bergson called a true emergent: a new event that cannot
be reduced to the sum of its parts nor explained away by
reference to its origins.

We have referred several times to basic trust and how it
develops out of the infant-mother relationship. Basic trust can
be cited once again to illustrate the synergistic character of
human structures. If, rising out of a profound biological need,
the infant and mother form a stable bond, sanctioned and
indeed shaped by the culture, and if growing out of that bond
basic trust develops, then this new human structure cannot be
reduced to either the mother's maternal instinct, or the infant's
dependency needs, or the positive reinforcement of the stimulus-
response bond in the mother-child transaction, or the social
institution of the family, or the physiological mechanisms
involved in feeding, or even the sum of all of these factors.
Moreover, once basic trust has developed, it must be taken into
account in the description of new psychic structures which
build on it, such as friendship, love, or self-confidence. These
structures, in turn, lead to others.

Nor is the process of creating utterly new and enduring
human structures confined to the growth of one's strengths;
it obtains for one's neuroses as well. Consider a neurosis like
hysteria. Psychoanalysts generally agree hysteria grows out of
the individual's abandonment of direct phallic gratification and
his subsequent preoccupation with symbolic substitutes. Like
basic trust, the stubborn and enduring structure of neurotic
hysteria is also created out of a complex of biological, interpersonal, developmental, and cultural factors. Basic trust may
be a prerequisite for mental health; hysteria may mean psychological distress. But both hysteria and basic trust have a synergistic quality: both are true emergents irreducible to their
origins, and both illustrate what is perhaps the most fundamental law of nature expressed in human life—the tendency
to form new wholes or structures.

This coming into being of new gestalts is the principle of
creativity in nature. The results are not always benign, and
there is often something inertial or blind in the process. But
no description of human experience is possible without taking
this phenomenon into account—as is well recognized in certain

branches of psychology. Gestalt psychology, holism, the organismic point of view, and even systems-analysis, all insist upon the irreducibility of wholes to their constituent parts. Indeed, since the advent of gestalt psychology, a large body of literature has grown up around this point of view. We are proposing a radical extension of holistic thinking to cover virtually every aspect of human experience, from the most minutely elaborated personality traits to the broadest social institutions.

Consider, now, the specific application of this principle to psychoanalytic theory. In the metapsychology, the concepts of sublimation (Freud) and secondary autonomy (Hartmann) attempt to account for roughly similar phenomena. But psychoanalysts have always had trouble with sublimation. Few other concepts in the Freudian corpus appear so ambiguous and uncertain. It flickers waywardly in and out of Freud's writings, never quite separated from the repression or suppression of instinctual impulses, until in the later stages of his thought it virtually disappears and is absorbed by other concepts. And Freud had good reason for hesitating, since sublimation does not really fit the metapsychology. Sublimation has always had a *deus ex machina* role of insuring that within the closed system of the metapsychology all of human experience could supposedly be related to libidinal origins. But if one begins by postulating atomistic charges of instinctual energy, then the question of how these become "sublimated"—that is, transformed—into the activities of ego and culture becomes an unintelligible mystery.

Hartmann's concept of secondary autonomy has virtually replaced sublimation and is somewhat closer to the mark (see Chapter Six). But it suffers from similar disadvantages. Like sublimation, it remains anchored to the energy theory; and it does not go nearly far enough. The doctrine of secondary autonomy maintains that a psychic structure like curiosity, which may have originated in infantile sexual wishes, can become an autonomous motive in its own right, apart from its origins. But suppose that a person's curiosity leads him to an intense interest in politics, and that interest, in turn, leads him to various values and goals associated with politics. Should we go on to compound the first distinction by labeling this accretion of values as tertiary and quadratic autonomy?

It would, perhaps, be better to put more emphasis on the new structure itself—its stability, its endurance, and what it has created that did not exist before—than to emphasize its origins. Psychoanalysts rely heavily upon the "genetic" point of view (the reconstruction of the past) because a neurotic conflict always bears the stamp of its origins. Thus, psychoanalysts become acutely sensitized to patients' references to their bodies, and to the symbolism of incorporating, penetrating, and expelling from the body. But it is a mistake to equate an adult personality trait that shows signs of infantile origins with these origins itself. In the jargon of psychoanalysis, a talkative, outgoing, giving person who likes to eat, drink, and smoke may be referred to as an oral personality, with the implication that these traits grow directly out of the so-called oral stage of development in infancy. Yet, even in the most severe neuroses there are, between infantile origins and adult personality, many intervening links. Furthermore, these oral characteristics do not define the whole person. They put too much weight on one aspect of personality; the same complex of traits is found in a wide variety of people. Between ordinary adult personality traits and infantile urges there are layers upon layers of relationships, experiences, values, and meanings. From infancy to adulthood is a long time, and there is a lot more going on by way of development, identifications, learning, and transformations of personality than is accounted for in the present metapsychology.

In brief, then, human experience is characterized by the dynamic development of synergistic structures over time, no one structure being reducible to any other. However inconvenient they may be, the neuroses are in and of themselves creative accomplishments—complex structures in their own right—growing out of the encounter between nature and culture. To call a neurosis dysfunctional is misleading when this label implies merely that some "normal" function is not working correctly or is absent. A neurosis is dysfunctional only in the sense that it may happen to interfere with the development of other structures or may be in conflict with them. The term "analysis" is itself misleading, implying as it does that a psychological datum is to be analyzed, i.e., broken down into its constituent parts and hence explained. What the psychoanalyst does in practice is not analysis but a bringing to light of old structures—and a creating of new ones.

2. MODES OF BEING

The study of human experience compels us to introduce abstractions different in kind from those used in describing physical reality. An abstraction such as "mode of being" will have an alien ring to American ears, especially to those accustomed to the language of science. While we could avoid controversy or misunderstanding with a less highly charged term such as "quality of experience," there is a clear-cut advantage to "modes of being": we need a phrase that will sharpen the contrast with the logic of attributes and simple location. The word "mode" has a family of meanings associated with "mood," "style," "state" and "manner." The word "being" is to be understood as a verb, not as a noun. It refers to how one exists in time.

In its application to psychoanalysis, the concept of modes of being makes explicit what is implied by Erikson's distinction between "modalities" and "zones" (Chapter Two of *Childhood and Society*). In treating severely constipated children, Erikson noticed that their toilet habits were characteristic of their total attitudes and behavior. The question thus became not one of explaining the child by reducing a complex pattern of behavior to the anal zone—more particularly, the zone connected with the anal sphincter—but the reverse: asking what meaning does this zone have within the total structure of the child's attitudes. Erikson attempted to explicate this structure in terms of certain "modalities" of meaning: enclosing or shutting oneself off had certain definite meanings for the child, and expelling and extruding had certain other definite meanings. A constipated child, for example, when playing with blocks, might wall himself in, seeking both to protect himself and shut himself off. In this connection, the child's preoccupation with the anal zone becomes a part of the larger whole, which is his relatedness to himself and to the world around him. Moreover, the urge to retain feces and the corresponding urge to release them at awkward and embarrassing moments turns out not to be a simply locatable drive. On the contrary, the meaning of these toilet symptoms is interwoven with other aspects of instinctual life: with erotic and aggressive urges as well as with basic fears against which he must prove some defense. (The expelling of feces, for example, may take on the significance of a death.)

In short, the child is not reduced to the anal sphincter, but this zone, and the peculiar meaning it comes to have for the child, is understood through his total modes of being in his world. Indeed, the whole of Erikson's discussion can be taken as a superb example of what the psychoanalyst should be doing, even though the metapsychology would have him look the other way.

An example outside of psychoanalysis may help to clarify further the concept of modes of being. We mentioned earlier that Sartre has observed that a person is a coward in a different sense from the way in which he is six feet tall. His height is an attribute that can be isolated from the rest of his qualities: we have only to stand him against the wall, make a mark with a pencil, run a ruler from floor to mark—and we have produced an altogether clear-cut and unambiguous measurement of this attribute. His cowardice, on the other hand, is a mode of being that implicates his whole personality—including attributes and qualities that are logical opposites.

The point is made vividly clear in Sartre's play *No Exit*. The character Garcin, a collaborator during the German occupation, had spent his life in virile and bold actions to prove his own courage. Then one night he had panicked and tried to escape from the country, only to be caught by the Resistance and shot. Now in Hell (where the play is set) he tortures himself with the question: Is he really a coward after all? His question is misdirected. It is as if we were dealing here with the human psyche on the model of a chemical analysis in which, after the chemist has boiled off or filtered away other components, he finds a simple substance—cowardice—at the bottom of his retort. But Garcin's cowardice-courage is not a simply isolatable substance or property. Here in Hell he might still be capable of launching himself into prodigies of heroism—provided there were an audience before whose eyes he could thus prove his courage. What is at issue is a total mode of being: Garcin's relationship with himself is such that he must, and

only can, exist in the eyes of others. So his courage, such as it
is, is inextricably entwined with the cowardly fear of how
he might look to other people. His courage-cowardice is a
single indecomposable modality, at once ambiguous and complex. Psychoanalysis, in its clinical writings, has taken a considerable step toward acknowledging these complex psychic
states by its persistent concern with ambivalence, paradox, and
the similarity of opposites (love-hate; gentleness-aggression;
sadism-masochism, etc.). But it has to take a further step and
recognize that phenomena such as ambivalence cannot be adequately conceptualized as conflicts of forces pushing in opposite directions.

Because of their commitment to the logic of attributes, psychoanalysts have great difficulty in generalizing beyond individual experience. It is traditional in their writings to rely on
typologies: paranoid personalities, schizoid types, manic-depres-
sives, hysterics, obsessive-compulsives, etc. The labels are convenient, for they quickly communicate something about the
patient's symptoms and style. Yet, most clinicians are uncomfortable with such typologies since they often find, for example,
that hysterics can be compulsive and compulsives can be hysterical, just as unhappy people are sometimes happy and vice
versa. One perceptive psychoanalyst commented on a paper
that clearly and accurately described the attributes of the so-
called psychopathic personality—his poor impulse control,
his amorality, etc.—that though he greatly admired the paper,
he realized that by paying too close attention to the psycho-
path's attributes, one lost important aspects of his experience.
The paper, for all its clarity, obscured those qualities of psy-
chopathy that are most relevant to therapy. The language of
typologies, nosologies, diagnostic entities, symptoms, and character traits, as rooted in the logic of locatable attributes, does
not do justice to patients' lives. Nowadays, analysts are often
less concerned with symptoms than with total modes of being
they can tune in to and help to change.

Structures such as basic trust and hysteria are not mere con-
catenations of attributes held together by a bond of energy.
Such an ontology is suitable only to the simplest inanimate
objects (and may not even be suitable to them). Complex human structures involve the entire person and his relatedness to

self and to the world. A person in a neurotic state is dominated by that neurotic mode of being and may, in therapy or in daily life, be struggling to free himself of it, to reduce its hold over him, or to force it to recede into the background so that other modes of being which simplify his relatedness to self and others may emerge.

Modes of being are drenched in the temporal aspect of experience. They do not represent a static cross-section of experience at any one point in time, but include present, past and future. When we describe a neurotic mode of being such as hysteria, we are not referring solely to the symptoms of conversion or phobia, the hysterical personality style, or to the oedipal conflict between phallic urges and a repressive ego, but to the past history, present state, and future possibilities of the hysterical qualities of experience.

3. HUMAN NATURE AND INSTINCT

In later chapters we will propose a theory at odds with the classic Freudian doctrine of instincts as endogenous and locatable drives that exist independent of experience and learning. It has become clear in recent years that instinctual and learned behavior in man cannot be rigidly separated; one cannot speak of an isolated instinct for this or that isolated behavior. With this qualification, we offer the principle of a *specific, knowable and instinctive human nature*, a doctrine that holds that the same instinctual and maturational tendencies are common to the species as a whole, and, though their forms of expression and extent of fulfillment may vary widely, they can be predicted wherever human beings are found, irrespective of race, geography, or culture. In contrast to older doctrines, however, human nature is not defined here as a matter of specific traits (e.g., "it is human nature to be selfish"), nor a matter of forces and energies (e.g., "the sex and aggression instincts are the main sources of psychic energy"). Indeed, the assumption that human nature can be adequately described by any one category—drives, instincts, reflexes, mechanisms, behaviors, predispositions, or traits of character—flies in the face of modern scientific knowledge. If the inventory of the single atom embraces so many multiple processes, just imagine the pluralism of forms embraced by our evolutionary heritage. (In a later chapter we shall indicate how modern science underscores the variety and complexity of the instinctual component in man.) Yet, however complex, man's instinctual nature is nonetheless so specific that no social scientist can ply his trade without some general conception of how it finds expression in the individual's personal and cultural experience.

Along with Lévi-Strauss, we shall use the example of language to illustrate the instinctual in man. An exclusive focus on sex or hunger or fear—the so-called basic drives—conceives of instinct in too narrow a mold. The position of language in the maturational schedule exemplifies how the instinctual and the cultural interact to create a typically human form of expression.

Another aspect of human nature concerns the trend of evolution. Evolution, far from being dominated by entropy, seems to point toward the creation of newer and more complex forms. For man, this aspect of nature is a mixed blessing. Because the so-called higher forms of life are so complex, they are also more fragile and vulnerable than forms lower on the phylogenetic scale. A simple organism like a sponge is far less easily destroyed—in its natural habitat a sponge can be torn to shreds and yet reconstitute itself, a gift not vouchsafed to man. When we look closely at man as a biological organism we see that the ecology of his life—the immense range of his symbiotic dependence on so many other forms of life, the complexity of his adaptation mechanisms, the great flexibility he has gained by virtue of his reliance on culture as well as instinct —all of these aspects of human evolution underscore man's vulnerability as well as his incredible complexity. But to have a fragile and flexible human nature is hardly the same as having no human nature at all. There is a direction, a purpose and an ancient biological heritage that play a weighty role in man's life. Of all of the human scientists, psychoanalysts are most familiar with this perspective since the neuroses and the instinctual are so closely bound together.

Though we wish to propose a far-reaching reformulation of instinct, we also want to preserve the traditional psychoanalytic emphasis on the instinctual. In neurosis, the derangement of some instinctual component is nearly always central.

4. THE MATURATIONAL SCHEDULE AND STRUCTURE FORMATION

A. MATURATION

Every organism grows on the basis of some equipment— genetic or acquired or both—from which development can take place. This rule also holds for human psychology. As the child grows, the biologically rooted tendencies that become prominent during his various stages must encounter fortunate environmental circumstances (for example, a loving and responsive parent) to permit the fundamental structures of personality to develop. This interactive process goes on throughout the whole of life.

In psychoanalytic theory, the concept of a maturational schedule is suggested both by Anna Freud's lines of development and Erikson's epigenetic principle. But Anna Freud holds her view within the traditional metapsychology, and Erikson has developed his own principle without at the same time challenging the orthodox metatheory. For this reason, the power of such concepts has not fully emerged; only when psychoanalysis is cleared of its old philosophical base will this all-important concept of a maturational schedule be free to generate the subtlety, depth of understanding and detail of documentation that it warrants.

B. STRUCTURE FORMATION

We propose to link the concept of a maturational schedule with a theory of learning and structure formation to form a single constitutive principle. One might urge that learning be made an independent principle since it represents the one branch of psychology that has been amply researched and is most adequately grounded. But there are several reasons, strategic and tactical, for treating learning and maturation together as a single principle. First of all, psychoanalytic theory is our main concern; and for psychoanalysis, the linkage will lead to more attention on the formation of values, meanings, identifications, symbols, and modes of being—topics that cannot be fairly treated within the present metatheory. In a later chapter we introduce the concept of a dependency-on-experience continuum to make the point that some maturational processes are more dependent on specific kinds of experience than others. (The child can learn to walk within almost any environmental setting; the development of self-esteem, however, depends on a narrower range of possible experiences.) Some forms of biologically rooted behavior develop independently of the quality of the culture. Breathing and eating are examples; yet even here, as psychosomatic studies of asthma and gastrointestinal disturbance show, these latter functions can also be severely affected by culturally influenced experience. As the individual matures, unless the society institutionalizes certain important experiences for him at an appropriate time in his own development, some of his biologically rooted potentialities will simply fail to develop and a basis for neurotic suffering will be set.

The concept of a dependency-on-experience continuum will be offered to replace Hartmann's concept of an "average-expectable environment." Freud gave us very few concepts to describe the influence of environment and culture. Hartmann, attempting to overcome the deficiency, acknowledged that people do not develop in an environmental vacuum and that some form of benign experience provided by the environment is needed, but here, once again, Hartmann's proposed solution has blurred the issue rather than opened it up to research. The question is not what constitutes an average-expectable environment but what specific experiences are required to elicit our maturational potential. Some cultures are good for maturation, and others are not. Some elicit more of the individual's maturational potential; others elicit a narrower range. Yet all are average-expectable environments for the individual born into them. We need to know far more than we now do about how the culture, mediated by personal experience, triggers and assists maturation. Particularly, we need to formulate laws of structure formation that regulate these complex processes in ways that are far less simplistic than the pleasure principle.

These laws must cover such important processes as the formation of ego identity, social role, hierarchy of motives, ethics and values, self-confidence, effectiveness, the neuroses, and also the specific mechanisms of displacement, introjection, identification, repression, condensation, substitution, assimilation, autonomy, splitting, spreading, formation of meaning, and similar structural forms within which development takes place.

Joining the concept of a maturational schedule with the laws of structure formation in the same constitutive principle enables us to avoid digging a chasm between the biological and the cultural. Also, this approach shifts emphasis away from the learning of skills that are peripheral to man's life; the learning processes that enter into the purview of psychoanalysis are central to the individual's life, his concepts of himself, and his relations to the larger society.

This principle is the key strategic concept linking nature to culture, insofar as the linkage concerns psychoanalysis. Sociologists and anthropologists will look for different linking concepts for their own metatheories (e.g., concepts such as social role, institutionalization, community, and the very notion of culture itself), but our focus on maturation and the learning associated with it is, we believe, most appropriate for psychoanalysis because of its urgent concern with the earlier years of growth.

Applying this dual concept of maturation and learning to psychoanalytic theory, we find that the neuroses are almost inevitably linked to early age-specific maturational stages and to the type of learning that is possible at those stages. A neurosis in which repressed rage is directed at the self, involving the complex mechanisms of introjection and projection, points to a structure formed at a very early stage of maturation with learning processes appropriate to that stage. This view is in keeping with clinical experience; but it does add a new focus of attention to the metapsychology on the specific nature of the maturation process and on how learning changes, both in form and in intensity, at each stage of growth.

The view of culture we propose differs radically from Freud's view as expressed in his *Civilization and its Discontents*. We emphasize not the opposition of culture to nature, but their unity. Such unity is inherently neither good or bad; it is simply that man's basic values depend utterly on what aspects of his maturational potential the culture is organized to elicit.

5. MEANING AND LANGUAGE

We have already spoken of the two separate theories in psychoanalysis: a theory of meanings, which is the clinical side of psychoanalysis, and a theory of forces, which is the metapsychology. We propose that the concept of meaning should be adopted as a primitive term within the new metapsychology with the same logical status as tissue states, instincts, or biological drives. This proposal is necessary in view of the fact that psychic processes are largely symbolic processes. Thus, the orthodox concept of cathexis will have to be redefined in terms of meaning and learning: when an object becomes "cathected" it acquires for the individual a meaning that it did not have before. Moreover, cathexes come and go; objects that were cathected—that had a positive attraction and interest for us— cease to be so; and this coming and going obviously involves processes of acquiring or learning.

It is remarkable that psychoanalysts have had so little to say about the nature of meaning in their metapsychology in view of the fact that Freud's turning from hypnosis and other manipulative methods to his patients' talk was a decisive step in the birth of psychoanalysis. Remarkable too, in view of the fact that every neurosis, whatever else it may be, produces somewhere a gap in communication. Either the patient cannot relate himself to another person sufficiently for real communication; or there are some hidden experiences whose full meaning he cannot comprehend for himself; or there may be an obsessive search for meaning that goes on and on but conceals rather than reveals. This connection between neurosis and communication points to an essential dimension of language and meaning that no analysis in terms of information theory can ever reach. Communication opens up to man the possibility of freedom. (See Chapter Twenty-Two.) In psychotherapy, any improvement in the patient will also be an improvement—an opening up—in communication.

Language and meaning play a vital role in forming, maintaining and modifying neurotic structures. In a very real sense, such structures are composed of meanings. And, while language and meaning should not be equated—meaning being the broader, more encompassing term—language is one of the few methods available to us for eliciting meanings and changing them.

6. IDENTITY AND THE HUMAN PERSON

The present metapsychology assumes that the human person is the sum of his ego, id, and superego, or more bluntly, that there is no such entity as a human person aside from the sum of these subdivisions of the psychic apparatus. Here the tendency to describe human experience with concepts derived from the study of objects shows up most poorly. The ontological premises built into the logic of analyzing a subject by breaking it down into units of energy, their aggregation, their spatial relations, their simple location, and the attributes to which they give rise, comes to grief in this strange inability to conceptualize the whole person whose ego, id, and superego we wish to understand.

In discussing Erikson we pointed to some of the ambiguities in his concept of identity, particularly in relation to the most elementary sense of identity—the sense of one's existence and continuity in time. Psychoanalyst Paul Myerson, in discussing hysteria (1968), remarks that in some patients activities such as excessive masturbation may be indulged not only for libidinal satisfaction (to compensate for the loss of the loved object), but also "as a frantic method deployed to cope with a state of distress." Myerson adds that in these instances, "the [patient's] act of masturbation does not represent an effort to find pleasure *but to convince himself that he himself at least is still there.*" (P. 14.) (Our italics.)

While Erikson has been the major figure in bringing identity to the fore in psychoanalytic thinking, the concept has to be carried further. We have to be prepared to think of the self as a whole without any vestige of reductionism. Consciousness, for example, has to be restored to a more central role in psychoanalytic thinking about the self. This superb gift of nature gives the individual a degree of control over his life which, though it has harsh limits, nonetheless exists and is one of the few resources available to him to bring about change. In psychoanalysis, the individual is often required to confront new aspects of his past consciously. What he accepts and what he rejects, what he preserves and how he goes beyond the past while yet preserving, are important facets of the psychoanalytic process that have received less attention than they should.

Only when the psychoanalyst has an adequate concept of self and identity, as distinguished from ego function, can he interpret a neurosis as the neurosis of that particular person and not a congeries of symptoms floating in the void.

7. FREEDOM AND EGO STRENGTH

Under the practical pressures of effecting a cure, as well as repeated exposure to clinical problems, psychoanalysts have been compelled bit by bit to modify the mechanism of their original theory—though without necessarily acknowledging that this was what they were doing. Beyond a doubt, the central concepts of contemporary psychoanalytic ego psychology, concepts such as ego autonomy, ego strength, and the therapeutic alliance, presuppose some degree of human freedom.

The premise of a limited but nonetheless effective human freedom is as justified philosophically as it is clinically. In earlier chapters we saw that the major reason for excluding will, choice, and decision, i.e., freedom, from official theories in psychoanalysis and from psychology generally, was an assumption that a belief in freedom and a belief in scientific lawfulness were incompatible. Taking issue with this viewpoint, third-force psychologist, Isidor Chein, states that he feels no contradiction in thinking of himself as a determinist and a believer in human freedom. (See Chapter Thirteen.) He suggests that the apparent contradiction between freedom and lawfulness might be due to the mistake of equating freedom with disorderliness and unpredictability, and points out, correctly, that freedom in the sense of choice and decision carries no such implication. But Chein stops too soon in his analysis. The freedom versus lawfulness dichotomy has deeper roots than mere semantic confusion over definitions. Indeed, the core of the problem is not logical but ontological. It has to do with one's conception of the nature of human experience in relation to the world of objects.

So long as the human person is characterized in analogy with objects, as a mechanism defined by the simple location of his body and acted upon by forces external to him, then lawfulness and freedom are indeed incompatible. Once the inadequacy of this view becomes apparent, one's conception of scientific lawfulness should broaden accordingly.

The view that the human person is self-determining within the boundaries of nature and culture is itself a lawful observation. It means that any description of human experience will be incomplete if it fails to include the individual's own existential decisions. Lawfulness has not been ravaged if, when we make predictions about what a person will do, we take into account his intentions as well as his instincts, habits, previous conditioning and social setting.

One immediate advantage of embracing this ontological premise is that it encourages the psychologist to investigate the precise conditions and limits of human freedom—without feeling that he has violated his credo as a scientist by so doing. The concept of ego strength (the ability to choose and make it stick) and the concept of the therapeutic alliance (the existential decision to trust and work with another human being) both have a secure ontological status that does not depend upon conjuring up borrowed quantities of psychic energy to support them.

8. VALUES AND ETHICS

On the face of it, one might have expected it to be apparent that a human being could never be fully described without including the esthetic and ethical values he holds. Nor are these values like ribbons stuck on the outside of something that at its center is without values and not valuing; on the contrary, they are part of the very warp and weft of life. Yet because the metapsychology taught analysts to look past it, it has taken the almost bruising impact of clinical experience to compel them to recognize the vital reality of values. Clinical experience has shown that every neurosis, besides being a gap in communication, is also somewhere along the line a *crisis in values*—if nothing more, a crisis in the value the individual places on himself. In the grip of neurotic conflict, a man may turn upon himself in revulsion, and let himself crumble in his own eyes in total valueless-ness. Or he may be thrust into an inflated and self-compensating valuation of himself in a tidal wave of narcissism. Usually, too, there are crises over the values he once found in the world outside himself. What had value for him may have lost its meaning; or he may run off in pursuit of the most self-destructive values. Man is the valuing animal as spontaneously and naturally as he is a breathing animal.

What has kept psychoanalysts from recognizing this fact long ago? The answer lies with a whole cluster of theoretical prejudices that have had a long and varied ancestry. For one thing, modern philosophy (since the seventeenth century) has not been much help. For all too long it has been laboriously digging a ditch between the ethical and the natural: the ethical must be made "autonomous"—that is, its roots in nature must be cut off. Against this background, and within the generally debunking atmosphere of late nineteenth century positivism, it was all too easy for Freud to think of values as nothing but commands imposed from without, represented by the stern Jewish father of the superego. Values (superego) were thus imposed by culture, and culture was looked at as something outside of, and alien to, nature (id). Yet the whole lesson of modern anthropology has been that man, even among the most primitive cultures we can find, is ever and always the value-seeking and the value-driven animal. There is no necessary conflict between ethical values (superego) and instinct (id). Like any other synergistic structure, values are the joint product of the instinctual and the cultural. The ethical and moral dimensions of man's life have a thoroughly natural basis not reducible either to infantile origins or to social custom. The reality of the ethical, as difficult as it may be to define and clarify, belongs as a primitive concept in any new metapsychology.

EIGHTEEN

The Core (Continued): The Modes of Psychoanalytic Knowledge

When we pass from the substantive to the regulatory, from ontology to epistemology, we find ourselves immediately faced with a puzzle: What, in fact, does explanation mean in psychoanalysis?

Explanation, it is generally assumed, has to do with discovering causes. Yet ever since Hume wrote his famous critique of causality, the matter has not been quite that simple. In the present century, quantum physics with its Indeterminacy Principle has made causality and explanation ever more problematic in the day-to-day conduct of science. Some years ago, the British philosopher, K. J. W. Craik, summarized four theories of explanation held by scientists, philosophers and the general public:

1. Explanation as causality (the traditional definition).
2. Relational theories, as in modern physics, which are uninterested in causes, but seek out instead those invariant relations between physical entities that will permit predictions to be made.
3. *A priori* theories which start from self-evident **principles** and deduce their logical consequences.
4. Explanation as description.

Psychoanalysis has adhered to the traditional view of explanation as a search for causes, and particularly causes behind the observable phenomena. The procedure is to take the terms in the clinical case history that are descriptive of what the patient experiences and replace them by other terms that refer to entities that do not figure in experience. (We have offered some concrete examples in Chapter Sixteen.) This procedure leads to very serious difficulties. It leads the analyst to think in terms that are remote from the patient's actual problems, with the result that the patient, in turn, may be led into conceptual structures remote from the concrete and living content of his experience. And it leads to a sharp split between the descriptive language of the case history and the theoretical language of the "explanation," with the result that the latter has moved so far from its data base that there is no longer any clear connection between the two. We therefore propose to scrap this sense of explanation and in its place substitute a variation upon one of the other views—explanation as a special kind of description.

Psychoanalysis, as a scientific body of knowledge, must begin with the case history. No matter how ingenious the theorizing, it will be irrelevant if it does not rest upon a data base provided by adequate case studies. Now, a case history happens in fact to be a history. It is easy to forget the force of this latter word of the compound; and psychoanalysts have often let themselves do so, whereas it might have been profitable to ponder some of the puzzles of causal explanation in the study of history.* Historians do in fact speak plentifully enough about "causes" in history. But when we look carefully at their texts, we find that these alleged causes are actually part of the historical narrative and not forces of another kind working behind what appears in history. Looking closer, indeed, we find that these so-called "causes" are really more or less selective and

---

* It would take us too far afield here to go deeply into the philosophical problems that surround history and historiography. Yet this chapter in philosophy, initiated by Dilthey, has great significance for the human sciences. For the goal that motivated Dilthey's critique was to show that in at least this one discipline about man, history, the imitation of the physical sciences was misconceived and could not work.

systematized descriptions of social structures and events interlinked in time.

Our view of explanation as a special kind of description is
clearly implied by our first two constitutive principles. Both
call attention to the fact that much of human experience
eludes such traditional abstractions as causes, attributes, aggregation, and simple location; and both point straight to explanation as a form of selective and generalized description. The
doctrine of synergism suggests that every trait of personality,
every meaningful human relationship, every lasting social in-
novation, introduces a structure that has never existed before.
Something new under the sun has been created, and all "explanations" of such structures must describe this new element.
Similarly, any full explanation of a mode of being such as a
depression must include a full description of the depressed person's world as it appears to him in that state of mind.

It is not enough, however, to say that explanation is mainly
description. We must specify what kind of description we
are referring to, for all descriptions do not explain. If a description is to have explanatory power, it must show a tightly
disciplined selectivity. There must, therefore, be an explicit
criterion of selection. The items described in an explanatory
case history, for example, will be selected out of the full and
shaggy details of the patient's total experience in the light of
both theory and metatheory. The metapsychology should suggest where to look; the clinical theory should sensitize the
analyst to the many possible meanings of his patient's unique
behavior. For example, a man who is being psychoanalyzed
dreams about his first day of school many years ago, recalling
with some distress the poignant quality of his separation from
his mother on the occasion. The psychoanalyst fits this memory
into a pattern along with his patient's anxious responses to himself whenever separation of any kind is threatened. A whole
series of seemingly unrelated incidents now fall into place that
show how this patient tends to cope with separation anxiety.
The analyst's metapsychology should sensitize him to the patient's maturational needs, and the clinical theory to the separation anxiety, the defenses against it, and the types of conflicts
it is likely to evoke. In presenting a case history which exhibits
these themes, the psychoanalyst brings both aspects of the

theory to bear on his data as criteria for selecting the incidents he chooses to describe.

Besides requiring selectivity, description that is explanatory must be able to present a case or a theory at several levels of generality at the same time. In the above examples, we referred to the separation anxiety of an individual considered in the light of his maturational needs. Yet, the very concepts of "separation anxiety" and "maturation" are high abstractions based on inductive generalization from large samples of human experience. In presenting a case, one need not refer explicitly to this broader source of data, but the very use of such concepts implies the reference. Psychoanalysis is utterly dependent upon generalized descriptions of human behavior, even though it lacks any rigidly systematic source for acquiring and refining them.

The concept of modes of being also illustrates how descriptions at several simultaneous levels of generality can take on explanatory power. Think of a psychoanalyst with a hysterical patient. The analyst, in attempting to understand his experience, senses his patient's constant efforts to make the analytical process, ordinarily an uncomfortable and distressing affair, into a source of positive enjoyment. He also notes other aspects of his patient's hysterical style: his openness about pleasure-seeking in all phases of his life, his emotionalism, labile and swiftly varying moods, exaggerated language to avoid genuine insight, flexibility, frequent shifts of attention, ability to converse about a mundane matter while ruminating on an unrelated erotic fantasy, anger hovering in the background momentarily covered up by his expectation that his doctor will relieve his tensions or provide some substitute forms of gratification, etc.* If the psychoanalyst extends these observations in time—to past and future as well as present—the full description of his patient's mode of being will become an indispensable part of its explanation.

This is not, however, the full explanation that is wanted in a case history. For that, we need the descriptive reconstruction of synergistic structures, the interactions of certain key

---

* Suggested by Dr. Paul Myerson and Dr. Robert Gardiner, Boston Psychoanalytic Institute, in a personal communication.

instinctual and maturational processes, <u>the full range of meanings associated with the patient's hysterical symptoms (e.g., migraines, muscle aches, phobias, impotence, etc.)</u>, his basic life values and his existential decisions about how to play out his hand so that he can hold on to his pleasure-seeking fantasies and at the same time accommodate himself to some of the demands made upon him by the rest of the world.

In such descriptions there will be a constant interplay between utterly concrete incidents unique to this one patient and general behavior patterns common to all so-called hysterics and, indeed, to mankind as a whole. Here, once again, the various levels of generality, from the unique to the universal, need not be isolated explicitly since they are implied by the very language of the description.

Another level of generality besides behavior patterns deserves special mention. In his case history, the psychoanalyst may make references to the mechanisms of introjection, displacement, self-object differentiation, and similar processes. Here the term "mechanism" may be properly used, for these are the more automatic and routine processes of the psyche. Furthermore, there is an orderliness and lawfulness to the operation of these mechanisms such that their full description, if systematically carried out, promises to be one of the major contributions psychoanalysis will make to a general psychology. Though these mechanisms are also based on inductive generalization, and hence are ultimately descriptive, their formal status is somewhat different from the other generalization we have discussed. Most generalizations in psychoanalysis take the form "y sometimes follows x and sometimes it doesn't," or at the very best, "y follows x under z conditions with n probability," where both z and n are grossly approximated. The mechanisms we have just cited may come closer to the norms of hard science; namely, that "under specified conditions an invariant relationship exists between x and y." But whether a relationship is believed to be invariant or whether it occurs with no known probability, the fact remains that generalizations about it are essentially descriptive.

A third requirement for explanatory description is that it <u>include purpose as well as process.</u> In probing separation anxiety, maturation, and hysterical modes of being, the psychoanalyst not only asks how the process unfolds but why. The adaptive point of view in psychoanalysis describes why a person's behavior or style helps him to cope with the world and its demands: it thus functions as an ultimate explanation of why a person behaves as he does. Its explanatory power also derives from inductive generalization, and hence is essentially descriptive. Here, however, the generalization broadens out to include species other than man, and time dimensions other than the present; namely, the immense backdrop of evolutionary history for virtually all forms of life.

Scientists are not as comfortable asking why as they are asking how. The influence of the natural sciences leads the human scientist to focus sharply, if not exclusively, on process: how the personality develops; how the genes affect heredity; how object relations are formed in infantile development. In so doing, this scientist may easily lose sight of one entire side of human experience. In human affairs the "how" does not tell the whole story; we have also to ask "why." We have to understand what the process or activity is for, what function it may serve, what final development it may lead to. Human life is the continuous interweaving of purpose and process. An adequate metapsychology must accord the first term just as basic and unprejudiced a status as the latter.

Our whole intention here may be summed up as an attempt to break down the hard and fast dichotomy between description and explanation. A description becomes explanatory to the degree that it is selective and multileveled in generality. Freud's case histories are not less "scientific" than his metapsychological treatises. Indeed, in our view, these case histories should prove more lasting in their scientific value. But the central source of confusion about causality as applied to human experience has still to be cleared up.

Historically, the concept of cause has been associated with a broad range of meanings: cause as a necessary and sufficient condition for an effect; cause as a blind mechanical force; cause as a single force; cause as an ultimate and unobservable entity; and cause as a means of predicting effect. As good a definition of strict causality as any has been offered by the theoretical physicist, Max Born. Causality, he tells us, is applicable when "the course of events in an isolated system is completely determined by the state of the system at the time, t = 0." (Born, 1937, p. 89.) Here causality and rigid determinism are held to be synonymous.

The concept of reasons, in contrast, carries other connotations: a reason is not generally thought of as a force but as a meaning, a predisposition, an interest. Most human events arise from a complex matrix of circumstances rather than one single factor; and a reason or set of reasons may often be a sufficient condition for human action but rarely a necessary condition. Therefore, reasons and rigid causal determinism are not synonymous. A description of the reasons for a man's actions will almost always differ from an explanation of their causes—where the latter are taken as blind forces pushing him from within or without. The tracing of reasons (values, conditionings, etc.) involves a different focus of interest and a different outlook from that found in an analysis of causes (hidden drives, forces, energies, etc.); hence a different ontology lies behind each. Such meanings and reasons—which, moreover, are not static, but genuinely develop from one another—are the actual and sometimes dramatic substance of the individual's life.

If we think of new and emergent human relations as structures of meanings, desires, and predispositions instead of assemblages of forces held together by energy, we introduce the thought that there may be an element of indeterminacy in human experience. If a synergistic relationship creates something new—a new feeling, outlook, belief or style of coping— then this new element as it acts upon subsequent events may not be "completely determined by the state of the system at the time, t = 0." One may never be able to predict its full chain of consequences. According to our ontological principles, a new element is introduced into human affairs that may not be implied by the most thorough analysis of causes. The new factor makes prediction of a long chain of such events fraught with theoretical as well as practical difficulties. And the more difficult prediction becomes, the more emphasis must be placed on description instead of causal "explanation."

In making predictions, the limits of change may be reasonably well hypothesized for a short time span; the processes within which change will take place can then be known with a

Indeterminancy

high degree of exactness. But the precise details of change over a long period of time in an individual or group grow ever more difficult to predict as synergistic possibilities increase. One reason why sick people and sick cultures lend themselves to a more "causal" type of analysis than healthy people and healthy cultures is that their capacity to create new relationships has been severely restricted. They become more like objects than like people, acted upon instead of actors.

In sum, predicting the path of a bullet in space is not the same as predicting the aftermath of a human tragedy that the bullet brings about. It is not simply that the tragedy is more complex than the trajectory of the bullet but nonetheless subject to the same sort of analysis; rather, the tragedy is different in kind. Objects, if defined narrowly, have only a mechanical aspect, while human experience has both a mechanical *and* a synergistic aspect. The mechanical aspects are susceptible to one type of explanation, the synergistic aspects to another. In reconstructing a human life, one may find ample reasons for an individual's behavior, but the reverse does not hold: one can rarely predict the detailed future behavior of a person from a thoroughgoing knowledge of that person as a child in his environment.

Some degree of indeterminism, it should be noted, need not undermine a belief in science. Quantum physicists, for example, regard indeterminism as an inherent characteristic of the microscopic events they study. This does not deter them from observing and predicting regularities, to which they sometimes assign surprisingly broad ranges of probability. Of course, it is possible that the quantum physicists are wrong and their difficulties in prediction are purely practical. The strategic point, however, is that psychology as a science should be based on a theory that will not be undermined if some margin of indeterminism figures in the picture.

The Nature of Psychoanalytic Knowledge

We come now to the troublesome issue of the nature of psychoanalytic knowledge. The problem here centers on the various modes of knowledge that psychoanalysts employ. Psychoanalysts rely upon both concepts and insight, which are not always clearly enough distinguished from one another. Psychoanalytic theory is codified in concepts such as defense, conflict, the dynamic unconscious, instinct, and aggression. Yet the direct encounter between doctor and patient calls upon a highly developed gift of insight and empathy which should be differentiated from conceptual knowledge. Both modes of knowing— by insight and by concept—are indispensable, but their relationship is complex.

In discussing knowledge it is usually assumed that insight is the more mysterious and suspect form, while knowledge by concept can be taken for granted. But in psychoanalysis, both types of knowledge require clarification. Actually, the process of insight is fairly well understood by psychoanalysts, its limitations are respected, and it is often wielded with impressive skill. Not so the conceptual side. Here there seems to be a less impressive understanding of the nature of theoretical abstraction. What, for example, constitutes psychoanalytic truth? Hartmann has urged his colleagues to accept the view that the sole criterion of a theory's worth lies in its heuristic value. He notes, correctly, that many propositions in science and in medicine are not literally true but have nonetheless proven their usefulness many times over. He seems to be saying: Let's not worry about truth in the abstract. Didn't Freud himself refer to the instinct theory as "our mythology"? If a theory leads to useful results, nothing more is required. After all, we are talking merely of concepts.

Hartmann's stand has had a strong appeal to his colleagues, and it seems so practical and down-to-earth that it would be easy to gloss over it. But to do so would leave unanalyzed one of the major sources of confusion on the regulatory side of psychoanalysis.

The Truth of Abstractions

Much of the confusion about truth in relation to pragmatic utility comes from the fact that psychoanalysis has several quite different objectives. It has one goal as a profession and another as an investigative science. The failure to keep them separate creates the confusion between truth and utility. A heavy emphasis on results may be satisfactory for the professional goals of psychoanalysis, but it collides head-on with its scientific goals.

As a profession, psychoanalysis pursues the goals of medicine, is imbued with its ethics and shares its commitment to "cure" the patient. In this role it seeks to develop a technique of therapy which has as its explicit purpose inducing change in its patients. Hence, as a profession, it is to be judged on its methods and results rather than on the objective truth of its insights and discoveries.

In assisting his patients, a psychoanalyst may offer interpretations that do not have to be true to be helpful. Psychotherapists of all schools are familiar with the dramatic changes that can transform a person's life should he come to believe intensely in some faith or ideology—whether it be Marxism or Christian Science or psychoanalysis itself—irrespective of the objective truth of his beliefs. *Indeed, there is no necessary relationship between revealing truth and creating change.* As practitioners, all psychotherapists can and do use a variety of techniques for creating change whose truth value is far from settled.

Psychoanalysts do not like to dwell on the distinction between truth and their form of therapy. Their method, they believe, brings the two together: in principle, a psychoanalyst creates the desired change in his patient by facilitating the patient's true insight—either as the forerunner of change or as its aftermath (which comes first is by no means clear).

In many instances psychoanalysis does work precisely this way. But one also finds many clinical interpretations justified by their results without regard to their truth. Unfortunately, theorists like Hartmann blur the distinction between truth and utility still further by defining truth itself in terms of utility—a true interpretation being one which creates the desired effect and a true concept being one which seems to work in practice. ⟨A technology of therapy may be quite useful without regard to its truth; change, not truth, is its objective. For eliminating symptoms and improving day-to-day functioning, the power of illusion, for example, cannot be minimized⟩ A man who believes his capabilities are slightly greater than they actually are may, within limits, feel better, function better and accomplish more than a man who believes his capabilities are slightly less than they are. The truth may help the second fellow and not the first. The beneficent effects of life without illusions have never been demonstrated, and the harmful effects of "the truth" are often among the skeletons in the closets of older psychoanalysts.

Perhaps psychoanalysts avoid distinguishing sharply between truth and utility because, consciously or otherwise, they tend to choose for psychoanalysis people who can be helped by the truth rather than those whom the truth might devastate or depress even further. Also, it is by no means clear whether those helped by psychoanalysis owe any positive changes in their life to the truth of the insights won in the course of their psychoanalysis, to the effects of the emotional experience that grew out of their relationship to the analyst, or to their having gained a new, more coherent and more emotionally meaningful way of ordering their lives, irrespective of its objective "factual" truth. In practice, all three influences operate simultaneously. All three are important to the technology of inducing change but not all are expressions of truth in a narrow, literal sense (which is how we are using the term).

When we turn from truth in therapy to truth in science we find a more subtle relationship between truth and utility. The main confusion between these terms stems from the map function of theories—a function whose importance has not, perhaps, been explored as systematically as it deserves to be. A good theory, like a good map, must, of course, serve a useful, pragmatic purpose. (As Kurt Lewin observed, nothing is more practical than a good theory.) The relevant question here is: Does a theory have any truth value apart from its pragmatic utility? If we understand him correctly, Hartmann would answer in the negative: his insistence on the heuristic value of concepts was formulated with the scientific goals of psychoanalysis in mind (Hartmann, 1959). It should be emphasized that Hartmann reflects the belief of many scientists from various fields. Indeed, some sciences have abandoned the pursuit of truth in the abstract in favor of pragmatic criteria of predictability, a tendency which blurs the distinction between truth and usefulness.

As a regulatory principle, we suggest that a theory's truth and usefulness are separate and distinct values, and that a good theory, like a good map, should insist upon having both. The truth of psychoanalytic propositions must be defined—and verified—other than by reference to utility. (If this standard were to be literally adhered to, how much of the metapsychology could be retained?) This requirement is not harsh, provided that what is meant by truth and verification can be formulated in some reasonable fashion.

The metaphor comparing theories to maps permits us just such a formulation, provided we understand how far we can carry the comparison. Maps are like theories in many respects: both are distinguishable from the phenomena they describe (which is easier to do with a map, but can be done with theories too); both are based on the principle of extreme selectivity; and both have a highly pragmatic character, a most important datum about a theory or a map being what purpose it is supposed to serve. Furthermore, both maps and theories may be (a) useless and false, (b) useless and true, (c) useful and false, or (d) useful and true. All four combinations are possible, and the history of science yields many examples of each. The two mixed cases—theories that are false but useful, or true but useless—are the most interesting. In the history of science the theory of epicycles and the theory of phlogiston have proven to be both useful (in their time) *and* false (a fate which Hartmann would presumably be willing to accept for his neutralized energies). On the other hand, the theory that mental life can be rendered in physico-chemical terms may be partly true

—but it is useless to psychoanalysts, in the same sense that a splendidly accurate map of New York City's subway system is useless to someone traveling through New York City's streets.*

The conception of truth we are proposing here derives from the premise that there are several modes of knowing and several definitions of truth, each mode of knowing having its own kind of truth. (The truth of a work of art is not the same as the truth of a scientific proposition.) Conceptual truths are truths of abstraction derivative from the mode of knowing by abstraction. If a scientific theory is a scheme of abstractions analogous in function to a map, then its truth (independently of its utility) lies in how well it depicts certain features of reality when reality's full concreteness and density can never be wholly captured by means of concepts, since abstractions, by definition, exclude full concreteness. In principle, we can verify truths about the abstract characteristics of any concrete event, since the event either does or does not possess the abstract characteristics attributed to it (in exactly the same sense that we can truly say that five apples, five days, and five beautiful women all possess the abstract attribute of fiveness). The operations for verifying abstractions encompass all of the various and multiform techniques possessed by science.

The Truths of Insight

Our earlier review of contemporary philosophers suggests the wisdom of not relying exclusively on abstract conceptual knowledge. After writing his epochal *Being and Time* in 1927, Heidegger turned away from philosophy toward poetry. Asked

---

* There is one crucial respect in which the comparison between maps and theories breaks down. When we visit a locale with which we are quite familiar, we can throw away the map and still find our way around. But it is never possible for us to discard our built-in cognitive maps, the modes of interpretation and meaning we have developed from infancy onward as our very means of perceiving reality.

for his reasons, he said simply: "I did not find what I was looking for in that direction." The result of his immersion in poetry was that he was eventually to recast the whole direction and emphasis of his thinking. Similarly, if not quite so drastically, Wittgenstein turned away from the rigid and oversimplified abstractions of his earlier period to a form of pointing at things and enjoining us to "Look!" Husserl's slogan, "To the things themselves!" summons us to the same effort to get behind abstractions, which as a mode of knowing can also be a mode of concealing—indeed, to get *behind traditional philosophy itself*, if need be, to a direct intuitive perception of the data as they evidence themselves in their full and concrete reality.

Perhaps it is the overemphasis on certain types of abstraction prevalent in our culture, especially in our science, that has led so many people to an interest in the philosophies of the East. Eastern thought does not depend on the same method of abstraction for gaining knowledge as do the philosophies and sciences of the West. In these Eastern philosophies everything is seen more dimly, but perhaps much is seen that we of the West have scarcely begun to learn. Our Western way of thinking, built up from clear and distinct abstractions, illuminates some aspects of reality in a sharp light, but plunges other aspects into darkness.

All of this is not to recommend a journey to the East. On the contrary, the Eastern countries themselves are aware of the limitations in their own philosophies; and far from rejecting our style of thought, are greedy to assimilate it. They perceive (correctly) that our material progress reflects our science, which in turn has sprung from our philosophy; and, further, that these fruits of Western civilization owe their great power (as well as their limitations) to the high development in Western countries of knowledge by our method of abstraction. In the future we may expect to see the ancient civilizations of the East torn by even more acute conflict than our own as they move inexorably to adopt our modes of clear and distinct abstract knowledge while at the same time seeking to hold on to their own precious intuitive heritage.

Modes of knowing other than by reductive abstraction are variously called insight, understanding, empathy, intuition, prehension, common sense, wisdom, etc. German psychiatrists, historians, and philosophers have long spoken of a mode of knowing they called *Verstehen*, a form of insight. None of these are well defined, or formalized, or purified of their mystical overtones, or universally accepted in Western science and philosophy. In fact, in academic "philosophy of science" courses they may even be lumped together with mysticism and superstition and relegated to second-class status. The main reason for their neglect is the difficulty of verifying intuitive knowledge by those "objective" methods which are the cornerstone of modern science. Forms of knowledge which do not lend themselves to verification by such methods are minimized or overlooked entirely.

Unfortunately, science has proven remarkably unimaginative about inventing new and more appropriate methods for verifying insights. All too often, scientists have assumed that insight is wholly private and subjective—an assumption belied by the fact that the most subtle insights can be shared by those who have had some common experience. Indeed, hard and fast distinctions between subjective and objective forms of knowledge fail to stand up to close scrutiny. Eventually, we will have to invent and codify new methods for verifying insights. When this is done, a grievous imbalance in our approach to psychological knowledge will have been corrected.

Psychoanalysis, however, cannot wait upon such a development. It is utterly dependent on nonconceptual modes of knowing which it seeks, not always successfully, to integrate with its theoretical abstractions. Whether we call the art of the clinician by the name of insight or *Verstehen* or intuition or empathetic understanding is less important than recognizing that the daily process of "tuning in" to a patient's fantasies and feelings often bypasses abstract concepts. In psychoanalytic circles it is recognized that the best theoreticians are not always the best clinicians—and vice versa. Nor should this be surprising, once we recognize how very different these modes of knowing are, though of course they are never found in absolute isolation from one another. Insight is always permeated with knowledge by abstraction, and theory degenerates into burlesque when it is uninformed by insight.

While there are a number of excellent descriptions of insight in the psychological literature, we are unaware of any systematic work on what the division of effort between insight and conceptual knowledge should be in a discipline such as psychoanalysis. It is clear, however, that insight must be given better credentials as knowledge and be divested of its mystery and vague overtones of unreliability.

At the present stage of scientific development, it is likely that the truths won by insight must first be translated into concepts in order to be verified. Even though a great deal is lost in such a translation, this compromise need not weaken its role; on the contrary, it gives insight an important place in the existing scheme of science in making discoveries and arriving at hypotheses to be verified by more systematic methods. It also helps to clarify the point that insight alone is not enough, just as verification of concepts is not enough. Psychoanalysts, among themselves, may feel little need for verification, but the acceptance of psychoanalysis as a science by others, and more important, its own progress, depends utterly upon establishing a firmer, more mutually supporting relationship between its two chief modes of knowing—insight and abstraction: insight for discovery and responsiveness to patients, abstraction for theory-making and verification.

Other Limitations on "Scientific Method"

Much of this book, in one way or another, has been concerned with dispelling the specter of "scientific materialism." So far, we have been mainly concerned with the materialism component. But real progress will not be made until both parts of this philosophy—the "scientific" as well as the "materialist" part—have been called into question. Workers in the human sciences must guard against the too narrow view of science and scientific method propagated by scientific materialism.

What scientific materialism overlooks is simply that every theory boils down to a set of abstractions and that the essence of abstraction lies in its selectivity. By excluding most aspects of a subject a scientific theory focuses on those highly selected aspects that happen to interest the science at the time. If we become interested in other aspects of the subject, stimulated perhaps by insight, the chances are that we will need a revised theory—one that is more general (subsuming the first) but is still highly selective. Thus, since theories are composed of abstractions and since abstractions exclude more than they include, no one theory can ever provide a complete picture. This conclusion is a more general formulation of Bohr's Principle of Complementarity. It implies that a single, unified, and systematic theory that purported to be a complete picture of a subject such as the nature of man and how to win knowledge about him is inherently impossible.

This warning must be sounded because at the present time many social scientists (and some psychoanalysts) have come to recognize the differences in subject matter between the human and the physical sciences, and hence the need for a new ontology. But they often fail to carry over the implications of this fact to regulatory principles and scientific strategies for dealing with this different subject matter. They wish to go on applying "the scientific method" to human experience—as if the phrase referred to one sacrosanct set of principles and procedures. It is as if in place of scientific materialism, they are willing to give us a version of scientific humanism—i.e., substituting a new set of ontological assumptions for the materialist ones, but leaving the regulatory assumptions (the methods of science) untouched.

This step is an improvement over scientific materialism, but does not go far enough. It thinks of method and subject matter as too easily detachable from each other. It is as if we were asked to think of scientific method as a spotlight, i.e., as an instrument that casts a clear illumination on whatever subject it is turned toward. Since the spotlight has worked well when turned on the physical world, why shouldn't it work equally well when its focus is turned on the human world (provided we have already recognized its inherent differences from the physical world)? Such thinking does not carry the difference between human experience and the world of objects far enough. It assumes, falsely, that the regulatory and constitutive aspects of human experience are detachable from each other, and that the regulatory principles of the physical sciences can be applied to human experience.

We have to recognize that materialist abstractions are by this time built into the very methods of science. We have seen that so-called scientific analysis—breaking a subject into its component parts—assumes that a subject is an aggregation of units—an assumption not valid for human experiences. The question remains: Can the conventional methods of science illuminate and measure human reality? The answer is that some can, while others cannot; some of the methods of science are truly general and transcend subject matter while others must be tied closely to the ontology of a particular subject. Thus, some abstractions required by the human sciences are not easily measurable by the methods of the physical sciences (e.g., describing and verifying modes of being).

Consider the radical ambivalence of human feelings; the coexistence of dialectical opposites such as love and hate; the prevalence of paradoxical meanings in certain human situations; the intricately woven strands of human motivation; the interplay among phylogenetic, maturational, and learned aspects of human behavior; the enmeshment of the human person in the many contexts of his life with others and with society; the ethical reality of human virtues and vices apart from their origins in the family drama; the differences between the identity of man and the identity of an object; man's awareness of his own being, etc. These facets of human life yield only clumsily to methods that may do quite well, say, for measuring changes in radiation.

The density and concreteness of human experience are such that existentialist philosophers doubt that a science of man is possible. Recognizing the dependence of science on abstraction, they call attention to the inherent limitations of abstraction as a legitimate mode of knowing human experience. We contend that a science of man is both possible and desirable, provided one takes a view of science that is neither too narrow nor too broad. If science is taken too broadly as being synonymous with knowledge itself, then it is unlikely that one can describe, know, and explain every facet of man's existence scientifically. Resorting to abstractions implies, by definition, that much of the concrete reality of human experience will be missed, and other modes of knowing will be required. But if there is even a vague sense of what is included and what is excluded by theoretical abstraction as applied to human experience, and if provision can be made for filling in what is excluded by other modes of knowing, then what is included can carry us very far indeed in our understanding of the human condition. We are suggesting here that "science" be given a very specific meaning—broader than one that equates science with formal techniques of verification but narrower than one that equates science with knowledge itself. The limitations of science are to be established as co-extensive with the limitations of practical certainty. There is a lot about man we will never know with practical certainty, but there is a great deal yet to be learned by a humanized science of man.

Any psychoanalytic theory must be defined within the inherent limitations of science. If abstractions can carry a science only one part of the way toward full understanding of the human world, then we must always keep in mind the relationship of science to nonscientific modes of understanding.

From the foregoing discussion we may distill the following six regulatory principles:

1. A theory of reasons: The causal theory of explanation to which psychoanalysis now subscribes is of marginal relevance; it should be supplanted by a theory of reasons. This is not mere semantic pettifoggery. The reasons for a person's acts and the causes of his acts are not simply different words for the same phenomena; as we define the two concepts, they refer to quite different, though interrelated, phenomena.
2. Explanation as a form of description: Explanation in psychoanalysis should be understood to mean description that is (a) selective (the theory being the criterion of selectivity); (b) multileveled in generality (the theory providing the more general levels of abstraction); (c) inclusive of purpose as well as process (the theory providing the relevant concepts of purpose); and (d) inclusive of past, present and future, rather than past alone or present alone.

3. Breaking down the dichotomy between description and explanation: While explanation in psychoanalysis is largely description, it should be understood that "pure description" is impossible, since all description is necessarily selective and general. A rigid distinction between description and explanation commits a double fallacy: it implies that a *tabula rasa*, presuppositionless type of description is possible, at the same time that it sets up a false conception of explanation (i.e., as being different from description).

4. Two modes of knowing: Psychoanalysis depends on at least two complementary but distinct modes of knowing—insight as well as knowledge by abstraction. Both are required for psychoanalysis as a profession and as a science, but the relationship between them differs in each instance. As a science, psychoanalysis depends mainly on knowledge by abstraction.

5. Truth in relation to utility: Psychoanalytic propositions must be true as well as useful, the criterion being standards of truth applicable to schemes of abstraction (not to insight). If psychoanalysis wishes to be a science, it must subscribe to standards of proof reflecting what the West has learned about methods for establishing practical certainty. These methods vary from subject to subject. Controlled experiments are appropriate to physics, less so to psychoanalysis. Inductive generalization and proof in psychoanalysis call for methods dictated by its own ontology and epistemology.

6. Relationship between theory and metatheory: Psychoanalytic theory and metatheory are distinguished from one another by their level of generality, not by a difference in their essential concepts. The same terms that appear in the metatheory should also be present in the clinical theory; two separate languages are not needed. The level of generality of the metatheory is philosophical in character, having to do with basic ontology and epistemology. However, its key concepts are selected for their relevance to psychoanalysis. A metatheoretical "map" of another subject, sociology, for example, would highlight different constitutive and regulatory features of its subject.

NINETEEN

Instinct and Human Nature

Strategically, the key to a new metapsychology is what is done with the instinctual drives, since the evolutionary influence lies at the heart of the psychoanalytic theory of human nature. Instinct is a cornerstone of the present metapsychology and a vital center of the clinical theory as well; it provides one of the few substantive links between the two. Also, since ego and superego are largely defined in opposition to instinct, reformulating these two concepts is critically connected with the definition of instinct. Despite the current fashion in ego psychology, the instinctual drives are never far from the center of attention of practicing psychoanalysts.

The psychoanalytic profession, to the surprise of some of its older members, is by and large accepted by the medical establishment, and is enjoying a certain amount of worldly success. Even so, it is undergoing a trying period of soul-searching. Throughout the profession a mood of uncertainty prevails, a questioning of future goals and fundamentals. The new mood arises from many contradictory pressures. Psychoanalytic ego psychology moves the theory toward fusion with other branches of psychology and, in the view of Hartmann and others, qualifies psychoanalysis to be a general psychology. As a branch of medicine, psychoanalysis moves away from psychology toward the medical model of the human person as a biological organism. Having barely won their long struggle for acceptance by the medical profession and having now assumed a dominant role in the psychiatry departments of many leading medical schools, psychoanalysts are also being drawn more deeply into the medical profession's current preoccupation with changing patterns of medical care. At the same time, the burgeoning concern with community mental health calls upon psychoanalysts to become more deeply involved in today's vast social problems. The legislation creating new mental health centers draws the psychoanalytic community into the problems of social pathology—delinquency, drug addiction, alcoholism, illegitimacy, criminality, abandonment, marital discord, and other forms of social distress and despair.

The most compelling pressure on the psychoanalyst, however, comes from his private practice. Typically, the psychoanalyst preoccupies himself not with global issues but with minute bits of behavior—a fragment of a patient's dream, the meaning of a hostile glance, a long pause in a patient's "free" associations. Contemporary adult problems, large and small, give way to the long-repressed childhood struggles of the solitary, middle-class, upper-income patient.

Despite the new claims on their time, the bulk of the analysts' energies in the future is likely to continue along the well-established path of private practice with a handful of well-to-do patients. It is estimated that the average psychoanalyst sees twenty-eight private patients a year, and that 90 percent of all psychoanalysts have a private practice. With approximately four thousand psychoanalysts in practice, this means that a maximum of 100,000 persons a year receive individual psychoanalytic care. Assuming that a thorough psychoanalysis takes two years to complete—three to four is actually closer to the mark—50,000 people a year at the most can be psychoanalyzed. A recent study suggests that more than 45 per cent of the population may have moderate to severe psychological disability (Srole, 1962); we can estimate that it would take 1,800 years for psychoanalysts to attend to the emotional needs of people existing now who might conceivably benefit from psychoanalysis. This logistics problem puts great pressure on psychoanalysts to modify their techniques and seek a wider application of their skills.

The conflict between the claims of private practice and the pressing demands of the larger world is forcing the profession to undergo some serious self-examination. What, they are asking themselves, is the essence of psychoanalysis? Wherein is it unique? What can it contribute that cannot be matched by other disciplines? Where does it fit—as a science and as a profession—in relation to psychiatry, psychotherapy, social welfare, and public policy? Where shall psychoanalysis find firm ground on which to stand so as to establish sound policies for its future?

Many older psychoanalysts—and some younger ones as well —go back to fundamentals for answers to such questions. They remind their colleagues that despite the recent emphasis on ego psychology and social psychiatry, the essence of psychoanalysis is the vicissitudes of the instinctual drives in the unique individual. Such a reminder is not meant to downgrade ego functioning—either the importance of the ego defenses or the positive ego resources built up from infancy on. It is meant to reconfirm the validity of Freud's unique discovery that the emphasis on the instinctual aspect of human experience distinguishes psychoanalysis from all other psychologies and psychotherapies.

Psychoanalysis shares with these other disciplines a keen interest in the patient's current reality, social circumstances, interpersonal relations, ego defenses, style of coping with experience, conceptions of self, and direct encounter with the therapist. But psychoanalysis is unique; it considers such concerns as way-stations en route to uncovering the hidden power of the instinctual drives. Sooner or later in the privacy of the psychoanalytic hour the realities of the patient's adult life recede; the remote past of his childhood becomes alive and vivid once again; the urgent circumstances of everyday problems take a back seat to old fantasies; and repressed instinctual impulses gradually loom larger than the defenses and habits presumably developed to prevent their direct expression.

This is the strange and, indeed, the unique world of psychoanalysis. It is a world still so unfamiliar that psychoanalysts who teach medical students and other uninitiated persons find it difficult to make believable, for it remains alien to common sense even after three-quarters of a century. Critics of psychoanalysis believe this emphasis upon the vicissitudes of the instincts during childhood to be overstressed, even totally exaggerated. Among the many eclectic students of human experience—social scientists, physicians, social workers, educators, and others who pick and choose among competing theories of human nature, this aspect of psychoanalysis is scanted in favor of its more accessible, common-sense aspects (i.e., its ego psychology). And yet it is this world and no other that forms the hard core of the psychoanalytic enterprise: the world of childhood fantasies deeply buried in the remote past of the adult's life, repressed from consciousness and society, and cut off from contemporary ego-syntonic experience.

Recent emphasis on ego psychology and on the indisputable importance of social and cultural forces may obscure this cardinal point. But if one de-emphasizes the repressed childhood world of sexual/aggressive fantasies and impulses in favor of various forms of environmentalism, one risks missing the very essence of psychoanalysis. Here is the essential contribution Freud made to human understanding, and the reason psychoanalysts always return to Freud. To misunderstand this point is to misunderstand psychoanalysis; the matter can be put as bluntly as that.

The reason instinct plays so dominant a role is that psychoanalysts are concerned with nothing less than basic human nature; and by basic human nature they mean the deposits of evolution in the form of hereditary factors; and by hereditary factors, they mean the instinctual drives. Thus, three key assumptions underlie the psychoanalytic theory of human nature:

1. There is a specific and definite human nature;
2. Such a human nature is rooted in hereditary forces in man called instincts;
3. These instincts have certain well-defined characteristics, i.e., they are peremptory, quantitative, acquire their aim and object through learning, and are sexual or aggressive in character.

Controversy rages around all three assumptions, although they are not always clearly distinguished from one another. Many divergent schools of thought bitterly dispute the very idea of a fixed human nature. Existentialism and behaviorism, in disagreement on virtually all else, meet on the common conclusion that there is no inherent human nature. The offshoots of psychoanalysis that emphasize interpersonal relations quarrel with the central importance Freud gave to instinct. Developmental psychologists, ethologists, behavioral geneticists, and others (including ourselves), agree with the emphasis but seriously question the content of psychoanalytic instinct theory.

The metapsychological doctrine of human nature is represented by four concepts—instinct, ego, pleasure principle, and psychic apparatus. Instincts are the motive forces of human life; ego is the psychic system which mediates between instincts and the world; the psychic apparatus defines the ontological status of the human person as an object in a world of objects; and the pleasure principle regulates the relation of ego and instinct to the psychic apparatus. Our quarrel with the metapsychology on its constitutive side is with all four of these concepts. Two of them, the psychic apparatus and the pleasure principle (the Newtonian elements), can readily be eliminated from the metapsychology without affecting either psychoanalytic clinical theory or practice. The relationship of ego to instinct is quite another matter. Here, reformulation rather than removal is called for. Instinct must continue to be one of the major connecting links between clinical practice and metapsychological theory.

How this intimate relationship between instinct and the psychoanalytic theory of human nature works, can be clearly seen in Anna Freud's statement:

> Where a little girl is described by her parents as an "affectionate, understanding, uncomplaining little thing," the analyst will note the conspicuous absence of the usual greed and aggression of childhood. Where the parents stress an older sibling's love for babies the analyst will look for the fate of the absent jealousies. Where a child is correctly described by the parents as "incurious and not interested in matters such as differences between the sexes, the origin of babies, the relationship between the parents," it is obvious to us that an insurmountable battle has been fought which has led to the conscious extinction of normal human curiosity. (A. Freud, 1965, p. 16.)

Anna Freud is assuming here that greed, jealousy, and curiosity are universal and inherent characteristics of childhood (i.e., of human nature); if they are absent, she assumes that they must nonetheless exist and she sets about looking for what happened to them. Rapaport refers to these givens in human nature as inherent maturational factors, occurring "prior to and independent of experience." He describes as the central achievement of psychoanalysis the disentangling of such factors "from the tangle of progressive changes apparently wrought by experience" (p. 211). And he further notes that it is this emphasis which distinguishes psychoanalysis both from the purer forms of environmentalism and from neo-Freudian schools whose theories "without exception lack such a factor." Rapaport goes on to state explicitly that inherent maturational factors are the instinctual drives. At a metapsychological level, the psychoanalytic theory of human nature is mainly a description of these drives and the forces that restrain their free discharge. (Note that Anna Freud's description above is clinical not metapsychological: nevertheless, according to the metapsychology, greed, jealousy, and curiosity are themselves derivative from the instinctual drives of sex and aggression.)

Such a postulation of inherent instincts serves the same purpose in psychoanalysis as is served by the measure of the speed of light in physics: it is a fixed point of reference, a constant to which other phenomena can be related. It is intended to save the clinical theory from degenerating into a shifting and rootless mass of data.

Curiously, the instinctual drives have proven just as troublesome for psychoanalysis to define as for other psychologists. (See Chapter Three for a brief history of Freud's struggle with instinct theory.) Inevitably, in defining the instincts, one runs up against the nature/nurture controversy—the age-old problem of relating heredity to environment. And here the trouble begins. Since the instincts represent the nature half of the nature/nurture dichotomy there can be no satisfactory formulation of instinct that does not also resolve the full nature/nurture dilemma.

The central importance given to the instinctual side of man has even caused controversy among orthodox psychoanalysts themselves. Yet, over the past few decades, psychoanalytic theory has quietly absorbed the lessons of its anti-instinct critics without basically changing its concept of the instinctual drives.

Much of what Adler, Horney, Sullivan, Reich, and Fromm discovered has been carried over into today's psychoanalytic ego psychology. For example, the importance of ego defenses and resistances stressed by Reich and Sullivan were adapted by Anna Freud and elaborated by Hartmann, Kris, and others, as vital parts of contemporary psychoanalytic theory.

However, the incorporation of their critics' good points has not eliminated disagreement on the importance of the instinctual drives. The position taken several decades ago by Harry Stack Sullivan (and by most American social scientists today) holds that man, of all the creatures on earth, is the one least dominated by instinct. They argue that we must give our attention to the forces that *do* dominate man—culture, society, and interpersonal relations. The Freudian system locates man's primary motivations within the human organism, specifically in the instinctual drives, while the environmentalist places his main emphasis on social forces outside the individual, on those social and interpersonal relationships that presumably shape his character and his behavior. The difference in emphasis is not easily resolved.

On the issue of heredity in relation to environment, orthodox psychoanalysis has shifted its own emphasis several times. The reader will recall that in the 1890's, Freud's work on hysteria seemed to deny the importance medical opinion placed on inborn factors as the source of mental disease. Freud's discovery of sexual traumas in childhood pointed to specific life experiences (e.g., seduction of the child) as the "cause" of hysteria. Then, suddenly, Freud learned that he had been wrong about the childhood seductions—which had occurred only in fantasy. This discovery shocked and depressed him for some time afterwards. Reacting to what he referred to as his "momentous mistake," he then swung to the other extreme: thereafter, and for at least a quarter of a century, he stressed the inborn (nature) against the experiential (nurture).

In the 1920's, in *The Ego and the Id*, he tried to correct the imbalance by assigning one set of life tasks to nature (personified by the id) and another to nurture (personified by the ego and the superego). Many psychoanalysts, especially in this country, responded enthusiastically to the renewed emphasis on the ego and the more important role Freud gave to experience and to social reality. American thought has usually supported a thoroughgoing environmentalism, rejecting restrictions on man's ability to master nature. Perhaps this is why the "decisive reorientation" in psychoanalysis caught on better here than abroad: it promotes the influence of nurture, and hence the environment, giving it more importance vis-à-vis the instincts. Indeed, the new ego psychology has been so enthusiastically embraced that many psychoanalysts now fear that it may bury Freud's major discovery, the centrality of the instinctual drives.

After Freud's redirection of the theory in the 1920's had had time to be absorbed, and while attention was focused on the ego, Hartmann and his co-workers advanced the suggestion that the ego too may have instinctual roots (a thought that also occurred to Freud in his final years). This possibility and the stress Erikson and others place on biologically rooted maturation processes, have once again stimulated interest among psychoanalysts in the study of the innate.

Our perspective will be broadened by a brief glance outside of psychoanalysis. These troublesome questions about instinct and human nature have been with us for many years. Long ago, Hegel suggested that man does not have a nature but only a history. In the present century, such different thinkers as Sartre and Watson have restated this same insistence on the total plasticity of the human person. Theirs is one extreme of the dominant environmentalist tradition, and they are joined by thinkers as disparate as Marx, Skinner, Sullivan, and Fromm. At the other pole one finds Freud, Darwin, Piaget, Werner, Lévi-Strauss, Boas, Lorenz, and others, whose work implies the presence of a definite human nature.

Freud's most implacable opponents come from the strict environmentalist group. Hardly bothering to attack the content of his instinct theory, they reserve their scorn for the prior assumption on which the instinct theory rests; namely, that there is a specific human nature. If one is so thoroughgoing an environmentalist as to reject the very notion of human nature, there is little need to pay attention to the details of how this nature is described.

The doctrine of a fixed human nature, it should be noted, is implied by many of the ideologies that dominate our intellectual history. From Hobbes and Machiavelli to the present day, a belief in an inherent human nature has usually accompanied politically conservative beliefs. Conservatism in politics and a belief in human nature (usually on its unsavory side) go hand in hand for the simple reason that environmentalism, on the surface, seems to imply the possibility of radical social change; a fixed human nature—again, on the surface—seems to imply that any large-scale social change will come to grief because "you can't change human nature." The presumption in the latter is that the existing social order accurately reflects human nature. Small wonder that radicalism, liberalism, and a faith in man's infinite plasticity have marched together. There is, however, no *necessary* relationship between political conservatism and the belief in a human nature; they have been bedfellows mainly because of circumstance.

Among scientists, the belief in geneticism, as the theory of human nature is sometimes called, has drawn fire for other reasons. Grave logical and methodological difficulties surround this position as it has been formulated in the past. It has frequently been accompanied by teleology, vitalism, and mysticism —pet hates of scientists trained in the tenets of scientific materialism. Surely, any doctrine that finds itself in the midst of political, philosophical, and scientific controversy is not likely to be approached coolly and dispassionately.

Nevertheless, the belief in a fixed human nature can be rescued from a needless alliance with any one political, philosophical, religious, or scientific posture. The doctrine that there is a specifically human nature does not by itself support any ideology. To be useful for ideological purposes, it is the content of that nature that counts. A belief in the inherent goodness of mankind (as in older deistic views), or in the incompatibility of society as now constituted with our inherent human nature, could just as readily support liberal or even radical ideologies (as it does today among student groups).

In sciences other than psychoanalysis, one finds the same polarization of belief about human nature in general and the nature/nurture issue specifically. In biology, one extreme view of nature in relation to nurture is known as Lamarckism. This doctrine holds that traits of character learned through specific life experiences (from environmental influences) will, within a brief span of generations, become part of our heredity. An outstanding and, in some quarters, a notorious example of Freud's commitment to the Lamarckian point of view, is the position he took in *Totem and Taboo*. There Freud suggested that the Oedipal conflict (the unconscious wish to destroy the father and possess the mother) had at one time in the past been acted out and has since become part and parcel of our phylogenetic inheritance, now presumably built into our genetic design. Although the Lamarckian doctrine is largely in scientific disrepute today, it is important historically (as Russian scientists of the Stalinist era learned when the biologist Lysenko, a Lamarckian, was in fashion and played the role of scientific dictator). Darwin himself believed the hereditary transmission of learned traits to be one of the major mechanisms of evolutionary adaptation.

The intense interest in evolution at the turn of the last century led to a spate of studies carried out by Galton and others, which had important social consequences. On the scientific side, these researches prepared the way for the modern science of behavioral genetics. On the social side, the efforts to account for genius and idiocy and for moral degeneration and uplift—all by hereditary transmission—proved to be bitterly controversial. Politically, the doctrine of innate characteristics was seized upon as evidence of the inherent superiority of certain races and social classes. Studies of hereditary patterns were used to promote programs of eugenics in order to purify and elevate the species. Each new advance in genetics, today as well as in the early years of the century, has brought with it an upsurge of a desire among evangelical biologists to breed a new and improved species of man by genetic control.

Inevitably, in a country with our intellectual and political traditions, opposition quickly arose to the theory that all men are *not* created equal—and that nothing can be done about it except by genetic control. The widespread belief in social Darwinism at the turn of the century generated strong feelings. The idea that we are predestined by our genes runs against the deepest traditions of American life. The traditional American optimism that we can, somehow, shape our own destiny, is reinforced by the ideals of American science: understanding, prediction, and control. It is no accident that behaviorism, which is both scientific *and* environmental, has become a dominant force in American psychology, since it represents these "enlightened" and "progressive" values to perfection. Moreover, American sociology has acquired a deep strain of Marxism, with its own strong emphasis on environmental economic factors as decisive in human history. (This emphasis becomes explicit in a thinker like Erich Fromm, who has watered down the instinctual side of his psychoanalytic beliefs to accommodate his Marxian commitments.)

Within science, the strongest opposition to an emphasis on heredity has come from behaviorist psychology—perhaps our most argumentative branch of science. Among the various dragons behaviorism has engaged in battle, the theory of innate characteristics is a favorite object of derision. Watson provided the most vehement polemics against theories that stressed heredity. He developed to its logical conclusion the *tabula rasa* concept of mind that is so central a theme in the history of British and American empiricism. "Give me a dozen healthy infants," said Watson in a famous quote, "well-formed and my own specified world to bring them up in, and I'll guarantee to take anyone at random and train him to become any type of specialist I might select—doctor, lawyer, artist, merchant-chief and, yes, even beggarman and thief, regardless of the talents, penchants, tendencies, abilities, vocations and race of his ancestors." (Watson, 1930, p. 104.)

The consequences of Watson's extreme anti-hereditary stand are aptly stated by the psychologist, McClearn:

. . . the theoretical frame of reference provided by the behavioral sciences has been, on the whole, an environmentalistic one. A key factor in this development was J. B. Watson's (1924) aggressive denial of the role of hereditary determinants in behavior. His challenging offer to produce people to specification by appropriate manipulation of environment—a bluff which, in the nature of things, could never be called—was accepted as though it were a demonstrated accomplishment. Because of Watson's great influence, and for a variety of other reasons [see Dobzhansky, 1962; McClearn, 1962; Pastore, 1949], psychology in particular and behavioral sciences in general

moved to a polar position with respect to the nature/
nurture issue. (McClearn, 1964, p. 433.)

McClearn adds that academic psychology began to take a
better balanced view of man's nature from about 1950 on, as
more evidence accumulated that for a broad range of behavior
a hereditary factor must be taken into account. In contemporary social science, the nature/nurture question is no longer
formulated as a sharp dichotomy. The acrimonious argument
between those who stress the biological side of man's nature and
those who emphasize his social and cultural life has quieted
down. And a clearer understanding of the complex interactions
between the biological and the social has gradually emerged.
Currently, the point of view of ecology prevails, a view that
recognizes the intimate interdependence and mutual interactions of both sets of factors, nature *and* nurture.

In the light of these historical developments, our claim that
the instinctual drives still form the vital center of psychoanalysis may seem exaggerated or outdated. Are we not today
caught up in the full tide of psychoanalytic ego psychology
with so much of its momentum channeled onto the ego and
the ego's functions? Might not our statement about the instincts have been truer of psychoanalysis thirty years ago, before the "decisive orientation" launched in *The Ego and the Id*
shifted psychoanalytic attention, long overdue, to other aspects
of the psyche? Perhaps, however, Freud's original insight—that
the instincts lie at the core of personal development—was, as
was so often the case with his first guesses, correct.

TWENTY

The Puzzle of Instinct

In seeking to clarify the puzzle of instinct in man we must keep in mind the astonishing fact that there does not exist today—within or outside of psychoanalysis—a clear-cut, well-defined, generally accepted concept of human instinct, or agreement on the importance that instincts have, or detailed understanding of how human instincts affect individual experience, or even agreement that the term "instinct" should be used at all in describing the human person.

The idea of instinct has proven to be as troublesome as that of race—both in the ideological fuss it kicks up and in the tedious search for definition. Pinning down the influence of environment and experience in relation to instinct is a horrendously difficult task. Nor are psychoanalysts alone in wrestling with it; almost every other branch of the human sciences has waffled around on this issue. Most workers will acknowledge that behavior relating to sex and hunger has instinctive roots. When aggression, however, enters the picture, or creativity, or the "territorial imperative" or specific male-female differences, agreement ceases abruptly. For example, psychoanalysts believe that aggression is instinctive while many psychologists believe that it is a learned response to frustration, and hence the result of environment and personal experience. The difference in viewpoint is fundamental.

So central is the idea of instinct to the metapsychology that we cannot bypass its many logical and factual difficulties. However bewildering it may be, we must face up to the puzzle of instinct.

Problems of Definition

Psychologists and psychoanalysts have tried to make a sharp distinction between instinctive behavior and learned experience, and the traditional definition of instinct holds that:

1. Behavior is instinctive when a whole species shows certain fixed behavioral patterns (e.g., beavers build dams, birds build nests, rats hoard).
2. These patterns occur universally in the species at a particular stage of the maturation process (e.g., at maturity moth caterpillars spin cocoons).
3. The behavior occurs as a response to specific stimuli (e.g., the epistogramma invariably follows any yellow and black pattern; the stickleback responds with a fighting response to any fish that is red underneath).
4. The behavior is invariant so that one can predict its occurrence whenever the appropriate stimuli are present.
5. The response can be demonstrated to be independent of experience (e.g., solitary wasps isolated from their species at birth nonetheless develop typical predatory behavior patterns).
6. The behavior appears to fulfill some phylogenetic purpose relating to adaptation, reproduction, survival, and the preservation of the species.

Among humans, there are few examples of behavior that meet all of these criteria. The infant's sucking response and the social smiling response (which occurs at about the third month of life) are usually cited as examples of pure instinctive behavior in humans unaffected by learning. On the surface, sucking, for instance, seems to be unlearned, to fulfill a self-evident survival purpose, and to be almost automatic when stimulated. But on closer examination, there are signs of learning. In a recent analysis of the research on the infant's sucking response (McKee and Honzik, 1962), the authors conclude that neither the sucking response nor any other human response can be described as a pure instance of nature or nurture—or even as a mix of the two in an additive sense. "There is no such thing," the authors conclude, "as a four-to-one mixture of heredity and environment."

Developmental psychologists now believe that all human behavior includes at least some traces of learning, that it is variable rather than fixed, and that it does not always follow as a response to the same stimuli. If, therefore, we insist that the instinctive in man be confined to behavior meeting all six of the traditional criteria, we might quickly—all too quickly—conclude that the instinctive plays a very small role in human life, confined to the most marginal aspects of human behavior. An example of precisely this conclusion is William James's great work on psychology where blushing, sucking, sneezing, and other incidental kinds of behavior make up the whole chapter on human instincts. In searching for inflexible behavior in response to specific stimuli uncontaminated by learning, James described responses that were later to be defined as unconditioned reflexes. But man's instinctive behavior is far more complex than early writers supposed. More impressive human characteristics than blushing or sucking show innate phylogenetic influences, and yet they elude the traditional criteria.

A newer formulation, which broadened the definition of instinct but at the same time made it less precise, came with Lashley's distinction between *instinct* and *reflex* (Lashley, 1938). He defined reflex as innately determined muscular contractions brought on by stimulating a specific group of receptors. He also showed that instinctive behavior did not necessarily require an environmental stimulus (e.g., deprived of sexual stimulation, sex behavior may arise "spontaneously"); nor need instinctive behavior be invariant: a bird building its nest will adapt itself to the material available and to where the nest is to be built. Most important of all, Lashley insisted that instinctive behavior is subject to modification by learning. More recent data from many sources back up this latter conclusion that the instinctual, in animals as well as in man, is rarely uninfluenced by experience.

With these discoveries, the old definition of instinct was left a shambles. The discovery that instinct does not refer solely to invariant and unlearned behavior is a scientific breakthrough,

~~and not, of course, a proof that instinct~~ is nonexistent. But it does add to the puzzle of instinct if instinct cannot be defined in sharp contrast to experience and learning.

There is another definitional problem in the question of what physical processes accompany instinctive behavior. In a series of experiments on appetite in rats, Richter (1941) destroyed the rats' physiological means of regulating homeostatic control and maintaining a constant internal environment—only to find that the rats made an effort to eat their usual diet and amount anyway. Richter explained this behavior by referring to the rats' so-called *drives,* which he clearly distinguished from the physiological organs or centers which were surgically removed. What the concept of drive means when divorced from a physiological basis (as in the hunger drive) is far from clear. On a similar quest for physical processes linked to instinct, the psychologist Hebb and the ethologist Lorenz have long been engaged in a fundamental controversy. Hebb claims that Lorenz moves in a vicious circle by defining the innate in terms of what is not learned, and the learned as what is not innate; he prefers to believe that behavior whose physical cause is not yet known will, once we have further knowledge, be revealed as the result of learning and not innate influences. This latter argument is not based on actual scientific work, but on Hebb's confidence in his own philosophical premises. (See Chapter Thirteen.)

Lorenz argues against Hebb with great vigor. Learning, he states, never takes place without being influenced by biogenetic factors. "It is an inescapable logical necessity," he writes, "to assume that learning . . . is performed by organic structures evolved in the course of phylogeny under the selection pressure of survival value. *All observational and experimental evidence goes to confirm this assumption. None contradicts it.*" (1965, p. 18.) (Our italics.) He is saying, of course, that all learning and all experience are affected by inborn factors. Lorenz believes that two quite different physiological processes are involved in phylogenetic and ontogenetic development (individual development and species development): the coded information stored in the genes and its decoding in phylogenetic development is different, he claims, from the information stored in the nervous system and its decoding by releasing a conditioned response or other form of learning. He sums up his differences with Hebb as follows: "Hebb in his criticism of ethology states that it would be hard to exaggerate the importance attributed by ethologists to the distinction between innate and learned, implying, of course, that we overestimate this importance. I could not agree more with the statement and less with the implication." (1965, p. 20.)

Whether information stored in the genes is decoded by different processes than information stored in the nervous system is an important question for empirical inquiry, one that behavioral genetics may ultimately be able to answer. But it is not crucial to our present concern. We may, therefore, set it aside at this time with the observation that current knowledge about the physical side of instinctive behavior in humans does not yet yield definitive information one way or the other. Furthermore, while future research may ultimately reveal the mechanisms of instinctive behavior, it cannot "explain" it away: such research can at best describe only one aspect of instinct.

Another sort of difficulty in defining instinct is exemplified in the work of the famous psychologist, William McDougall. Apart from Freud, McDougall was once the major proponent of an instinct theory. It is he whom the behaviorists most vehemently attack on the grounds that his theory is circular and tautological. The argument against McDougall was pungently stated by Holt many years ago:

> . . . man is impelled to action, it is said, by his instincts. If he goes with his fellows, it is "herd instinct" which activates him; if he walks alone, it is the "anti-social instinct"; if he fights, it is the "pugnacity instinct"; if he defers to another it is the instinct of "self-abasement"; if he twiddles his thumbs, it is the thumb-twiddling instinct; if he does not twiddle his thumbs, it is the thumb-not-twiddling instinct. Thus, everything is explained with the facility of magic—word magic. (Holt, 1931.)

The point, though cruelly made, has merit. If we start with behavior as it presents itself—walking, fighting, thumb sucking and so on—we must fight off the compulsion to look for some underlying invisible force that must "explain" the behavior (e.g., mothering is "caused" by a maternal instinct conceived of as a subcutaneous unit of force).

It is too bad that great psychologists like McDougall, who were aware of the sterilities of mechanistic explanations for human behavior, should themselves have been undermined by the very philosophy they opposed. There are many other lists of instincts, drives, and needs prepared by psychologists, and most of them share McDougall's logical vulnerability. The trouble with such quasi explanations is that they give the investigator a premature sense of closure; he feels satisfied too quickly that an answer has been found, and the careful work of observing phenomena under a variety of conditions is cut short. What is wanting is a more complete description of the phenomenon rather than a too quick causal explanation of it.

Ethologists like Tinbergen and Lorenz have carried out some marvelously detailed descriptions of instinctive behavior among a wide variety of species. Without attempting to generalize from their animal studies to human behavior, we can nonetheless pick up some hints as to how phylogenetic influences might make themselves felt in various forms of life. Lorenz warns us specifically about working backwards from any one overt example of behavior à la McDougall to postulate a specific "instinct" as its cause. Writing about the so-called maternal instinct, he urges us to resist the temptation of assuming that various forms of mothering behavior are caused by a specifically maternal instinct. He cites the remarkable behavior of the inexperienced turkey hen, who, guarding a new brood, will viciously attack any object in or near the nest that moves and does not utter the characteristic chirp of the infant turkey. Deaf turkey hens will even destroy their own young; they have no means of recognizing their brood except by sound. And it is a blood-chilling sight, Lorenz writes, to see a turkey hen destroy one of her own infants who is dumb and cannot chirp, and at the same time nestle under her wings a huge stuffed polecat who has been specially fitted with a mechanical chirp. The turkey hen's reaction suggests the presence of an instinctive process, but we must exercise great care before we label it as a specifically *maternal* instinct. In fact, Lorenz suggests that the turkey's behavior is not the expression of a maternal instinct at all but the inhibition of an aggressive instinct, which is cut off from expression by the signal of the infant's chirp. Unless the signal is given, the "normal" aggressive response to an

intruder who comes too close will be forthcoming. In turkeys
and in many other species, mothering behavior is not elicited
by any innate recognition of one's own young but by a network of highly specialized part-processes, some of which are
unrelated to mothering. Thus, it would be as incorrect to refer
to a mothering instinct or even to a survival instinct as to
explain the motion of an automobile by reference to an auto-
motive force or instinct—the movement of the automobile
being the result of many different processes interacting with
one another and not a single force pushing from behind. In
animals and humans as well, the complex functions of mothering or surviving or even eating are the end product of a
whole series of interacting part-processes only some of which
are phylogenetically based, and even these may have evolved to
fill other purposes.

Problems of Method

An even more bewildering aspect of the puzzle is related to the
methods for studying instinct. If instinct cannot be sharply
differentiated from learned behavior, how does one identify it
and isolate it for scientific research?

A cursory glance at the psychoanalytic method will show
that it is not a good research strategy for studying instinct
scientifically; its focus on the single individual limits the scope
of its methods too greatly. Typically, the psychoanalyst will
start out with some urgent problem in his patient's life, then
work backwards in time, tracing its antecedents and reconstructing the same sort of solutions to the problem that the
patient tried when it occurred in the past. The further back
in time the psychoanalyst penetrates, the stronger becomes his
impression that some instinctive or inherent maturational factor
is operating in his patient's life. Finally, he reaches back to
the patient's childhood and to what he regards as evidence of
strong instinctual pressures.

Repeated with one patient after another, these clinical impressions can be very persuasive. But a vivid experience is not
wholly viable as scientific method. Quite apart from the prob-

lem of validation, the retrospective reconstruction of a single person's past by analyzing his defenses, transferences, and associations in a psychoanalytic setting does not permit one to isolate what is and what is not instinctive in man. For it is almost impossible with such a method to sort out the phylogenetic from the ontogenetic, learned, and cultural aspects of behavior—all these are inextricably intertwined in any one person living in any one historical epoch in any one culture. To focus on the instinctual we need a perspective going beyond the single individual in the single culture. We need macrocosmic data on total populations, controlled for culture and social class. We also need more formal methods of description, analysis, and measurement.

Psychoanalysis is not alone in having a problem. Though both ethologists and behavioral geneticists have gathered an impressive body of knowledge on instinctual behavior in animals, it is difficult for them to apply their findings. In extrapolating from animals to man, these sciences run up against the well-known fact that as one moves up the phylogenetic scale, fixed, automatic, and invariable responses of a species become increasingly rare. Furthermore, we cannot assume that what is instinctive in animals will also be instinctive in man. The mechanism that stimulates the turkey hen to attack all creatures that do not emit a characteristic sound is not present in the human female. Women have other ways of recognizing their own offspring.

Still, animal behavior is an excellent illustration of the instinctive in a relatively pure form. For, as we move *down* the phylogenetic scale, learning and culture become less important and innate processes more autonomous. Since it is the interposition of learning, experience, and the effects of culture that make instinct so difficult to isolate in man, other species give us the opportunity to see the dynamics of instinct under simpler conditions. Hopefully, as we move back up the phylogenetic scale we can then trace, step by step, the interplay among learning, culture, experience, and instinct, in the higher animals and in man.

A more serious problem of method than extrapolating from animal to human behavior is central to the issues raised in this work. Though one finds in sciences such as biology increasing sophistication in defining what is instinctive, the sophistication is not often carried over to research methods. The well-known work of Dr. T. C. Schneirla of the Museum of Natural History in New York City illuminates this point. In an important paper, Schneirla presents a highly technical discussion of the interrelationships that obtain among instinctive behavior, maturation, experience, and development. (Appropriately, his paper is titled, "Instinctive Behavior, Maturation, Experience and Development," 1960). His formulation of the entire nature/nurture issue shows a nice awareness of the logical pitfalls to which this controversy is prey. And yet, Schneirla himself appears to be caught in a basic incompatibility between his own definition of instinct and the methods of investigation he favors.

Discussing the role of the instinctive in human life, Schneirla emphasizes how hard it is to pinpoint any one factor as a cause of instinctive behavior, and concludes that we cannot trace an instinctive act back to any one physical source, such as a particular complex of unaltered genes or set of cells. He quotes the embryologist Eduardo Weiss to the effect that cells do not develop independently but go through chains of environmental interactions with neighboring cells (and even distant ones), and that at any one stage of development the entire cellular system can be understood only by reference to its earlier history of transformations and modifications. In other words, in living organisms, even so simple an entity as a cell, though it seems to enjoy the characteristic of simple location, cannot be understood except by reference to the entire system, and to the antecedent history of the system and its transformations in time.

Schneirla takes Weiss's conclusion into account in formulating his own position on instinct. His point of view is stated precisely but abstractly:

> Our premise is that the hypothetical genic effects are mediated at each ontogenic stage by systems of intervening variables characteristic of that stage in that species under prevalent developmental conditions, and that from initial stages these variables include both factors indirectly dependent on the general type and others primarily dependent on the situation and environs of development. (Pp. 307–08.)

Now, to expand this highly condensed statement. Schneirla places the greatest possible emphasis on the importance of the innate: "It is a strong probability that heredity is basically involved in the development of all behavior." (P. 304.) He acknowledges that behaviorists such as Watson, to whom he is otherwise sympathetic, went too far in their anti-instinctivist opposition, and as a result genetics was virtually "locked out of the discussion." Like Hebb, whose point of view he largely shares, Schneirla believes that ethologists such as Lorenz oversimplify the processes whereby genetic influences make themselves felt in behavior. The Lorenz theory that the genes pass on a code that directly determines the development of instinctual patterns is not, he states, justified by available evidence.

Biologists use the terms genotype and phenotype. The genotype is an individual's inborn genetic design and the phenotype is the observable and measurable set of characteristics of the species, both with regard to its physical make-up and its behavior. In Schneirla's view, which is probably typical of the majority view today, vastly complex systems mediate between each person's unique genetic make-up and his overt behavior, making it difficult to trace the relationship between genotype and phenotype. From the fertilized egg onward there are so many stages of man's development, and at each stage so many processes interact with each other before the organism enters the next stage, that each of the stages is comprehensible only in relation to preceding and even subsequent stages. We are not justified, Schneirla argues, in leaping directly from phenotype to genotype; we cannot assume from observing a creature's behavior that there are "species templates"—that is, direct instructions—in the genes (à la Lorenz) that are directly uncoded into that behavior. Schneirla concludes with the lament that "no infallible rules exist for differentiating the innate from the acquired." (P. 305.)

Despite its complexity, Schneirla's main point is unambiguous: nature is so inextricably tied up with nurture that one cannot say that *this* human trait is inherited, and is unaffected by learning and experience; *that* human trait is caused by experience without regard to heredity.

Schneirla takes strong issue with Lorenz on the physiological processes underlying instinctive behavior. But both Schneirla and Lorenz, and most workers in this field, would readily agree that all too little is known about such processes. And Schneirla's formulation is also not inconsistent with a good deal of contemporary scientific thinking. (It is also in harmony with our own position.) It stresses:

1. The inseparability of genes from their medium.
2. The intervention of mediating factors between genotype and phenotype.
3. The strong phylogenetic basis of individual development.
4. The presence of a more or less fixed schedule of development.
5. The need to take prior and future stages into account when describing development.
6. The difficulty of distinguishing nature's influence from nurture's.
7. The pervasive importance of innate factors generally.

But as soon as Schneirla moves beyond this formulation to research methods, his philosophical commitments enter the picture and create a stumbling block. Though he acknowledges that the early behaviorists went too far in embracing a total environmentalism, he cites their research methods approvingly. "Their principal contribution was," he states, "their emphasis on objective experimental investigations of behavior development to replace the phenomenistic-descriptive type characteristic of the classical instinctivists." (P. 304.) There seems to be some misunderstanding here between "phenomenistic" and "phenomenological." Schneirla is confusing the McDougall type of description, where an "instinct" or "inner need" is assigned in a simple one-to-one relation with behavior, with true phenomenological description, which seeks to follow the patterns of behavior as these are overtly revealed within their natural conditions. (Ironically, phenomenology was created to counter precisely these kinds of misapplications of causal explanation that are too quick to postulate forces acting behind the scenes.) In rejecting a "phenomenistic-descriptive" type of investigation in favor of laboratory experiments, Schneirla holds fast to the conventional wisdom in science. Unfortunately, the method of laboratory experiment may be least applicable to the condition that Schneirla has taken such great pains to identify as inherent in the study of instincts—the resistance of the instinctive to being artificially isolated.

It is worth pondering this question of what method is most appropriate for studying instinct to illustrate the point that the social sciences, including psychoanalysis, all too often fail to recognize that methods (regulatory principles) are utterly dependent on subject matter (constitutive principles) and not on some *a priori* concept of Scientific Method. Behind Lorenz's arguments against the behaviorists in his *Evolution and Modification of Behavior* there is a telling point bearing on the issue of laboratory experiments that comes only indirectly to the surface. Perhaps just because it is a point that involves a fundamental issue of philosophy it can appear only in the background of a technical work devoted to the relative roles of innate and learned behavior. Let us try to catch it in a few brief quotations:

> This type of psychologist (*viz.*, the behaviorist) probably finds it so very easy to forget the questions of survival function and phylogenetic origin of behavior in general and of learning in particular, because their experimental setups deviate from the natural surroundings of the species investigated to such an extent that it becomes all too easy to overlook the survival function of behavior altogether and, therewith, the selection pressure which caused its mechanisms to evolve. (P. 13.)

Later in this same work Lorenz points out how animals in captivity or in artificial experimental circumstances may lose some of their instinctive élan (birds build nests half-heartedly, for instance). He concludes:

> Ethology loses its character of a biological science if the fact is forgotten that adaptedness exists and needs an explanation. (P. 31.)

And further:

> What we want to elucidate are the amazing facts of adaptedness. Life is a steady state of enormous general improbability and that which does need an explanation is the fact that organisms and species miraculously manage to stay alive.

What is the difference of fundamental orientation involved here? Lorenz, as a good Darwinian, confronts the reality of millions of years of evolution, and the survival and adaptiveness that have taken place within that long span. The behaviorist, of course, does not deny these tremendous facts of evolutionary history. Nevertheless, he proceeds as if he had forgotten them, as if the structure of his own concepts, as they program his experiments, takes precedence even over the realities of evolution. We may formulate this in classical philosophical language as the tendency into which the human mind easily slips—first manifest in Platonism and subsequently given systematic expression in the scientific program of Descartes—of giving priority to Thought over Being. The Being, in this case, is the staggering process of evolution as it has taken and is taking place in millions of species on this planet; the Thought is the man-made system of laboratory concepts and requirements for which the behaviorist tends to forget the greater natural reality that he was trying to understand.

Fitting the Puzzle Together

Thus far we have been able to arrive at only negative conclusions about instinct:

1. One cannot work backwards from behavior (e.g., mothering) to deduce a specific "instinctual force" as its cause;
2. The physical processes that accompany instinctive behavior are complex and largely unknown; and
3. Neither the psychoanalytic method of the individual case history nor the behaviorist bias in favor of the laboratory experiment is suitable for studying the instinctive in man.

Herein lies the puzzle of instinct: ethologists, zoologists, psychoanalysts, developmental psychologists, biologists, and many others believe that human life is shot through and through with instinctual influences, but to no single instance of human behavior—not even the infant's sucking of the breast—can they point and say, "This is instinct, pure and unaffected by learning." Nor are they able to agree even on appropriate methods for investigating instinct.

In seeking a solution to this puzzle, let us draw upon the philosophical principles set forth in earlier chapters. Our regulatory principles, it will be remembered, call for a descriptive theory of explanation, and hence for methods designed to describe phenomena (as distinct from manipulating or controlling them). By implication, therefore, progress in studying instinctive behavior in humans may come through the very method Schneirla derides—the method he has confused with the McDougall approach to clarifying instincts. Nowhere, perhaps, is the so-called "phenomenistic-descriptive" method needed so much as for describing (and explaining) stages of human development that have an instinctual aspect.

Schneirla's excellent, if abstract, account of human development, which complements Anna Freud's and Erikson's accounts, implies that any satisfactory method for investigating stages of development must take into account what we have called the principle of synergism. His conclusion that one can understand an advanced stage of development only by referring to both antecedent and future stages (plus interaction with the environmental medium) requires a philosophical framework that is radically at variance with scientific materialism. The philosophy we propose assumes that certain forms of relatedness, especially those that take place in human growth, create entirely new states of being which cannot be accounted for solely by their antecedent "causes." Each time a new stage of development occurs there is a transformation of the whole person-in-his-environment (the two are inseparable). A synergistic effect results from the transformed relationship, creating a new state of human affairs, irreducible to its antecedents.

This is not to deny that human growth is lawful enough that statistical regularities can be used to predict stages of development. Such lawfulness is not, however, of the Max Born type (where the behavior of the system at all stages can be predicted from the initial stage), since the new stage of development is *not* wholly contained in the system at the time, t = o, and it does *not* take place in an isolated system.

Our point becomes clearer if we expand our time-space perspective. If we turn from the unique individual in a single culture to man as a species, the idiosyncrasies of the individual wash out and the broad uniformities of the human condition emerge more starkly. We may some day be able to understand evolution retrospectively and even measure some of its remarkable uniformities. But with what we know, we could not have predicted its past development nor can we now predict its future development.

It should be noted that this nondeterministic viewpoint collides with current theories of evolution, which are mainly based on principles of mechanism and which hold that evolution can be explained by two variables—chance variation and natural selection. As philosopher Marjorie Green has pointed out, the *a priori* "explanatory" elements imbedded in these variables are chance and necessity. Mutations are assumed to be chance failures of nature's duplicating mechanism; and natural selection is assumed to be the agent of necessity which eliminates the less well-adapted variants (Green, 1966).

Why chance variation and mechanism? A man would have to be blindly prejudiced not to acknowledge the large element of mechanism in all forms of nature. But it is equally blind to presuppose that whatever is unknown in nature must be due to the operations of simple mechanism, i.e., nature considered as a mechanically interacting aggregate of machines. The main argument against mechanism as the exclusive agent of evolution is that mechanism by itself can create nothing new. Yet evolution is precisely the history of the emergence of the new amid the massive repetition of the old. So strong is the grip of the old philosophy that current theorists of evolution feel they must explain the appearance of the new by introducing the wildly implausible premise that failures in nature's duplicating mechanisms account for novelty (mutations). The theory then reverses itself by holding that evolution moves forward when natural selection happens to favor those "failures." An odd terminology, to say the least, that labels evolution's awesome creativity as the result of "failures" created by chance.

The principle of natural selection, Darwin's major contribution, is well documented and almost surely valid, though there is some question as to its proper level of generality. But the principle of chance variation—the theory of how and why mutations come about—is less well validated and suggests assumptions deduced from an *a priori* philosophy of science rather than from observation of biological data. Despite its lack of hard evidence, the doctrine of chance variation remains persuasive to scientists. To those reared in the materialist tradition the idea of a mechanism failing occasionally and thereby producing a chance mutation has far more surface validity than the idea that evolutionary change might reflect purpose and direction. The latter seems to imply "mysticism" and "teleology," but it may be merely a more pragmatic description of nature's true complexity. Surely the clear-cut trend of evolution toward flexibility and toward higher and more complex forms of organization cannot blandly be assumed to be the artifact of chance mutations preserved by natural selection.

The one-time popularity of Lamarckism was an effort to redeem the theory from precisely this implausibility. Hereditary transmission of acquired traits has today been widely and justly discredited; but instead of leaving open the vital question of how novelty and change come into being, scientific materialism rushes in to fill the vacuum of knowledge by assuming that mechanism, operating solely on a chance basis, is the answer to the mystery of evolution. Brilliant and otherwise open-minded scientists will go to all lengths to preserve their metaphysical commitments.

As a consequence, acceptance of the evolutionary hypothesis has often been a matter of lip service and ideology rather than of genuine response to the awesome reality that the theory taught. If evolution is true, and confirmation now leaves it virtually unassailable, then it is not merely one ideology among others; it points to a great process of change of which man has been and is still only a small part. The fact of evolution cannot be filed away in some mental cabinet while we then proceed to forget it. Above all, it should engender in us a sense of awe before the vastness and intricacy of nature's processes—an awe, too, at the incompleteness of human concepts and of the technologies that embody them.

The discoveries of science since Darwin have deepened our understanding of the adaptive point of view he developed and documented so meticulously. (The rereading of Darwin's own works is always refreshing, dealing as they do with descriptions of the world of fossils and geological strata and with the lives of organisms in the wild.) The sciences of anthropology and ethology have now broadened our perspective beyond Darwin. The single most important fact about human evolution they dramatize is that human change reflects the interaction of the innate with the cultural. Quite fundamental shifts in our orientations and behavior can be effected within the span of generations simply by modifying child-rearing patterns and other culturally determined meanings. The lower the position on the phylogenetic scale, the more complete and autonomous the organism appears to be in relation to its surroundings. Man's plasticity, though not so complete as the environmentalists have insisted, is nonetheless far greater than that of any other creature, and it derives from his utter dependence on some sort of culture. Indeed, outside of a cultural setting man can hardly exist. He is truly a psychosocial being; he needs a culture to complete himself biologically.

This is the concept of culture biologized; that is, of culture imbued with evolutionary purposes and processes which in lower animals are more vested in the animals' biological make-up. Consequently, instead of looking at instinct as an independent, isolatable entity, we must look at total phases of development which take place in culture considered as an inseparable aspect of evolution—man as inherently enmeshed in a psychosocial setting as well as in a biosphere; and beyond that, the psychosocial setting itself as a part of the evolutionary process.

As this point of view, which is very much in the air, gains currency, its methodological implications will become evident. More emphasis will be placed on phenomenological, cross-cultural and longitudinal studies. The laws of human development, hypothesized by psychoanalysis and other disciplines, will be validated not mainly by laboratory experiments whose artificial conditions maim or destroy the very variables being investigated, but by means of large-scale field studies based on scientific sampling techniques. Descriptive statistics will extend the generalizing power of phenomenological methods. The laboratory experiment will cease to be regarded as the ideal of scientific inquiry for the human sciences, in any event. It will continue to play a role, but a far less central one than in the physical sciences. Furthermore, experimentation itself will have a different use in the human sciences—not so much for providing proof as for extending observation. When experimentation is conceived broadly enough, then any form of systematic intervention can be considered as an experiment. A psychoanalyst who creates a transference relationship is creating an experimental situation that extends the range of his observations to include what happens to the individual under the new set of circumstances. Hebb's and Lorenz's deprivation experiments are valuable for the same reason: they immensely enhance the range of observation.

Progress in science as in other disciplines rarely proceeds at a steady pace. Long static periods are followed by sharp spurts forward. In the present instance, the long period of immobility in the study of human instinct is drawing to an end, and the ground is prepared for a leap forward. The scientists discussed in this chapter are approaching a more accurate definition of instinctive behavior even though they have not yet adjusted their methods to fit their new understanding. Paradoxically, training in science sometimes makes it easier to be open-minded about one's subject than about methods for studying it. But now that there exists a more complex sense of the interdependence of nature and nurture, the method gap will eventually be closed.

There are many signs in the air that it is being closed now. Curiously, the best lead we have to future research on the instinctive in man comes from an unexpected quarter—from the behaviorist Hebb, who usually chafes at the notion of the instinctual. For behaviorists, the concept of the instinctual goes against the grain of their environmentalist beliefs. But just because of this theoretical bias the testimony from this other side of the fence on the subject of instinct can be valuable, since it clearly does not start from any attraction to the innate or instinctual. From behaviorist writing on instinct, there can be expected at most a grudging and minimal concession. But for our purposes this seems to us all to the good, since a minimal concession may be the best guiding principle for trying to understand a subject on which so many romantic and semi-mystical words have been shed.

Here is Hebb:

> The term "instinctive" will be used to refer to behavior other than reflexes in which innate factors play a *predominant* part. Empirically, this is behavior in which the motor pattern is variable but *with an end result that is predictable from a knowledge of the species without knowing the history of the individual animal.* (1949, p. 166.) (Our italics.)

This brief passage warrants careful study. Hebb's conception of instinctive behavior has very clear advantages over earlier definitions: it does not dichotomize learning and instinct nor equate the instinctive with the automatic and the invariant, and, with its reference to knowledge of end results, it even weakly implies the relevance of purpose.

All of these are distinct advantages, yet there is an even more significant one that follows from his words. Transform what he says to apply to man: the instinctive in the human being would be what we can know of the individual simply as a member of the species without knowing anything about his individual development. No doubt, the behaviorist may be operating on the tacit assumption that individual and cultural variation are so enormous that there will be left only a residue of the most "elementary" drives, such as hunger, sex, etc. But this imputation turns out to be unwarranted. Hebb's minimal concession is not so grudging after all. The door that was supposed to be opened only a merest fraction of an inch is in fact thrown wide open. Let us place beside Hebb's statement the quotation taken earlier from Lévi-Strauss: "Whoever says 'man,' says 'language' . . ." If we follow Hebb's guiding principle to the letter, we must conclude that language belongs to the inherent—or instinctual—nature of man. For we do know of any member of the human species, without knowing anything about his individual development, that he has a language, however inadequate and deficient that language may be.

This possibility of considering language within the instinctual equipment of man has very wide consequences—the details of which we will try to unfold in the next chapter. We mention it here only to indicate the first step we have won in our effort to indicate a new orientation and a new approach to the complex and puzzling phenomenon of instinct. For the fact of language, if it be taken as inherent in man, places the phenomenon of the instinctual within the world of significant meanings rather than blind drives. The logic that surrounds this position has now become widely accepted in scientific circles and is quite compelling. It is based on the premise we have discussed throughout this chapter, that the learned and the instinctive cannot be dichotomized—that it is extraordinarily difficult, if at all possible, to exhibit instinctive behavior in man that can be known to be absolutely free of all learned components. But this premise cuts two ways—both for the behaviorist notion of learning and against the notion of oversimplified drives. For if the instinctive and the learned can never be absolutely separated, and if the universal fact of language has an instinctive base, then the concept of instinct as a peremptory drive loses much of its meaning. While it may seem to make sense to characterize hunger and sex as drives, it is more difficult to fit aggression under this rubric, and even more implausible to postulate a "language drive." Furthermore, as anthropology makes abundantly clear, even the drives of sex and hunger—so commonly thought of as "peremptory," or "basically biological"—are fulfilled within a world of meanings.

We may close this discussion of the puzzle of instinct by attempting to unsnarl a serious problem of logic in the relationship of instinct to the larger context of the nature/nurture issue.

The nature/nurture problem belongs with freedom/determinism and the mind/body problem as among the oldest, the most important, and the most troublesome puzzles in both psychology and philosophy. Actually, all three are so closely interrelated and their formal difficulties are so much alike that any light shed on one will illuminate the others as well.

Consider the nature/nurture problem. For many years, its traditional formulation has harbored a subtle but all-pervasive fallacy relating to the misuse of abstractions. We shall call this the fallacy of false categorization. This fallacy has gone undetected for so long because identifying it depended on first isolating a prior type of misused abstraction—the fallacy of simple location, which Whitehead brilliantly clarified in the 1920's. (Whitehead, 1925.) The fallacy of simple location, it will be recalled, is the assumption that whatever is real must occupy a definitely circumscribed space. A corollary assumption is that events not having a specific locus (e.g., values, the passage of time, consciousness) are not "really real" and must be reduced to something that does have a specific location. This view underlies the belief in certain branches of psychology that all mental events must ultimately be reduced to physico-chemical processes.

Once we are liberated from such an arbitrary piece of metaphysics we are free to mix abstractions that refer to meanings, values, and time with abstractions that refer to physical states, without presupposing that the former must be explained in terms of the latter. We can then talk about meanings and tissue states and consciousness in the same breath within the same theory and at the same level of abstraction. While this practice may shock those brought up in the Cartesian tradition, it follows from the philosophic consensus that we discussed earlier, for that consensus was concerned with showing that all the items within experience enjoy, at least at the starting-point of inquiry, the same status in reality. They are equally real because they are equally there in experience.

The fallacy of false categorization is exposed once we move from physical objects to human experience: a whole world of new relationships opens up for which we do not have adequate descriptive abstractions, as we have seen in our discussion of synergism and modes of being. This failing was covered up as long as the fallacy of simple location prevailed, but with it out of the way the need for new types of abstractions becomes imperative. Consider the experience of human love. If we treat love as an attribute (analogous to weight, good looks, and viscosity) instead of as a mode of being, we imply that it shares with other attributes certain relationships common to the world of objects. But love is not an attribute in this sense at all. By the abstraction "love" we are selecting out of the matrix of concrete human experience certain emotions, behaviors, moods, and complex states of relatedness. Among these are physical states such as palpitations and various forms of excitation. Also, there are the dialectic opposites to love considered as an attribute, namely, hatred, ambivalence, jealousy, and oral aggressiveness ("I could eat you up"), as well as the more familiar states of affection, tenderness, gentleness and wanting to be with and near the loved person. Present also are other relationships—a heightened sensitivity to the loved one, distortions of veridical perception ("love is blind"), exclusion of other people from attention, and shifts in basic life values ("I'll give up all this for you").

Being in love is neither an attribute nor a category; nor is it merely a physical state, though it involves physical processes. It is a mode of being—it engages the entire being of the person and involves a new organization of his total field of meanings and relationships. It is a new gestalt, a totality that alters all previous forms of psychic organization; and it leads to a synergistic relationship with the loved one, in that it creates a new state of being. Thus, terms such as "love" and "hate," though abstractions, are not categories in the same sense that abstractions like "fruits" and "nuts" refer to categories of physical objects; nor are they attributes in the same sense as are abstractions like "height" and "weight."

This mistaking of a mode of being abstraction for a category or attribute abstraction is even more prevalent than the fallacy of simple location since one might overtly reject materialist reductionism and still be prey to those of its premises that are built into the very structure of our language. As long as our grammar assumes that reality is divisible into constituent parts or attributes, then all abstractions automatically become categorical in form. Thus, according to most psychological theories (including psychoanalysis), the human person, though acknowledged to be a unified whole enmeshed in a social and organic world, is nonetheless always divided into categories—categories of mind and body, of organism and environment, of id and ego. Each of these notions is a high abstraction, a concept, a segment of a map. But by implying that human experience can be sliced into pieces like a salami, they become false abstractions, however useful they may be.

As we have insisted throughout, the key feature of abstractions is their selectivity; their power depends utterly on their ability to draw attention to certain limited aspects of events and away from others. In this sense, all abstractions are poten-

tially untruths—or at least half-truths or tenth-truths or twen-
tieth-truths. They are surely untruths when they call attention
to aspects of events which the events do not possess.

Most abstractions are categorical. But the concepts of
"mind," "body," "ego," "id," "heredity," and "environment"
are not. They are abstractions but they are not categories or
attributes. There are many kinds of abstractions—category
abstractions, attribute abstractions, abstractions that refer to
aspects of events, modes-of-being abstractions, etc. Unfortunately, we are most comfortable, especially in scientific discourse, with types of abstractions that reflect the world of
objects rather than human experience.*

As long as science concerns itself with simple objects, there is
no grave problem of false categorization. Under the old metaphysics, many noncategorical abstractions could be forced into
a categorical mode without badly falsifying the experience being described because fundamental explanations were made in
terms of physico-chemical processes, i.e., processes having the
property of simple location, and thereby enjoying spatial relationships among their various abstract characteristics. And, as
Newton and others discovered, it is an interesting property
of physical objects, especially those which are larger than
atoms and smaller than galaxies, that so many interesting things
can be said about them merely in terms of their spatial relationships. In other words, as long as we can usefully break down a
whole into parts which occupy space, then we are perfectly safe
in using category abstractions. Among the various ways of analyzing a body of water, one way is to categorize it chemically
into a compound of two parts of hydrogen for one part of
oxygen. In theory, and in practice as well, one can separate the
hydrogen from the oxygen, a feat made possible by the fact
that the basis for the categorical relationship is spatial and additive. But if an analysis of spatial relationships is inapplicable, as
in analyzing love, then categorical abstractions are misleading

---

* The concept of a physical object is itself a high abstraction, selecting
out of the flux of experience certain highly stable forms of organization. Indeed, we cannot think or perceive except in abstractions. The
process of abstracting (selecting, organizing, and generalizing) is a
fundamental characteristic of mind.

and lead to false concepts (such as Freud's concept of a complemental series).

Curiously, thinkers who share this fallacy nonetheless disagree violently over the false problems it creates for them. We have already discussed the controversy bred by the false mind/body categorization. Materialists take the position that only one category—the body—is real. Idealists take the position that only the other category—mind—is real. Psycho-physical parallelists take the position that both mind and body are real but are separate categories working in miraculous coordination with one another. This point is relevant to our present concerns because Freud wavered between outright materialism and psycho-physical parallelism, while many of his followers have been accused (not always unjustly) of lending reality only to the mind.

Dividing the human psyche into an ego and an id is a particularly lovely instance of the fallacy of false categorization. The psychological modes of being of the individual designated by ego and the id are obviously neither additive nor spatially related. Referring to them as *systems of functions* (the current terminology) sounds impressive, but does not in any way mitigate the original categorical error. The instincts, which are said to be part of the id, are not a substantive category; nor are ego processes.

Many psychological experiences, such as trust, hope, and identity, must be described in terms of their *instinctual* aspects, their *learned* aspects, their *meaning* aspects and their *maturational* aspects, without any implication that the instinctual, the learned, the meaning, and the maturational refer to separate categories of entities like fruits in a basket. The distinction between abstractions that refer to categories and abstractions that refer to modes of being is fundamental to clarifying a proper definition of instinct.

TWENTY-ONE

Toward a Theory of Human Nature

Two great insights of the human sciences stand out above all others. First is the evolutionary perspective. Scientists now believe that the earth was formed four billion years ago and that life on this planet traces back two billion years, human existence two hundred million years. Hardly a year passes without new discoveries about man's origins and the continuities that relate him to the past. Scientists disagree on precisely how evolution works, but they concur that man is the product of evolution and that the gains of this great process are somehow recorded in his genetic make-up and form the framework within which his individual development takes place.

The other insight concerns the unique importance in human life of culture—the transmission by social means of symbols, meanings, traditions, rituals and institutions from one generation to the next. Though man is rooted in his biological past he lives out his life in the context of a specific culture. And since culture is man-made, he enjoys a degree of control, flexibility, and variability vouchsafed to no other species. Some animals—jackdaws, graylag geese and rats—are able to teach their young how to recognize simple paths and the enemies of their species. Among rats, knowledge of the danger of poison and even of specific poisons is taught by one generation to the next. But with simple exceptions such as these, symbols are not transmitted in other species by tradition and culture. It is

a remarkable fact that the differences among men are far
greater than the differences among the strongest and the weakest animals. Culture creates the great variability among civilizations, and among individuals. It is this insight environmentalists
have fought so vigorously to safeguard against the strict advocates of genetic determinism.

These two great insights are frequently formulated so as to
appear contradictory to each other, which they are not. Much of
the controversy in the human sciences is over a false problem.
Fortunately, science has begun to reject the artificial alternatives of evolution *or* culture and to seek instead a synthesis that
will bring these two truths into harmony with each other.

Freud's structural point of view is a brilliant effort to achieve
such a synthesis. The ego-id-superego formulation incorpo-
rates in a single statement man's experience (ego) in relation
both to his culture (superego) and his evolutionary heritage
(id). This division of personality, which embodies Freud's
theory of nature in relation to nurture, delineates also the kinds
of conflicts most frequently encountered by the analyst. It
covers the core of individual experience—the exercise of individual consciousness within the constraints of nature and
culture. Historically, this structural division opened up a vast
new perspective for psychoanalysis. It is still the most popular,
influential and best-known aspect of Freud's metapsychology—
among the lay public as well as in psychoanalytic circles.

Yet, despite its prestige and despite the fact that it brings
evolution, culture, and individual experience together, the ego-
id theory is open to serious question. Does the concept of
id truly describe the evolutionary basis of human nature?
Does culture impinge on the individual through a quasi-inde-
pendent set of functions (superego)? Is the psychoanalytic
concept of ego adequate to individual experience and freedom
in relation to culture and evolution? The preceding chapters
and, indeed, this entire work, raise serious doubts that these
questions can be answered affirmatively.

Some psychoanalysts will regard tampering with the structural point of view as a near heresy. They are prepared to
question the pleasure principle, the energy theory, and even
the psychoanalytic definition of instinct. But to challenge the
ego-id distinction is to cut through the fat of the metapsy-

chology to the bone and marrow of clinical practice. Indeed, many psychoanalysts adhere to the ego-id doctrine precisely because it *is* so useful in clinical practice: it demarcates the lines of cleavage of the conflicts they most often encounter—an advantage that cannot lightly be dismissed; and, as a set of shorthand symbols for describing neurotic conflict it does seem to work: instinctual, cultural, and experiential elements do enter into any serious human conflict and the ego-id-superego division symbolizes this fact.

Yet, on balance, the defects of the structural point of view may well outweigh its great advantages. Even its clinical practicality may, to some degree, be spurious: the psychoanalyst is beguiled into believing that he has explained a conflict when he defines it as a collision of ego with id, or id with superego, or ego with superego. As we have noted, however (e.g., McDougall's doctrine of instincts), to have a name for something is not the same as a scientific explanation. Although one must always consider basic human conflict in the light of evolution, culture, and individual experience, there is not more correspondence between these abstractions and specific intrapsychic processes than there is between religious belief and a soul substance, or between love of music and a music muscle. A man's greed may conflict with his sense of justice, and we then speak metaphorically of a conflict between Greed and Justice. But it adds not a jot to our scientific understanding to give them pseudo-scientific names and to label them as explanatory concepts.

The fatal weakness of the ego-id doctrine, however, is not that it harbors mere logical difficulties. Its problems are more fundamental. They concern nothing less than the soundness of the psychoanalytic theory of human nature. We enter, then, upon the most important and far-reaching phase of the reconstruction—a reformulation of the theory of human nature and a proposal for revising the structural point of view.

The Developmentals

One of the most serious flaws in the structural point of view is the concept of id. As the repository of our instinctual nature, the id stands for evolution in the life of the single individual. The viability of ego-id doctrine depends utterly upon a sound conception of instinct. But at least seven basic assumptions orthodox psychoanalysis holds about instinct and id are either too restrictive or overgeneralized or plainly incorrect:

1. That the evolutionary side of man's life (the id) is a "seething cauldron" of unruly impulses pressing for release.
2. That all instincts are alike in being quantities of forces.
3. That the list of human instincts can be largely confined to sex and aggression.
4. That the id is "archaic" and serves no adaptive purpose (this function being assigned to ego).
5. That the instinctual is less susceptible to change than the experiential.
6. That the id is not affected by experience.
7. That culture is inherently alien to instinct.

Most of these assumptions have already been discussed in earlier chapters. Compositely, they raise so many obstacles that we propose replacing the id with a new concept we shall call the developmentals. To define the developmentals we must begin with a revised understanding of instinct.

Psychoanalysis conceives of instinct in analogy with the hunger drive, assuming (a) that the instincts of sex and aggression seek peremptory relief when aroused and (b) that they are linked with specific physiological states. Actually, man's sexual urges do have enough in common with the hunger drive to lend some credibility to the comparison. What happens in the theory, however, is that the attributes shared in common by sex and hunger become sharply delineated, while those aspects of sexuality that are unlike the hunger drive fade into a vague background. The analogy with hunger becomes even more questionable when one turns to aggression. It is difficult to identify specific tissue states or physiological deficits with the arousal of aggression; there is great artificiality in attributing to aggression the peremptory character of the hunger drive; and one cannot so readily claim that aggression is endogenous, arises spontaneously, and exists irrespective of experience. These considerations have made some psychoanalysts uncomfortable, but as long as they identify aggression as having some instinctual basis (correctly, we believe) they have no other way to describe aggression in view of their peculiar concept of instinct.

One common association with aggression is that of some violent explosion of force. Along this line aggression would be most clearly manifest in a case like that of the American student Charles Whitman, thought of as "a nice guy" by all who knew him, but who one day barricaded himself in the tower at the University of Texas and proceeded to gun down thirty people before he himself was killed. Here is a case where seething and hidden aggressions did break explosively into the open. Presumably, then, if we follow this explosion-of-force line of thinking, the same aggressions are in all of us, but we are not so "sick" and manage to control them.

In fact, however, we should think of human aggressiveness as more complexly structured. Consider two executives competing for the same high position within a business corporation. Suppose one wins out; and suppose, further, that he triumphs because he is more "aggressive" in going at his goal. This aggressiveness does not mean a greater explosion of force. Quite the contrary: a display of physical force, within the elaborate protocol of corporation life, would almost surely lose the job for him. No; aggressiveness here may manifest itself in a greater will to subordinate all impulses to the constraint of his aim, in an unrelenting concentration upon what he is after and a willingness to bend every bit of energy, intellectual and moral, to that single goal. Nietzsche, with great insight, singled out this type of aggressiveness as one of the prime manifestations of the will to power as it has shaped human history: the individual who acquires power by humbling himself, by standing back, by being willing to wait and if necessary wait a long time until he can secure the upper hand. This kind of aggressiveness, obviously, is not a simply locatable drive, but an aspect of a total psychic structure, and it fuses intimately with every aspect of that structure from top to bottom.

Similar considerations on the sexual instinct arise when one examines some anthropological investigations of the subject. Malinowski, in *The Sexual Life of Savages*, remarks:

> Sex is not a mere physiological transaction to the primitive South Sea Islander any more than it is to us . . . Sex, in its widest meaning, . . . is rather a sociological and cultural force than a mere bodily relation of two individuals. (Introduction, p. *xxiii*.)

The whole of Malinowski's book documents this contention. In writing about sexual behavior, Malinowski begins with tribal and family structure (Lévi-Strauss has acknowledged him as a predecessor of his own structuralism); passes on to rites and games; and finally to the whole structure of meanings embedded in magic and mythology without which we would not understand the significance of sexuality to the "savage." His inclusion of so many topics under the heading of sex is not a mere wandering from the point for the sake of an encyclopedic compilation. On the contrary, Malinowski is sticking to the point throughout—that sex, even more than aggression, does not usually manifest itself as a simply locatable drive but pervades the whole life-structure of the primitive. It may well be that only the most limited aspects of sexuality and aggression can be thought of in analogy to a peremptory hunger drive seeking discharge.

Consider now the forms of instinctual expression represented by language and language development, which cannot be even remotely compared to the hunger drive. Hebb has suggested that the domain of the instinctive may be located by statements one can make about individuals or a group without knowledge of their life history or culture but in the light of knowledge about the species as a whole. Language development fits this prescription in that one can make reliable statements about language development in peoples of all cultures without knowing their particular life histories. And yet, language development shares few characteristics with the hunger drive: it is not peremptory; it is not mainly concerned with energy discharge; it is not endogenous; it is not periodic; it is not associated with a tissue deficit; it is not fixed; and it does not exist independently of experience in the same sense that hunger does.

Instead, it has other interesting properties. Some years ago Dorothea McCarthy (1954), reviewing the immense descriptive literature on language development, pointed out some of its universal characteristics: (1) language is a uniquely human capacity unshared by other species; (2) it is phase-specific in that all human children make babbling sounds as a precursor to speech at about the same age; (3) there is a greater capacity for language learning in young children than in highly trained adults; (4) its development cannot be explained by imitation and conditioning alone; and (5) once the child has acquired a rudimentary vocabulary he begins to form propositions which are syntactically correct even though they may not be meaningful, i.e., accuracy in form may precede correctness in content.

More recently, the noted expert in structural linguistics, Professor Noam Chomsky, has insisted upon the radical premise (radical, at least, to many of his philosophic colleagues) that one cannot understand language development without introducing the premise of innate structures (which we label as instinct). This position dovetails rather remarkably with some of the ideas advanced by ethologists such as Lorenz.

On the face of it, the disciplines of ethology and linguistics would seem to have little to do with each other; and such independence is a fact. Hence, their convergence on one single point —the presence of innate language structures—seems to us all the more remarkable. Indeed, this convergence makes the hypothesis of innate structures more plausible, since it is reached along two different avenues of evidence.

Chomsky's position, briefly put, is that the child must have an innate scanning device that enables him, amid the welter of sounds he hears, to learn the grammar of the language. It is not necessary here to enter into the full intricacy of his arguments; it will suffice if we indicate the general direction of his reasoning. He begins by attempting to construct a learning model to represent how the child is able to acquire a language:

Specifically, we must ask how, on the basis of the limited data available to him, the child is able to construct a grammar of the sort that we are led to ascribe to him, with its particular choice and arrangement of rules and with the restrictive principles of application of such rules.

This model must meet two empirical conditions:

First, we must attribute to the organism, as an innate property, a structure rich enough to account for the fact that the postulated grammar is acquired on the basis of the given conditions of access to data; second, we must not attribute to the organism a structure so rich as to be incompatible with the known diversity of languages. We cannot attribute knowledge of English to a child as an innate property, because we know that he can learn Japanese as well as English.

These last words imply a general principle that must be kept in mind in all our discussion of innate structures. These structures do not contain specifically differentiated products within themselves as if in a box. Rather, the innate programming is an incomplete structure such that only after a definite process of maturation (which will include cultural stimuli) does it terminate in a definite end product.

Chomsky goes on to make his crucial point that the child's learning of a language is not confined to the limited number of sounds he has actually heard:

The child's ultimate knowledge of language obviously extends far beyond the data presented to him. In other words, the theory he has in some way developed has a predictive scope of which the data on which it is based constitutes a negligible part. The normal use of language characteristically involves new sentences, sentences that bear no point-by-point resemblance or analogy to those of the child's experience. Furthermore, the task of constructing this system is carried out in a remarkably similar way by all normal language learners, despite wide differences in experience and ability. The theory of human learning must face these facts.

In other words, in learning a language the child does not acquire meanings passively. On the contrary, he builds meanings as he learns. Man does not passively inhabit a world of meanings; he is, rather, an active builder of meanings.

Chomsky concludes that any attempt to reconstruct this learning situation must postulate pre-existing linguistic structures within which the learning takes place. (If, for example, we could duplicate this learning model on a computer, we would have to program the computer with a considerable prior equipment of language, both with regard to grammar and a basic discrimination of phonemes.) Moreover, this pre-existing structure would have to be of considerable scope:

> Roughly, I think it reasonable to postulate that the principles of general linguistics regarding the nature of rules, their organization, the principles by which they function, the kinds of representations to which they apply and which they form, all constitute part of the innate condition . . . If this suggestion is correct, then there is no more point asking how these principles are learned than there is in asking how a child learns to breathe, or, for that matter, to have two arms.

If we take these last words literally, language is as natural to man as breathing.

Chomsky's position here accords exactly with that of the ethologist Arnold Gehlen. The latter starts from the general view that man is by nature a being of culture. That is to say, while man's whole system of innate potentialities is phylogenetically constructed, it nonetheless must be complemented by culture. Gehlen, like Chomsky, uses language as a case in point. The whole extensive neuro-sensory apparatus of human speech is phylogenetically evolved; at the same time it is so constructed that the existence of a culturally developed language is necessary if the infant is to learn. In other words, we are phylogenetically programmed for language; but we learn to speak English, Japanese, or Swahili accordingly as we are born into one culture rather than another.

Curiously enough, though Chomsky draws his materials from an altogether different range of experience, there is a striking similarity between the ultimate form of his argument and that

of the ethologists. Consider, for example, the debate between
Lorenz and Hebb over the question of innate versus learned
behavior. Hebb, the behaviorist, alleges that there is some un-
discovered process of learning that accounts for the behavior
which the ethologist claims is innate. The ethologist, Lorenz, in
response, seeks to make his deprivation experiments more precise, and thereby to exclude all possibilities of learning. In reply, the behaviorist will find evidence of learning *in utero* or
even *in ovo.* Ultimately, then, the ethologist invokes the basic
principle that learning can take place only for an organism that
has already been programmed or structured so that it is able to
learn. And this principle, as Lorenz correctly states, is exactly
the philosopher Kant's doctrine of the *a priori.* It is the identical
principle that Chomsky seeks to exemplify in linguistics.

We find it revealing that Chomsky's conclusions have created
a considerable uproar among certain philosophers. In particular,
he has upset those steeped in the tradition of British empiricism,
who swear allegiance to Locke's doctrine of the *tabula rasa,*
according to which the mind begins as an absolutely blank
tablet on which experience writes. In this view, any talk of
"innate ideas" is "repugnant" and "nonsensical." The old
bromide of the *tabula rasa* seems to die very hard. It is, of
course, a presupposition that lies at the basis of all behaviorism.
If the mind begins as a blank tablet, then an extreme behaviorist
can claim that by writing on it as he pleases he can make us
into any kind of person he chooses. Yet, if we set the facts of
behavioral genetics and child development alongside Chomsky's investigations, then the inherent implausibility of the
tabula rasa concept becomes even more evident. Indeed, from
the evolutionary point of view, if man were to enter this world
as an absolute *tabula rasa,* he could not survive for a day.

Many other generalizations about the instinctual basis of
language development can be made; these are merely illustra-
tive. Compositely, they lead to the conclusion that language
development flows from an interaction between inherent maturational structures and experience. Experience alone—the individual's exposure and response to language—is a necessary
but not sufficient condition for language development. Some
inherent process, which the child brings to the task, must also
be postulated.

Breathing and hunger on one end and language development on the other represent the two extremes of an immensely broad spectrum of inborn processes. Ethology, in its study of animals, has identified some of the forms of instinct that lie in between hunger and language. Lorenz describes a marvelous variety of instinctive inhibitions against aggression in animals. In lizards, a chemical stimulus in the form of a smell inhibits the male from biting the female. In birds, the inhibition is elicited by sound. In coral fish it is evoked by the fish's brilliant flag colors. In other animals the inhibition takes the form of appeasing behavior: a cock beaten in a rival fight will put his head in a corner to remove the fight-eliciting stimuli of its red cone and wattles; a wolf vanquished in a fight with a rival will turn his powerful teeth and jaws to one side and offer to his opponent the most vulnerable part of his body—the jugular in the arch side of the neck; the beaten jackdaw proffers the unprotected base of his skull. In each instance the inhibition is so powerful that it can abruptly stop the attack of a wild beast in midbattle. Furthermore, says Lorenz, there is a direct correlation between the effectiveness of each animal's weapon and the strength of the inhibition. In animals whose claws, beak, or teeth can be lethal, the inhibition is proportionately greater than in animals who are less powerful (Lorenz, 1952).

The widespread existence of instinctual inhibitions suggests a point of far-reaching significance for the metapsychology. Freud always assumed that instinct connoted discharge of energy, not its inhibition. This premise caused him to subsume all inhibiting phenomena under the ego and superego. The ego and superego belong to culture, which Freud dualistically set off against nature. Instinctive inhibiting mechanisms in animals raise the possibility, entertained by some psychoanalysts such as Rapaport, that inhibiting behavior in man, too, may not be the product of learning alone but may also have instinctive roots. (There are many other forms of instinctive behavior in animals that show no sign of peremptory energy discharge, such as when young baboons present their marvelously colored behinds—not as sexual stimuli but as a way of saluting the higher rank of an older or stronger baboon.)

When we turn from animals to humans, we also find a wide variety of inborn processes. Spitz points out that some human

infants are born with form perception: from the very first
second of life the infant, without learning, is able to perceive
shape, size, and three-dimensionality (Spitz, 1965). Hamburg
hypothesizes that infant females may have better genetic pro-
tection against blood-clotting disorders and color-vision defects
than infant males. Scientists at the National Institute of Mental
Health, observing infants right after birth, have noted sharp
differences (seemingly inborn) between males and females as
registered on skin conductance tests (Yolles, 1967). Infants of
both sexes are born with a constitutionally high threshold designed to ward off unwanted stimuli and they manifest the
rudiments of cognitive processes Freud called the primary processes. The tendency to seek peremptory relief from tension, on
which Freud counted so heavily, is also an innate characteristic;
so are the reflexes and fixed response patterns such as crying
and thrashing about. The infant also inherits a variety of motor
patterns, a wide range of tensions, and a need for pleasurable
stimulation.

A full inventory of inborn human characteristics would run
on indefinitely. It would contain a mix of prepatterned behavioral responses, periodic tensions, reflexes, generalized needs,
unlearned mechanisms, and other mental and physical characteristics. Furthermore, all such characteristics have been seen
to have different properties and belong to different part-processes. A generalized need for stimulation, for example, may not
be experienced as a tension and may not have rhythm or pe-
riodicity or urgency. Peremptory discharge may apply to hunger and urination, but not to the desire for stimuli which the
infant actively seeks out. These varied manifestations of the
inborn are part of our phylogenetic inheritance; they represent
the gains of millions of years of human evolution. They cannot
be described by any one categorized form of "instinct" or any
one type of process.

In brief, then, any definition of instinct modeled on the
hunger drive as fixed, peremptory, endogenous, associated with
specific physiological organs or functions, and developing irrespective of individual experience, is altogether too restrictive.
The "instinctive" in man does not refer to a single, unitary
item, but a bewildering variety of inborn processes. Hunger,
sexuality, aggression, thumb-sucking, language development,

SYNERGISM

basic trust, moral restraint, form-perception, classification, and many other human characteristics are species-wide, yet each innate predisposition has a different underlying structure.

Keeping this pluralism of innate structures in mind, we come now to one special group of them. Clearly, the psychoanalyst is not concerned with the full sweep of man's instinctive life. (He is, for example, only marginally interested in language development.) Some psychic structures, however, especially those linked to maturation, are all-important to his work. Aspects of aggression and sexuality and basic trust—the primary processes as they relate to the development of personal meanings, a sense of order, and many other instinct-based processes—directly link the evolutionary to the cultural side of man's life. We shall call these processes "developmentals" since they emerge in the species as part of the individual's progress through experience from one stage of development to the next. They are the joint product of evolution and culture collaboratively.

Erikson's epigenetic principle singles out for special attention what is perhaps the most complex of the developmentals: a maturational schedule according to which a person's development proceeds normally phase by phase—if he is lucky enough to have the right experience at each stage. These developmentals differ from wholly unlearned processes such as hunger, breathing, urination, and unconditional reflexes, in that they depend on the occurrence of critical life experiences and at the same time on inherent maturational factors. Though they are partly the results of learning, experience by itself cannot account for them. Because they involve both learning and inborn structures in complex interaction, they are peculiarly difficult to investigate. Yet they cannot be neglected, for they constitute the core of the human personality.

To locate the developmentals among the variety of instinct-based processes, let us use as an organizing abstraction a dependency-on-experience continuum. At one end of such a continuum will be found hunger and the other instinctual drives. Though these may be channeled by learning, they find a way to express themselves irrespective of individual experience; unlike the developmentals, their very existence does not depend on circumstance. At the other end of the continuum are those processes whose development will be stunted unless the individual passes through certain critical experiences (which he could readily miss if the culture did not provide them through its social institutions). Basic trust may fail to grow unless the infant enjoys a period of prolonged mothering, while hunger (like walking) is hardier and more autonomous: it does not depend for its very existence on the quality of individual experience.

When instinct and experience are held to be mutually exclusive, i.e., when it is erroneously assumed that a psychic process is either instinctual in the sense of being unlearned or learned in the sense of being independent of inborn structures, then a developmental such as basic trust cannot even be defined. The developmentals require both learning and an inborn factor to bring them into being. We define the developmentals, therefore, as structures that grow only when phylogenetic factors interact with critical individual experience at specific stages in the life cycle. Experience and instinct are here regarded as inseparable aspects of a single unified event: in one sense, the infant "learns" basic trust from being mothered, but in another sense mothering elicits and brings to fulfillment an instinctive potential for basic trust.

Many lasting developmentals are formed during the child's long period of helplessness—an extraordinarily prolonged phase of dependency in comparison with other species. As has often been stressed, this period of dependency is the major source of man's vulnerabilities. But it is also the source of his strengths and his freedom. Man's great adaptability—and his freedom of choice as well—grows directly out of the learning that takes place during the human child's phase of helplessness. But instinct is not for that reason absent. In the forming of developmentals, learning is always selective and experience never elicits a merely random response. The culture does not implant its influence on an infinitely plastic medium, a *tabula rasa*; there are inherent limitations to man's plasticity. The infant starts out life with a complex of inbuilt predispositions and potentials—a maturational schedule—which his unique experience (within a culture) structures along highly selective lines.

The correct understanding of this point, which has long been a source of confusion in the human sciences, is central both to the reconstruction of psychoanalytic metapsychology and to a viable theory of human nature. It can be made more concrete by returning once again to our paradigm of language development.

Language development is instructive because of the babbling stage. Apparently, children go through a period of babbling which slowly grows into recognizable and meaningful sounds. The sounds, in turn, gradually become words and symbols with precise denotative meanings. The initial babbling is unlearned (though it presupposes the development of physical capabilities), the transformation of babbling behavior into spoken language is learned. But if the babbling stage passes without the child's having learned to speak, verbal fluency and language ability are far more difficult to acquire later on. If we, therefore, say that the human child has an instinctive capacity or innate potential for language (demonstrated by the babbling stage) the meaning of such terms becomes quite specific. (The analogue to babbling in the development of basic trust is more diffuse and therefore more difficult to specify concretely.)

We are now gaining more information about human traits that demand the interaction of experience with phase-specific inborn structures. Freud brilliantly described infantile sexuality, Lorenz described aggression in animals, Erikson described basic trust, and Lévi-Strauss described how classificatory systems develop. In the future, we may expect to see more of such fundamental descriptions, and eventually the radical concept of inborn potential will be accepted as a precise generic term for referring to all phylogenetic processes that require a critical experience to bring to fruition.

In scientific discourse, such potentials can be described in the form of contrary-to-fact conditionals which specify the experiences in the absence of which the potential would not have become actual. ("If such and such a condition had not been present, then a certain definite structure would not have developed.") Hartmann's notion of a general and unspecified average expectable environment will not do because it is too undifferentiated: it fails to identify the specific experiences the culture must provide to develop the inborn potential. In certain cultures (including some of our own poverty subcultures), the mothering that is needed to elicit basic trust is neither average nor expectable. Scientifically, it is of vital importance to be able to state that given a certain stage of development, if X experience does not occur, Y characteristic will not develop with Z probability. (The negative form of the statement is more appropriate than the positive, for it is easier to specify that certain traits will *not* develop than that they will. For example, if a boy lacks an effective father or father substitute with whom to identify, the probability that certain personality traits will fail to develop is quite high. The positive form of the statement may not have the same high probability.)

When in common parlance we speak of "human nature," very often what is meant are the developmentals—as when Anna Freud referred to the fact that if a child lacked curiosity one would not take its absence for granted but would actively search for what happened to it. In all likelihood, the developmentals should be the main concern of psychoanalysis (and its primary research interest). In childhood, when we are most vulnerable, and must undergo certain critical experiences to pass successfully from one developmental stage to the next, the opportunities for things to go wrong are very great. The timing of critical experiences may be out of synchronization with the child's maturation schedule; the relationship with a parent may be too intense or not intense enough; sexual arousal may be premature and overly disturbing; the parents may rush in too quickly to soothe a child instead of showing him how to cope with his own distress; or the parents may go to the other extreme and encourage an excessively high degree of control which the child cannot yet manage without sacrificing other aspects of his personality; death, sickness, or separation may occur at a particularly sensitive time. In short, any one of a thousand mishaps may lead ultimately to neurosis—due to the close link between critical experiences and inborn development schedules. It is this latter qualification that makes all the difference. Sometimes the same experience occurring a year later or even a year earlier will have far less impact on a person's life. It is not the content of the experience that counts—this view leads to a superficial environmentalism—but its relation to an instinctive factor at a particular stage of development. Moreover, since the most basic aspects of personality are at stake, structures formed when the child is in vulnerable transition from one development stage to the next may have long-enduring consequences.

DEVELOPMENTALS DISCOVERED BY CROSS-CULTURAL RESEARCH

Given their importance, how can we isolate these developmentals from the dense stream of human experience? How can we avoid playing a McDougall game with a new set of labels, leading to pseudo explanation instead of true understanding? Fortunately, the conditions for true descriptive explanation are present: the *criteria* for identifying developmentals can be made clear and specific since they are related to a maturational timetable; the necessary *research methods* are at hand; and the *analytical procedures* for understanding how these structures are formed lie well within the range of scientific description and explanation. Indeed, the subject desperately cries out for this type of research and analysis.

The research methods required are implied by Hebb's operational definition of where to start looking for instinct. (His formulation does not, of course, define instinct substantively; it does tell us how to go about tracking it down.) We are to look for those facets of human experience that one can know without knowing the individual's life history (or by extension, the history of the culture). If we reflect on the lead Hebb has given us, we see immediately that the required research points away from the psychoanalytic method, which is exclusively concerned with the individual's life history, and toward social research. Such research must, however, be more flexible and sophisticated than much of what we have today. It must mix phenomenology with statistics, evolutionary theory with the analysis of social structure, direct psychoanalytic experience with anthropological cross-cultural surveys. It must, of course, be interdisciplinary, since it is working at the interface of several disciplines. The methods for carrying it out, it should be stressed, lie well within the existing capabilities—and practices —of the human sciences. To illustrate how fruitful such cross-cultural perspectives can be, we describe below the results of several research efforts by prominent social scientists.

The social psychologist Hadley Cantril has reported (1964) on a research study of thirteen different societies and cultures. Cantril was looking for what he called common "functional uniformities." He found a number of such uniformities, which he attributed, at least in part, to a "genetically built-in design." With the qualification that his categories overlap, intertwine, and are interdependent, Cantril identifies the following common human characteristics in all thirteen cultures:

1. The quest for food, shelter and for other means of satisfying the survival needs.
2. The quest for security both in a territorial and an emotional sense.
3. The need for order, certainty, and form—the assurance of experience that is repeatable, and the pressing need to preserve some semblance of order and pattern.
4. The quest, particularly striking when survival needs are well met, to enlarge the range and quality of human satisfactions. (In this connection, Cantril endorses approvingly the observation many social scientists have made that human behavior is caricatured when represented merely as adaptation to the environment. There is, says Cantril, an intense desire for development in a specific direction. "People are hungry for good and new experiences," is the way one respondent summed it up for him.)
5. Man is a creature of hope, oriented toward the future and always needing a feeling of surety and confidence that the society of which he is a part holds out the hope that his aspirations will be fulfilled.
6. The capacity to make choices and an urgent requirement for at least a limited freedom to be able to do so.
7. The common need to reconfirm his own ego identity within a framework of meanings the individual creates for himself within the culture.
8. The common need, however diverse the culture, to experience a sense of his own worthwhileness, to build up a conviction that he is valued by others.
9. The need for a system of values and beliefs to which he can commit himself and even sacrifice himself.

Now then, Cantril's conclusion that *all* of these "functional uniformities" are genetically inbuilt may be open to question; his data may be too impressionistic; they may lack rigorous validation; they may be interpreted from a somewhat ethnocentric point of view, projecting our own values onto other people's societies; his sample of cultures and societies may be skewed toward some common historical root such that investigation of other societies would oblige him to modify his list radically, etc., etc. But even if all of this happened—and it is not likely, since Cantril is a researcher of sophistication and sensitivity—the research strategy is basically sound. We can survey cultures as readily as individuals. If our sample of cultures is sufficiently broad and varied and if our techniques for identifying uniformities are well designed, we have the statistical means of control for variations in physical environment, past history, cultural institutions, and individual learning. By these techniques we can ultimately formulate, and even verify, the "if . . . then" statements that identify man's instinctive potentials and the critical experiences needed to bring them to completion.

An example of a different sort is found in the work of Lévi-Strauss. Juxtaposing Lévi-Strauss with Cantril affords us a broad representation of points of view, since the former holds to an out-and-out materialist position in the classical scientific sense, while Cantril's philosophical views are closer to the nondeterminist position presented in this work. (It is sometimes easier for scientists to agree on concrete empirical findings than on their metaphysics.)

In his book *The Savage Mind*, Lévi-Strauss examines a wide variety of totemic beliefs and methods of classification employed by nonliterate societies. The fact that a culture may be poor or undeveloped in its social institutions does not mean, he says, that it is intellectually impoverished. A richness of abstract terms, complex rules of syntax, and highly elaborate methods of naming and taxonomy characterize even the simplest "savage" societies. So-called primitive peoples show a great thirst for objective disinterested knowledge. The universe is as much an object of thought for them (as well as a means of satisfying needs) as it is for our own culture. Whether we look at the pygmies of the Philippines, the North American Hopi Indians, or the Luchozi of northern Rhodesia, the picture is similar: an incredibly detailed wealth of knowledge about plants, animals, and natural surroundings, ordered around organizing principles at high levels of generality. The ordinary Negrito male (Philippines) can identify 450 plants, 75 birds, 20 species of ants, 45 types of edible ground mushrooms, and more than 50 types of arrows. (R. B. Fox, quoted by Lévi-Strauss, p. 5.) The Aymara Indians of the Bolivian Plàteau have developed a system of dehydration which served as a model for processes ultimately adapted by the American army. Living at an altitude of 12,000 feet, they worked out an elaborate taxonomy of the maizelike plant, solanum, distinguishing over 250 varieties and classifying them on the basis of sex, color, texture, form, and a generalized dichotomy distinguishing those that can be eaten after simple cooking and those that need more elaborate processing (p. 47).

The thought of the primitive, just as our own, reflects a demand for order that is found across cultures, and that illustrates one of Cantril's "functional uniformities." And yet, despite the similarity in systems of classifications, the concrete characteristics of any culture's totemic classifications are not identical. The Navaho Indians classify living creatures into those endowed with speech and those not endowed with speech. The Hanunóo of the Philippines classify colors not as we do, by brightness (value) and intensity (chroma), but on the basis of colors found in fresh and succulent plants compared with those found in desiccated plants. Bees are associated with pythons and red ants are linked with cobras in the totemic system adopted by the Nuer of Africa because of similar markings in the first instance and common color in the second. Menstruation is associated with successful eagle hunting by the Hidatsa of North America (for complex reasons, which Lévi-Strauss elucidates in detail) while among the Pueblo, menstruation suggests the death of the eagle hunter rather than his success. From a great wealth of such illustrations, Lévi-Strauss draws the important conclusion: "The principle underlying a classification can never be postulated in advance. It can only be discovered *a posteriori* . . . by experience." (P. 58.)

The systems of logic employed by primitive peoples tend to

work on two or more axes at the same time. They might combine the principles of contiguity (snakes and anthills) with physical resemblance (red ants and red cobras) and with the possession of common characteristics (creatures with wings). The connections may be close or distant, synchronic or diachronic, static or dynamic. The number and nature of these logical axes are not the same in every culture. However, even a culture that is poor in classificatory systems will use complex methods of naming and employ more than one principle of taxonomy. The content of such systems is never the same (unless cultural diffusion or shared circumstance intervenes) but their structures *are* alike.

We have here yet another instance of a developmental (anticipated, incidentally, by Kant) that the "mind" brings to experience forms (innate structures) which are rooted in man's evolutionary heritage. But individual experience, mediated by the culture, must elicit them and give them concrete embodiment. We may therefore include among the developmentals the tendency of the human mind to impose order on the surroundings by the application of inborn taxonomic abilities. These latter exist as instinctive potentials: they must be stimulated by the culture and in the culture; and in any one culture, some develop and others fail to do so.

Identifying what the developmentals are may be the least difficult part of the research task. We must then isolate three analytically distinguishable aspects of each one. The first is in the form and nature of the instinctive components. These may be clearly correlated with physically based changes such as in adolescence. They may involve changes in mode and zone, as Freud and Erikson suggest when describing how the infant passes from the oral to the anal modality of experience. Or they may be like the babbling stage in language development. Among animals, we have seen, aggression is inhibited in one instance by smell, in another by sound, and in another by appeasing behavior. In each instance the structure, Lorenz tells us, is a different form of an innate releasing mechanism that must encounter certain forms of experience to be elicited. Furthermore, there is no reason to believe that innate structures relating to human aggression, trust, language, identification, love, etc., are similar. On the contrary, the likelihood is that each is finely differentiated.

The second aspect of each developmental that must be researched is the critical experience needed to translate an inborn potential into an actual synergistic structure—a trait of personality, an enduring predisposition, a lasting bond, a sense of competence, a sense of ego identity, a capacity to form ethical judgments, etc. Thanks to many researchers, we know something about the quality of the symbiotic experience that must take place between mother and child to form the structure of basic trust. But what sort of experience do we need for a sense of order, a capacity to enlarge the range and quality of experience, a gift for building friendships, bridges, revolutions, or a sense of self-worth? No fact about the social sciences is more surprising than the dearth of research on the relationship of critical experiences to inborn structures and how they come together to form personality and basic life values.

The third aspect of the developmentals that needs research is the nature of the connecting link between critical experiences and inborn structures, the always scientifically important question of process. We propose that the instinctive side of human life be conceived as incomplete psychic structures. The great advantage of this concept is that it cuts through the traditional nature/nurture dichotomy. It implies a radical incompleteness in all inborn intrapsychic processes apart from their development in individual and cultural experience. If instinct cannot be conceived apart from experience, the split between them disappears, as do a number of false issues. No longer need we be concerned with unanswerable questions such as "Which is more important, nature or nurture?" or "Is science violated if man is treated as a subject instead of as an object?" Instead, some immensely productive specific research questions arise as to precisely how the individual's instinctive potential is completed by experience. How, we must ask, does each person's unique experience impinge upon the natural endowments he shares with the rest of the species so as to develop unique controls, habits, skills, meanings, personality traits, knowledge and values? And once this question is posed we enter the all-important domain of adaptation, learning, and structure formation.

The Laws of Structure Formation

An even more serious weakness of the structural point of view than the troubled concept of id is a thin and inadequate theory of how psychic structures are formed, i.e., how nurture interacts with nature to shape the enduring structures of personality. Nowhere, perhaps, has the influence of Freud's borrowed philosophy so weakened psychoanalysis as in leading to false assumptions about how psychic structures are formed and interconnect.

The concept of a complemental series is a prime example of how Freud interrelated the structure of instinct with ego. He invoked the "complemental series" idea to describe the strength of instincts relative to the strength of the ego's learned controls. Sheer logic then led to the unwarranted conclusion that the chances of curing the neuroses were not good for people whom nature had endowed with strong sexual and aggressive instincts —on the grounds that it would be harder for them to "tame" their instincts than for people whose instincts were average or weak.

This equation of mental health with the ego's power to control instinct permeated Freud's thinking throughout his career, although it is most explicit toward the end of his life. A complemental series implies, of course, an additive relationship between nature and nurture—the very embodiment of the fallacy of false categorization. Fortunately, in recent years psychoanalytic writers have begun to work their way out of this conceptual dead end. As psychoanalyst John Benjamin has written, the question is not properly nature *or* nurture but "*What* experiences interact with *what* innate variables and universals at *what* time leading to *what* behaviors?" (P. 15.)

Benjamin's effort to correct this point of theory illustrates a familiar process. Individual psychoanalysts often make new discoveries or come up with important reformulations of theory. Their writings constitute the public theory of psychoanalysis. Yet, for all their intrinsic worth, these contributions must remain as idle appendages so long as the basic metapsychology is unchanged, for they cannot be integrated with it. They mislead psychoanalysts into thinking "Well, we've taken that issue into account"—when they have, in fact, passed it by. It is not that most analysts wish to ignore change (some may; it is beside the point), but that they have little choice in the matter. Even though the structural point of view sharply categorizes psychic functions, the clinician will admit: "Actually it's not that simple; id and ego processes overlap. Freud himself said as much." At first glance, the qualification seems to make sense, taking into account the always complex nature of human responses. But on close examination, it becomes evident that such a qualification does not modify the theory so much as contradict it. Psychoanalysts must contend with the fact that a basic nature-versus-nurture dichotomy is inescapably built into the structural point of view.

Remember that psychoanalysis is, first and foremost, a conflict theory. According to the metapsychology, normal human development (as well as neurosis) grows out of a nature-nurture conflict from the very first days of life: the infant's frustration of his need to gratify his instincts instantly leads to the control mechanisms that become the basis for the adult ego. Freud came to emphasize the nature against nurture conflict late in life. He had not always conceived the core of human personality in these terms. True, his was a conflict theory from the beginning, but it took him many years before he was sure that the fundamental collisions of human life were mainly those of nature pitted against nurture. In his earliest formulations (e.g., the topographical point of view), the nature-nurture dichotomy was not drawn nearly so sharply as it was to be later. What were repressed, according to this early theory, were thoughts, memories, and perceptions associated with painful experiences, which were not linked with instinct. Even in his middle period, the nature-nurture opposition was blurred; at that time, Freud opposed instincts to each other (sex in the sense of regulating the preservation of the species, was said to conflict with the instinct for individual survival). This is the doctrine of nature against itself—nature versus nature. But after 1923, the issue was settled to Freud's satisfaction: the nature versus nurture characterization of conflict became formally enshrined in the structural point of view.

Hartmann, we have seen, sensed that the ego-id relationship should not be drawn exactly along the lines of a nature-nurture conflict, and he struggled strenuously with this problem. He solved it to his own satisfaction by introducing the concept of conflict-free ego functions and by emphasizing the biological roots of the ego. Typically, he did not alter the basic ego-id dichotomy itself. Here, once again, Hartmann used his great skill as a theorist to patch up and preserve a doctrine that cries out for more radical change. Let us grant that what psychoanalysts see time and again in their clinical practice is, in fact, a derangement of instinct and a failure to integrate instinctive impulses into acquired personality structures. Here is where the descriptive utility of the ego-id point of view is most convenient. The mischief comes when psychoanalysts then generalize this view of neurosis to normal development and to essential human nature—on the assumption that neurosis is not different in kind from normal development but simply in degree. The result is an upside-down theory; or more precisely, a special theory masquerading as a general theory. Instead of describing neurosis as a special case of normal development, the nature of normal development is deduced from neurosis. The difference is crucial: the observation of a broken family charged with hatred and misunderstanding cannot, by inference, give us a picture of what successful family life is like. This impasse accounts for the absence in the metapsychology of a general theory of structure formation which would apply equally to normal and neurotic structures.

A theory of structure formation is indispensable to a viable metapsychology: it is the study of the how—how culture works in collaboration with evolution to create the psychic life of man. We refer to "structure formation," instead of the more traditional term "learning," because in academic psychology learning has had a narrower meaning, colored by the metaphysical assumptions of behaviorism. Learning, in this latter sense, usually refers to skills and responses acquired by one or another form of conditioning. Structure formation is a broader term, encompassing not only isolated skills but all that is learned by the individual from the interplay of experience with nature. Such structures include traits of personality, habits, language, perceptual abilities, controls over impulse, values, and enduring human bonds with others. All develop in a highly patterned sequence, mediated through social institutions such as the family, the economy, and the larger groupings of tribe, state, and nation.

We now enter what ought to be the most orderly aspect of psychology, for here if anywhere the human sciences can come closest to realizing their dream of an objective science where laws of great generality can be applied to human experience. A systematic statement of such a theory would, however, carry us too far beyond the scope of this work and would, in any case, represent a large-scale scientific enterprise. What follows below, therefore, is a brief sketch of the kinds of laws such a theory would seek to formulate.

Any theory that describes how incomplete psychic structures complete themselves and are influenced by experience should probably start with principles of selectivity. Piaget's principle of assimilation may be taken as an example. The gifted psychoanalytic researcher, Peter Wolff, has written extensively on how this contribution of Piaget's might be integrated into psychoanalysis. Piaget holds to a doctrine of experience impinging upon inborn schemas in accordance with certain general principles of selectivity. He maintains that the inborn schemas themselves are modified by the encounter with experience— a doctrine of great importance. Piaget thereby opens up a fruitful way of tracing the development of each individual's unique cognitive style, yet remaining within a framework that takes into account both innate structures and experience.

One inborn schema described by Piaget relates to how the child assimilates new experience within his limited repertoire of actions. The newborn infant will suck on the breast, the pacifier, the rattle, and almost any object that comes within his grasp. A broad miscellany of objects which we, from an adult perspective, would classify as grossly dissimilar are, according to Piaget, initially experienced by the child as similar because they share the same action pattern, i.e., they are all suckable.

Piaget states that discriminations take place in the second to fourth month when the infant discovers that an object may be suitable for two or more action patterns—it can be seen *and* grasped *and* sucked. Objects then begin to be divorced from their context of pure action and to assume a constancy in their own right.

Piaget states that the infant's every encounter with novelty slightly modifies the schema to which it is assimilated, so that the new is always experienced in relation to a schematized past which it, in turn, changes. He points out that it is not until the seventh or eighth year of life that the child experiences objects as fully differentiated from their original action context, thereby giving childhood memory a totally different quality from adult memory.

Piaget's theory postulates a variety of inborn capabilities, including action patterns such as grasping, looking, and sucking, whose repeatability is inbuilt; schemas for distinguishing between similarity and difference; and innate capabilities for assimilating the new to the old and modifying the old at the same time. These capabilities manifest themselves in an orderly sequence as the child grows, and they bring into development a rudimentary sense of object permanence, the schemas of space, time and causality, and the capacity for language. At each stage, new maturational patterns emerge in accordance with an inborn developmental schedule, modifying the organism's previous patterns of organization. Thus, the child progresses from classification based on action patterns, to classification based on more abstract principles of similarity and difference. If, as Lévi-Strauss suggests, man is the classifying animal, then Piaget has helped us to reconstruct the complex developmental sequences that underlie classification.

We have here an instance of how a general principle of structure formation, closer to observed behavior than the pleasure principle, may be fashioned. The innate side of human life is abundantly represented; it is recognized that, unlike mechanical objects, the "instincts" or inborn schemas are influenced by experience; a wide variety of maturational processes are seen to work together in order to constitute and differentiate objects; and evolving structures take on an increasingly stable, but not wholly rigid, form. Culture is also represented. As Lévi-Strauss has shown, each culture from the most primitive to the most sophisticated, evolves its own modes of classification, which then become part of the child's early experience. Yet, since each person's experience is different, unique individual experience is stamped into every encounter and every classification.

The process of linking nature to experience is shot through and through with selectivity, since every object constituted in perception and every classification based on similarity and difference selects out of the flux of experience certain limited aspects of it, pushing all others into the background. Each basis of classification—whether it relates eagle-hunting to female menstruation, or breast to thumb, or neurotic symptoms to dreams or mathematical sets to one another—represents a high principle of selectivity. No theory of forces is entailed, no strange ghost which lies behind the phenomena is invoked. The description of each individual's history of classification, when fully detailed and generalized, merges imperceptibly into explanation; it becomes explanation when we generalize from inborn schemas plus principles of selectivity plus critical experience to account for the growth of the individual's structures of meaning. We have lost some simplification, but we have gained immensely by faithfulness to the data and have taken a step toward new levels of generality.

Another point of importance to be made about a general theory of structure formation is that pluralism in learning principles is as desirable as pluralism in conceiving forms of innate influences.   •

In psychoanalytic theory, how the individual acquires impulse control is regarded as the core of ego development. (See Chapter Four.) Even if one accepts the classic psychoanalytic model of how impulse control is established, one sees that there is a great deal more going on than can be accounted for by the pleasure principle. There is stimulus generalization, extending from feeding to other forms of satisfaction; there are the effects of reinforcement as the experience is repeated over and over again; there is the development of affective ties with the mother, which may contribute more to the infant's ability to tolerate delay than the failure of hallucinated satisfaction does; there is a complex process of synthesis as various forms of experience are integrated into unified patterns; there is the development of object differentiation, and the mutual exchange of nonverbal signals between mother and child—and many other processes of learning.

At the present stage of knowledge it is important to avoid a false parsimony. We must start off by introducing the broadest possible array of learning principles at comparatively low levels of generality. Piaget's principle of assimilation is but one example of a whole body of principles of selectivity and structure formation. Many others are to be found in the various branches of the human sciences. Behaviorist psychology presents us with a corpus of work almost exclusively concerned with another principle of learning, that of reward and punishment, on which many variants of reinforcement theory are based. Biological studies describing the transmission of genic codes, read in the light of information theory and modern computer technology, promise to open up new insights into the crucial questions of how information is stored, retrieved, and used by the organism. The processes of identification and imitation contain yet another set of principles relating to development: identification with others is perhaps the most powerful agent for shaping human growth and change. We must come to understand much more than we do now about how identification operates in assimilating experience, working it through, unifying it, rejecting some aspects and bringing others into harmonious balance. (One of the many difficulties of Freud's structural point of view is that it is almost impossible to account for identification in ego-id-superego terms.) Even the nineteenth century laws of association by contiguity, although they have less general applicability than was once believed, suggest some useful principles of selectivity.

Over and above these examples, the research of developmental and personality psychologists, cognitive theorists, gestaltists, and others, yields many insights into structure formation. Freud's own descriptions of the primary processes, though underresearched and inadequately conceptualized, also provide instances of laws of structure formation within psychoanalysis itself.

At the present time, then, each of the many fragmented branches of psychology possesses one or two principles of learning and structure formation, which it inevitably overgeneralizes. If psychoanalysis is to realize its ambition of becoming a general psychology, it must break down the barriers to other disciplines, for they cast much light on the full complexity of human adaptation, learning, meaning, and structure formation.

Our proposal for a radical pluralism of learning principles does not imply that human science must abandon its dream of arriving at a few laws of supreme generality. It does suggest that the laborious task of describing the diversity of forms of psychic structure formation must come first. The direction presently taken by contemporary schools of psychology suggests that sooner or later a synthesis will emerge that will integrate the now fragmented descriptions of human learning within some cohesive framework. When such a synthesis is achieved, it is likely, we believe, to be formulated as descriptions of the formal and abstract characteristics of psychic structures. We witness today an ever-increasing emphasis on levels of organization, differentiation, individuation, autonomy, stabilization, etc. These terms describe the morphological characteristics of structures, independently of their content. Here a new kind of map begins to emerge—a map not of forces or conditioning, or even of isolated meanings, but of structures and their formation and interactions.

An emphasis on form permeates those psychoanalytic writings that most directly reflect clinical experience. Sterba, in an important paper written some years ago, describes splitting and separation as fundamental characteristics of ego structure (1934). Nunberg (1936) has written extensively on the synthesizing processes of the ego. More recently, Mahler and other child-development workers have discussed the process of separation-individuation in great detail. In other psychoanalytic writings, the hierarchical structure of human strivings is frequently emphasized; there appears to be an order of priority in human cravings such that the failure to achieve basic feelings of security, continuity of self, and satisfaction of dependency needs, will keep the individual from striving after other satisfactions. Once these primary needs are filled, other motivations appear and become dominant.

Within psychoanalysis itself we catch brief glimpses of fundamental laws of structure formation at the highest levels of generality. The terms are abstract and formal, and yet they denote a morphology of structure radically at variance with the old conception of objects divisible into the sum of their parts and describable in terms of energy and quantity.

Among key formal characteristics of psychic structure are those of:

1. Integration.
2. Separation.
3. Diffusion.
4. Autonomy.
5. Degrees of stability.
6. Hierarchy of levels of organization.
7. Regression.
8. Individuation and fusion.
9. Withdrawal and transcendence.
10. Potential and completion.
11. Deficit.
12. Conflict.
13. Forms of relatedness.

These are different in kind from atomistic units, their combinations and their spatial relationships.

An emphasis on the formal characteristics of structure formation is congenial to the philosophical position we have taken: they exemplify a conception of nature as constantly creating new forms and structures at every conceivable level of organization—organic and inorganic forms of life, intrapsychic processes, interpersonal relations, and social and cultural institutions. They apply to the broad sweep of evolution as well as to the brief span of an adolescent love affair. They encompass relationships as diverse as the therapeutic alliance, the ties of old friendships, and the loyalty of soldiers to their army. And they apply to simple structures such as muscular coordination as well as to complex structures such as self-respect and neurosis.

Freedom and Cure

Thus far in this chapter, we have discussed two basic flaws in the structural point of view: the faulty psychoanalytic conception of instinct built around the id concept, and the lack of an adequate theory of structure formation to describe how nature and nurture work together. By means of such concepts as "developmentals" we have illustrated how these difficulties might be overcome. We turn now to the third fundamental objection to the structural point of view: the fact that it leaves out any conception of the human person as a whole (as distinct from the sum of his parts) and hence any concrete, detailed account of the nature of human freedom. One chief consequence of such an omission is that psychoanalytic cure is almost impossible to define or assess. And since curing people is what psychoanalysis is all about (at least as a profession), the problem is severe.

A discussion of cure will lead us toward a new metapsychological conception of man as a free being. For it is in enhancing the scope of his freedom that all the aspects of man's being previously discussed—man as biologically limited, as creature of his culture, and as individual ego—are brought to their fulfillment.

For a discipline that prides itself on its determinism, the assumption of freedom plays a surprisingly crucial role in psychoanalysis. Just how crucial it is becomes obvious when we look at the psychoanalytic doctrine of cure. What it means to "cure" a person by psychoanalytic methods has changed considerably from Freud's early probes into buried trauma to today's more subtle—and far more ambiguous—notions of cure. Beneath all the ambiguity, however, one point stands out sharply and clearly: as it is understood today, psychoanalytic cure, whatever else it may be, seeks to enlarge the scope of the individual's freedom. And it seeks to do so in large measure by bringing him face to face with certain truths about himself.

Psychoanalysis stands squarely in a classical Western tradition that goes all the way back to the Bible. In the words of Scripture, "You shall know the truth and the truth shall make you free." There is indicated in this saying an intimate and essential connection between truth and freedom. Within philosophy, the same connection appears at the dawn of Western thinking, when Socrates states that the unexamined life is not worth living. In our own epoch, Heidegger has stressed this same close relationship between truth and freedom. Man's understanding of himself, says Heidegger, is an essential part of his being. If a man conceives of himself as a robot or as a free being, the difference is not merely between two theoretical positions but between two concrete modes of experiencing one's life.

Truth and freedom—and truth as the way into freedom—have been the two great themes of Western philosophy. They happen also to be the real, though hidden, themes of Freud's own achievement. Psychoanalysis is in this sense an elaboration of the rationalist, humanist views of the Enlightenment: it extols reason as a method of understanding, and also as a means ultimately of exercising our freedom. What Freud built was essentially a rational method for getting at truths about the self in the interests of greater freedom. But what psychoanalysts mean by truth and by freedom is not the same as what Socrates meant, or what the philosophers of the Enlightenment meant, or what Heidegger meant.

How psychoanalysts actually use truth and freedom to cure people is probably the most ambiguous part of this whole thoroughly ambiguous discipline. As a result, every facet of psychoanalytic cure is shot through and through with ambiguity—its objectives, its methods, and its degree of practical success (or failure).

With respect to objectives, Freud himself is responsible for one major misunderstanding. His famous dictum on cure runs: "Where id is, there shall ego be"; and he adds to this Delphic pronouncement one of his most striking metaphors: "It is reclamation work—like draining the Zuyder Zee." The work of analysis here would be simply to dredge up all the silt that lies buried in the unconscious. This slogan for the aims of psychoanalytic cure can be paraphrased in a number of ways: (1) "Where impulses are, there controls shall be"; (2) "Where the pleasure principle is, there shall the reality principle be"; (3) "Where instincts are, there the structures formed by learning and culture shall be." Though each of these phrases conveys slightly different shades of meaning, the core idea in all of them is the same: the dominance of the instinctive is to be lessened. We are to recognize the great power of the instincts and acknowledge their all-pervasiveness—but all this merely as a means of bringing the instincts under the ego's control.

This view of therapy and cure is, as we have seen, thoroughly in line with Freud's conception of ego and id. Since these two are taken to be antithetical in most neurotic conflicts, and since the forces of the id are blind, to cure a person one must build up the strength of his ego and its control over his archaic nature. When Freud speaks of the "reality principle" as set over the "pleasure principle," the emphasis upon the former is almost always anti-instinctual. Here, Freud reveals himself to be unwittingly the prisoner of another cultural tradition besides the scientific materialism of the Helmholtz circle. His reality principle is the Protestant ethic incarnate, with all of its stress on the primacy of impulse control over expressiveness, on the virtues of husbanding one's resources prudently for the future, and on the high value of work and calculation. Of course, these values are not to be lightly dismissed, for they have helped to create a great civilization. But clearly, psychoanalytic cure is unfairly represented as a prolonged struggle to gain control over one's impulses so that a hostile world can be prudently milked of a little satisfaction. Given the present state of disrepair in our society, it should be recognized that the values of the Protestant ethic are subject to questioning (certainly our college youth are subjecting them to downright disrespectful questioning).

Once we move out of the aura of Freud's genius to his gifted but more literal-minded followers, the extreme ethnocentricity of this formulation of cure becomes more evident. Thus, we find the biographer of Freud, the noted psychoanalyst Ernest Jones, presenting the criteria of psychoanalytic cure in these terms: "Mental health and the capacity for continence go together," he writes. In psychoanalytic therapy, the patient, to gain control of himself, "must have dealt satisfactorily with the evil and aggressive side of his nature." (In Glover, 1958, p. 332.) Such an interpretation of the slogan, "where id is, there shall ego be," shows its Protestant-ethic implications far more vividly than Freud's own language.

Jones's discussion of cure also illustrates how the metalanguage adds to the ambiguity of this as well as other psychoanalytic topics. Describing the patient's desires to enhance his own self-confidence and well-being, Jones adds: "By well-being I mean, of course, the potential capacity for enjoyment and happiness since the actual amount of happiness obtainable will not depend on internal factors only. This objective sense signifies that *more energy is at the disposal of the ego than was previously, although there is correspondingly less cathexis of id and superego . . . independent of ego control.*" (Metalanguage in italics.) Once the burden of assessing cure is shifted from subjective well-being to measuring how much new energy has been released by therapy for use by the ego, we might as well kiss goodbye to any realistic hope of fixing the meaning of cure, or evaluating it.

Jones wrote these words some years ago. More recently, one of Freud's most prominent followers, Sandor Rado, has taken a fresh crack at translating Freud's cryptic formula. The goal of psychoanalytic cure, Rado states, is "enlightened hedonic control of [the patient's] behavior on the level of self-reliance and aspirations." (In Weigert, 1962, p. 260.) Rado's phrase "enlightened hedonic control" captures the meaning of the psychoanalytic reality principle precisely. We see in this formula several converging themes. There is the classical Freudian theme of strengthening the battalions of the ego to counterbalance instinctual forces; there is the Protestant-ethic theme implicit in the concept of the reality principle; and there is the theme of man pictured as a kind of human centaur—a creature with a beastly lower half, surging with animalistic urges, and an upper half full of rational virtue. The humanist tradition tends to exalt the "upper" half, which it equates with man's unique characteristics, and at the same time to denigrate the "lower" half, which he shares with other species. Such a view must lead ultimately to a conception of man as most human when he is most estranged from the natural roots of his being. It is a peculiar and one-sided view, wholly arbitrary in the low valuation it places on that side of our nature which we purportedly share with the rest of creation.

Though we may disagree with it, the Jones-Rado interpretation of Freud is quite clear. However, many other strands of psychoanalytic thought are vehemently at odds with it. Freud and his followers have always rejected equating psychoanalytic cure with any ideology, good or bad. Quite apart from the virtues of the Protestant ethic, psychoanalysis is explicitly agnostic on the subject of what positive values the patient should embrace. Freud resisted basing a *Weltanschauung* on the findings of psychoanalysis, since he was alert to the dangers of unwittingly "selling" an ideology to patients. At its best, psychoanalytic therapy does not suggest what the patient should do with his life; it seeks simply to leave him freer than he was to do what he will.

Few psychoanalysts, therefore, consciously equate the cure of neurosis with the patient's acceptance of specific values. Indeed, psychoanalysts constantly warn each other against interjecting their personal values into the therapeutic situation. While a value-free therapy may be neither possible in practice nor even desirable in theory, it is difficult to think of an experienced psychoanalyst today who would confuse Jones's equation of continence with virtue, and instinct with evil.

The ambiguity in objectives, therefore, centers on the relationship of cure to control over impulse. When psychoanalysis became popular in this country in the 1920's, it stimulated a revolution in sexual mores that is still going on—a movement to encourage the freer expression of sex in particular and impulse in general. Nor was this interpretation by the general public a misreading of psychoanalysis. In discussing cure, the English psychoanalyst Charles Rycroft stresses as the main objective of mental health that it puts the patient once more in touch with "his basic inner nature," his instincts. The essence of cure, Rycroft insists, is overcoming alienation from instinct. He admits, of course, that there is much ignorance and disagreement about what instinct in man really is. But Rycroft's experience with "instinct" as it unfolds phenomenologically in his practice tells him that the core of neurosis is not the inability of the ego to control instinct but our alienation from our own "inner nature." Between Rycroft's view and Rado's stress on hedonic control lies a world of difference.

We must emphasize that we are not pointing to contradictions. One can reconcile both points of view—gaining greater control over instinct *and* overcoming alienation from one's own instinctive nature. We are simply making clear that such varied formulations add up to a highly ambiguous statement of the objectives of psychoanalytic cure.

Even when we turn from these theoretical considerations to the clinical aspects of cure, the ambiguity, if anything, increases. Psychoanalyst Anthony Storr, in a perceptive account of this subject, is most lucid when he discusses what psychoanalytic cure does *not* mean. Storr emphasizes the difference between mental illness and physical disease. Obviously, or perhaps not so obviously, one does not eliminate emotional distress and despair in the same sense that one eliminates a diseased appendix. We are able to grasp quite readily what is involved in removing an appendix: the patient feels pain and distress in a certain area of his body, the doctor diagnoses the complaint, the surgeon performs the operation, the pain disappears, the patient leaves the hospital feeling fit and healthy. Psychoanalysis does not work this way.

Storr stresses the little-known fact that in psychoanalysis the cure of symptoms is infrequent and even irrelevant. Most psychoanalysts can cite a favorite case where a neurotic symptom (e.g., adult bed-wetting) dramatically disappeared shortly after the patient began therapy. But, Storr states: "The majority of patients who present themselves to psychoanalysis cannot expect that their symptoms will easily depart. Or, if this should happen, that they will then be freed from emotional problems and willing or able to discontinue their analytic treatment." (P. 52.) Unlike a diseased appendix, most neurotic symptoms are not "parts of the patient which he can well be without."

As an example, Storr cites the symptom of agoraphobia common to postadolescent girls who are afraid to leave the house or cross the street or go anywhere unaccompanied. Such a symptom may be the only visible sign of a deep-rooted character disorder that pervades the girl's entire being:

Accompanying her overt fears of being left alone without support, it will regularly be discovered that she is frightened of any instinctual response which might incur parental disapproval. The fear of crossing the street alone will often be associated with fears that men will make sexual advances to her, and also that she will respond to such approaches. It will also be discovered that she is fearful of her own aggressive feelings toward her mother. If at an earlier stage in her development she had been able to display that normal degree of self-assertiveness which is essential if children are to reach independence, she would have learned to be more self-reliant. In such cases, however, it is generally discovered that the mother has both discouraged a show of active rebellion against her authority, and has also over-protected the child by habitually doing for her innumerable daily tasks which she should have learned to carry out for herself.

Note that in this brief description, Storr not only generalizes the emotional problem beyond the symptoms of agoraphobia, but he also makes reference to inherent human nature ("that normal degree of self-assertiveness which is essential if children are to reach independence"). He points out that her symptoms are inevitably linked with the patient's whole personality and that success in curing the agoraphobia would not relieve the patient of most of her emotional problems—a conclusion that unfortunately holds true of most neurotic symptoms.

We cannot, therefore, find in the alleviation of neurotic symptoms a clear and unambiguous definition of the objectives of cure. The reader will see how far psychoanalysis has traveled from the simplicities of Miss Lucy's hysteria to the ambiguities of the modern girl's fear of mother.

Storr also discusses other nondefinitions of psychoanalytic cure. One traditional demand psychoanalysts make of "cured" patients is that they achieve "full genitality"—a blessed state of sexual maturity. As he points out, however, a Don Juan, who is surely possessed of "full genitality" in the narrow technical sense, would not be considered by psychoanalysts to have reached maturity but merely to have remained fixated at an early narcissistic phase of development. Such phrases as "full genitality" mask a perfectionistic demand for an ideal state of mental health of which genital sexuality is only a sign. These ideals, when made explicit, are seen to be unattainable—not only for the patient but for most mortal human beings, including psychoanalysts. Similar ideal standards of perfection are hidden behind terms like "full emotional maturity," "self-realization," "self-actualization," and "mature object-relationships."

In discussing the topic of cure, the gifted and utterly sympathetic psychoanalyst, Edith Weigert, approvingly cites Rado's prescription of "enlightened hedonic control." But then she adds: "the goal of psychoanalysis is the adaptation of the patient to the world in which he is thrown." (Weigert, p. 254.) And then, a few pages later, she quotes the language of Alfred North Whitehead as he describes that "reverence and respect for man as man which . . . secures liberty of thought and action for the upward adventures of life." Instilling this reverence and respect for man as man is the true goal, says Weigert, of psychoanalytic cure (p. 267). These are noble words, and they may well reflect the ideals of many psychoanalysts. But one would find it difficult to abstract from the varied objectives of enlightened hedonic control, better adaptation to the society, and reverence for man as man, any unambiguous sense of what in the world psychoanalysts are up to when they seek to cure their patients.

Incidentally, in recent years some resistance to psychoanalysis has built up among college youth: they react against Weigert's implication that the purpose of psychoanalysis is to help the individual adjust to a society which many of them believe to be seriously flawed. Here, once again, the ambiguities of psychoanalysis have led to misunderstanding. In practice, psychoanalysis is neutral on the issue of social change versus conservatism. A better adaptation to the society may be a consequence of cure; but it is certainly not its objective.

Let us now turn to another kind of ambiguity—the aura of doubt about the practical success of psychoanalytic cure. Many unfriendly critics like to point out that scientific assessments of psychoanalytic cure are either nonexistent or inconclusive or negative. And they are joined in this harsh judgment by some psychoanalysts. Storr, who is a partisan of psychoanalysis, states: "The evidence that psychoanalysis cures anybody of anything is so shaky as to be practically nonexistent." (P. 58.) The American Psychoanalytic Association had a survey made some years ago on the number of cures effected by analytic treatment; it is rumored that the report was never issued because the results were so depressing. One will also find that the most experienced psychoanalysts often express themselves diffidently and indeed, pessimistically, on psychoanalysis as a practical method of cure. Apart from the length of time it takes and its high cost, these experienced practitioners are all too aware of the stubborn and intractable character of man's neuroses and how little can be done, often, to change them.

One wonders, however, whether these psychoanalysts, quite unwittingly, may be underestimating their own accomplishments by subscribing to artificial standards. Some of the objectives psychoanalysts set for themselves call, in effect, for a cure of the human condition itself. But is there any cure for that, except death? Moreover, by subscribing to their antagonists' requirements, they may be introducing standards that are irrelevant to what psychoanalytic therapy does achieve. For at the same time that experienced analysts express pessimism about its curative powers, they also cite one instance after another of patients' lives that have been made freer by psychoanalysis. The apparent contradiction may come from an unwitting equation of freedom with happiness and pleasure (as in the Jones-Rado formulations). The transition from a neurotic state of being to a free state of being—an exquisitely meaningful, if intangible, change—does not always bring greater happiness. It may, and often does. But it may also bring a less-than-blissful response to life's real problems. Awakened from his preoccupations with his own private hangups, the postneurotic may confirm for himself what he has long suspected: that the world which he is now prepared to take straight is no bargain. Greater freedom may even, as we point out in the final chapter of this book, bring tragedy with it.

Any rigorous measure of psychoanalytic cure should not, therefore, be based on increased happiness or on the disappearance of symptoms or on abstract ideals of perfect mental health. The sole standard that can be brought to bear is the person's ability to confront the human condition with greater freedom from neurotic distress. It is not an exaggeration to state that no valid measures of psychoanalytic success (or failure) exist today, since both the criteria of cure and the methods for measuring it are yet to be formulated.

The ambiguity that surrounds the notion of cure is paralleled by ambiguities in the methods that psychoanalysts use to bring about change in their patients' lives. These methods are many: and though they are all part of the "talking cure," each psychoanalyst utilizes some or all of the following "therapeutic agents." Which of these is emphasized and which is pushed into the background is a matter of individual style.

1. *The transference and its interpretation*. The patient projects his neurotic feelings and attitudes upon the analyst, who functions as a surrogate parent, sibling, etc., around whom the neurotic constellation was originally formed. As this past is relived, its distortions become clear to patient as well as physician and hence susceptible to interpretation. Interpretation of the transference is today the most universally accepted agent of cure in psychoanalysis.

2. *Insight*. It is possible to relive the past emotionally through the transference without gaining true insight. Conversely, insight (into his own personality and his problems) can be achieved by the patient, as it often is, outside of the transference relation. Hence the expanding of insight has to be listed as a separate therapeutic agent at the disposal of the analyst.

3. *Working through*. Although this is usually spoken of in connection with "working through" the transference, it should be singled out as a separate therapeutic agent by itself. Most of the time spent in psychoanalysis is devoted to working through a wide range of feelings, attitudes, and changes that do not fall strictly within the orbit of the transference relation.

4. *The therapeutic alliance*. This is the most elusive but perhaps the most important of all the curative agents, since it already involves the notion of the patient as a free being. The patient chooses to collaborate with the doctor in the task of curing himself, and entrusts himself to another human being with whom he develops a genuine relationship, as distinct from an artificial "transference" relationship.

5. *The adoption of some general life-view*. What will emerge from the prolonged and arduous confrontation with himself may be a new set of life-values for the patient. He will now have a new set of meanings—some general interpretive scheme—by which to understand the world around him and his place in it. We might almost call this a philosophic change, if philosophy is understood as the totality of one's concrete life-attitudes. This is one of the most underesti-

mated agents of change in psychoanalytic and other forms of therapy, and it is easy to see why: it seems too diffuse, formless, and intangible in comparison with the more specific devices of psychoanalysis. Yet, in a good many cases, it may be the most effective agent in bringing about change.

6. *Abreaction*. In effect, this is a modern version of the ancient concept of catharsis. One becomes purged of a troubling or burdensome emotion. Today abreaction is regarded as a relatively minor agent of psychoanalytic cure.

All of these varied therapeutic means work toward helping the individual to achieve a greater degree of freedom to change himself. For the moment, let us think of such change in purely negative terms as freedom *from*; i.e., the psychoanalyst seeks to free the patient from being whipped about by depressions, passions, and obsessions rooted in buried experiences of the past. And yet, paradoxically, psychoanalysts are ever mindful of the conclusion reached by Freud and reiterated even more strongly by Rapaport to the effect that psychic structures, once formed, rarely change. Here, once again, we confront the most impenetrable ambiguity. If change is the objective and yet change is not possible, where are we? Perhaps, if the individual cannot change himself, he can at least change his circumstances. If a man lives on a mountain and has a fear of heights, presumably he can move to a flatter terrain. But here, too, change is blocked. Psychoanalysts recognize that people are rarely cured of deep-seated neuroses by changes in circumstance. The fellow who moves off the mountain carries his fears with him: he creates his own heights. The repetition compulsion, one of Freud's most brilliant insights, suggests that people will return again and again to gnaw away at the problems that obsess them, recreating and reliving the troubles of the past however painful they may be. As long as something fundamental is unresolved in a person's life, he will come back to it whatever his practical change of circumstance may be.

To complicate matters still further, some of these therapeutic means may help to achieve freedom for the individual without truth necessarily being at issue. The emotional reliving of experiences in the transference relationship, the adoption of a congenial interpretive framework, and the ability to relate

meaningfully to another person in the therapeutic alliance—
these may be vital methods for advancing therapy, but their
relationship to truth remains ambiguous. On the other hand,
the gaining of valid insights into one's past in the context of
emotions stimulated by the transference, the abreaction that
accompanies the lifting of repressions, the integration of truths
about the self in "working through"—these are direct routes
to enhancing freedom by means of truth. Note, however, that
the kind of truth at issue is not merely a theoretical and conceptual affair. On the contrary, it has to do with very special
kinds of truths about the self. Not Truth with a capital T, but
plural truths, and for the most part truths of a gritty and unpleasant kind—truths of the toilet, of sibling hatred, of sexual
conflict. More important still: the truth that secures deliverance
from one's neurotic demons cannot be a merely detached one.
What is at the core of the whole psychoanalytic process is *lived*
truth: the patient must carry through the arduous course of
his treatment from day to day, endure the turmoil of the transference process, and work it through. There is no intellectual
shortcut to cure. In some cases, a brilliant intelligence can be an
obstacle to the patient's becoming open to the truths that could
make him free. Only the lived truth, gained through the labor
and sweat of life itself (as part of which we must count the
analytic process), can help to enlarge individual freedom.

Our discussion of cure lets us see that the psychoanalytic concepts of "cure," "change," "truth," and "freedom" are inextricably interwoven with each other, but ambiguous and even
paradoxical in their interrelationships. Psychoanalysis seeks to
enhance man's freedom by truth, and yet some of its methods
do not depend on truth. Its concepts of cure involve "internal"
change, and yet the theory insists that psychic structures, once
formed, do not change. The changes at which it aims have
essentially to do with enhancing man's freedom, and yet the
theory denies that freedom is possible. Some of the most experienced and thoughtful psychoanalysts are diffident, if not
downright pessimistic, about the practical success of psychoanalytic therapy, and yet these same persons believe that they
help their patients and that their therapy leads to profound human changes. Is there any positive resolution for these ambiguities and paradoxes? We believe that there is, and that it

centers on the concrete and specific meaning of human freedom in the psychoanalytic context. Psychoanalysts have too long avoided the subject because there is no place for it in their metapsychology. Clearly, however, the issue is the very core of psychoanalytic therapy.

THE MEANINGS OF PSYCHOANALYTIC FREEDOM

In the present scientific climate of opinion, it is no longer so disreputable as it once was to presuppose human freedom. Several decades ago, to do so would have seemed like a denial of science itself. In the 1920's and 1930's, when positivism was at the peak of its prestige, if one started with its premise of scientific materialism it inevitably followed that to believe in freedom was to deny the lawfulness of nature. At that time modern physics was still too new to convey the significance of its break with Newtonian philosophy. And psychoanalysis was too new to reveal its deeper implications. Paradoxically, those who believed that man's free choices were nothing but epiphenomena caused by invisible forces, were able to hail Freud's discoveries as confirmations of their own philosophy of science.

Today, the supports for rigid determinism have grown less firm. Logical positivism as an ideology has receded in influence; and even though the philosophy of scientific materialism remains entrenched, the chief effect of the "consensus" is to reduce drastically its generality of application. Whatever aspects of the world of objects this philosophy may illuminate, it casts no light on the nature of human experience. Once we bypass scientific materialism, there is no longer any need to assume that a belief in freedom undermines faith in the lawfulness of nature. The apparent contradiction comes from an overly restrictive view of lawfulness. It disappears once we break the bad habit of treating the lawfulness of human life in strict analogy with physical objects.

The revolution in modern physics has also helped to put the issue of freedom in better perspective; a good deal of the traditional argument over determinism versus freedom now appears quite beside the point. It is not that physics has established the reality of human freedom; any such proof would be beyond its scientific province and competence. Nevertheless, the changes in physics have altered the intellectual situation in which philosophers felt called upon to prove freedom against what seemed to be the overwhelming authority of the most exact of the sciences. In the past, a great philosopher like Kant thought that he had to ground freedom on the existence of a type of causality and type of causal agent—the non-empirical or noumenal Self—that stood outside the rigid chain of Newtonian causation. In contrast to such heroic lifting by one's own bootstraps, the philosopher today can simply discern freedom as a plain empirical fact within the day-to-day world of man and his actions. Some parts of physics (e.g., traditional molar mechanics) postulate determinism, other parts (e.g., nuclear physics) postulate indeterminism. In both cases the postulate is not an ultimate revelation about the realities underlying experience, but a definition of the kinds of entities with which the particular branch of science is concerned. When physical theory is thus understood, the problem posed by human freedom is no longer that of proving its existence but of describing its features as they exhibit themselves within our ordinary experience.

Finally, it should be clear by now that as psychoanalysis has developed, its findings hardly suggest that human freedom does not exist. On the contrary; its integrity as a branch of the medical profession depends upon presupposing that the patient's freedom can be enhanced through psychoanalytic therapy. Certain other forms of therapy do not presuppose human freedom. Behavioral therapy does not: it seeks to modify psychic structures in a somewhat mechanical fashion by systematically manipulating the stimulus situation. Various forms of drug therapy surely do not presuppose human freedom: they work mainly by physico-chemical interventions. There is, of course, nothing incompatible among these various approaches. They complement each other, each one taking a different route to accomplishing a similar end. But psychoanalysis and psychotherapy, far from refuting freedom, show us its specific nature . . . and its limits. Of course our freedom is limited by unconscious motives—just as it is limited by the frailty of our bodies and by the human condition itself. Freedom is meaningless unless defined by its constraints. Constraints characterize all things under the sun. But to be constrained is not to be non-existent; a denial of human freedom on scientific grounds is a metaphysical leap, not an empirical judgment based on facts.

As the scientific climate of opinion continues to change, in the coming decades we can expect a more relaxed attitude towards human freedom as part of nature's lawfulness. It is not too much to hope that in the near future arguments about whether human freedom is or is not compatible with science will appear beside the point. Students will say: "Why are they flogging that dead horse?" And when students of scientific psychology and scientific sociology and scientific psychoanalysis do finally arrive at this judgment, then one of the strangest eras in our intellectual history will have passed from the scene. We are now, in fact, reaching its end; a tradition of three hundred years is slowly dying. Psychoanalysis has been prominent among the chief victims of that tradition. Uniquely as a science of man, it has struggled with the existential core of the human person; and at that core, the place of human freedom is unmistakable.

What, then, are the specific forms of human freedom revealed by psychoanalytic experience?

FREEDOM AS A STRUCTURE OF MEANINGS

To begin with, freedom as revealed by psychoanalysis most emphatically does not mean what Jean-Paul Sartre defines as freedom in his version of existential psychoanalysis. A rather odd irony haunts a theory like Sartre's that would make freedom a pure and absolute spontaneity. Such freedom, Sartre declares, opens dizzying prospects before us. It is like the vertigo we might face on the edge of a cliff: we can hurl ourselves into the abyss, since in fact nothing prevents us from so doing. And just as abruptly, in his life the individual can tear himself up by the roots and launch himself, out of pure freedom, into another career or path. The irony in such dizzying and absolute freedom is that it dialectically cancels itself and turns into non-freedom. Pure spontaneity is no more the basis of freedom than would be the undetermined jump of an electron in the brain that sets off an unpredictable chain of neural events. Sartre would be above offering such a bit of popular physics as a justification for freedom; yet his own theory, supposedly conceived under existentialist blessings, has just as little to say about how freedom can and does function in the continuity in being of the individual person.

The traditional way of talking about freedom has perhaps led to this emphasis upon freedom as the unpredictable jump. The question of freedom has usually been put in the form of asking whether an individual is free to follow one or another course of action. Two roads diverge in the yellow wood, as Robert Frost puts it, and whether we take one or the other will "make all the difference." No doubt, the anguish of choice does strike more forcefully upon us in such a situation, and consequently it would be the aspect that would claim most attention when people come to think about the subject at all. This tendency was also abetted by the penchant of philosophers to think in the pattern of simple location: one would seem to be pinning down this whole matter of freedom more precisely if one could reduce it to the question of whether an individual human body can move in one path or another. These tendencies have, nevertheless, served to conceal the more significant and pervasive kind of freedom at work within a human life.

In Dostoevski's *Crime and Punishment* the young hero Raskolnikov chooses himself, for very intellectual reasons, as a murderer. He commits the crime but cannot live with it. His "free" choice has been at violent odds with his own unconscious ego identity. For Raskolnikov is also a sensitive, compassionate, and generous person who weeps at the flogging of a horse, helps a wounded drunk, and compulsively thrusts his last kopeks on a poor family. To be sure, these gestures are spontaneous; and Raskolnikov, retreating back into his own mind, can sneer and jeer at them. But that is just the measure of how far his conscious mind is from knowing what he himself is really like as a person. Would Raskolnikov have been less free if he had recognized that it was impossible for him to live with the murder, and therefore had chosen not to do it? Of course not; and Dostoevski's whole novel makes it clear that this godlike and Sartrian stroke of freedom was in fact the outcome of sickness and aberration.

At the end of the road, in his Siberian prison, Raskolnikov finally finds enlightenment; feelings that had been unconscious and inaccessible to him break through at last, and his first response is to try to understand them intellectually:

> But he could not think for long together of anything that evening, and he could not have analyzed anything consciously; he was simply feeling. Life had stepped into the place of theory and something quite different would work itself out in his mind.

"Life had stepped into the place of theory." Dostoevski could not have put it more simply or more effectively. Through that contact with the hitherto unconscious and inaccessible current of his life, Raskolnikov has become more, not less, intelligent; more, not less, free. The level of consciousness itself has been raised through the emerging of the unconscious.

To turn from literature to more mundane matters, consider the case of a friend or neighbor who has so settled into his life that he would not think of changing it. Tomorrow, hopefully, will resemble today; and such variation in the days as may come, again hopefully, will not be too far from a regular pattern. Is such a man deprived of freedom? Would more freedom come into his life only if he could violently pull up stakes, remove himself to another scene, and launch himself on another way of life? Not at all. So long as what he is doing is meaningful to him, he is pursuing his path day by day in freedom. Routine and habit are not in essential conflict with freedom; they seem to be a prison only when this daily round has become meaningless. Then the openness of the future closes and the world shuts in around us. But in what does this openness consist? Not in the fact that there is a jet plane waiting to take us in a few hours to a spot on the other side of the globe in order to pursue an altogether different way of life. In such frantic attempts at flight we only manage to flee back to servitude to a self that is still imprisoned. Human freedom is not a question of enlarging the sphere of our physical capabilities; it may, in fact, persist through a life as externally routine as Immanuel Kant's, by whose daily walks his fellow townsmen set their clocks.

In our discussion of cure we stressed the negative side of

psychoanalytic freedom—freedom from the paralysis, the misery, the depression, the hangups of the developmental past. There is, however, a positive quality to psychoanalytic freedom. We can best describe it in the language of one of our key ontological principles: psychoanalytic freedom is a shift in mode of being. A neurotic person typically lives in a world whose quality and meaning to him will change in essential ways if he can break out of his neurotic bind. He may even retain some of his neurotic symptoms (like Freud's own phobias), but his world will have changed in a decisive fashion. Where he was closed off before, he now becomes open. A neurotic person is a prisoner: the bars may be invisible but they are there. To be neurotic is to be locked in—into oneself, into compulsive rituals, into depressions, into distorted ways of thinking, into repetitive fantasies, into false states of exaltation, into relationships that repeat *ad nauseam* old patterns of response. The ways one can be an emotional prisoner are infinitely varied. The transition from a neurotic state of being into a free one (relatively free, at any rate) opens up a new world of possibilities, the possibilities of freedom in the most practical, mundane sense of the word.

During a considerable early period of treatment the psychoanalyst will usually recommend, and recommend quite firmly, that the patient make no radical change in his life-situation, such as getting married, divorced, shifting his occupation, or any other abrupt response to what may loom as the more galling facts of existence at the moment. Analytic experience has made it all too clear that in most cases the trouble lies "inside" the patient and not in the external situation on which he is venting his frustrations and confusions. Besides, if he is going to change his external way of life, it is most prudent to make the decision when the smoke and clouds of inner turmoil have lightened a little. It is essentially toward a change in the mode of being of the patient that the analyst is working.

Psychoanalysts rarely write about this dimension of change. They offer a theory of the mechanism by which it is supposed to be achieved: the working off of repressed material in the transference, and the incorporation of newly released energies into the structures of the ego. But even if this description were valid it would only tell us how the patient came to be changed, not what the change consisted in. This is why evaluation studies of psychoanalytic cure are so elusive and misleading, since they do not capture the quality of change in mode of being.

Quite often change will be described in terms of what happens to the patient's symptoms. But as we have seen, the symptoms are frequently beside the point, whether they remain or disappear. That patient's trouble is at once more diffused and more total; his sense of frustration is general: the world is closed and flat around him, his life has ceased to be meaningful. Obviously, it is more difficult to describe what the lifting of this condition consists in. Wittgenstein has remarked with considerable insight that "when a man has passed through a period in which he found life meaningless and now has come to find it meaningful again, he cannot say wherein the change consists." Quite right; he cannot specify the change in terms of things, objects, or particular behavior. The course of his external life may not have altered at all; he remains married or unmarried as the case may be, he has the same job, lives in the same place, etc., etc. It is a change that cannot be specified in terms of any simply located object or objects within his world. And yet, his whole world has changed.* Here in the simple difference of these two statements we are at the heart of the matter: his world has indeed changed; it has become open to him even though he pursues his old regular path through it.

Of course, this kind of change will seem an "intangible" one for people who can think only in terms of solid and simply located objects. But to the patient it may be a change that is, quite simply, the difference between life and death. And it is freedom in this fundamental sense to which the whole dialogue between analyst and patient ultimately appeals, and on which it is ultimately predicated. It is in examining the nature of this transition from a neurotic to a freer mode of being that we begin to clarify the ambiguities which relate truth to freedom and freedom to truth. Man is free insofar as he can become open to the possibility of truth. The truth may make us free, but the converse is, perhaps, the more striking insight: freedom—

---

* It may be noted in passing that practical research techniques for measuring such intangibles do exist, if only psychoanalysts would avail themselves of them.

the shift from neurotic to a freer mode of being—makes truth itself possible for us.

These are highly abstract formulations; yet the practicing psychoanalyst, who must often wait for a long time for the patient to become open to the meaningfulness of some disclosure, will know that this is the basic freedom without which all the tedious and painful labor of psychoanalysis would never bear fruit.

On this issue perhaps the most powerful human document ever written is Tolstoi's *My Confession,* which ought to be required reading for any psychoanalyst. In middle age Tolstoi felt himself suddenly assailed by the futility of life and the meaninglessness of the world. He was in excellent health at the time; he could work vigorously in the fields alongside the peasants and then concentrate for hours at his writing desk; he had already won great fame as an author; he was rich; and he had a wife and children who catered to him. Yet with all this, the feeling of meaninglessness struck him with such power that it was almost like the physical sensation of being thrust into a dark sack. Still, with that extraordinary energy and directness that was characteristic of his genius, he flung himself headfirst at this mysterious impasse, reading and pondering all that philosophers and religious teachers had to say about life and its meaning—but always coming out again at the bottom of that closed sack.

In the midst of this personal anguish, Tolstoi pauses at one point, turns his gaze from himself to mankind at large, and observes that there are millions of simple folk, like the peasants he knew, who endure hardships, raise families, and pass the torch of life on to their descendants. These people show no signs of faltering in the continuous struggle for the life of the species. They have experienced Tolstoi's question, but have found a response to it through "instinct." (Not, of course, in the sense of sexual and aggressive drives, but in the broader meaning toward which Rycroft is groping.) Their answer, as Tolstoi puts it, comes through "life itself." And by this response, they are able to stand open to the larger life of mankind, to the past of ancestors and the future of descendants. They are free to recognize and respond to the most elemental truths of life. Even when we discount this nineteenth century romanticizing of peasant life, the essential value of Tolstoi's insight comes through to us. Truth and freedom, and the truth of freedom, are not mere intellectual exercise, but a basic response to life.

The testimony of these two great Russian novelists, Dostoevski and Tolstoi—both overlapping contemporaries of Freud—focus, as Freud himself did, on man's "inner nature," but the meanings they ascribe to it are quite different.

Another facet of psychoanalytic freedom as a structure of meanings is exhibited when we relate it to identity. And here we come back, as we have so often, to the thought of Erik Erikson.

One of Erikson's contributions is to have seen psychic life in analogy with the epigenetic development of a biological organism. Epigenesis implies that later stages of development are not contained completely or mechanically in earlier stages. The later phase is a genuine and further development—sometimes even a startling metamorphosis—of the earlier situation, though it will be preformed and shaped by the earlier stage. It is the identical individual who goes through these phases, despite the fact that characteristic traits and problems at one stage may be markedly different from what they are at another. (Analogously, it is the identical insect who passes from caterpillar to butterfly even though the latter is so extraordinary a transformation of the former that a person ignorant of the metamorphoses of this species would not recognize it as in any way the same creature.)

Thus, in Erikson's scheme, it is the identical individual who is first the helpless infant dependent upon maternal care, from which he emerges either capable or not of basic trust; who passes through the various childhood stages of initiative, guilt, and the struggle for competence; the identical individual who at puberty goes through the first full-scale and explicit crisis of identity; and the same individual who in old age encounters the crisis of integrity—the last battle to retain his human wholeness against the threat of meaninglessness and non-being that looms with his imminent dissolution. The identity of the individual lies in the continuity of this life-pattern. The aged man, struggling to be intact in the face of death, is unrecognizable from the infant in arms, yet he is the identical individual because he has issued from one process of change and development.

With all due respect for the depth and suggestiveness of this leading idea of Erikson's, we do not believe that it brings forward certain basic concepts that are required to describe identity in its full human concreteness. Epigenetic continuity gives us identity at a basically biological, rather than fully human, level; and it does not exhibit the part played by freedom in human identity.

First of all, epigenetic identity lies in the continuity of a single time-structure. With the human being, however, there emerges a time-structure that is intrinsically different from this mere biological continuity—and the difference is not merely of degree but of kind. Time enters in a more radical way into the structure of a human life than into biological development. The biological process preserves the earlier stages as schemas that are in turn bases for later phases. Past, present, and future are spread out in a sequential and causally related order. But the three dimensions of time enter into human existence in a far more internal way than as a sequence whose parts are externally compartmentalized one from another. Human existence always stretches—possibly backward and forward over the whole of its time. The whole of a man's past may appear to him at a certain moment as meaningless, and he finds himself in an impasse without any future. Since human development involves meanings and intentions, the fact of possibility plays a quite different role here than in the mere potentiality of an earlier for a later phase that is the case in epigenetic continuity. At certain moments our past can emerge before us as a rather nightmarish jumble of fragments; that possible aspect of the past is at the same time a future possibility for redeeming and making that past meaningful. And such possibilities are not extrinsic attachments to a being who is otherwise whole and self-contained in the present. The self-identity of a human being is a time-structure that must hold past and future meaningfully together as one—a far different matter from preserving past traces as steps in a biological sequence.

The openness to these possibilities of establishing oneself meaningfully in time or falling away into meaninglessness is a fundamental condition of our human freedom. But here as elsewhere, nature's gift of a capacity for freedom is at the price of considerable risks and dangers. Human identity is menaced by more dangers than the natural causes that can destroy a wolf or lion. Primitives speak of "the perils of the soul," as Sir James Frazer pointed out, that have to be circumvented by fairly elaborate social rituals. Man can "lose his soul" even where he retains the identity of development as an organism. Most of us have at some time or another the feeling of being "not quite ourselves"; and for many people the experience may be a prolonged one without even becoming pressingly conscious. As Heidegger has remarked, a person can, and often does, exist in the manner of loss-of-self. The self thus understood is not a substance-subject underlying its various states and enduring through time; rather, it is a meaningful structure never finished but always open to the future. In this openness to the future, which goes hand in hand with the precariousness of self-identity, there lies the ever-present possibility of threat to the integrity of the self.

At the same time, this self exists within a concrete world of other people, things, and institutions, and thereby has to find its meaning (and consequently identity) within this world. A solitary and isolated ego would be incapable of any meanings, and therefore of any identity at all.* To find one's identity in one's world, however, does not signify a routine conformism by which we would mechanically take some allotted place in the group. Our identity may find itself in a struggle against our environment. Yet this struggle is ultimately meaningful only where it invokes some potential direction in which the present environment ought to be changed.

Here again we find ourselves required to make use of bridging concepts to explicate what might appear to be purely "psychological" realities. A person's identity might seem to be the most individual, unique, and private thing about him. But since this identity is developed both from and within culture, it is always essentially related to social and historical factors.

Thus, the idea of human identity, as distinct from epigenetic

---

* This is the basic insight behind Kant's famous "Refutation of Idealism" in the *Critique of Pure Reason*.

continuity, brings forward three interrelated concepts that bear on human freedom defined as structures of meaning:

1. An openness in time toward past and future, in such a way that these temporal dimensions may hold together or disintegrate into fragments.
2. Meanings or meaningfulness which hold the time-structure together.
3. The cultural context as the concrete totality within which the human person defines himself and finds his niche (either at peace with the culture or creatively at odds with it).

FREEDOM FROM NARCISSISM

As we explore the positive meanings of psychoanalytic freedom, the need for some unified conception of the human person as a whole becomes ever more pressing. Only within such a framework can the meaning of human freedom be fully grasped. Up to now psychoanalysis has lacked such a conception, being content either to assume that a man is simply the sum of his id, ego, and superego, or else to equate him with his ego alone.

Under such circumstances, it is not surprising that psychoanalysis has no formal concept of freedom. Instead, it speaks of strengthening the ego. But what does it mean to strengthen an ego unless it becomes strengthened for acquiring freedom—or at least more freedom than it was previously capable of? The post-Freudians have shied away from introducing freedom directly; they have skirted the issue with euphemisms such as ego strength and ego autonomy. But unless the concept of a human person who is capable of freedom is introduced squarely into the forefront of the theory, all developments within psychoanalytic ego psychology remain so much patchwork lacking in organic unity.

Can one legitimately speak of a human person apart from the specific psychic structures of ego, id, and superego? We answer with a strong unqualified "yes," on the grounds that when one shifts from objects to people the whole must not be defined in terms of its parts. Time and again psychology has found itself forced to give up the atomistic notion that putting together the parts will add up to a whole. Even in the simplest experiments on perception it has been found impossible to decompose the perceiver into elementary sensors, or to fix the perceived datum in itself apart from the contextual whole in which it appears. Grudgingly, and step by step, psychologists have been forced to admit both the existence of man as the whole perceiver as well as the whole situation in which he perceives. But why stop there? If you admit the whole perceiver, what about the whole person? The whole person does more than perceive, and—if we are to carry the gestalt principle forward—then what he does in those other areas will be specifiable in terms of the totality that he is. If psychology is to give up reductionism once and for all, then it cannot shrink ultimately from dealing with the whole human person as the ultimate subject it seeks to understand.

We are defining the person not merely as the bones, brains, symptoms, and structures, enclosed within the envelope of a skin, but as being inseparable from a context which includes other persons, objects, and institutions. Freedom is a mode of being, a form of the person's total relatedness to himself, to others, and to his world.

We come then to the most significant meaning of human freedom as revealed by psychoanalytic experience. Angyal used the term "homonomy" to describe man's profound desire to belong to something larger and more significant than himself. The contrasting term is "autonomy," the independence of self. The sickness that is neurosis, at least in our times, is largely a cutting off of relatedness to meanings outside the narcissistic self, leading to withdrawal, self-involvement, alienation, and a profound dislocation of the human spirit.

A passing reference to the human spirit in the present era calls for comment. The term is suspect to many of us; the notion of spirit has no place in science and it has all but disappeared from contemporary philosophy. The long-standing secular stance of our culture tends to make us regard the "spiritual" as a vestigial remain of sectarian religion.

Yet Freud himself—in that conversation with Ludwig Binswanger which we have taken as a dramatic and pivotal episode for understanding the history of psychoanalysis—speaks of the "spiritual" (*geistige*). "Man has always known that he has spirit," he remarked to the younger psychiatrist, "it has been for me to show him that he is instinctual." Confronting the contemporary situation, we are hardly likely to agree with him that man today knows he has spirit. In fact, a large part of psychoanalytic ego psychology is devoted to recapturing qualities of the human person which Freud simply took for granted in his reference to spirit but which we can no longer take for granted today.

In this search for the human qualities essential to a psycho-analytic metapsychology (essential because they are related to cure) we may not wish to use the word "spirit." We may prefer to use terms less loaded with historical connotations. We can readily coin new words or enrich the meaning of words like "identity" and "homonomy." But whether we use these up-to-date terms with their more specific meanings or fall back on old-fashioned and more global terms such as Erikson's resur-rection of the word "virtue," we must have some practical means of referring to these qualities of the human person. One such quality is, of course, relatedness to something or someone outside the self, when such relatedness is relatively free of narcissism. Basically, the individual seeks from psychoanalysis the freedom to form such relations. By way of contrast, con-sider a relationship between two people that lacks this dimen-sion. To the extent that it is neurotic, it will be self-centered, dominated by egoism. Distortions and projections will charac-terize it; each of the parties will play out an artificial role vis-à-vis the other; each will use the other to satisfy personal needs that properly belong with relationships long past. In such situations, each person is truly alone even when he appears to be most intimate with the other; he is locked into a self from which he cannot escape.

So it is with all neurotic relationships: with one's work, for example. To the extent that a work relationship is neurotic, it too is exclusively self-centered. There is little interest in the work itself; rather, the interest is devoted to gaining recogni-tion, being praised, acquiring power and status and becoming the center of attention. We are not implying that the desire for attention, status, and power are neurotic per se. They need not be; and even if they were, the most healthy of us would not be free of their claims. The point at issue, rather, is that in the non-neurotic aspects of relationships there is to be found a meaning over and above these motives. To be free from neurosis means to succeed in transcending narrow ego gratifications in order to develop a genuine concern with something outside oneself. Man thus emerges as free insofar as he freely allows himself to be bound and limited by values and relationships that have validity for him beyond the narrow life of his own ego.

Such values do not connote freedom where they are merely routine traces left in the superego by parental and social commands. The person must be able to give himself to these values, freely and spontaneously, even though the struggle to do so may have been long and arduous. Science, for example, can be a pursuit of interests beyond the self, and in the case of most scientists it probably is. A young scientist, however, might be led into a certain field by his natural gifts and he might strive to excel in it merely as a matter of ego gratification, or because he had been conditioned to seek a respectable eminence. Science, in this case, would be a worldly profession but hardly a form of relatedness to something other than one's own needs.

At what point does such relatedness pass beyond mere self-involvement? Common sense answers simply, and quite rightly: when it becomes a matter of dedication; i.e., when the scientist subordinates his own ego to the claims of truth, and when he pursues these claims as if there were neither time, death, nor personal disturbances to harass him—and sometimes against the remonstrances of parental, marital, and social voices. Science does not become a genuine value until the scientist is capable of self-sacrifice (which, in another sense, is his self-fulfillment as scientist) to something larger and more enduring than himself—i.e., to the continuing and growing body of scientific truth.

The pursuit of art beyond self and neurosis—to use another clarifying example—requires a similar dedication to truth, though its own mode of truth. On this subject we have some marvelously revealing pages in the novel of Marcel Proust where he describes the death of an imaginary novelist named Bergotte who had drifted into less than his best work through the desire for fame and social prominence. Toward the end of his life, Bergotte becomes obsessed with the thought of the painter Vermeer, who had died poor and obscure but who had given his life to the production of paintings that transcend time. In one of these paintings, "The View of Delft," Bergotte remembers one patch of yellow wall that, as it marvelously catches the light, seems to outbrave time. And, as the aged novelist collapses on a sofa in a fashionable salon, he sees in his mind's eye that single patch of painted wall cast on a balance and outweighing all the façile and fashionable volumes that he had written.

This incident is in line with the central preoccupation of Proust's novel: how man achieves meaning through, and if necessary against, time. Proust is therefore a good witness on this question, which happens also be ours at the moment. He is not saying that Vermeer painted that patch of wall out of a conscious desire to be immortal. Perhaps he did; it really doesn't matter. Over and above such desires, there is in the finished canvas the painter's urge "to make it right," forgetful of all private troubles and deprivations in this single-minded pursuit. The free artist, like the free scientist, acts as if he were immortal in the sense that he expends himself for a value that endures beyond him. Many artists are almost as famous for their neuroses as for their art, and innumerable books have been written celebrating the linkage between the two. But if we are to avoid reductionism, we must not confuse the artist's neurosis with his work; rather, we must understand how so many works of art transcend neurosis to achieve a value outside of the self. Indeed, the artist may be able to maintain his precarious balance only by breaking out of the bonds of neurosis through his art.

These examples of using one's freedom to break out of narcissism were chosen from the highest levels of cultural activity: science and art. But what about the average citizen who is not engaged in such lofty pursuits? Is his life untouched by such possibilities? On the contrary, the freedom of ordinary life probably surpasses that of artists and writers. In carrying forward his life from day to day, the average person carries on the life of his community and through the latter—though he may never venture to put it in such lofty language to himself —the continuing and larger life of mankind.

The smallest group in which the average person participates is the family. Psychoanalysts have got so used to the idea of the family as an area of conflict that they may find it hard to think of family life as involving ideals and values at all. Yet the role of parenthood clearly involves dedication beyond the self. Indeed, it is precisely in this relationship of parents toward children that the instinctual (what is due to nature) and the ethical (what, supposedly, is due only to cultural inhibition) intersect. That parents are moved to care for their children may be said to be merely a matter of instinct; the kind and degree of care they give will then, presumably, be a matter determined by the culture. But obviously, it is impossible to establish any hard and fast dichotomy here. At what precise point does the parental care for offspring pass from the instinctual to the ethical plane that has been fostered by the educating forces of the culture? As soon as we put such a question, we realize how artificial it is, and how unreal the dichotomy from which it springs. The biological uniqueness of the human person (as we have stressed in previous chapters) lies in the fact that culture, or the capacity for culture, is one of his chief evolutionary resources. How, then, could one bifurcate the biological altogether from the cultural? To be good human parents, fathers and mothers must do more than merely feed and protect the young until they are physically mature. Parents feel called upon to educate their young mentally, shape them morally, and also to be concerned in providing, so far as they can, a stable world into which the young will enter. Thus, the world of the parents opens toward that larger world of mankind through the persons of their children.

And here the conclusion seems inevitable: the freedom from neurosis which one seeks in psychoanalysis is a freedom to choose other persons, values, and callings that point beyond the individual to the continuing life of mankind. But is this not an expression on one level of the bond which ties the individual into the biological life of the species? And are we not back once again to Rycroft's concept of cure as consisting in a more harmonious relationship with one's "inner nature"—except that we may now refer to a broader conception of "inner nature" than the Freudian doctrine of the instinctual drives?

With this conclusion, we round off the line of reasoning that we have been pursuing in this long chapter. In examining the instincts, we find that they are not blind forces essentially inimical to human and cultural values. And in examining the higher values of the ego—those characteristics that single out man from the rest of nature—we find that these are not rootless constructions in the void, but are tied in to a natural and instinctual basis. Man is not a being cleft in two, whose higher part is altogether alien in nature from his lower. The human person is an integral being for whom the claims of freedom, identity, and the possibility of dedication beyond the self are in fact part of his nature.

This question of how man, bound by time, achieves meaningfulness through continuing time, has been at the center of all philosophical reflections from Plato to Heidegger, no matter how their answers have varied. And it is significant that in the first thinker in whom this question becomes fully explicit, namely Plato, there emerges the famous Eros doctrine, according to which man naturally and instinctively longs for the good, and further a good that will endure beyond his own brief and numbered days.

How is it then that in our contemporary climate of opinion, freedom and instinct, the ethical and the natural, have been dropped neatly into antithetic compartments? When we look at the history of philosophy, we are astonished to find how late in origin is the dichotomy between nature and morality. We do not find that dichotomy in the earlier Greek philosophers; and in the greatest of the Greek philosophers, Plato and Aristotle, the tie between the natural and the moral is never broken: moral education is intended to fulfill and complete the individual's nature; and, ultimately, evil is condemned because it is destructive of human nature. Throughout the Christian Middle Ages, particularly where the Greek inheritance is preserved, the natural basis of all morality is still stressed. St. Thomas Aquinas, for example, holds that man, as a creature of God, has a natural tendency toward the good. It is only when we come to the end of the eighteenth century with Immanuel Kant that we find a fully developed formal theory of ethics in which the moral and the natural are cleft apart.

Several reasons have been given why this took place with Kant. He was an heir at once of Lutheran Protestantism and the rationalism of the Enlightenment, and in his ethical theory he attempted to do justice to both inheritances. On the one hand, he could continue the Lutheran condemnation of human nature by rejecting the desires of human nature as irrelevant to virtue; on the other hand, he could fulfill the rationalism of the Enlightenment by a theory in which only the strictly formal character of human reason, and not the needs and desires of human nature, were decisive on moral matters. But there seems to us another, less conspicuous but perhaps more significant influence that led Kant into this dualism of the natural and the moral: the complete Cartesian-Newtonian picture of the universe that he inherited allowed no place for anything like a specific human nature (molded by evolution) that would be directed toward the goals of the species. Man was a machine, like all other bodies in nature, except that this particular machine was inhabited by a ghost, called mind or spirit. Naturally, the ghost and the machine could have nothing to do with each other.

The existence of the alienated personality unable to form a relatedness to something outside of himself might seem to argue against the universality of the individual's reaching out to form some link between himself and the species. In fact, however, the studies of the delinquent and rebellious personality help to confirm this conclusion. Great alienated souls, like a Kierkegaard or Nietzsche, were indeed painfully cut off from their times and the society around them; but their isolation and rebellion would have only been meaningless self-destruction if they had not borne meaning for a mankind that would eventually be able to listen to their voices. The delinquent personality, on the other hand, is the unsuccessfully alienated; nothing meaningful comes of his revolt. Nevertheless, he is always driven, unconsciously or not, to caricature this larger meaningfulness of the heroically alienated: in the absurd stances, costumes, or rites that delinquents adopt, they appear to link themselves to another world than that of mere social conformity. After all, if the longing for meaningfulness is as much a part of man's nature as his drive toward sexual discharge, there is no reason why the former could not become just as repressed or distorted in its expression as the latter. In many cases of urban delinquency it seems that we have a breaking out of the craving for identity, meaningfulness, and free comradeship that social conditions had prevented from a more positive expression.

Readers habituated to psychoanalytic literature may feel uncomfortable with these references to instinctively based ethical values reaching beyond the self. Nevertheless, we would claim that psychoanalysis was bound to invoke this dimension of human existence from the day that Freud, in his modest consulting rooms, took the momentous step—and indeed one of the most momentous he ever took—of replacing hypnosis and the laying on of hands with the free talk of the patient. In the climate of mechanistic thought in which he started his practice, it would be natural for a young doctor of the mind to have his own specialized tools like the usual medical practitioner, and therefore to throw emphasis upon one such special tool—in this case hypnosis—as a mechanism that would somehow set in motion the healing process. But in later turning to the patient's talk, "mere" talk, Freud took a decisive step into the whole domain that opens to man with language. And between patient and doctor, as they entered that domain, there was set up a new relation.

Current psychoanalytic theory has gone so far as to recognize the implication of freedom in the concept of the "therapeutic alliance." Yet one cannot take this half-step without going the whole way. As we have suggested, the "therapeutic alliance" must be more than an honest gentleman's agreement between doctor and patient to work together on the patient's problems with a view to a "cure" or at least relief. The problems the patient brings before the analyst are highly personal and subjective, and they eventually touch the innermost nerve of personal identity. Ultimately too, the patient's sense of his own validity and meaning as a personal being is always at stake. There may not always be, and perhaps there need not always be, an ultimate "I-thou" encounter between patient and analyst in Martin Buber's sense, yet that possibility is always there in the background. The person who comes to a psychoanalyst for help is generally regarded as a patient in the strict medical sense. Most often, however, he is not so much a passive recipient of medical services as a seeker who may not at first know what he is seeking. There is in him a hunger to break out of a self-enclosed ego: this is almost always the residue left over once specific symptoms have been put into perspective. Inseparable from the truth and freedom toward which he gropes is his reaching out to touch the psychoanalyst himself—to form a human bond in which the psychoanalyst himself must participate. This encounter provides the final context within which all the painful comings and goings of the psychoanalytic transaction can have meaning.

Summary

The metapsychology we are proposing lies halfway between a general philosophy of human nature and a specialized theory within a single branch of science. In its concern with nature, culture, freedom, and science—the basic concepts of the debate between Sartre and Lévi-Strauss—it merges into philosophy. In its concern with the developmental crises of the individual it merges into the clinical theory of psychoanalysis.

It is important to emphasize that the perspective of psychoanalysis is severely limited to the individual and to certain highly specific aspects of his life. The individual's struggles to make a living, the expression of his creative impulses, the routine pattern of his everyday life—these fade into the background in the clinical theory, and to a lesser extent even in the traditional metapsychology. So do the complex processes of accommodation to, and resistance against, the political life of the nation, the great issues of war and peace, of technology and population explosion, and the huge social problems of a complex, technological society. Any full-scale ontology of the human person would take these broader contexts of individual life into account. The inclusion in the metapsychology of a concept of the human person, his freedom and his development, provides at least the scaffolding for relating the private emotional life of the single individual to the larger world in which he participates.

One should, therefore, realize how very selective such a metapsychology will be. For to be useful as a *psychoanalytic* tool, it should not compete with sociology or history or biology or a general philosophy of human nature. The neuroses are derangements of the individual and his basic psychic structures. While these may reflect flaws in the society or in the physical make-up of the individual, the purpose of the metapsychology is to mediate between the disciplines which encompass these latter subjects and the individual, placing its sharpest focus on that small piece of ground occupied by the single individual in his own private world.

We have taken three of the four steps needed to construct a new metapsychology. The first step was to identify the need for a metapsychology as distinct from either a general philosophy or a clinical theory of psychoanalysis (Chapter Eleven). As a second step, we proposed new constitutive and regulatory principles to replace the philosophy of scientific materialism (Chapters Seventeen and Eighteen). We then proceeded, in the third step, from philosophical principles to empirically rooted bridging concepts linking psychoanalysis with philosophy and with the other sciences of man (Chapters Nineteen through Twenty-One). The major bridging concepts proposed were:

1. Multiple forms of instinct, arrayed on a dependency-on-experience continuum.
2. The developmentals, defined as incomplete psychic structures; i.e., as the class of instinctively based processes that is most dependent on experience.
3. The critical experience needed to bring a developmental into being.
4. Cultural institutions designed to ensure the occurrence of critical experiences.
5. A specific sequence of human development.
6. The morphology of psychic structures, and the general laws of structure formation.
7. Cure defined as enhancement of freedom.
8. Freedom as the ability to modify identity, other structures of meaning, and narcissism.
9. The human person with whom the therapist establishes his therapeutic alliance.

There remains the fourth and final step of adapting, adjusting, and modifying the new metapsychology to fit clinical experience. So much of the clinical theory now resides unformulated in the minds of a few thousand therapists that integrating it with a new metapsychology cannot be accomplished by outsiders. If psychoanalysts see merit in the proposals made here, they themselves may wish to assume the difficult task of adaptation.

In brief, then, the handful of concepts proposed here leads to a theory of human nature that brings together instinct, culture, and individual freedom. Hopefully, it will prove more faithful to psychoanalytic experience than the system of cranks, levers, and pulleys of the present metapsychology.

PART FIVE

BEYOND
PSYCHOANALYSIS

TWENTY-TWO

Tragedy—Private and Social

The patients who first came to the consulting rooms of the unknown Dr. Freud were not people fulfilled or made happy by their civilization. One historian has called the period from 1870 to 1914 "The Generation of Materialism." There were no major European wars during that period; technology and industrialism had advanced and the prosperity of the middle classes had risen; democracy and literacy were being extended and ideas of Enlightenment and progress were everywhere in the air. Yet within this period of relative bourgeois euphoria psychoanalysis was born; and the people who came for this new therapy, whatever the private sources of their frustration and wretchedness, were not among the disadvantaged of society. Whatever else may bear upon the origins of psychoanalysis, we cannot forget that it came into being at a time of peace and prosperity for the privileged classes.

The frenetic social climate of the United States today bears little resemblance to pre-World War Europe. Our society may be stable in its political structure and it is prosperous, but there is radical discontent, and there are racial violence, poverty, crime, war, destruction, pollution of our natural environment, and student unrest. Our attention therefore tends to shift away from the personal conflicts which psychoanalysts are concerned with—they seem too remote from our societal crises. In our universities, students have grown impatient with purely private and personal perspectives because these appear irrelevant to the upheavals taking place around us. Yet, when we probe into the nature of the social changes that are taking place in our country, we must return to some basic truths about the individual and his culture. Psychoanalytic experience does have something important to tell us about our own lives and civilization.

Several decades ago a sharp controversy split the circles devoted to psychoanalytic thought. The partisans on one side were psychiatrists like Sullivan and Horney who were attempting to modify the original Freudian scheme; on the other side stood the strict Freudians, holding fast against deviations from the orthodox. The first camp made little use of Freud's theory of instincts; stressing the importance of cultural and social factors in understanding the human personality, they seemed to shy away from any notion of a residual human nature and any limitations on man's plasticity. Also, in opposition to the reductive tendencies of Freudian thought, they emphasized the relevance of the so-called "higher" aspects of man's behavior— our social values as well as personal goals and purposes.

The orthodox response to this humanism was sharply critical. The "revisionists" were accused of being Pollyannas who turned their backs on the darker side of human nature. The strict Freudians emerged as presenting the "hard line" on human nature, the revisionists as offering a "soft line." And where the polarities are set in terms of hard and soft lines, the initial advantage always seems to lie with the hard-liners, for the soft line suggests the secret wish to find solace and optimism by glossing over hard facts, whereas the hard line seems to vibrate with the sterner bravery of pessimism that would face reality at all costs.

Inevitably, a number of literary intellectuals entered the lists and, interestingly enough, nearly all on the side of psychoanalytic orthodoxy. The reasons for this partisanship did not spring from scientific evidence but from the vital needs of the imagination. Freud, they felt, had provided a profound and pessimistic vision of the human condition, which cut across the varieties of culture as well as the historical epochs of the ancient and modern worlds. In comparison, the point of view of the reformers seemed to speak within the much narrower compass of the progressive and optimistic mentality of the Western Enlightenment.

Since the position advanced in this book affirms a certain form of human freedom and calls attention to the fact that man is as much a builder of meanings as a seeker of pleasure, it might appear to belong to the camp of the "optimists" and of the "soft line." On the other hand, since it dwells on the restrictions on human freedom and the limitations on man's plasticity imposed by his biological heritage, it might be said to take a hard line. Actually, the soft line-hard line and optimist-pessimist dichotomies are, we believe, irrelevant to the real issues, and distort the complexity of the human condition. For some aspects of our lives, the outlook is promising, and for others, it is bleak. The human condition cannot be so easily categorized as rosy or dark.

Tragedy, for example, is the other face of freedom. Without freedom there is no tragedy, only mechanical breakdown. When human tragedy occurs, it does so in a different sense than when a computer collapses on the job. The tragic, as understood from the time of the Greeks onward, has always implied freedom: Oedipus chooses blindly and succumbs to his fate; but he does choose, nevertheless, and viewed as a whole, his defeat is in some profound sense self-chosen.

Besides his famous family drama, another fact about Oedipus we must remember is that he grew up lame. (The myth can serve as a parable to psychoanalysis in many ways.) We are thus reminded that none of us escapes the possibility of severe crippling in early childhood or in growing up. Because of the long maturation period required for his powers, man is exposed to a prolonged infancy of fragility and weakness in which any number of things can go wrong—and the rest of his life cannot escape those traces. Here is another dimension of the truly human meaning of tragedy that Freud brought into the open. Though we have always known, as Erikson observed, that "every adult was once a child," Freud has forever changed the meaning of this truism. The human race renews itself by passing through a biological cycle which involves the exposure of each child in turn to the hazards of fortune in growing up. No matter how admirable the aspirations of humanists, liberals, and Marxists, mankind will never succeed in abolishing the tragic possibilities inherent in this condition.

This fact is driven home to the psychoanalyst every day of his professional life. He is constantly exposed to human tragedy even as he presses forward in dedication to the possibilities of amelioration and "cure." He encounters people caught in the toils of their past, struggling within their own self-laid traps, who are as definitely imprisoned as if they carried their own barred cells around with them. One psychoanalyst remarked privately: "With some patients I have the sense of hands raised above the water for the last time just before sinking under; and I cannot dive in and pull them out." The patient may struggle with his whole will and mind, but yet not make it to the other shore—and succumb to the crippling conditions of his illness.

In the example with which this book began, we referred to a noted public figure who took his own life despite the ministrations of a famous and skillful psychoanalyst. Freud, who understood very well the truly human sense of tragedy, had known similar cases. In the conversation with Ludwig Binswanger to which we have returned several times, the two men began by discussing a similar case: a patient known to them both seemed to make definite progress all along the way, but was unable to take the last decisive step toward cure, and so succumbed to a self-destructive neurosis. Binswanger ventured to suggest that the failure might be understood as a "deficiency of spirit." Then, as Binswanger reports it, "I could hardly believe my ears when I heard him [Freud] say, 'Yes, spirit (*geist*) is everything.'" What Freud is acknowledging as tragic here is clearly not the failure of a mechanism but a defeat of the whole human person.

There is evidence that psychoanalysis can leave some patients worse off, as well as be dramatically helpful to others. This finding is hardly surprising. If psychoanalysis has any potential for good, it also has a potential for harm. Yet it is a disconcerting thought, one that runs counter to any easy melioristic point of view. The psychoanalytic encounter may, by revealing the nature of one's illness in relation to the world, make one's total experience more meaningful, but it cannot always avoid tragedy.

The possibility of defeat and tragedy haunts not only the individual in his personal life but whole cultures and civilizations, even the species itself. At the end of the nineteenth century, science presented us with two different pictures of the cosmic process. On the one hand, the prophecy of thermodynamics portrayed a universe leveling off in a homogeneous diffusion of energy that meant an eventual heat-death. The evolution of life on this planet, on the other hand, brought a quite different vista before the mind: organic development consisted in the ceaseless elaboration of more varied, complex, and differentiated forms. For some thinkers, this latter picture provided the springboard for a leap into a kind of cosmic optimism: the course of nature, it seems, must ever be "onwards and upwards." Unfortunately, there is no suggestion that the "upward" course of evolution will ensure survival and avoid disaster. Evolutionary history is littered with the corpses of species that failed to make it; and human history carries the debris of cultures and civilizations that have perished.

When we look beyond the individual to total populations, it becomes painfully clear that the quality of culture holds the key to the eventual success or failure of people's instinctive potentials. There are cultures that thwart instinctual development and those that bring it to full expression; there are dynamic cultures and stagnant cultures; cultures that Freud described as repressing sexuality, and cultures that Gabriel Marcel characterized as repressing man's sense of being; cultures that lead to the lopsided overdevelopment of one set of instincts, and cultures that lead to contradictions and dead ends. In other words, culture is to be seen as the continuation of the evolutionary process by other means.

Each individual culture brings into balance a great number of needs and instinctive potentials, and represents—no matter how deeply grounded in basic human nature—a genuinely contingent creation. In the metaphor of anthropologist Stanley Diamond, every culture is a kind of rope bridge (in analogy to the primitives' handiwork) that carries man across the chasm of nature. And like such a rope bridge it must be carefully built and constantly repaired.

In works like *Civilization and its Discontents* and *Beyond the Pleasure Principle,* Freud presented us with his own vision of culture in relation to instinct—seen, however, from the perspective of nineteenth century Middle Europe.

If we look at these works carefully, especially from the vantage point of today, we find something striking and even paradoxical taking place in Freud's thinking. On the one hand, the whole thrust of his discoveries had been to find invariants of human nature that cut across historical epochs and cultures. On the other hand, he came to believe that his discoveries had a topical relevance to the historical situation of his own day. Human culture, he argued, always involved the burden of repressing instincts. Looking at his own society, he concluded that the social sanctions (in the past, mainly religious) that compensated the individual for such instinctual sacrifice had become shaky in the Western society of his day. That civilization, therefore, was bound to show increasing signs of uneasiness and unrest. The quandary of civilized man thus presented itself in the form of the European bourgeois of the turn of the century struggling to carry on his social tasks while fettered by a cramping and repressive sexual code.

Looking at our own society from the same point of view of an invariant human nature, we realize that Freud overgeneralized his own historical epoch. To understand the contemporary scene we must bring to bear a broader perspective on instinct and culture than that of sexual and aggressive energy pressing for discharge against a bulwark of institutionalized defenses. Indeed, our contemporary society exhibits facets of our lives that hardly concerned Freud at all. We see today the outlines of a vast social conflict that is at least as fundamental as the clash of social mores with sexual tensions, and yet is radically different.

In what follows we will briefly characterize the two sides of this conflict within the framework of our proposed metapsychology, i.e., as a clash of instinctively rooted developmentals with culture, where culture is seen as the agent, not the opponent, of instinct.

In our chapter on the Cartesian epoch, we described a powerful developmental elicited in a unique form by our culture. The psychological roots of what we called Cartesianism relate to an instinctive readiness to impose order on the environment, to control and master it, and to systematize, classify, and objectify reality. In our society, these tendencies are nourished and shaped by an interlocking series of cultural institutions that include our child-rearing practices, our schools, our economic institutions, and our long tradition of Western philosophy. While we stressed the highly abstract philosophical form of this tendency no one has documented its social manifestations as well as Max Weber, a founder of modern sociology and a contemporary of Freud's. Weber was fascinated with the singularity of Western culture. Bringing all of his learning to bear on a comparison between our culture and others', he concluded that the uniqueness of Western culture consisted in the implacable unfolding of what he called rationalization. He meant by this latter term a broader version of what a modern plant manager tries to do when he "rationalizes" his production line; i.e., organizes it so that it can produce the most products at the greatest speed for the least effort at the minimum cost— with all the standardization and controls that this process implies.

Weber is the historian *par excellence* of rationalization. He documents its impact on areas as diverse as music, religion, economics, law, and politics; and he describes its many forms and consequences for specific social structures. Our bureaucracies and other complex organizations, he observes, tend toward inexorable systematization. In a rationalized society, the external relations among men are ruled by standards of utilitarian proficiency. The role of the individual in such large-scale organizations becomes ever more formalized and "intellectualized" in order to contribute more efficiently to the whole. And a false sense of progress, to which we attribute the highest of moral purposes, accompanies the entire process.

Weber recognizes the psychological motive for rationalization to be the thrust toward mastery of the environment. He foresaw that the attainment of such mastery might further stimulate man's unreasoning confidence in his own works and thereby create a peculiarly modern form of *hybris*. The modern individual, he notes ironically, far from advancing his understanding of his world, ends up being more ignorant of it and yet more complacent about the conditions of life he takes for granted. Observing the high price in human satisfaction exacted by rationalization, Weber wondered whether so much activity might not cover up an underlying despair. He notes that one of the most far-reaching consequences of rationalization is the secularizing of life—the stripping from it of all mystery and charm. Even death—a break in efficiency—becomes robbed of its fully human significance in a fully rationalized society.

In his scientific writings Weber was careful to avoid judging society against some implicit and supraordinate system of values. But in his public statements his broader philosophical vision of where the society was tending stands out sharply. Nowhere perhaps was he more explicit than in his fear that rationalization might become more burdensome to man than the situation it sought to remedy; he feared above all that it might extend beyond the regulation of man's external activities to stifle his private and personal life.*

If we translate Weber's theory of rationalization into our own frame of reference, he is saying that the traditions of our culture have overdeveloped and overinstitutionalized one of man's most potent developmentals—his need to order, systematize, and master his world—and that, even though this trait is survival-related, it risks being overdeveloped and defeating its original purpose.

Without sharing Weber's vision unqualifiedly, we can say that enough time has passed since his death to see that our technological mastery of the environment is, indeed, a mixed blessing. When we look at the contemporary American scene we quickly see many of the consequences he anticipated. The most obvious of these, perhaps, are those facts that have to do with mankind's pollution of our natural environment. These matters come under the purview of ecology, the biology of man's natural environment. In a matter of decades, we in America have transformed Lake Erie—a body of water of more than 300,000 square miles—into what is virtually a Dead Sea. Ecologists have estimated that even with a crash program of restoration it would take some five hundred years to bring this lake back to its condition at the beginning of this century. The processes of life, once set askew by human carelessness, are not easily reversed, even by all our technological competence. After

---

* Weber's vision of the world is superbly summed up in Julian Freund's *The Sociology of Max Weber*, Pantheon Books, 1968.

a detailed study of the lake's destruction, one biologist offered this searching and philosophical observation:

> The deterioration of Lake Erie warns of a great impending crisis in our environment, one that threatens to destroy the suitability of the earth for human habitation. It is a crisis born of our unwitting destruction of the natural system that supports us. The lake damage suggests that the conviction that science and technology can "conquer" nature is indeed a dangerous illusion. If we are to survive, we must remake our urban, industrial, and agricultural technologies so that they will conform to the unconquerable demands of the natural environment on which human welfare and survival depend. (Commoner, 1968.)

We should remember that there are many ways of relating ourselves to the environment other than conquering it. Consider, for example, the windmill in relation to the bulldozer. The windmill has to accommodate itself to the wind and to the terrain. To fulfill its function as a windmill it has to fit into a part of nature; it makes use of this region even as it accommodates itself to it. It also makes use of the wind. But it uses the wind in such a way as not to consume it. The wind continues on and remains the wind. The windmill can use the wind only by giving itself to it; it lets the wind be wind. In putting the wind to use, it does not suppress, repress, or otherwise level or convert the wind into something else.

The bulldozer is a human artifact of a very different kind. Its name conveys appropriately the idea of power: it does not accommodate itself to the objects of nature, but overpowers them. It bursts through obstacles, pushes them aside, levels them. The word "leveling" is significant here: as it levels, the bulldozer reduces trees, hills, and terrain into a uniform rubble. This rubble, of course, can become the site on which roads and houses are built. The human habitat is thus extended a little farther over the earth. All of this we unquestioningly call progress. The bulldozer has powers of transforming the conditions of life quite beyond the feeble achievements of the old-fashioned windmill.

But power is accompanied by responsibility, as has been said before. The uprooting of trees leads to soil erosion, inadequate drainage, and easy flooding. A superhighway becomes a congested procession of automobiles and trucks belching fumes and noise. Nearby communities, which once had a life of their own, are transformed into mere traffic intersections. The bulldozer has the power to create new conditions of life, but also to disrupt the whole fabric of life, which already has a balance of its own. A fateful burden weighs upon the wisdom of the men who make use of it.

By contrast, a mistaken windmill has no such frightening possibilities. Perhaps the windmill has been put up in the wrong place to catch enough of the wind, or it is too far for the convenience of the neighboring farmers. But no permanent damage has been done. The mistakenly built windmill has not disrupted irreparably the life of the community around it. It need not even be taken down. It may be left where it is, an attactive though not very useful edifice gracing a landscape. On the other hand, the consequences of the misuse of the bulldozer are not so easily amended. In some cases, indeed, they might be irreparable.

The windmill may well be a symbol of an archaic past—gentle, old-fashioned, and somewhat ineffectual; but the bulldozer is not necessarily a mark of progress in human evolution; and our human freedom does not, we have tried to show, consist in manipulating our natures and ourselves any way we wish (as Sartre, Marx, and myriad other thinkers have mistakenly believed). The central point of psychoanalysis and the philosophy of human nature set forth in this work is that we are not putty to be molded to the specifications of some technologically inspired utopia.

To understand all of the many forces urging total rationalization we must look beyond the drive to "conquer nature." There are other forces at work that bear even more directly on contemporary American culture. We must not, for example, underestimate the conscious social and political goals of American society, the most potent of which is to distribute broadly the fruits of our industrial achievements. The great inequities that still exist in our society should not mask the fact that as a nation we subscribe to, and tend eventually to make steps toward, the goals of broader distribution of goods and services, education, political rights and material well-being.

The unique feature of our society is the way we blend politics with technology. With each passing generation we lean more heavily on technology to achieve our political goals. And as technology advances, we broaden these goals. Today we seek not only to secure a high standard of living for the mass of citizens, but we have also added new goals such as the mass distribution of higher education, leisure, health, and culture, all of which have been made practical, directly or indirectly, by technology and complex organization.

This process of broadening goals and harnessing technology to achieve them defines the vital thrust of our society. Meeting the new goals, however, calls for an extreme form of rationalization. Without a rationalized economy and giant bureaucracies (business, trade unions, government, etc.), the wide distribution of so many benefits on so vast a scale would not be possible. In other societies only a small minority have benefited from technological progress. We are trying to distribute its benefits on a massive scale, in keeping with our democratic ideals.* The goals of justice and equality are deeply embedded in our social ethics and they are compatible with technological progress. If we become more faithful to them, given our technology and distributive institutions, we can quickly reach the point where poverty in this country can be obliterated and every man can be assured a passable living, an education, decent housing, good medical care, and security in his old age. This is the reality that lies behind the rhetoric of the "Revolution of Rising Expectations," "Affluent Society," "Great Society," etc., etc.; it expresses one of the most deep-rooted values in our historical ethic; and there is no doubt that it mirrors basic human needs.

But our methods of fulfilling these goals create havoc because they are based on two of the same false assumptions we have run up against time and again in our discussion of the false

---

* Even if one believes that the process works the other way—that we advance our technology and then broaden our goals to utilize it—the net effect would be about the same.

philosophy that dominates our social sciences. The first is that man is altogether plastic and can adapt himself to any rationalized system that has the public good at heart; the second is that we can apply the same scientific techniques to the mastery of our social environment that we have to our physical environment. If the assumptions were true we would not have to worry about such facts as these: that as society grows more rationalized, man's work and his private life become dangerously separate and distinct from each other; important social groupings become large and impersonal; social belonging becomes precarious and subject to constant change; nature becomes more remote; crowding in the urban megalopolis becomes ever more intense (70 percent of our people are squeezed into 2 percent of the land mass); the physical environment of our cities grows more unlivable; huge organizations even as they become a dominant part of a person's life grow less responsive to individual needs; the service institutions of the society develop an anti-service orientation and man's work slowly degenerates into being "just a job." If we were infinitely adaptable to the environment, these consequences might not matter so much. But we are not, and they do.

Looking at the individual in the light of the concept of human nature developed in this work, we find that many current trends toward rationalization in American society seem to collide head on with other human needs. As illustration, several years ago, a UNESCO-sponsored study of various countries and cultures derived four criteria for a healthy society. These are as follows:

1. "All aspects of life are closely integrated—work, for instance, is not something separate and distinct."
2. "Social belonging is automatic."
3. "Change is slow" and its purpose and direction are apparent.
4. "The important social groupings are small." (Scott and Lynton, p. 15.)

If you think about these, you will note that our society is rapidly moving away from all four of them. Visualize a young married programmer working in the aerospace industry in suburban Los Angeles, having recently moved there from a small town in the Midwest. Think of him as a symbol of modern trends in his choice of job, choice of industry, and choice of home. In all likelihood, his work and his family life (criterion 1) are not closely integrated. His social belonging (criterion 2) is far from automatic; he and his wife struggle daily to maintain it. Change (criterion 3) is rapid, not slow—and its purpose and direction are ambiguous. And if he succeeds in keeping his important social groupings small (criterion 4), he does so by straining against the thrust of both his company and his city.

These four criteria may be possible to achieve in simpler societies or in a simpler age. They are not easy to meet today, and will become even less so in the final third of the twentieth century. But they say something fundamental about our human needs; needs that do not change so rapidly as the society changes. At the present time we do not know either how to meet these criteria or how to replace them. But we cannot ignore them: they are a touchstone; they reflect basic needs of the individual that must be met in one form or another.

One side of the conflict, then, is that an instinctively based need for order, control and mastery, shaped by our Western society in the mold of rationalization, has been institutionalized in business, government, education, science, and all of the other large complex organizations that characterize our modern world. In the United States, to a greater extent than in other countries of the West, this tendency fuses with, and is given impetus by, our conscious political goals and ideals. The overdevelopment of forms of rationalization threatens to prevent other instinctive needs and potentials from finding full expression in our society.

When we turn to the other side of the conflict, we quickly realize that opposition to the excesses of rationalization has a long history. Such opposition is hardly new to the West. From the middle of the nineteenth century on, the prophetic voices of Kierkegaard and Nietzsche prepared the way for what was to become in the Europe of the 1920's and 1940's the existential movement. European existentialism has both a philosophical and a sociological aspect. We make mention here solely of its sociological aspect, whose themes are these:

—That Western man has become triply estranged—from nature, from his fellow man, and from himself.

—That having exalted the rational intelligence above all else, modern science and technology have created a monster. The technological mind has entered into a demoniacal struggle to master nature—a struggle which it falsely equates with progress.

—That with the decline of religion, man is deceiving himself in looking outside of himself to ideologies like democracy or communism or science for his values. Dependence upon such sources for values leads only to despair and to the anxiety of meaninglessness.

—That the widening gap between the pretensions of technological man and his finitude creates the absurdity of human life.

—That mass culture, along with modern technology, causes us to live an existence lacking in authenticity. The individual becomes a mere dehumanized object. He loses his identity and becomes swallowed up by his social and economic functions.

In short, this facet of existentialism presents us with a depressing image of modern man: cut off from his roots in nature by science and technology, falsely related to his fellow man by mass culture, and closed off to meaning in life by the counterfeiting of values. Worshiping false gods, modern man stands forlorn before the gaping void of nothingness—fragmented, dehumanized, estranged, alienated, anxious and guilty.

This vision of modern life has attracted many people who feel that the times are out of joint. We should recognize, however, that it is the voice of a period that is past. We are hearing echoes of T. S. Eliot writing *The Waste Land;* echoes of Nietzsche and Kierkegaard acting out an intense personal crisis that is somehow involved in the larger nineteenth century European crisis of Christian belief; and echoes of Jean-Paul Sartre reacting to the fall of France and to the Nazi terror—a debilitating moral crisis that, fortunately, is not part of our American experience. These are sensitive men protesting against the emergence of a world that they feel is destroying their personal culture.

No doubt there is much truth to these protests; but as expressed in existentialist literature, they belong to the mood of another epoch and another continent. The idiom of this sociological side of existentialism sounds a false note to our ears. As Americans, at least up until the last few years, we have not been responsive to its language, nor to its mood of despair, nor to its aristocratic mistrust of technology and mass culture. For these reasons, existentialism never really caught on in the United States. Instead, the revolt against rationalization was delayed and has now taken another form, better adapted to our idiosyncratic American culture. It has finally found one form of expression in the unrest on our campuses. Underlying the specific issues of the student revolt in this country—from the trivial emphasis on freer parietal rules to the profound bitterness and dismay aroused by the Vietnam War—is a powerful, if somewhat inarticulate, revolt against the same values challenged by the existential crisis in Europe. It is a revolt that draws its potency from frustrations of needs that are deeply rooted in basic human nature.

To understand the real issues of the present student crisis in this country we must, as in any truly fundamental human problem, call upon the twin concepts of culture and developmentals.

It is always easy to see the effects of a culture at one remove. Anthropologists like Oscar Lewis speak, for example, of "a subculture of poverty," referring to the unique pattern of mores, traditions, values, and institutions that dominate the lives of the very poor no matter which country they live in. But we must also learn to see the effects of a culture when it is our own and we are stuck in it up to our necks. There is an upper-middle-class subculture in this country that is just as distinct from the culture of the country as a whole and just as powerful in its influence on those who are part of it as any subculture of poverty. We will refer to it as the "post-affluent" subculture, for it creates and reinforces values that affluence has made possible, such as taking for granted one's ability to make a good living—a luxuriant feeling that eludes the culture at large. Some of the values that characterize this subculture are an intense longing for greater self-expression, self-fulfillment, and social justice; a desire for work that is meaningful beyond its economic significance; and an insistence of the prerogatives of the individual.

The articulate children of the upper middle class comprise most of the college students who are pressing hard for social reform or even social revolution today—a revolt that is incomprehensible to the great mass of Americans who envy these young people their opportunities and their privileges, and who regard them as ingrates, at best, or spoiled brats or even anarchists.

Let us emphasize that the vast majority of college students are not part of this subculture, and are quite content with the way things are: they provide the stability and continuity between the generations. (Yankelovich, 1969.) But a significant minority, most of them the children of well-to-do, college-educated parents, raise fundamental questions about the quality of American life and its most treasured institutions, beliefs, and good faith. And although rationalization in all of its forms is their true target, they frequently miss this target because they lack a historical perspective.

Thus, they accuse their parents of hypocrisy, and out of bad conscience, the parents too readily accede to this misleading half-truth. But hypocrisy is beside the point. The older generation is faithful (more or less) to its own values and to the institutions that purportedly embody them. Individualism, for example, is highly cherished; so is fair play; so is giving people a voice in decisions that relate to their lives and their future; so is the sacredness of individual human life, the belief in success, hard work and saving for the future. The old values of the Protestant ethic are as powerful as ever and are not notably characterized by hypocrisy on the part of the private upper-middle-class individual. (Yankelovich, 1967.)

These values are also, of course, official "establishment" values. The predominant institutions in American life—political, economic and social—are assumed implicitly to embrace them. And it is primarily these institutions that militant college youth attack, their sharpest attack being directed against university administrations, the military draft, the war in Vietnam and the "military-industrial" complex. Here, the student attack comes closer to its mark. Unlike most private individuals, these institutions often violate in practice the very values they espouse in principle—and radical youth leaps to the conclusion that hypocrisy must be at work. Since the students believe the establishment consists of like-minded, homogeneous, decisive persons who have deliberately shaped our institutions to their own personal values, what else are they to assume? Yet, when they perceive, correctly, that their parents share some of their own yearnings for work that is more than just a job, for greater self-expression, for moral dedication to something outside of themselves, for fewer restrictions, and for more of a voice in decisions that affect their lives, they add to the charge of hypocrisy the even graver charge of moral cowardice, vowing that they at any rate will not "sell out" or compromise with the establishment.

It is doubtful that these youthful attitudes represent a rejection of parental values, a real "generation gap." More often than not, the son of a successful business executive who decides against following in the old man's footsteps, is not rejecting or rebelling against his father so much as he is reflecting one side of his father's own ambivalence. The very economic and social success of the father gives the son the luxury of identifying with the suppressed yearning of the father for expressing another side of his nature.

The sympathetic response of the upper middle class to the student protest—and it *is* largely sympathetic, in contrast to that of other social classes—reflects a deep intuitive understanding that the new generation has a different task to perform than their own. But the true magnitude of this task is not yet evident. For it consists in nothing less than realigning many of our social institutions so that they will be less violently dissonant with other facets of our inherent human nature. We cannot credit college youth with being wiser and more perceptive than their elders; we *can* credit them with a more energetic, less ambivalent response to the contradictions in their own subculture. Freed of the demoralizing influence of the Depression, taking affluence for granted, searching for new challenges against which to test themselves, pressed by an intense, age-specific need (in fact, *a part of their human nature*) to identify themselves with some person, some idea, some institution outside of themselves, and unimpeded by the restraints of family responsibilities, they are able to protest, loudly and noisily, against institutions which they see as no longer responsive to basic human needs.

Indeed, our post-affluent culture elicits precisely those developmentals that are reflected in many of the ideals of today's radical youth. The demands for participatory democracy express to perfection the desire to extend to other arenas beyond the family the tendency for family decisions to reflect the point of view of its youngest members as much as, and sometimes above, those of other members. Similarly, other developmentals associated with testing and proving oneself against stringent demands; reaching beyond the boundaries of the individual ego to form lasting relations with others; contributing something meaningful to the larger society; achieving self-fulfillment by developing one's expressive gifts—these potentials of inherent human nature have already been developed by the time the privileged young student reaches college. There, the discontinuity he confronts when he encounters a whole new set of social institutions is a violent "culture shock," against which he reacts according to his own personality style—either with bewildered acceptance, or with dogged determination to adapt himself, or with the vehement anger of the New Left, or with withdrawal into privatism, or with loud, self-confident protest. The student revolts at Berkeley, Columbia and Harvard show that the protesters admire and cherish these institutions. (Barton, 1968.) They do not demonstrate despair or the indifference of anomie, but the anger of those who care and are sure—often cocksure—that they will be listened to. The fact is that the ideals of youth that bring them into sharpest conflict with the institutional demands of the society for greater rationalization often express the underlying needs of human nature better than the institutions with which they collide.

The confrontation between the post-affluent values of the upper-middle-class student and our rationalized institutions need not be destructive and embittered; on the contrary, it is probably the best chance our society has for self-renewal and for correcting the historical overdevelopment of the dehumanizing, impersonalizing, compartmentalizing, logicizing effects of a one-sided philosophy. If we see this conflict as a decisive shift in bringing new aspects of human nature to the fore, then we may eventually succeed in civilizing the hidden barbarism of our contemporary civilization.

In the years that lie ahead we will need new guideposts to replace those "liberal" ideologies that are tied to an unreasoning faith in environmentalism, in rationalization, in technology, and in one-sided social planning. The utopia of B. F. Skinner's *Walden II*—a logical extension of this faith—is a modern nightmare growing straight out of some of the old philosophy. It is the *reductio ad absurdum* of the old liberalism which so many students now reject. Bringing these issues into clear focus is the intellectual task that faces the next generation of social philosophers and social scientists; resolving it through new and modified institutions is the social task that faces the society at large—especially the younger members of our post-affluent subculture.

We are heading into a period of increasingly tense social conflict. Though we have achieved feats impossible for earlier generations, in doing so we have created a mass of new problems. Worse than this: for a long time now our culture has come to think that the solving of problems is a procedure that lies exclusively within the domain of what can be objectively calculated and manipulated. Freud and psychoanalysis turn our gaze toward another dimension and another kind of reality: toward the recalcitrant and galling facts of our human nature and its imperatives. That is why, despite all the criticisms made in this book, we believe that the further development of psychoanalytic knowledge is a necessity for this civilization. The door that Freud budged ajar must be opened wider. Freud's greatness as a cultural figure can be measured almost by the depths of the scandal he uncovered: that a European civilization boasting of its enlightenment and progress harbored within itself, and indeed tended to produce, individuals crippled by neurotic suffering, suffering that sprang from frustrated and maimed instincts. After him, we can no longer fling ourselves into the spectacular visions of the technology of tomorrow without keeping an eye on the human nature that is still with us, and is supposed to be the recipient of all those imaginary marvels. What shall it profit man if he gains the whole world, technologically speaking, but enters that glittering future impoverished and stunted in his individual experience?

Bibliography

Allport, G. W. (1937), *Personality: A Psychological Interpretation.* New York: Holt.

Allport, G. W. (1955), *Becoming.* New Haven: Yale University Press.

Angyal, A. (1956), *Neurosis and Treatment: A Holistic Theory.* New York: John Wiley & Sons, 1965.

Arlow, J. A., and C. Brenner (1964), *Psychoanalytic Concepts and the Structural Theory.* New York: International Universities Press.

Austin, J. L. (1962), "Other Minds." In *Philosophy in the Twentieth Century,* eds. H. Aiken and W. Barrett, Vol. II. New York: Random House, p. 820.

Barton, A. (1968), *Student and Faculty Response to the Columbia Crisis.* New York: Bureau of Applied and Social Research, Columbia University.

Benjamin, J. (1959), *The Innate and the Experiential in Development.* In Brosin, H. W. (ed.): Lectures in Experimental Psychiatry. Pittsburgh: University of Pittsburgh Press, 1961.

Berelson, B., and G. A. Steiner (1964), *Human Behavior.* New York: Harcourt, Brace & World, Inc.

Berneld, S. (1944), "Freud's Earliest Theories and the School of Helmholtz." In *Psychoanalytic Quarterly,* 13:341–62.

Bibring, E. (1936), "The Development and Problems of the Theory of the Instincts." In *Imago,* 22:147.

Binswanger, L. (1927), *Selected Papers,* ed. Jacob Needleman. New York: Basic Books.

Blanck, G. (1966), "Some Technical Implications of Ego Psychology." In *International Journal of Psycho-Analysis,* 47, 6.

Born, M. (1937), *Atomic Physics.* London: Black.

Bowlby, J. (1951), *Maternal Care and Mental Health,* 2. Geneva: World Health Organization.

Bowlby, J. (1960), "Grief and Mourning in Infancy." In *The Psychoanalytic Study of the Child,* Vol. 15.

Brandchaft, B. (1966), "Herbert Rosenfeld: Psychotic States." In *International Journal of Psycho-Analysis,* Vol. 47, Part 4, p. 569.

Cantril, H. (1955), "Toward a Humanistic Psychology." In *ETC.: A Review of General Semantics,* 12, 4.

Chomsky, N. (1968), *Linguistics and Philosophy.* To be published by New York University Press.

Commoner, Barry (1968), *Science & Survival.* New York: Viking Press.

Craik, K. J. W. (1952), *The Nature of Explanation.* Cambridge: Cambridge University Press.

Dewey, J. (1929), *The Quest for Certainty.* New York: Putnam, 1960.

Dobzhansky, T. G. (1962), *Mankind Evolving; The Evolution of the Human Species.* New Haven: Yale University Press.

Erikson, E. H. (1950), *Childhood and Society.* New York: W. W. Norton.

Erikson, E. H. (1958), *Young Man Luther.* New York: W. W. Norton.

Erikson, E. H. (1959), "Identity and the Life Cycle." In *Psychological Issues,* 1 (1). New York: International Universities Press.

Erikson, E. H. (1964a), *Insight and Responsibility.* New York: W. W. Norton.

Erikson, E. H. (1964b), "The Nature of Clinical Evidence." In *Insight and Responsibility.* New York: W. W. Norton.

Erikson, E. H. (1964c), "Psychological Reality and Historical Actuality." In *Insight and Responsibility.* New York: W. W. Norton.

Erikson, E. H. (1965a), "Identity, Psychosocial." *International Encyclopedia of the Social Sciences.*

Erikson, E. H. (1965b), "The Human Life Cycle." Prepared for the *International Encyclopedia of the Social Sciences.*

Fisher, A. L. (1963), "Freud and the Image of Man." In *Insight,* 1, 13–26.

Freud, A. (1936), *The Ego and the Mechanisms of Defense.* New York: International Universities Press, 1946.

Freud, A. (1965), *Normality and Pathology in Childhood.* New York: International Universities Press.

Freud, S. (1895), *The Project for a Scientific Psychology, Standard Edition,* Vol. 1. London: Hogarth Press, 1966.

Freud, S., and J. Breuer (1895), *Studies on Hysteria*, *Standard Edition*, Vol. 2. London: Hogarth Press, 1955.

Freud, S. (1896), *The Aetiology of Hysteria*, *Standard Edition*, 3:191–221. London: Hogarth Press, 1962.

Freud, S. (1887–1902), *The Origins of Psychoanalysis: Letters, Drafts and Notes to Wilhelm Fliess* (1887–1902). New York: Doubleday Anchor Books, 1957.

Freud, S. (1900), *Interpretation of Dreams*, *Standard Edition*, Vols. 4 and 5. London: Hogarth Press, 1953.

Freud, S. (1905), *Three Essays on the Theory of Sexuality*, *Standard Edition*, 7:130–243. London: Hogarth Press, 1953.

Freud, S. (1911), *Formulations on the Two Principles of Mental Functioning*, *Standard Edition*, 12:213–226. London: Hogarth Press, 1958.

Freud, S. (1913), *Totem and Taboo*, *Standard Edition*, 13:1–100. London: Hogarth Press, 1955.

Freud, S. (1914), *On Narcissism: An Introduction*, *Standard Edition*, 14:73–102. London: Hogarth Press, 1957.

Freud, S. (1915), *Instincts and Their Vicissitudes*, *Standard Edition*, 14:117–140. London: Hogarth Press, 1957.

Freud, S. (1917[1915]), *Mourning and Melancholia*, *Standard Edition*, 14:243–58. London: Hogarth Press, 1957.

Freud, S. (1920), *Beyond the Pleasure Principle*, *Standard Edition*, 18:7–64. London: Hogarth Press, 1955.

Freud, S. (1921), *Group Psychology and the Analysis of the Ego*, *Standard Edition*, 18:69–143. London: Hogarth Press, 1955.

Freud, S. (1922), *Two Encyclopedia Articles*. "A. Psycho-Analysis," *Standard Edition*, 18:235–54. London: Hogarth Press, 1955.

Freud, S. (1923), *The Ego and the Id*, *Standard Edition*, 19:12–66. London: Hogarth Press, 1961.

Freud, S. (1926), *The Problem of Anxiety*, *Standard Edition*, 20:87–172. London: Hogarth Press, 1959.

Freud, S. (1929), "Psychoanalysis." In *Encyclopaedia Britannica*, 14th Edition, 1929.

Freud, S. (1930[1929]), *Civilization and its Discontents*. In *Standard Edition*, 21:64–145. London: Hogarth Press, 1961.

Freud, S. (1932), *New Introductory Lectures on Psycho-Analysis*. New York: Norton, 1933.

Freud, S. (1937), *Analysis: Terminable and Interminable*, *Standard Edition*, 23:216–53. London: Hogarth Press, 1964.

Freud, S. (1940[1938]), *An Outline of Psychoanalysis*, *Standard Edition*, 23:144–207. London: Hogarth Press, 1964.

Freud, S. (1964), *Future of an Illusion*. New York: Doubleday.

Freud, S., and W. C. Bullitt (1966), *Thomas Woodrow Wilson, Twenty-eighth President of the United States: A Psychological Study*. New York: Houghton.

Freund, J. (1968), *The Sociology of Max Weber*. New York: Pantheon.

Gamow, G. (1966), *Thirty Years That Shook Physics*. Garden City: Doubleday & Co. Inc.

Gibson, J. J. (1941), "A Critical Review of the Concept of Set in Contemporary Experimental Psychology." In *Psychology Bulletin*, 38:781–817.

Gill, M., and M. Brenman (1959), *Hypnosis and Related States*. New York: International Universities Press.

Glover, E. (1958), *The Technique of Psycho-Analysis*. New York: International Universities Press.

Green, M. (1966), *The Known and the Unknown*. New York: Basic Books.

Greenacre, P. (1952), *Trauma, Growth and Personality*. New York: Norton.

Greenacre, P. (1958), "Early Physical Determinants in the Development of the Sense of Identity." In *Journal of the American Psychoanalytic Assn.*, 6:612–27.

Grunbaum, A. (1953), "Causality and the Science of Human Behavior." In *The Philosophy of Science*, ed. H. Feigl and M. Brodbeck. New York: Appleton-Century-Crofts.

Hamburg, D., quoted in *The Development of Sex Differences*, ed. E. Maccoby. (In preparation. Stanford.)

Hartmann, H. (1939), *Ego Psychology and the Problem of Adaptation*. New York: International Universities Press, 1958.

Hartmann, H. (1950), "Comments on the Psychoanalytic Theory of the Ego." In *Essays on Ego Psychology*. New York: International Universities Press, 1964, p. 120.

Hartmann, H. (1959), "Psychoanalysis as a Scientific Theory." In *Psychoanalysis, Scientific Method and Philosophy*, ed. S. Hook. New York: Grove Press.

Hartmann, H. (1964), *Essays on Ego Psychology*. New York: International Universities Press.

Hebb, D. O. (1949), *Organization of Behavior: A Neuropsychological Theory*. New York: Wiley.

Hegel, G. (1954), "Philosophy of Law." In *Philosophy of Hegel*, ed. C. Friedrich. New York: Modern Library, p. 226.

Heidegger, M. (1927), *Being and Time*. New York: Harper, 1962.

Heidegger, M. (1962), *Kant and the Problems of Metaphysics*. Bloomington, Indiana: Indiana University Press.

Holt, E. B. (1931), *Animal Drive and the Learning Process*. New York: Holt.

Home, H. J. (1966), "The Concept of the Mind." In *International Journal of Psycho-Analysis*, 47, 42.

Hook, S. (1959), *Psychoanalysis, Scientific Method and Philosophy*. New York: Grove Press.

Jacobson, E. (1964), *The Self and the Object World*. New York: International Universities Press.

James, W. (1890), *Principles of Psychology*, 2 vols. New York: Dover, 1950.

Jones, E. (1953), *The Life and Work of Sigmund Freud*, Vol. 1. New York: Basic Books, p. 29.

Jones, E. (1936), quoted in "Criteria of Success in Treatment." In Glover, E., *The Technique of Psycho-Analysis*. New York: International Universities Press, 1958, pp. 331–32.

Kant, I., *Critique of Pure Reason*. Translated by Norman K. Smith. New York: Humanities Press, 1934.

Kardiner, A. (1949), *The Psychological Frontiers of Society*. New York: Columbia University Press.

Kerly, A. and Krish, *et al.* (1966), *Physical Review Letters*.

Klein, G. (1965), "Empiricism and Ego." In *Contemporary Psychology*, 10:358.

Klein, G. (1966), "Perspectives to Change in Psychoanalytic Theory." Presented to the Psychoanalysts of the Southwest in Galveston, Texas, March 1966.

Koch, S. (1959), *Psychology: A Study of a Science*, Vol. 1. New York: McGraw-Hill.

Koch, S. (1964), "Psychology and Emerging Conceptions of Knowledge as Unitary." In *Behaviorism and Phenomenology*, ed. T. W. Wann. Chicago: The University of Chicago Press, pp. 1–45.

Koyré, A. (1965), *Newtonian Studies*. Cambridge: Harvard University Press.

Kris, E. (1952), "The Development of Ego Psychology." In *Samiksa, the Indian Journal of Psychoanalysis*.

Laing, R. O. (1962), "Ontological Insecurity." In *Psychoanalysis and Existential Philosophy*. New York: E. P. Dutton & Co.

Lashley, K. S. (1938), "Experimental Analysis of Instinctive Behavior." In *Psychological Review*, 45, pp. 445–71.

Lévi-Strauss, C. (1964), *Tristes Tropiques*. New York: Atheneum.

Lévi-Strauss, C. (1967), *The Savage Mind*. Chicago: University of Chicago Press.

Loevinger, J. (1966), "Three Principles for a Psychoanalytic Psychology." In *Journal of Abnormal Psychology*, 71, 6, pp. 432–43.

Lorenz, K. (1963), *On Aggression*. Translated by M. K. Wilson. New York: Harcourt, Brace & World, 1966.

Lorenz, K. (1965), *Evolution and Modification of Behavior*. Chicago: The University of Chicago Press.

Lorenz, K. (1952), *King Solomon's Ring; A New Light on Animal Ways*. New York: Crowell.

Mahler, M. and K. LaPerriere (1965), "Mother-Child Interaction During Separation-Individuation." In The Psychoanalytic Quarterly, 34:483–498.

Malinowski, B. (1929), *The Sexual Life of Savages*. New York: Harcourt, Brace & World.

Marcel, G. (1949), *Philosophy of Existence*. New York: Philosophical Library.

McCarthy, D. (1954), "Language Development in Children." In *Manual of Child Psychology*, 2nd Edition, pp. 492–630.

McClearn, G. E. (1964), "The Inheritance of Behavior." In *Psychology in the Making*, ed. L. Postman. New York: Alfred A. Knopf, 1963.

McDougall, W. (1960), *An Introduction to Social Psychology*. New York: Barnes and Noble.

McKee, J. P., and M. P. Honzik (1962), "The Sucking Behavior of Mammals: An Illustration of the Nature/Nurture Question." In *Psychology in the Making*, ed. L. Postman. New York: Alfred A. Knopf, 1963.

Merleau-Ponty, M. (1962), *Phenomenology of Perception*. London: Routledge and Kegan Paul, Ltd. New York: The Humanities Press.

Miller, G. A., *et al.* (1960), *Plans and the Structure of Behavior*. New York: Holt, Rinehart & Winston, Inc.

Miller, G. A. (1962), *Psychology: The Science of Mental Life*. New York: Harper.

Murray, H. A. (1962), "The Personality and Career of Satan." In *The Journal of Social Issues*, Vol. 18, No. 4. Ann Arbor: The Heffernan Press, pp. 36–54.

Myerson, P. (1968). Unpublished paper, "Discussion of the Nature of Hysteria."

Nagel, E. (1959), "Methodological Issues in Psychoanalytic Theory." In *Psychoanalysis, Scientific Method and Philosophy*, ed. S. Hook. New York: Grove Press.

Nunberg, H. (1936), *Principles of Psychoanalysis*. Translated by M. Kahr and S. Kahr. New York: International Universities Press.

Oppenheimer, R. (1966), "Physics and Man's Understanding." In *Encounter*, April 1966, p. 39.

Pastore, N. (1949), *The Nature-Nurture Controversy*. New York: King's Crown Press.

Perry, R. B. (1948), *Thought and Character of William James.* Cambridge: Harvard University Press.

Piaget, J. (1950), *The Psychology of Intelligence.* Translated by M. Piercy and D. E. Berlyne. London: Routledge & Kegan Paul, 1950.

Piaget, J. (1950), *The Construction of Reality in the Child.* Translated by M. Piercy and D. E. Berlyne. London: Routledge and Kegan Paul.

Piaget, J. (1952), *The Origins of Intelligence in Children.* New York: International Universities Press.

Piaget, J. (1960), "The General Problems of the Psychobiological Development of the Child." In *Discussions on Child Development,* eds. J. M. Tanner and B. Inhelder. Vol. IV. New York: International Universities Press, pp. 3–27.

Proust, M. (1927), *Remembrance of Things Past.* New York: Random House.

Rapaport, D. (1954), "The Autonomy of the Ego." In *Psyche, Psychiatry and Psychology,* Austin Riggs Center, Vol. 1. London: International Universities Press.

Rapaport, D. (1958), "The Theory of the Ego Autonomy: A Generalization." In *Bulletin of the Menninger Clinic,* 22:13–35.

Rapaport, D. (1959), "A Historical Survey of Psychoanalytic Ego Psychology." In *Psychological Issues,* Vol. 1, No. 1, ed. G. S. Klein. New York: International Universities Press, pp. 5–17.

Rapaport, D., and M. M. Gill (1959), "The Points of View and Assumptions of Metapsychology." In *The International Journal of Psycho-Analysis,* 40:153–62.

Rapaport, D. (1960), "Psychoanalysis as a Developmental Psychology." In *Perspectives in Psychological Theory,* ed. B. Kaplan and S. Wapner. New York: International Universities Press.

Richter, C. P. (1954), "Behavioral Regulators of Carbohydrate Homeostasis." In *Acta Neurovegetativa,* 9:247–59.

Ross, L. (1960), *Vertical and Horizontal.* New York: Hearst.

Rycroft, C. (1967), *Psychoanalysis Observed.* New York: Coward-McCann.

Ryle, G. (1949), *The Concept of Mind.* New York: Barnes & Noble.

Sanford, N. (1965), "Will Psychologists Study Human Problems?" In *The American Psychologist.*

Schneirla, T. C. (1960), "Instinctive Behavior, Maturation-Experience and Development." In *Perspectives in Psychological Theory,* ed. B. Kaplan and S. Wapner. New York: International Universities Press.

Scott, J. F. and R. L. Lynton (1952), *The Community Factor in Modern Technology.* New York: UNESCO.

Scriven, M. (1964), "Views of Human Nature." In *Behaviorism and*

Phenomenology, ed. T. W. Wann. Chicago: The University of Chicago Press, pp. 163–90.

Sears, R. R. (1943), *Survey of Objective Studies of Psychoanalytic Concepts*. New York: Social Science Research Council.

Shakow, D., and D. Rapaport (1964), "The Influence of Freud on American Psychology." In *Psychological Issues*, Vol. 4, No. 1, ed. G. S. Klein. New York: International Universities Press.

Sinnott, E. W. (1966), *The Bridge of Life*. New York: Simon and Schuster.

Skinner, B. F. (1953), *Science and Human Behavior*. New York: Macmillan & Company.

Skinner, B. F. (1960), *Walden II*. New York: Macmillan.

Spitz, R. (1965), *The First Year of Life*. New York: International Universities Press.

Srole, Langer, *et al.* (1962), *Mental Health in the Metropolis*. New York: McGraw-Hill.

Sterba, R. (1936), "The Fate of the Ego in Analytic Therapy." In *International Journal of Psychoanalysis*, Vol. 15, Parts 2 and 3: 117–26.

Storr, A. (1967), "The Concept of Cure." In *Psychoanalysis Observed*. London: Rycroft, Constable & Co. Ltd.

Taylor, H. O. (1925), *The Medieval Mind*, 4th Edition, Vol. 1. Cambridge: Harvard University Press, 1962.

Thurber, J. (1961), *Lanterns and Lances*. New York: Harper.

Tinbergen, N. (1952), *Instinktlehre*. Berlin: Paul Parey.

Tinbergen, N. (1963), "On Aims and Methods of Ethology." In *Z. Tierpsychol.*, 20:404–33.

Tinbergen, N. (1955), "Some Aspects of Ethology, the Biological Study of Animal Behavior." In *Advanced Science*, 12:17–27.

Tinbergen, N. (1951), *The Study of Instinct*. London: Oxford University Press.

Tuchman, B. (1967), "Can History Use Freud?" In the *Atlantic Monthly*, March 1967, pp. 39–45.

Von Senden, M. (1932), *Space and Sight. The Perception of Space and Shape in the Congenitally Blind before and after Operation*. London: Methuen, 1960.

Watson, J. B. (1924), *Psychology from the Standpoint of a Behaviorist*. Philadelphia: Lippincott.

Weigert, E. (1962), "Goals in Psychoanalysis." In *New Perspectives in Psychoanalysis, Sandor Rado Lectures (1957–1963)*, ed. G. Daniels. New York and London: Grune & Stratton, 1965.

Weisman, A. (1965), *The Existential Core of Psychoanalysis*. Boston: Little Brown.

White, R. (1963), "Ego and Reality in Psychoanalytic Theory." In *Psychological Issues,* Vol. 3, No. 11. New York: International Universities Press.

Whitehead, A. N. (1925), *Science and the Modern World.* New York: Macmillan Company.

Whitehead, A. N., and B. Russell (1925), *Principia Mathematica.* Cambridge: Cambridge University Press.

Wittgenstein, L. (1953), *Philosophical Investigations.* Translated by G. E. M. Anscombe. New York: Macmillan Company.

Wolff, P. H. (1960), "The Developmental Psychologies of Jean Piaget and Psychoanalysis." In *Psychological Issues,* Vol. 2, No. 1. New York: International Universities Press.

Wolff, P. H. (1959), "Observations on Newborn Infants." In *Psychosomatic Medicine,* Vol. 21.

Yankelovich, D. (1965), *Young Adults: The Threshold Years.* New York: Institute of Life Insurance.

Yankelovich, D. (1967), "A Study of American Basic Life Values." Unpublished.

Yankelovich, D. (1969), *Profile of a Generation.* New York: For CBS News.

Yolles, S. (1966). Quoted in *The New York Times,* February 5, 1967, p. 64.

Index

About the Authors

DANIEL YANKELOVICH, age forty-four, was born in Boston and educated at Harvard and studied philosophy and psychology at the Sorbonne. He is President of his own social research firm, Daniel Yankelovich, Inc., and in addition, is Adjunct Professor of Psychology at N.Y.U., Lecturer in Psychiatry at the Tufts Medical School and Co-Chairman of the Basic and Applied Social Research Center at Columbia University. He is married, has a nine-year-old daughter, and lives in Manhattan.

WILLIAM BARRETT is Professor of Philosophy at New York University, and the author of *Irrational Man*, among other books. He was at one time an editor of *Partisan Review*, and literary critic for the *Atlantic Monthly*. His *What is Existentialism?* was the first introduction of this subject to the American audience. Other books: *Zen Buddhism* (with D. T. Suzuki) and *Philosophy in the Twentieth Century* (with H. D. Aiken).

VINTAGE WORKS OF SCIENCE
AND PSYCHOLOGY